Foundations for Success

IDIS - G104

IPFW Edition

ON COURSE
Skip Downing

CENGAGE
Learning™

Australia • Brazil • Japan • Korea • Mexico • Singapore • Spain • United Kingdom • United States

**Foundations for Success:
IDIS - G104, IPFW Edition**

ON COURSE
Skip Downing

Executive Editor:
Maureen Staudt
Michael Stranz

Senior Project Development Manager:
Linda de Stefano

Marketing Specialist:
Sara Mecurio
Lindsay Shapiro

Production/Manufacturing Manager:
Donna M. Brown

PreMedia Supervisor:
Joel Brennecke

Rights & Permissions Specialist:
Kalina Hintz
Todd Osborne

Cover Image:
Getty Images*

ISBN-13: 978-1-4240-7774-8

ISBN-10: 1-4240-7774-5

Cengage Learning
5191 Natorp Boulevard
Mason, Ohio 45040
USA

Cengage Learning is a leading provider of customized learning solutions with office locations around the globe, including Singapore, the United Kingdom, Australia, Mexico, Brazil, and Japan. Locate your local office at: **international.cengage.com/region**

Cengage Learning products are represented in Canada by Nelson Education, Ltd.

For your lifelong learning solutions, visit **www.cengage.com/custom**

Visit our corporate website at **www.cengage.com**

Printed in the United States of America
1 2 3 4 5 6 7 12 11 10 09 08

Contents

Look for the **Wise Choices** in College feature to help you learn the essential **study skills** necessary to succeed in college – reading, note taking, studying, memorizing, test taking, writing, and researching.

Preface   *xii*

1 Getting On Course to Your Success   *1*

Taking the First Step   *2*
  What Is Success?   *2*
  The Power of Choice   *3*
  Write a Great Life   *4*
  Assess Yourself   *5*
  Self-Assessment   *6*
  Forks in the Road   *10*
  A Few Words of Encouragement   *10*
  Journal Entry 1   *12*

ONE STUDENT'S STORY Jalana Onaga   *13*
On Course Principles at Work   *13*
Believing in Yourself: **Develop Self-Acceptance**   *15*
  Self-Esteem and Core Beliefs   *15*
  Know and Accept Yourself   *16*
  Journal Entry 2   *17*

  WISE CHOICES IN COLLEGE: Learning College Customs   *18*

2 Accepting Personal Responsibility   *22*

Case Study in Critical Thinking: The Late Paper   *23*
Adopting the Creator Role   *24*
  Victims and Creators   *25*
  Responsibility and Choice   *26*
  Journal Entry 3   *28*
ONE STUDENT'S STORY Brian Moore   *29*

Mastering Creator Language   *29*

  The Language of Responsibility   *32*

  Journal Entry 4   *32*

Making Wise Decisions   *34*

  The Wise-Choice Process   *35*

  Journal Entry 5   *37*

Personal Responsibility at Work   *38*

Believing in Yourself: **Change Your Inner Conversation**   *40*

  The Curse of Stinkin' Thinkin'   *40*

  Disputing Irrational Beliefs   *43*

  Journal Entry 6   *44*

ONE STUDENT'S STORY Dominic Grasseth   *45*

  Why Learn Study Skills?   *45*

WISE CHOICES IN COLLEGE: Effective Reading   *48*

  Embracing Change: Do One Thing Different This Week   *51*

3   Discovering Self-Motivation   *53*

Case Study in Critical Thinking: Popson's Dilemma   *54*

Creating Inner Motivation   *55*

  A Formula for Motivation   *56*

  Value of College Outcomes   *57*

  Value of College Experiences   *58*

  Journal Entry 7   *60*

ONE STUDENT'S STORY Chee Meng Vang   *62*

Designing a Compelling Life Plan   *62*

  Roles and Goals   *62*

  How to Set a Goal   *63*

  Discover Your Dreams   *65*

  Your Life Plan   *66*

  Journal Entry 8   *67*

Committing to Your Goals and Dreams   *68*

  Commitment Creates Method   *68*

  Visualize Your Ideal Future   *69*

  How to Visualize   *70*

Journal Entry 9   *71*

ONE STUDENT'S STORY **Amanda Schmeling**   *72*

Self-Motivation at Work   *73*

Believing in Yourself: **Write a Personal Affirmation**   *75*

Claiming Your Desired Personal Qualities   *77*
Living Your Affirmation   *78*

Journal Entry 10   *78*

ONE STUDENT'S STORY **Donna Ludwick**   *80*

 WISE CHOICES IN COLLEGE: Effective Note Taking   *81*

Embracing Change: Do One Thing Different This Week   *85*

4   Mastering Self-Management   *87*

Case Study in Critical Thinking: The Procrastinators   *88*

Acting on Purpose   *89*

Harness the Power of Quadrant II   *89*
What to Do in Quadrant II   *91*

Journal Entry 11   *92*

Employing Self-Management Tools   *93*

Monthly Calendars   *94*
Next-Actions Lists   *94*
Tracking Forms   *95*
The Rewards of Effective Self-Management   *96*

Journal Entry 12   *97*

ONE STUDENT'S STORY **Allysa LaPage**   *101*

Developing Self-Discipline   *101*

Staying Focused   *102*
Being Persistent   *103*

Journal Entry 13   *105*

ONE STUDENT'S STORY **Holt Boggs**   *107*

Self-Management at Work   *107*

Believing in Yourself: **Develop Self-Confidence**   *109*

Create a Success Identity   *109*
Celebrate Your Successes and Talents   *110*
Visualize Purposeful Actions   *110*

Journal Entry 14 *112*

 WISE CHOICES IN COLLEGE: Effective Writing *113*

Embracing Change: Do One Thing Different This Week *118*

 5

Employing Interdependence *120*

Case Study in Critical Thinking: Professor Rogers' Trial *121*
Developing Mutually Supportive Relationships *122*
    Ways to Relate *123*
    A Sign of Maturity *123*
    Giving and Receiving *124*
    Journal Entry 15 *125*
ONE STUDENT'S STORY Jason Matthew Laden *126*
Creating a Support Network *126*
    Seek Help from Your Instructors *127*
    Get Help from College Resources *127*
    Create a Project Team *128*
    Start a Study Group *128*
    Journal Entry 16 *130*
ONE STUDENT'S STORY Neal Benjamin *131*
Strengthening Relationships with Active Listening *131*
    How to Listen Actively *132*
    Use Active Listening in Your College Classes *133*
    Journal Entry 17 *134*
Interdependence at Work *135*

Believing in Yourself: **Be Assertive** *137*
    Leveling *138*
    Making Requests *139*
    Saying "No" *140*
    Journal Entry 18 *140*

 WISE CHOICES IN COLLEGE: Effective Studying *142*

Embracing Change: Do One Thing Different This Week *145*

Gaining Self-Awareness *147*

Case Study in Critical Thinking: Strange Choices   *148*

Recognizing When You Are Off Course   *149*

The Mystery of Self-Sabotage   *149*
Unconscious Forces   *150*
Journal Entry 19   *151*

Identifying Your Scripts   *152*

Anatomy of a Script   *153*
How We Wrote Our Scripts   *154*
Self-Defeating Habits   *155*
Journal Entry 20   *157*

ONE STUDENT'S STORY James Floriolli   *158*

Rewriting Your Outdated Scripts   *159*

The Impact of Outdated Beliefs   *159*
Doing the Rewrite   *160*
Journal Entry 21   *160*

Self-Awareness at Work   **164**

Believing in Yourself: **Write Your Own Rules**   *166*

Three Success Rules   *167*
Changing Your Habits   *168*
Journal Entry 22   *168*

ONE STUDENT'S STORY Brandeé Huigens   *169*

 WISE CHOICES IN COLLEGE: Effective Test Taking   *170*

Embracing Change: Do One Thing Different This Week   *174*

Adopting Lifelong Learning *176*

Case Study in Critical Thinking: A Fish Story   *177*

Becoming an Active Learner   *178*

How the Human Brain Learns   *178*
Three Keys to Deep and Lasting Learning   *180*
Your Learning Choices   *183*

Journal Entry 23   *183*

Discovering Your Preferred Learning Style   *184*

Self-Assessment: How I Prefer to Learn   *184*
A. Thinking Learners   *187*
B. Doing Learners   *189*
C. Feeling Learners   *190*
D. Innovating Learners   *191*

Journal Entry 24   *192*

ONE STUDENT'S STORY **Melissa Thompson**   *193*

Learning to Make Course Corrections   *194*

Change requires self-awareness and courage   *194*
Change and lifelong learning   *195*

Journal Entry 25   *196*

ONE STUDENT'S STORY **Jessie Maggard**   *197*

Lifelong Learning at Work   *198*

Believing in Yourself: **Develop Self-Respect**   *201*

Live with Integrity   *201*
Keep Commitments   *202*

Journal Entry 26   *204*

 WISE CHOICES IN COLLEGE: Effective Memorizing   *205*

Embracing Change: Do One Thing Different This Week   *208*

---

8   Developing Emotional Intelligence   *210*

Case Study in Critical Thinking: After Math   *211*

Understanding Emotional Intelligence   *212*

Four Components of Emotional Intelligence   *213*
Knowing Your Own Emotions   *214*

Journal Entry 27   *215*

Reducing Stress   *215*

ONE STUDENT'S STORY **Lindsey Beck**   *216*

What Is Stress?   *216*
What Happens When Stress Persists?   *217*
Unhealthy Stress Reduction   *218*
Healthy Stress Reduction   *218*
Choose Your Attitude   *223*

Journal Entry 28   *224*

ONE STUDENT'S STORY Jaime Sanmiguel   *225*

Creating Flow   *225*

College and Flow   *226*
Work and Flow   *227*

Journal Entry 29   *228*

Emotional Intelligence at Work   *229*

Believing in Yourself: **Develop Self-Love**   *231*

Design a Self-Care Plan *232*

Journal Entry 30   *233*

WISE CHOICES IN COLLEGE: Effective Money Management   *235*

Embracing Change: Do One Thing Different This Week   *242*

9 Staying On Course to Your Success   *244*

Planning Your Next Steps   *245*

Commencement   *246*
Assess Yourself, Again   *247*
Self-Assessment   *248*

Journal Entry 31   *252*

Bibliography   *255*
Acknowledgments   *257*
Index   *259*

Preface

On Course is intended for college students of any age who want to create success both in college and in life. Whether you are taking a student success or freshman seminar course, a composition course, or an "inward-looking" course in psychology, self-exploration, or personal growth, *On Course* is your instruction manual for dramatically improving the quality of your life. In each chapter, you'll learn essential study skills—reading, note taking, studying, memorizing, test taking, writing, and researching—for success in college. However, that's just the beginning. Through self-assessments, articles, guided journals, case studies in critical thinking, and inspiring stories from fellow students, *On Course* will empower you with time-proven strategies for creating a great life—academic, personal, and professional. You are about to learn the techniques that have helped many thousands of students create extraordinary success! Get ready for the only course you'll probably ever take where the subject of the course is . . . YOU!

New and Proven Features of the Fifth Edition

- **Self-Assessment Questionnaires.** *On Course* begins and ends with a self-assessment questionnaire. By completing the initial questionnaire, you see areas of growth that need attention. By completing the concluding questionnaire, you see your semester's growth. You have the option of completing the questionnaire either in the text or online. The online version gives you an immediate print out of your scores, and, for comparison, the average scores of everyone else who has taken it. To access the self-assessment online, go to the Online Study Center for On Course at *college.hmco.com/pic/downing5e*.
- **Articles on Proven Success Strategies.** Thirty-one brief articles explain powerful strategies for creating success in college and in life. Each article presents a success strategy from respected figures in psychology, philosophy, business, sports, politics, and personal and professional growth. In these articles, you'll learn the "secrets" of the extraordinarily successful.
- **NEW! Updated Articles on Self-Motivation and Lifelong Learning.** These sections present the practical application of the latest research in two areas critical to college (and life) success. You'll learn what studies in achievement motivation reveal and how you can apply this knowledge to thrive in college over the long journey. Additionally, you'll learn some of the latest brain research that provides keys to learning your subjects in deep and lasting ways.

- **Guided Journal Entries.** A guided journal entry immediately follows each article, giving you an opportunity to apply the success strategy to enhance your personal outcomes and experiences in college and in life. *Believing in Yourself* journal activities appear in each chapter, reinforcing the importance of developing strong self-esteem for long-term success. Many of the Journal Entries have been revised for more focused learning.
- **NEW! Embracing Change Activities.** Another feature new to the 5th edition, these activities encourage you to experiment for a week with one of the specific success strategies you have just learned. In this way, you can assess the results that this new choice creates in your life. In many cases, you'll want to add it to your toolbox of success strategies and use it for the rest of your life.
- **NEW! One Student's Story.** A new feature in this edition, these short essays are written by students who have used *On Course* strategies to improve the quality of their college outcomes and experiences. These stories show the positive and dramatic results achieved when students apply what they learn in this course to overcome the multitude of challenges that can sabotage success in college . . . and beyond.
- **Wise Choices in College.** This feature will help you learn the **essential study skills** necessary to succeed in college—reading, note taking, studying, memorizing, test taking, writing, and researching. Additionally, you'll find sections on learning college customs and making wise choices with money, both important factors for success in college.
- **Case Studies for Critical Thinking.** Case studies help you apply the strategies you learn to a real-life situation. As such, they help prepare you to make wise choices in the kinds of challenging situations you will likely face in college. Because case studies don't have "right" answers, they also encourage you to think critically and creatively.
- **On Course Principles at Work.** These sections show how important the *On Course* success strategies are for choosing the right career, getting hired, and succeeding in the work world.
- **Quotations.** Marginal quotations express the timeless wisdom of famous and not-so-famous people regarding the success strategies under consideration in articles throughout the text.
- **Cartoons.** Cartoons throughout the book are thematically linked with the success strategies being explored. Plus, they're fun!

Support for Students

At the Online Study Center (*college.hmco.com/pic/downing5e*) you will find many resources to support your success in college and in life. There you will find the electronic version of the self-assessment from the text, as well as additional ways to *Improve Your Grade* and *Prepare for Class*. Also, you'll find practice quizzes, additional articles on success strategies, downloadable self-management tools, a learning styles inventory, and many other tools that will help you create success in college and beyond.

Support for Instructors

At the **Online Teaching Center (*college.hmco.com/pic/downing5e*)** you will find many resources to offer a course that empowers your students to become active, responsible, and successful learners.

1. Facilitator's Manual. The facilitator's manual, now offered online in the Online Teaching Center, offers educators specific suggestions for using *On Course* in various kinds of courses, and it endeavors to answer questions that educators might have about using the text. It also includes numerous in-class exercises that encourage active exploration of the success strategies presented in the text. These exercises include role playing, learning games, dialogues, demonstrations, metaphors, mind-mappings, brainstorms, questionnaires, drawings, skits, scavenger hunts, and many others.

2. New Eduspace Course Cartridge. Powered by BlackBoard, a new Eduspace Course Cartridge allows flexible, efficient, and creative ways to present *On Course* in classes that are fully or partially online. This online course management system was created by the author for use exclusively with *On Course*. Specific features include journal activities, essays topics, samples of student work, personal research assignments, workplace related activities, technology exercises, discussion board topics, quizzes, links to the student web site and several interactive reflection tasks. Instructors have the option of using the electronic grade book, receiving assignments from students via the Internet, and tracking student use of the communication and collaboration functions.

The *On Course* Eduspace course also includes the interactive Video Skill Builders. These online exercises combine video clips featuring discussions with students, instructors, and experts, with articles and activities designed to give students a fully engaging learning experience. Topics include: time management, test taking, note taking, and health and wellness. Request that your textbook come packaged with the etoken for access to the *On Course* Eduspace course.

3. Houghton Mifflin Assessment and Portfolio Builder. This resource provides your students with online access to a personal assessment tool that assists them in preparing for lifelong learning. Students build a portfolio by responding to questions about their skills, attitudes, values, and behaviors in three key life areas: **Personal Growth, Career Growth,** and **Community Growth.** Each of these modules asks students to provide supporting evidence for questions where they rate themselves as highly proficient—great practice for critical thinking skills, as well as creating a résumé or preparing for interviews. An **Accomplishments Report** summarizes the results of their responses. The HMAPB also provides access to Houghton Mifflin's web-based **Career Resource**

Center, which includes tips, exercises, articles, and ideas to help students succeed on their journeys from college to career. Request that your book come packaged with the etoken for the HM Assessment and Portfolio Builder.

4. Houghton Mifflin Success Planner. This compact book, available packaged with *On Course*, contains an eighteen-month, week-at-a-glance academic planner. The Success Planner assists students in making the best use of their time both on and off campus, and includes additional reading about key learning strategies and life skills for success in college and beyond.

5. Videos to support your course are available to adopters of *On Course. The Interviewing Process: Strategies for Making the Right Impression* (ISBN: 0-618-37982-7) takes students through the interviewing process from start to finish, with strategies to be successful in a job search with simulated interview scenarios. This video supplements the text's sections relating *On Course* strategies to success at work. *Money and Finances* (0-618-38255-0) discusses strategies to help students develop the skills of good money management, including the pitfalls of credit-card spending and a discussion of financial aid. This video supplements the text's section on Effective Money Management. Contact your sales representative, or call Faculty Services at 1-800-733-1717 to get a copy of these videos for your classroom.

6. Assessment Tools. Package *On Course* with one of our assessment tools. *The Retention Management System™ College Student Inventory* (CSI from Noel-Levitz) is an early-alert, early-intervention program that identifies students with tendencies that contribute to dropping out of school. Students can participate in an integrated, campuswide program. Houghton Mifflin Company offers you three assessment options that evaluate students on 19 different scales: Form A (194 questions), Form B (100 questions), or an online etoken (that provides access to either Form). Advisors are sent three interpretive reports: The Student's Report, the Advisor/Counselor Report, and The College Summary and Planning Report.

The *Myers-Briggs Type Indicator ® (MBTI ®) Instrument*[1] is the most widely used personality inventory in history—and it is also available for packaging with *On Course.* The standard Form M self-scorable instrument contains 93 items that determine preferences on four scales: Extraversion-Introversion, Sensing-Intuition, Thinking-Feeling, and Judging-Perceiving. Talk to your Houghton Mifflin sales representative about completing our qualifications form for administering the MBTI on your campus.

7. College Survival Consulting Services: College Survival is the leading source of expertise, support services, and materials for student success courses. We are

[1] MBTI and Myers-Briggs Type Indicator are registered trademarks of Consulting Psychologists Press, Inc.

committed to promoting and supporting effective success courses within the higher education community.

Houghton Mifflin's College Survival consultants have provided consultation and training for the design, implementation, and presentation of student success and first-year courses for nearly two decades. Our team of consultants has a wide variety of experience in teaching and administering the first-year course. They can provide help in establishing or improving your student success program. We offer assistance in course design, instructor training, teaching strategies, and much more. Did you know that requiring a Houghton Mifflin Student Success text in your course allows you to attend our College Survival conferences for free? Contact us today at 1-800-528-8323, or visit us on the Web at *http://college.hmco.com/collegesurvival/resources/instructors/ consulting_services/index.html* for more information.

8. Instructor Trainings: Skip Downing, the author of *On Course*, offers faculty development workshops for all educators who want to learn innovative strategies for empowering students to become active, responsible, and successful learners. An online graduate course (3 credits) is available as a follow up to the 4-day On Course Workshops. For information, contact the author toll-free at 1-888-597-6451, or go to his web site at *oncourseworkshop.com*.

9. On Course Newsletter. All college educators are invited to subscribe to the free *On Course Newsletter*. Thousands of subscribers worldwide receive biweekly emails (monthly in the summer) with innovative, learner-centered strategies for engaging students in deep and lasting learning. To subscribe, simply go to *www.oncourseworkshop.com* and follow the easy one-click directions.

Acknowledgments

This book would not exist without the assistance of an extraordinary group of people. I can only hope that I have returned (or will return) their wonderful support in kind.

At Houghton Mifflin, I would like to thank Shani Fisher, Andrew Sylvester, and Amanda Nietzel for their unflagging attention to details and encouraging guidance. At Baltimore City Community College, my thanks go to my colleagues, the amazing teachers of the College Success Seminar. At On Course Workshops, thanks to the extraordinary support and wisdom of my colleagues and friends Jonathan Brennan, Robin Middleton, Deb Poese, and Gabrielle Siemion. Thanks also to the On Course Ambassadors, some of the greatest educators in the world who work tirelessly to introduce their students and colleagues to *On Course*. And especially Carol—your unwavering love and support keep me on course. You are my compass.

A number of wise and caring reviewers have made valuable contributions to this book, and I thank them for their guidance:

Jennifer Ankerholz, Barton County Community College, KS
Judy Cusumano, Jefferson College of Health Sciences, VA
George Daniel, The University of Tennessee at Martin
Elaine Davis, Flathead Valley Community College, MT
Stephen Davis, Ohio University
Marnice Emerson, Sierra College, CA
Sharon L. Gorman, University of the Ozarks, AR
Thomas Hale, NEO A & M College, OK
Sharon Juenemann, Mt. Hood Community College, OR
Brenda Kutz, Iowa State University
Cheri Maben-Crouch, Buena Vista University, IA
Mark McBride, Brevard Community College, FL
Shirley Melcher, Austin Community College, TX
Dana Murphy, National Park College, AR
Maxwell Ndigume Kwenda, Cameron University, OK
Gregory S. Ochoa, Shippensburg University, PA
Joan O'Connor, New York Institute of Technology
Shelley H. Palmer, Rowan Cabarrus Community College, NC
Taunya Paul, York Technical College, SC
Mary Parthemer, Lane Community College, OR
Jennifer M. Reitz, Mercy College, OH
Gabrielle Siemion, Santa Barbara City College, CA
Virginia Smith, Carteret Community College, NC
Dr. S. M. Snyders, Nelson Mandela Metropolitan University, South Africa
Holly J. Susi, Community College of Rhode Island
Louise Walkup, Three Rivers Community College, CT
Celia Young, Montgomery College, MD
Eileen Zamora, Southwestern College, CA

Finally, my deep gratitude goes out to the students who over the years have had the courage to explore and change their thoughts, actions, feelings, and beliefs. I hope, as a result, you have all lived richer, more personally fulfilling lives. I know I have.

Travel with Me

On Course is the result of my own quest to live a rich, personally fulfilling life and my strong desire to pass on what I've learned to my students. As such, *On Course* is a very personal book, for me and for you. I invite you to explore in depth what success means to you. I suggest that if you want to achieve your greatest potential in college and in life, dig deep inside yourself where you already possess everything you need to make your dreams come true.

During my first two decades of teaching college courses, I consistently observed a sad and perplexing puzzle. Each semester I watched students sort themselves into two groups. One group achieved varying degrees of academic success, from those who excelled to those who just squeaked by. The other group struggled mightily; then they withdrew, disappeared, or failed. But, here's the puzzling part. The struggling students often displayed as much academic potential as their more successful classmates, and in some cases more. What, I wondered, causes the vastly different outcomes of these two groups? And what could I do to help my struggling students achieve greater success?

Somewhere around my twentieth year of teaching, I experienced a series of crises in both my personal and professional life. In a word, I was struggling. After a period of feeling sorry for myself, I embarked on a quest to improve the quality of my life. I read, I took seminars and workshops, I talked with wise friends and acquaintances, I kept an in-depth journal, I saw a counselor, I even returned to graduate school to add a master's degree in applied psychology to my doctoral degree in English. I was seriously motivated to change my life for the better.

If I were to condense all that I learned into one sentence, it would be this: **People who are successful (by their own definition) consistently make wiser choices than people who struggle**. I came to see that the quality of my life was essentially the result of all of my previous choices. I saw how the wisdom (or lack of wisdom) of my choices influenced, and often determined, the outcomes and experiences of my life. The same, of course, was true for my struggling students.

For nearly two decades, I have continued my quest to identify the inner qualities that empower a person to make consistently wise choices, the very choices that lead to success both in college and in life. As a result of what I learned (and continue to learn), I created a course at my college called the College Success Seminar. This course was a departure from traditional student success courses because, instead of focusing primarily on study skills, it focused on empowering students from the inside out. I had come to realize that most students who struggle in college are perfectly capable of earning a degree and that their struggles go far deeper than not knowing study skills. I envisioned a course that would empower students to develop their natural inner strengths, the qualities that would help them make the wise choices that would create the very outcomes and experiences they wanted in college . . . and in life. When I couldn't find a book that did this, I wrote *On Course*. A few years later, I created a series of professional development workshops to share what I had learned with other educators who want to see their students soar. Then, to provide an opportunity for workshop graduates to continue to exchange their experiences and wisdom, I started a listserv, and this growing group of educators soon named themselves the On Course Ambassadors, sharing On Course strategies with their students and colleagues alike. Later, I created two online graduate courses that further help college educators learn cutting-edge strategies for empowering their students to be more successful in college and in life. To launch the second decade of *On Course*, the On Course Ambassadors hosted the first On Course National Conference, bringing together an overflow crowd of educators hungry for new ways to help their students achieve more of their potential in college and in life. Every one of these efforts appeals to a deep place in me because they all have the power to change people's lives for the better. But that's not the only appeal. These activities also help *me* stay conscious of the wise choices I must consistently make to live a richer, more personally fulfilling life.

Now that much of my life is back on course, I don't want to forget how I got here!

Getting On Course to Your Success

1

|

SUCCESSFUL STUDENTS . . .	STRUGGLING STUDENTS . . .
■ **accept personal responsibility,** seeing themselves as the primary cause of their outcomes and experiences.	■ see themselves as Victims, believing that what happens to them is determined primarily by external forces such as fate, luck, and powerful others.
■ **discover self-motivation,** finding purpose in their lives by discovering personally meaningful goals and dreams.	■ have difficulty sustaining motivation, often feeling depressed, frustrated, and/or resentful about a lack of direction in their lives.
■ **master self-management,** consistently planning and taking purposeful actions in pursuit of their goals and dreams.	■ seldom identify specific actions needed to accomplish a desired outcome. And when they do, they tend to procrastinate.
■ **employ interdependence,** building mutually supportive relationships that help them achieve their goals and dreams (while helping others do the same).	■ are solitary, seldom requesting, even rejecting, offers of assistance from those who could help.

Taking the First Step

 FOCUS QUESTIONS What does "success" mean to you? When you achieve your greatest success, what will you **have,** what will you be **doing,** and what kind of person will you **be?**

Congratulations on choosing to attend college! With this choice, you've begun a journey that can lead to great personal and professional success.

What is success?

I've asked many college graduates, "What did success mean to you when you were an undergraduate?" Here are some typical answers:

When I was in college, success to me was . . .

. . . getting all A's and B's while working a full-time job.

. . . making two free-throws to win the conference basketball championships.

. . . having a great social life.

. . . parenting two great kids and still making the dean's list.

. . . being the first person in my family to earn a college degree.

College is a place where a student ought to learn not so much how to make a living, but how to live.
Dr. William A. Nolen

Notice that each response emphasizes *outer success:* high grades, sports victories, social popularity, and college degrees. These successes are public, visible achievements that allow the world to judge one's abilities and worth.

I've also asked college graduates, "If you could repeat your college years, what would you do differently?" Here are some typical answers:

If I had a chance to do college over, I would . . .

. . . focus on learning instead of just getting good grades.

. . . major in engineering, the career I had a passion for.

. . . constantly ask myself how I could use what I was learning to enhance my life and the lives of the people I love.

. . . discover my personal values.

. . . learn more about the world I live in and more about myself . . . especially more about myself!

Notice that the focus some years after graduation often centers on *inner success:* enjoying learning, following personal interests, focusing on personal values, and creating more fulfilling lives. These successes are private, invisible victories that offer a deep sense of personal contentment.

Only with hindsight do most college graduates realize that, to be completely satisfying, success must occur both in the visible world and in the invisible spaces within our minds and hearts. This book, then, is about how to achieve both outer and inner success in college and in life.

To that end, I suggest the following definition of success: **Success is staying on course to your desired outcomes and experiences, creating wisdom, happiness, and unconditional self-worth along the way.**

As a college instructor, I have seen thousands of students arrive on campus with dreams, then struggle, fail, and fade away. I've seen thousands more come to college with dreams, pass their courses, and graduate having done little more than cram thousands of facts into their brains. They've earned degrees, but in more important ways they have remained unchanged.

Our primary responsibility in life, I believe, is to realize the incredible potential with which each of us is born. All of our experiences, especially those during college, can contribute to the creation of our best selves.

On Course will show you how to use your college experience as a laboratory experiment. In this laboratory you'll learn and apply proven strategies that will help you create success—academically, personally, and professionally. I'm not saying it'll be easy, but you're about to learn time-tested strategies that have made a difference in the lives of thousands of students before you. So get ready to change the outcomes of your life and the quality of your experiences along the way! Get ready to create success as *you* define it.

To begin, consider a curious puzzle: Two students enter a college class on the first day of the semester. Both appear to have similar intelligence, backgrounds, and abilities. The weeks slide by, and the semester ends. Surprisingly, one student passes and the other fails. One fulfills his potential; the other falls short. Why do students with similar aptitudes perform so differently? More importantly, which of these students is you?

Teachers observe this puzzle in every class. I bet you've seen it, too, not only in school, but wherever people gather. Some people have a knack for achievement. Others wander about confused and disappointed, unable to create the success they claim they want. Clearly, having potential does not guarantee success.

What, then, are the essential ingredients of success?

The power of choice

The main ingredient in all success is wise choices. That's because the quality of our lives is determined by the quality of the choices we make on a daily basis. Successful people stay on course to their destinations by wisely choosing their beliefs and behaviors.

Do beliefs cause behaviors, or do behaviors lead to beliefs? Like the chicken and the egg, it's hard to say which came first. This much is clear: Once you choose a positive belief or an effective behavior, you usually find yourself in a cycle of success. Positive beliefs lead to effective behaviors. Effective behaviors lead to success. And success reinforces the positive beliefs.

There is only one success—to be able to spend your life in your own way.
Christopher Morely

The deepest personal defeat suffered by human beings is constituted by the difference between what one was capable of becoming and what one has in fact become.
Ashley Montagu

© Tee and Charles Addams Foundation.

Here's an example showing how the choice of beliefs and behaviors determines results. Until 1954, most track-and-field experts believed it was impossible for a person to run a mile in less than four minutes. On May 6, 1954, however, Roger Bannister ran a mile in the world-record time of 3:59.4. Once Bannister had proven that running a four-minute mile was possible, within months, many other runners also broke the four-minute barrier. In other words, once runners chose a new belief (a person can run a mile under four minutes), they pushed their physical abilities, and suddenly the impossible became possible. By the way, the present world's record, set in 1999 by Hicham El Guerrouj of Morocco, is an amazing 3:43.13. So much for limiting beliefs!

Consider another example. After a disappointing test score, a struggling student thinks, "I knew I couldn't do college math!" This belief will likely lead the student to miss classes and neglect assignments. These self-defeating behaviors will lead to even lower test scores, reinforcing the negative beliefs. This student, caught in a cycle of failure, is now in grave danger of failing math.

In that same class, however, someone with no better math ability is passing the course because this student believes she *can* pass college math. Consequently, she chooses positive behaviors such as attending every class, completing all of her assignments, getting a tutor, and asking the instructor for help. Her grades go up, confirming her empowering belief. The cycle of success has this student on course to passing math.

Someone once said, "If you keep doing what you've been doing, you'll keep getting what you've been getting." That's why if you want to improve your life (and why else would you attend college?), you'll need to change some of your beliefs and behaviors. Conscious experimentation will teach you which ones are already working well for you and which ones need revision. Once these new beliefs and behaviors become a habit, you'll find yourself in the cycle of success, on course to creating your dreams in college and in life.

Life is a self-fulfilling prophesy . . . in the long run you usually get what you expect.

    Denis Waitley

Write a great life

College offers the perfect opportunity to design a life worth living. A time-tested tool for this purpose is a journal, a written record of your thoughts and feelings, hopes and dreams. Journal writing is a way to explore your life in depth and discover your best "self." This self-awareness will enable you to make wise choices about what to keep doing and what to change.

Because you'll be writing about your life and your success, consider carefully where and how you want to record these important ideas. You may want to buy a blank book especially for journal writing. Or you may prefer to keep an electronic journal on a computer. Whatever your choice, I urge you to put your mind and heart into your writing and keep all of your journal entries together in one book or document. If you do, someday many years from now, you'll have the extraordinary pleasure of reading this autobiography of your growing wisdom about college and life.

Journal work is an excellent approach to uncovering hidden truths about ourselves . . .

Marsha Sinetar

Many people who keep journals do what is called "free writing." They simply write whatever thoughts come to mind. This approach can be extremely valuable for exploring issues present in one's mind at any given moment.

In *On Course*, however, you will write a guided journal. This approach is like going on a journey with an experienced guide. Your guide takes you places and shows you sights you might never have discovered on your own.

Before writing each journal entry, you'll read an article about proven success strategies. Then you'll apply the strategies to your own life by completing the guided journal entry that follows the article. Here are five guidelines for creating a meaningful journal:

- *Copy the directions for each step into your journal (just the bold print):* When you find your journal in a drawer twenty years from now, having the directions in your journal will enable you to make sense of what you've written. (You may want to use different-color inks for the directions and for your response.)

- *Be spontaneous:* Write whatever comes to mind in response to the directions. Imagine pouring liquid thoughts into your journal without pausing to edit or rewrite. Unlike public writings, such as an English composition or a history research paper, your journal is a private document written primarily for your own benefit.

- *Be honest:* As you write, tell yourself the absolute truth; honesty leads to your most significant discoveries about yourself and your success.

- *Be creative:* Add favorite quotations, sayings, and poems. Use color, drawings, and photographs. Express your best "self."

- *Dive Deep:* When you think you have exhausted a topic, write more. Your most valuable thoughts will often take the longest to surface. So, most of all—DIVE DEEP!!

For easy reference, these important guidelines are also printed on the inside back cover of this book.

Assess yourself

Before we examine the choices of successful students, take a few minutes to complete the self-assessment questionnaire on the next two pages. Your scores will identify behaviors and beliefs you may wish to change to achieve more of your potential in college and in life. In the last chapter, you will have an opportunity to repeat this self-assessment and compare your two scores. I think you're going to be pleasantly surprised!

This self-assessment is not a test. There are no right or wrong answers. The questions simply give you an opportunity to create an accurate and current self-portrait. Be absolutely honest and have fun with this activity, for it is the first step on an exciting journey to a richer, more personally fulfilling life.

Self-Assessment

You can take this self-assessment on the Internet by visiting the *On Course* web site at *http://collegesurvival.college.hmco.com/students.* Select Downing's *On Course* from the list of textbook sites. You'll receive your score immediately...and see how others scored as well.

Read the statements below and score each one according to how true or false you believe it is about you. To get an accurate picture of yourself, consider what **IS** true about you (not what you want to be true). Obviously there are no right or wrong answers. Assign each statement a number from zero to ten, as follows:

Totally false 0 1 2 3 4 5 6 7 8 9 10 Totally true

1. ___ I control how successful I will be.
2. ___ I'm not sure why I'm in college.
3. ___ I spend most of my time doing important things.
4. ___ When I encounter a challenging problem, I try to solve it by myself.
5. ___ When I get off course from my goals and dreams, I realize it right away.
6. ___ I'm not sure how I learn best.
7. ___ Whether I'm happy or not depends mostly on me.
8. ___ I'll truly accept myself only after I eliminate my faults and weaknesses.
9. ___ Forces out of my control (like poor teaching) are the cause of low grades I receive in school.
10. ___ If I lose my motivation in college, I know how to get it back.
11. ___ I don't need to write things down because I can remember what I need to do.
12. ___ I have a network of people in my life that I can count on for help.
13. ___ If I have habits that hinder my success, I'm not sure what they are.
14. ___ When I don't like the way an instructor teaches, I know how to learn the subject anyway.
15. ___ When I get very angry, sad, or afraid, I do or say things that create a problem for me.
16. ___ When I think about performing an upcoming challenge (like taking a test), I usually see myself doing well.
17. ___ When I have a problem, I take positive actions to find a solution.
18. ___ I don't know how to set effective short-term and long-term goals.
19. ___ I remember to do important things.
20. ___ When I have a difficult course in school, I study alone.
21. ___ I'm aware of beliefs I have that hinder my success.
22. ___ I don't know how to study effectively.
23. ___ When choosing between doing an important school assignment or something really fun, I usually do the school assignment.
24. ___ I break promises that I make to myself or to others.

Totally false 0 1 2 3 4 5 6 7 8 9 10 Totally true

25.____ I make poor choices that keep me from getting what I really want in life.
26.____ I have a written plan that includes both my short-term and long-term goals.
27.____ I lack self-discipline.
28.____ I listen carefully when other   people are talking.
29.____ I'm stuck with any habits of mine that hinder my success.
30.____ When I face a disappointment (like failing a test), I ask myself, "What lesson can I learn here?"
31.____ I often feel bored, anxious, or depressed.
32.____ I feel just as worthwhile as any other person.
33.____ Forces outside of me (like luck or other people) control how successful I will be.
34.____ College is an important step on the way to accomplishing my goals and dreams.
35.____ I spend most of my time doing unimportant things.
36.____ When I encounter a challenging problem, I ask for help.
37.____ I can be off course from my goals and dreams for quite a while without realizing it.
38.____ I know how I learn best.
39.____ My happiness depends mostly on what's happened to me lately.
40.____ I accept myself just as I am, even with my faults and weaknesses.
41.____ I am the cause of low grades I receive in school.
42.____ If I lose my motivation in college, I don't know how I'll get it back.
43.____ I use self-management tools (like calendars and to-do lists) that help me remember to do important things.
44.____ I know very few people whom I can count on for help.
45.____ I'm aware of the habits I have that hinder my success.
46.____ If I don't like the way an instructor teaches, I'll probably do poorly in the course.
47.____ When I'm very angry, sad, or afraid, I know how to manage my emotions so I don't do anything I'll regret later.
48.____ When I think about performing an upcoming challenge (like taking a test), I usually see myself doing poorly.
49.____ When I have a problem, I complain, blame others, or make excuses.
50.____ I know how to set effective short-term and long-term goals.
51.____ I forget to do important things.
52.____ When I have a difficult course in school, I find a study partner or join a study group.
53.____ I'm unaware of beliefs I have that hinder my success.
54.____ I've learned to use specific study skills that work effectively for me.
55.____ I often feel happy and fully alive.
56.____ I keep promises that I make to myself or to others.
57.____ I make wise choices that help me get what I really want in life.
58.____ I live day to day, without much of a plan for the future.
59.____ I am a self-disciplined person.
60.____ I get distracted easily when other people are talking.
61.____ I know how to change habits of mine that hinder my success.
62.____ When I face a disappointment (like failing a test), I feel pretty helpless.
63.____ When choosing between doing an important school assignment or something really fun, I usually do something fun.
64.____ I feel less worthy than other people.

Transfer your scores to the scoring sheets on the next page. For each of the eight areas, total your scores in columns A and B. Then total your final scores as shown in the sample.

Self-Assessment Scoring Sheet

SAMPLE

A		B	
6.	8	29.	3
14.	5	35.	3
21.	6	50.	6
73.	9	56.	2

__28__ + 40 − __14__ = 54

SCORE #1: Accepting Personal Responsibility

A		B	
1.		9.	
17.		25.	
41.		33.	
57.		49.	

_____ + 40 − _____ = _____

SCORE #2: Discovering Self-Motivation

A		B	
10.		2.	
26.		18.	
34.		42.	
50.		58.	

_____ + 40 − _____ = _____

SCORE #3: Mastering Self-Management

A		B	
3.		11.	
19.		27.	
43.		35.	
59.		51.	

_____ + 40 − _____ = _____

SCORE #4: Employing Interdependence

A		B	
12.		4.	
28.		20.	
36.		44.	
52.		60.	

_____ + 40 − _____ = _____

SCORE #5: Gaining Self-Awareness

A		B	
5.		13.	
21.		29.	
45.		37.	
61.		53.	

_____ + 40 − _____ = _____

SCORE #6: Adopting Lifelong Learning

A		B	
14.		6.	
30.		22.	
38.		46.	
54.		62.	

_____ + 40 − _____ = _____

SCORE #7: Developing Emotional Intelligence

A		B	
7.		15.	
23.		31.	
47.		39.	
55.		63.	

_____ + 40 − _____ = _____

SCORE #8: Believing in Myself

A		B	
16.		8.	
32.		24.	
40.		48.	
56.		64.	

_____ + 40 − _____ = _____

Carry these scores to the corresponding boxes in the chart on the next page, writing them in the "Your Score" column.

Choices of Successful Students

Your score	Successful students...	Struggling students...
Score _____	**accept self-responsibility,** seeing themselves as the primary cause of their outcomes and experiences.	see themselves as Victims, believing that what happens to them is determined primarily by external forces such as fate, luck, and powerful others.
Score _____	**discover self-motivation,** finding purpose in their lives by discovering personally meaningful goals and dreams.	have difficulty sustaining motivation, often feeling depressed, frustrated, and/or resentful about a lack of direction in their lives.
Score _____	**master self-management,** consistently planning and taking purposeful actions in pursuit of their goals and dreams.	seldom identify specific actions needed to accomplish a desired outcome. And when they do, they tend to procrastinate.
Score _____	**employ interdependence,** building mutually supportive relationships that help them achieve their goals and dreams (while helping others do the same).	are solitary, seldom requesting, even rejecting, offers of assistance from those who could help.
Score _____	**gain self-awareness,** consciously employing behaviors, beliefs, and attitudes that keep them on course.	make important choices unconsciously, being directed by self-sabotaging habits and out dated life scripts.
Score _____	**adopt lifelong learning,** finding valuable lessons and wisdom in nearly every experience they have.	resist learning new ideas and skills, viewing learning as fearful or boring rather than as mental play.
Score _____	**develop emotional intelligence,** effectively managing their emotions in support of their goals and dreams.	live at the mercy of strong emotions, such as anger, depression, anxiety, or a need for instant gratification.
Score _____	**believe in themselves,** seeing themselves as capable, lovable, and unconditionally worthy human beings.	doubt their competence and personal value, feeling inadequate to create their desired outcomes and experiences.

Interpreting your scores: A score of . . .

0–39	Indicates an area where your choices will **seldom** keep you on course.
40–63	Indicates an area where your choices will **sometimes** keep you on course.
64–80	Indicates an area where your choices will **usually** keep you on course.

Forks in the Road

Why are these eight qualities so important? Because the road of life is rich with both opportunities and obstacles. At every opportunity or obstacle, the road forks and we have to make a choice. Some of those choices are so significant they will literally change the outcomes of our lives. In college, students encounter opportunities such as new ways of thinking, scholarships, work-study, lunch with an instructor, study groups, social events, sports teams, new friends, study-abroad programs, romantic relationships, academic majors, all-night conversations, diverse cultures, challenging viewpoints, and field trips, among others.

For a long time it had seemed to me that life was about to begin — real life. But there was always some obstacle in the way. Something to be got through first, some unfinished business, time still to be served, a debt to be paid. Then life would begin. At last it dawned on me that these obstacles were my life

Fr. Alfred D'Souza

Possible obstacles include disappointing grades, homesickness, death of a loved one, conflicts with friends, loneliness, health problems, endless homework, anxiety, broken romances, self-doubt, lousy class schedules, lost motivation, difficult instructors, academic probation, confusing tests, excessive drinking, frustrating rules, mystifying textbooks, conflicting work and school schedules, paralyzing depression, jealous friends, test anxiety, learning disabilities, and financial difficulties, to name a few.

In other words, college is just like life. There are always opportunities and obstacles, and the choices we make at each of these forks in the road determine whether we sink or soar. It takes a lot more than potential to excel in college or in life. And you're about to find out how to succeed in both . . . despite inevitable challenges. You see, while life is generating a dizzying array of options, successful people are making one wise choice after another.

A few words of encouragement

In the next few months, you'll be taking a personal journey designed to help you develop the empowering beliefs and behaviors that will help you maximize your potential and achieve the outcomes and experiences you desire. However, before we depart, let's see how you're feeling about this upcoming trip. Please choose the statement below that best describes how you feel right now:

1. I'm excited about developing the inner qualities, outer behaviors, and academic skills that have helped others achieve success in college and in life.

2. I'm feeling okay about this journey because I'll probably learn a few helpful things along the way.

3. I can't say I'm excited, but I'm willing to give it a try.

4. I'm unhappy, and I don't want to go!

In nearly every *On Course* group I've worked with, there have been some reluctant travelers. If that's you, I want to offer some personal words of encouragement. First, I can certainly understand why you might be hesitant. Frankly, I would have been a reluctant traveler on this journey when I was a first-year college student. I can tell you, though, I sure wish I'd known then what you're about to learn. Many students after completing the course have asked, "Why didn't they teach us this stuff in high school? It sure would have helped!" Even some of the reluctant travelers have later said, "Every student should be required to take this course!"

I can't promise that you'll feel this way after finishing the course. But I can promise that if you do only the bare minimum or, worse yet, drop out, you'll never know if this course could have helped you improve your life. So, quite frankly, my goal here is to persuade you to give this course a fair chance.

Maybe you're thinking, "*I don't need this success stuff. Just give me the information and skills I need to get a good job.*" If so, you're going to be pleased to discover that the skills you'll learn in this course are highly prized in the work world. In fact many companies pay corporate trainers large fees to teach these same skills to their employees. Think of the advantage you'll have when you bring these skills with you to the job.

Or, perhaps you're thinking, "*I already know how to be successful. This is just a waste of my time.*" I thought this, too, at one time. And I had three academic degrees from prestigious universities and a good job to back up my claim. Hadn't I already proven I could be a success? But when I opened myself to learning the skills that you'll discover in these pages, the quality of both my professional and personal life improved dramatically. I've also taught these skills to successful college educators (perhaps even your own instructor) and many of them have had the same experience I did. You see, there is success . . . and then there is SUCCESS!

Or, maybe you're thinking, "*I don't want to examine and write about myself. That's not what college should be about.*" I understand this objection! When I was in college, self-examination was about the last thing on my to-do list (right after walking backwards to the North Pole in my bathing suit). Of course I had a "good" reason: Athletes like me didn't look inward. I labeled it "touchy feely" and dismissed self-exploration. I'm sure you have reasons for your reluctance: shyness, your cultural upbringing, or a host of other explanations that make you uncomfortable when looking within for the keys to your success. I urge you to overcome your resistance. Today, I'm sorry it took me so long to realize that success occurs from inside out, not outside in. *You* are the key to your success, and apparently your instructors agree or they wouldn't have chosen this book for you to read.

The battles that count aren't the ones for gold medals. The struggles within yourself— the invisible battles inside all of us—that's where it's at.
Jessie Owens, Winner of four gold medals at the 1936 Olympics

So, I hope you'll give this course your best effort. Most likely, it's the only one you'll ever take in college where the subject matter is YOU. And, believe me, if you don't master the content of this course, every other course you take (both in college and in the University of Life) will suffer. I wish you a great journey. Let us begin!

Journal Entry 1

n this activity, you will take an inventory of your personal strengths and weaknesses as revealed by your self-assessment questionnaire.

All glory comes from daring to begin.

Eugene F. Ware

1. **In your journal, write the eight areas of the self-assessment and record your scores for each, as follows:**

_____ 1. Accepting personal responsibility

_____ 2. Discovering self-motivation

_____ 3. Mastering self-management

_____ 4. Employing interdependence

_____ 5. Gaining self-awareness

_____ 6. Adopting lifelong learning

_____ 7. Developing emotional intelligence

_____ 8. Believing in myself

Transfer your scores from the self-assessment to the appropriate lines above.

2. **Write about the areas on the self-assessment in which you had your highest scores.** Explain why you think you scored higher in these areas than in others. Also, explore how you feel about these scores. Your entry might begin, "By doing the self-assessment, I learned that I . . ."

3. **Write about the areas on the self-assessment in which you had your lowest scores.** Explain why you think you scored lower in these areas than in others. Also, explore how you feel about these scores. Remember the saying, "If you keep doing what you've been doing, you'll keep getting what you've been getting." With this thought in mind, write about any specific changes you'd like to make in yourself during this course. Your entry might begin, "By doing the self-assessment, I also learned that I . . ."

My journal from this course is the most valuable possession I own. I will cherish it always.

Joseph Haskins, student

The five suggestions for creating a meaningful journal are printed on the inside back cover of *On Course*. Please review these suggestions before writing. **Especially remember to copy the directions for each step (printed in color) into your journal before writing.**

It's amazing how fast someone can go from being excited about college to flunking out. A year and a half ago, I received a letter from the University of Hawaii at Hilo informing me that I was being dismissed due to my inability to maintain a GPA of at least 2.0. I wasn't surprised because I had spent the whole semester making one bad choice after another. I hardly ever attended classes. I didn't do much homework. I didn't study for tests. And I never asked anyone for help. Mostly I just hung out with friends who told me I didn't need to go to college. But, fast-forward to today and you'll see a woman who has clear goals for her future, the motivation to reach those goals, and a plan to carry her to her dreams. However, it took a lot of learning in order for me to make such a huge change in my life.

After taking courses for a while at a community college, I got permission to re-enroll at the university. I was so nervous! I worried that I'd get dismissed again and I'd never do anything with my life. A counselor suggested that I take the University 101 course, and I'm so thankful I did. While writing the *On Course* journals I learned so much about myself and how I can succeed. I realized that when I first enrolled at the university, I was taking nursing courses because my parents wanted me to and I couldn't get motivated.

ONE STUDENT'S STORY
Jalayna Onaga,
*University of
Hawaii-Hilo, Hawaii*

This time I got inspired because my journals helped me look inside myself to figure out my own dreams for the future and to create a plan to reach them. For the first time, the plans I made were coming from my heart, not from someone telling me what I should do. I realized that I really love kids and *my* dream is to teach second or third graders. That's when I made a personal commitment to attend every class and learn as much as I could. In later journals I learned that making a schedule and writing everything down helped me get the important things done. I even learned to ask for help, and when I was absent because my car broke down, I met with the teacher to find out what I had missed. Before tests, I found it inspiring to read over my journal because my own words reminded me of my dreams and why I should study hard to get them.

Best of all, my new choices really paid off. When the semester ended, I had three A's and a B+ and I made the dean's list. My University 101 course and the *On Course* textbook really changed me as a student and as a person. Not long ago, I was a student without a direction. Now I can envision myself in the near future teaching a class full of eager students, watching them learn and grow, just like I was able to do.

On Course Principles at Work

I think we have to appreciate that we're alive for only a limited period of time, and we'll spend most of our lives working.

Victor Kiam, Chairman, Remington Products

Applying the strategies you're about to learn in *On Course* will not only improve your results in college, they'll also boost your success at work. You're about to explore dozens of proven strategies that will help you achieve your goals both in college and in your career.

This is no small matter. Career success (or lack of it) affects nearly every part of your life: family, income, self-esteem, who you associate with, where you live, your level of happiness, what you learn, your energy level, your health, and maybe even the length of your life.

Some students think, "All I need for success at work is the special knowledge of my chosen career." All that nurses need, they believe, are good nursing skills. All that accountants need are good accounting skills. All that lawyers need are good legal skills. These skills are called HARD skills, the knowledge needed to perform a particular job. Hard skills include knowing where to insert the needle for an intravenous feeding drip, how to write an effective business plan, and what the current inheritance laws are. These are the skills you'll be taught in courses in your major field of study. They are essential to qualify for a job. Without them you won't even get an interview.

But, most people who've been in the work world a while will tell you this: Hard skills are necessary to get a job but often insufficient to keep it or advance. That's because nearly all employees have the hard skills necessary to do the job for which they're hired. True, some may perform these skills a little better or a little worse than others, but one estimate suggests that only 15 percent of workers lose their jobs because they can't do the work. That's why career success is often determined by SOFT skills, the same strategies you'll be learning in this book. As one career specialist put it, "Having hard skills gets you hired; lacking soft skills gets you fired."

A United States government study agrees that soft skills are essential to job success. The Secretary of Labor asked a blue-ribbon panel of employers to identify what it takes to be successful in the modern employment world. This panel published a report in 1992 called the Secretary's Commission on Achieving Necessary Skills (SCANS). The report presents a set of foundation skills and workplace competencies that employers consider essential for work world success, and the report's timeless recommendations continue to be a valuable source of information for employers and employees alike. No one familiar with today's work world will find many surprises in the report, especially in the foundation skills. The report calls for employees to develop the same soft skills that employers include in job descriptions, look for in reference letters, probe for in job interviews, and assess in evaluations of their work force.

The SCANS report identifies the following soft skills as necessary for work and career success: taking responsibility, making effective decisions, setting goals, managing time, prioritizing tasks, persevering, giving strong efforts, working well in teams, communicating effectively, having empathy, knowing how to learn, exhibiting self-control, believing in one's own self worth. The report identifies these necessary skills but doesn't suggest a method for developing them. *On Course* will show you how.

Learning these soft skills will help you succeed in your first career after college. And, because soft skills are portable (unlike many hard skills), you can take them with you in the likely event that you later change careers. Most career specialists say the average worker today can expect to change careers at least once during his or her lifetime. In fact, some 25 percent of workers in the United States today are in occupations that did not even exist a few decades ago. If a physical therapist decides to change careers and work for an Internet company, he needs to master a whole new set of hard skills. But the soft skills he's mastered are the same ones that will help him shine in his new career.

So, as you're learning these soft skills, keep asking yourself, "How can I use these skills to stay on course to achieving my greatest potential at work as well as in college?" Be assured, what you're about to explore can make all the difference between success and failure in your career.

Believing in Yourself: Develop Self-Acceptance

 FOCUS QUESTIONS Why is high self-esteem so important to success? What can you do to raise your self-esteem?

The foundation of anyone's ability to cope successfully is high self-esteem. If you don't already have it, you can always develop it.

Virginia Satir

Roland was in his forties when he enrolled in my English 101 class. He contributed wonderful ideas to class discussions, so I was perplexed when the first two writing assignments passed without an essay from Roland.

Both times, he apologized profusely, promising to complete them soon. He didn't want to make excuses, he said, but he was stretched to his limit: He worked at night, and during the day he took care of his two young sons while his wife worked. "Don't worry, though," he assured me, "I'll have an essay to you by Monday. I'm going to be the first person in my family to get a college degree. Nothing's going to stop me."

But Monday came, and Roland was absent. On a hunch, I looked up his academic record and found that he had taken English 101 twice before. I contacted his previous instructors. Both of them said that Roland had made many promises but had never written an essay.

I called Roland, and we made an appointment to talk. He didn't show up. During the next class, I invited Roland into the hall while the class was working on a writing assignment.

"Sorry I missed our conference," Roland said. "I meant to call, but things have been piling up."

"Roland, I talked to your other instructors, and I know you never wrote anything for them. I'd love to help you, but you need to take an action. You need to write an essay." Roland nodded silently. "I believe you can do it. But I don't know if *you* believe you can do it. It's decision time. What do you say?"

"I'll have an essay to you by Friday."

I looked him in the eye.

"Promise," he said.

I knew that what Roland actually did, not what he promised, would reveal his deepest core beliefs about himself.

Self-esteem is the reputation we have with ourselves

Nathaniel Brandon

Self-esteem and core beliefs

So it is with us all. Our core beliefs—true or false, real or imagined—form the inner compass that guides our choices.

At the heart of our core beliefs is the statement *I AM ___.* How we complete that sentence in the quiet of our souls has a profound effect on the quality of our lives.

High self-esteem is the fuel that can propel us into the cycle of success. Do we approve of ourselves as we are, accepting our personal weaknesses along with our strengths? Do we believe ourselves capable, admirable, lovable, and fully worthy of the best life has to offer? If so, our beliefs will make it possible for us to make wise choices and stay on course to a rich, full life.

For example, imagine two students: one with high self-esteem, the other with low self-esteem. Picture them just after they get very disappointing test scores. What do they do next? The student with low self-esteem will likely choose options that protect his fragile self-image, options such as dropping the course rather than chancing failure. The student with high self-esteem, on the other hand, will likely choose options that move her toward success, options such as persisting in the course and getting additional help to be successful. Two students, same situation. One focuses on weaknesses. One focuses on strengths. The result: two different choices and two very different outcomes.

The good news is that self-esteem is learned, so anyone can learn to raise his or her self-esteem. Much of this book is about how you can do just that.

Self-esteem is more than merely recognizing one's positive qualities. It is an attitude of acceptance and non-judgment toward self and others.

Matthew McKay and
Patrick Fanning

As smart as he was, Albert Einstein could not figure out how to handle those tricky bounces at third base.

© ScienceCartoonsPlus.com

Know and accept yourself

People with high self-esteem know that no one is perfect, and they accept themselves with both their strengths and weaknesses. To paraphrase philosopher Reinhold Niebuhr, successful people accept the things they cannot change, have the courage to change the things they can change, and possess the wisdom to know the difference.

Successful people have the courage to take an honest self-inventory, as you began in Journal Entry 1. They acknowledge their strengths without false humility; they admit their weaknesses without stubborn denial. They tell the truth about themselves and take action to improve what they can.

Fortunately for Roland, he decided to do just that. On the Friday after our talk, he turned in his English 101 essay. His writing showed great promise, and I told him so. I also told him I appreciated that he had let go of the excuse that he was too busy to do his assignments. From then on, Roland handed in his essays on time. He met with me in conferences.

He visited the writing lab, and he did grammar exercises to improve his editing skills. He easily passed the course.

We cannot change anything unless we accept it.
Carl Jung

A few years later, Roland called me. He had transferred to a four-year university and was graduating with a 3.8 average. He was continuing on to graduate school to study urban planning. What he most wanted me to know was that one of his instructors had asked permission to use one of his essays as a model of excellent writing. "You know," Roland said, "I'd still be avoiding writing if I hadn't accepted two things about myself: I was a little bit lazy and I was a whole lot scared. Once I admitted those things about myself, I started changing."

Each of us has a unique combination of strengths and weaknesses. When struggling people become aware of a weakness, they typically blame the problem on others or they beat themselves up for not being perfect. Successful people, however, usually make a different choice: They acknowledge the weakness, accept it without self-judgment, and, when possible, take action to create positive changes. As always, the choices we make determine both where we are headed and the quality of the journey. Developing self-acceptance helps us to make the choices wisely.

Journal Entry 2

In this activity, you will explore your strengths and weaknesses and the reputation you have with yourself. This exploration of your self-esteem will allow you to begin revising any limiting beliefs you may hold about yourself. By doing so you will take a major step toward your success.

Be what you is, not what you ain't, 'cause if you ain't what you is, you is what you ain't.
Luther D. Price

1. **In your journal, write a list of ten or more of your personal strengths:** For example, Mentally: *I'm good at math*; Physically: *I'm very athletic*; Emotionally: *I seldom let anger control me*; Socially: *I'm a good friend*; and Others: *I am almost always on time.*

2. **Write a list of ten or more of your personal weaknesses:** For example, Mentally: *I'm a slow reader*; Physically: *I am overweight*; Emotionally: *I'm easily hurt by criticism*; Socially: *I don't listen very well*; and Others: *I'm a terrible procrastinator.*

3. **Using the information in Steps 1 and 2 and score #8 on your self-assessment, write about the present state of your self-esteem.** On a scale of 1 to 10 (with 10 high), how strong is your self-esteem? How do you think it got to be that way? How would you like it to be? What changes could you make to achieve your ideal self-esteem?

To create an outstanding journal, remember to use the five suggestions printed on the inside back cover of *On Course*. **Especially remember to dive deep!**

Entering college is like crossing the border into another country. Each has new customs to learn. If you learn and heed the following college customs, your stay in higher education will be not only more successful but more enjoyable as well.

1. Read your college catalogue. This resource contains most of the factual information you'll need to plot a great journey through higher education. It explains how your college applies many of the customs discussed in this section. Keep a college catalogue on hand and refer to it often. Catalogues are usually available in the registrar's or counseling office, and many colleges post a copy of the catalogue on their web site.

2. See your advisor. Colleges provide an advisor who can help you make wise choices. Sometimes this person is a counselor, sometimes an instructor. Find out who your advisor is, make an appointment, and get advice on what courses to take and how to create your best schedule. Students who avoid advisors often enroll in unnecessary courses or miss taking courses that are required for graduation. Your tuition has paid for a guide through college; use this valuable resource effectively.

3. Understand prerequisites. A "prerequisite" is a course that must be completed before you can take another course. For example, colleges require the completion of calculus before enrollment in more advanced mathematics courses. Before you register, confirm with your advisor that you have met all of the prerequisites. Otherwise you may find yourself registered for a course you aren't prepared to pass. Prerequisites appear within each course description in your college catalogue.

4. Complete your general education requirements. Most colleges require students to take a minimum number of general education courses such as freshman composition, speech, history, psychology, and mathematics. Find a list of these required courses in your college catalogue, and check off each requirement as you complete it. Regardless of how many credits you earn, you can't graduate until you've completed the general education requirements.

5. Choose a major wisely. You usually choose a major area of study in your first or second year. Examples of majors include nursing, early childhood education, biology, teaching, mechanical engineering, and art. Even if you've already picked a major, you may want to visit the counseling center to discover what other majors might interest you more or be a better steppingstone to your chosen career. For example, majoring in English is great preparation for a law degree. All majors and their required courses are listed in your college catalogue. Until you've entered a major, you're wise to concentrate on completing your general education requirements.

6. Take a realistic course load. I once taught a student who worked full-time, was married with three small children, and had signed up for six courses in her first semester. After five weeks, she was exhausted and withdrew from college. There are only 168 hours in a week. Be realistic about the number of courses you can handle given your other responsibilities. Students often register for too many credits because of their mistaken belief that this choice will get them to graduation more quickly. Too often the actual result is dropped and failed classes, pushing graduation farther into the future.

7. Attend the first day of class (on time). Of course it's wise to attend *every* day, but whatever you do, be present on the first day! On this day instructors usually provide the class assignments and rules for the entire semester. If you're absent, you may miss something that will come back to bite you later.

8. Sit in class where you can focus on learning. Many students focus best sitting up front. Others prefer sitting on the side about halfway back where they can see all of their classmates and the instructor during a discussion. Experiment. Try different places in the room. Once you find the place that best supports your learning, sit there permanently . . . unless you find that changing seats every day helps you learn better.

9. Study the syllabus. In the first class, instructors usually provide a syllabus (sometimes called a first-day handout). The syllabus is the single most important handout you will receive all semester. Typically, it contains the course objectives, the required books and supplies, all assignments and due dates, and the method for determining grades. This handout also presents any course rules you need to know. Essentially, the course syllabus is a contract between you and your instructor who will assume that you've read and understood this contract; be sure to ask questions about any part you don't understand.

10. Buy required course books and supplies as soon as possible. College instructors cover a lot of ground quickly. If you don't have your study materials from the beginning of the course, you may fall too far behind to catch up. To get a head start on their classes, some students go to their college bookstore weeks before the semester or quarter begins and purchase course materials. If money is tight, check with the financial aid office to see if your college provides temporary book loans. Or, as a last resort, ask your instructors if they will put copies of the course texts on reserve at your college library.

11. Introduce yourself to one or more classmates and exchange phone numbers and email addresses. After an absence, contact a classmate to learn what you missed. Few experiences in college are worse than returning to class and facing a test that was announced in your absence.

12. Inform your instructor before an absence. Think of your class as your job and your instructor as your employer. Professional courtesy dictates notifying your employer of anticipated absences. The same is true with instructors.

13. If you arrive late, slip in quietly. Don't make excuses. Just come in and sit down. If you want to explain your lateness, see the instructor after class.

14. Ask questions. If the question you don't ask shows up on a test, you're going to be upset with yourself. Your classmates are equally nervous about asking questions. Go ahead, raise your hand and ask one on the first day; after that, it'll be easier.

15. To hold an extended conversation with your instructors, make an appointment during their office hours. Most college instructors have scheduled office hours. Ask your instructor for his or her office hours and mention that you'd like to make an appointment to discuss a specific topic. Be sure to show up (or call beforehand to reschedule).

16. Get involved in campus life. Most colleges offer numerous activities that can broaden your education, add pleasure to your life, and introduce you to new friends. Consider participating in the drama club, school newspaper, intercultural counsel, student government, athletic teams, band or orchestra, literary magazine, yearbook committee, science club, or one of the many other organizations on your campus.

17. Know the importance of your Grade Point Average (GPA). Your GPA is the average grade for all of the courses you have taken in college. At most colleges, GPAs range from 0.0 ("F") to 4.0 ("A"). Your GPA affects your future in many ways. At most colleges a minimum GPA (often 2.0, a "C") is required to graduate, regardless of how many credits you have accumulated. Students who fall below the minimum GPA are usually ineligible for financial aid and cannot play intercollegiate sports. Academic honors (like the Dean's List) and some scholarships are based on your GPA. Finally, potential employers often note GPAs to determine if prospective employees have achieved success in college.

18. Know how to compute your grade point average (GPA). At most colleges, GPAs are printed on a student's transcript, which is a list of courses completed (with the grade earned). You can get a copy of your transcript from the registrar's office. Transcripts are usually free or available for a nominal charge. Computing your own grade point average is simple using the formula on page 20.

19. If you stop attending a class, withdraw officially. Students are enrolled in a course until they're

---

Formula for Computing Your Grade Point Average (GPA)

$$\frac{(G1 \times C1) + (G2 \times C2) + (G3 \times C3) + (G4 + C3) + \ldots (Gn + Cn)}{\text{Total \# of Credits Attempted}}$$

In this formula, G = the grade in a course and C = number of credits for a course. For example, suppose you had the following grades:

"A" in Math 110 (4 Credits) G1 ("A") = 4.0

"B" in English 101 (3 Credits) G2 ("B") = 3.0

"C" in Sociology 101 (3 Credits) G3 ("C") = 2.0

"D" in Music 104 (2 Credits) G4 ("D") = 1.0

"F" in Physical Education 109 (1 Credit) G5 ("F") = 0.0

Here's how to figure the GPA from the grades above:

$$\frac{(4.0 \times 4) + (3.0 \times 3) + (2.0 \times 3) + (1.0 \times 2) + (0.0 \times 1)}{4 + 3 + 3 + 2 + 1} = \frac{16 + 9 + 6 + 2 + 0}{13} = 2.54$$

officially withdrawn. A student who stops attending is still on the class roster at semester's end when grades are assigned, and the instructor will very likely give the non-attending student an "F." That failing grade is now a permanent part of the student's record, lowering the GPA and discouraging potential employers. If you decide (for whatever reason) to stop attending a class, go directly to the registrar's office and follow its official procedures for withdrawing from a class. Make certain that you withdraw before your college's deadline. This date is often about halfway through a semester or quarter.

20. Talk to your instructor before withdrawing. If you're going to fail a course, withdraw to protect your GPA. But don't withdraw without speaking to your instructor first. Sometimes students think they are doing far worse than they really are. Discuss with your instructor what you need to do to pass the course and make a step-by-step plan. If you

discover that failing is inevitable, withdraw officially.

21. Keep a file of important documents. Forms get lost in large organizations like colleges. Save everything that may affect your future: course syllabi, completed tests and assignments, approved registration forms, scholarship applications, transcripts, and paid bills. If you're exempted from a college requirement or course prerequisite, get it in writing and add the document to your files.

22. Finally, some college customs dictate what you should *not* do. Avoiding these behaviors shows respect for your classmates and instructors.

- Don't pack up your books or put on your coat until the class is over.
- After an absence, don't ask your instructor, "Did I miss anything?" (Of course you did.)
- Don't wear headphones during class.

- Don't let a pager or cellular phone disturb the class.
- Don't talk with a neighbor while the instructor or a classmate is talking.
- Don't make distracting noises in class (e.g., clicking pen, popping gum, drumming fingers, and so on).

College Customs Exercise

Ask an upperclassman, "What is the one thing you now know about college customs that you wish you had known on your first day?" Be prepared to report your findings.

Accepting Personal Responsibility

2

I accept responsibility for creating my life as I want it.

SUCCESSFUL STUDENTS . . .	STRUGGLING STUDENTS . . .
■ **adopt the Creator role,** believing that their choices create the outcomes and experiences of their lives.	■ accept the Victim role, believing that external forces determine the outcomes and experiences of their lives.
■ **master Creator language,** accepting personal responsibility for their results.	■ use Victim language, rejecting personal responsibility by blaming, complaining, and excusing.
■ **make wise decisions,** consciously designing the future they want.	■ make decisions carelessly, letting the future happen by chance rather than by choice.

The Late Paper

Professor Freud announced in her syllabus for Psychology 101 that final term papers had to be in her hands by noon on December 18. No student, she emphasized, would pass the course without a completed term paper turned in on time. As the semester drew to a close, **Kim** had an "A" average in Professor Freud's psychology class, and she began researching her term paper with excitement.

Arnold, Kim's husband, felt threatened that he had only a high school diploma while his wife was getting close to her college degree. Arnold worked at a bakery, and his coworker **Philip** began teasing that Kim would soon dump Arnold for a college guy. That's when Arnold started accusing Kim of having an affair and demanding she drop out of college. She told Arnold he was being ridiculous. In fact, she said, a young man in her history class had asked her out, but she had refused. Instead of feeling better, Arnold became even more angry. With Philip continuing to provoke him, Arnold became sure Kim was having an affair, and he began telling her every day that she was stupid and would never get a degree.

Despite the tension at home, Kim finished her psychology term paper the day before it was due. Since Arnold had hidden the car keys, she decided to take the bus to the college and turn in her psychology paper a day early. While she was waiting for the bus, **Cindy,** one of Kim's psychology classmates, drove up and invited Kim to join her and some other students for an end-of-semester celebration. Kim told Cindy she was on her way to turn in her term paper, and Cindy promised she'd make sure Kim got it in on time. "I deserve some fun," Kim decided, and hopped into the car. The celebration went long into the night. Kim kept asking Cindy to take her home, but Cindy always replied, "Don't be such a bore. Have another drink." When Cindy finally took Kim home, it was 4:30 in the morning. She sighed with relief when she found that Arnold had already fallen asleep.

When Kim woke up, it was 11:30 A.M., just 30 minutes before her term paper was due. She could make it to the college in time by car, so she shook Arnold and begged him to drive her. He just snapped, "Oh sure, you stay out all night with your college friends. Then, I'm supposed to get up on my day off and drive you all over town. Forget it." "At least give me the keys," she said, but Arnold merely rolled over and went back to sleep. Panicked, Kim called Professor Freud's office and told **Mary,** the secretary, that she was having car trouble. "Don't worry," Mary assured Kim, "I'm sure Professor Freud won't care if your paper's a little late. Just be sure to have it here before she leaves at 1:00." Relieved, Kim decided not to wake Arnold again; instead, she took the bus.

At 12:15, Kim walked into Professor Freud's office with her term paper. Professor Freud said, "Sorry, Kim, you're 15 minutes late." She refused to accept Kim's term paper and gave Kim an "F" for the course.

Listed below are the characters in this story. Rank them in order of their *responsibility for Kim's failing grade in Psychology 101*. Give a different score to each character. Be prepared to explain your choices.

Most responsible ← 1 2 3 4 5 6 → Least responsible

___ **Professor Freud,** the teacher	___ **Philip,** Arnold's coworker
___ **Kim,** the psychology student	___ **Cindy,** Kim's classmate
___ **Arnold,** Kim's husband	___ **Mary,** Prof. Freud's secretary

DIVING DEEPER: Is there someone not mentioned in the story who may also bear responsibility for Kim's failing grade?

Adopting the Creator Role

FOCUS QUESTIONS   What is self-responsibility? Why is it the key to gaining maximum control over the outcomes and experiences of your life?

When psychologist Richard Logan studied people who survived ordeals such as being imprisoned in concentration camps or lost in the frozen Arctic, he found that all of these victors shared a common belief. They saw themselves as personally responsible for the outcomes and experiences of their lives.

I am the master of my fate; I am the captain of my soul.
William E. Henley

Ironically, responsibility has gotten a bad reputation. Some see it as a heavy burden they have to lug through life. Quite the contrary, personal responsibility is the foundation of success because, without it, our lives are shaped by forces outside of us. **The essence of personal responsibility is responding wisely to life's opportunities and challenges, rather than waiting passively for luck or other people to make the choices for us.**

Whether your challenge is surviving an Arctic blizzard or excelling in college, accepting personal responsibility moves you into cooperation with yourself and with the world. As long as you resist your role in creating the outcomes and experiences in your life, you will fall far short of your potential.

I first met Deborah when she was a student in my English 101 class. Deborah wanted to be a nurse, but before she could qualify for the nursing program, she had to pass English 101. She was taking the course for the fourth time.

"Your writing shows fine potential," I told Deborah after I had read her first essay. "You'll pass English 101 as soon as you eliminate your grammar problems."

"I know," she said. "That's what my other three instructors said."

"Well, let's make this your last semester in English 101, then. After each essay, make an appointment with me to go over your grammar problems."

"Okay."

"And go to the Writing Lab as often as possible. Start by studying verb tense. Let's eliminate one problem at a time."

The more we practice the habit of acting from a position of responsibility, the more effective we become as human beings, and the more successful we become as managers of our lives.
Joyce Chapman

"I'll go this afternoon!"

But Deborah never found time: *No, really . . . I'll go to the lab just as soon as I . . .*

Deborah scheduled two appointments with me during the semester and missed them both: *I'm so sorry . . . I'll come to see you just as soon as I . . .*

To pass English 101 at our college, students must pass one of two essays written at the end of the semester in an exam setting. Each essay, identified by social security number only, is graded by two other instructors. At semester's end, Deborah once again failed English 101. "It isn't fair!" Deborah protested. "Those exam graders expect us to be professional writers. They're keeping me from becoming a nurse!"

I suggested another possibility: "What if *you* are the one keeping you from becoming a nurse?"

Deborah didn't like that idea. She wanted to believe that her problem was "out there." Her only obstacle was *those* teachers. All her disappointments were *their* fault. The exam graders weren't fair. Life wasn't fair! In the face of this injustice, she was helpless.

I reminded Deborah that it was *she* who had not studied her grammar. It was *she* who had not come to conferences. It was *she* who had not accepted personal responsibility for creating her life the way she wanted it.

"Yes, but . . ." she said.

Victims and Creators

When people keep doing what they've been doing even when it doesn't work, they are acting as **Victims.** When people change their beliefs and behaviors to create the best results they can, they are acting as **Creators.**

When you accept personal responsibility, you believe that you create *everything* in your life. This idea upsets some people. Accidents happen, they say. People treat them badly. Sometimes they really are victims of outside forces.

This claim, of course, is true. At times, we *are* all affected by forces beyond our control. If a hurricane destroys my house, I am a victim (with a small "v"). But if I allow that event to ruin my life, I am a Victim (with a capital "V").

The essential issue is this: Would it improve your life to act *as if* you create all of the joys and sorrows in your life? Answer "YES!" and see that belief improve your life. After all, if you believe that someone or something out there causes all of your problems, then it's up to "them" to change. What a wait that can be! How long, for example, will Deborah have to wait for "those English teachers" to change?

If, however, you accept responsibility for creating your own results, what happens then? You will look for ways to create your desired outcomes and experiences despite obstacles. And if you look, you've just increased your chances of success immeasurably!

The benefits to students of accepting personal responsibility have been demonstrated in various studies. Researchers Robert Vallerand and Robert Bissonette, for example, asked one thousand first-year college students to complete a questionnaire about why they were attending school. They used the students' answers to assess whether the students were "Origin-like" or "Pawn-like." The researchers defined Origin-like students as seeing themselves as the originators of their own behaviors, in other words, Creators. By contrast, Pawn-like students see themselves as mere puppets manipulated by others, in other words, Victims. A year later, the researchers returned to find out what had happened to the one thousand students. They found that significantly more of the Creator-like students were still enrolled in college than the Victim-like

Blaming . . . is a pastime for losers. There's no leverage in blaming. Power is rooted in self-responsibility.

Nathaniel Branden

Every time your back is against the wall, there is only one person that can help. And that's you. It has to come from inside.

Pat Riley,
Professional Basketball Coach

students. If you want to succeed in college (and in life), then being a Creator gives you a big edge.

Responsibility and choice

The key ingredient of personal responsibility is **choice.** Animals respond to a stimulus because of instinct or habit. For humans, however, there is a brief, critical moment of decision available between the stimulus and the response. In this moment, we make the choices—consciously or unconsciously—that influence the outcomes of our lives.

Numerous times each day, you come to a fork in the road and must make a choice. Even not making a choice is a choice. Some choices have a small impact: Shall I get my hair cut today or tomorrow? Some have a huge impact: Shall I stay in college or drop out? The sum of the choices you make from this day forward will create the eventual outcome of your life.

The moment of choice looks like this:

I believe that we are solely responsible for our choices, and we have to accept the consequences of every deed, word, and thought throughout our lifetime.
Elisabeth Kübler-Ross

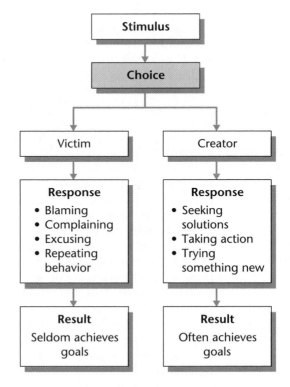

In that brief moment between stimulus and response, we can choose to be a Victim or a Creator. When we respond as a Victim, we complain, blame, make excuses, and repeat ineffective behaviors. When we respond as a Creator, we pause at each decision point and ask, "What are my options, and which option will best help me create my desired outcomes and experiences?"

The difference between responding to life as a Victim or Creator is how we choose to use our energy. When I'm blaming, complaining, and excusing, my efforts cause little or no improvement. Sure, it may feel good in that moment to claim that I'm a poor Victim and "they" are evil persecutors, but my good feelings are fleeting because afterwards my problem still exists. By contrast, when I'm seeking solutions and taking actions, my efforts often (though not always) lead to improvements. At critical forks in the road, Victims waste their energy and remain stuck, while Creators use their energy for improving their outcomes and experiences.

But, let's be honest. No one makes Creator choices all of the time. I've never met anyone who did, least of all me. Our inner lives feature a perpetual tug of war between the Creator part of us and the Victim part of us. My own experiences have taught me the following life lesson: The more choices I make as a Creator, the more I improve the quality of my life. That's why I urge you to join me in an effort to choose more often as a Creator. It won't be easy, but it's worth it. You may have to take my word for it right now, but if you experiment with the strategies in this book and continue using the ones that work for you, in a few months you'll see powerful proof in your own life of the value of making Creator choices.

Here's an important choice you can make immediately. Accept, as Creators do, this belief: *I am responsible for creating my life as I want it.* Of course sometimes you won't be able to create the specific outcomes and experiences you want. The reality is that some circumstances will defy even your best efforts. But, believing that you always have a way to improve your present situation will motivate you to look for it, and by looking you'll often discover options you would never have found otherwise. For this reason, choosing to accept personal responsibility is the first step toward your success.

Here's a related choice. Set aside any thought that Creator and Victim choices have anything to do with being good or bad, right or wrong, smart or dumb, worthy or unworthy. If you make a Victim choice, you aren't bad, wrong, dumb, or unworthy. For that matter, if you make a Creator choice, you aren't good, right, smart, or worthy. These judgments will merely distract you from the real issue: Are you getting the outcomes and experiences that *you* want in *your* life? If you are, then keep making the same choices because they're working. But, if you're not creating the life you want, then you'd be wise to try something new. We benefit greatly when we shift our energy from defending ourselves from judgments and put it into improving the outcomes and experiences of our lives.

I am a Shawnee. My forefathers were warriors. Their son is a warrior. . . . From my tribe I take nothing. I am the maker of my own fortune.

Tecumseh

"Oh, I get what you mean!" one of my students once exclaimed as we were exploring this issue of personal responsibility, "You're saying that living my life is like traveling in my car. If I want to get where I want to go, I better be the driver and not a passenger." I appreciate her metaphor because it identifies that personal responsibility is about taking hold of the steering wheel of our lives, about taking control of where we go and how we get there.

Ultimately each of us creates the quality of our life with the wisdom or folly of our choices.

Journal Entry 3

In this activity, you will experiment with the Creator role. By choosing to take responsibility for your life, you will immediately gain an increased power to achieve your greatest potential.

1. **Write and complete each of the ten sentence stems below.** For example, someone might complete the first sentence stem as follows:

1. IF I TAKE FULL RESPONSIBILITY FOR ALL OF MY ACTIONS, I will accomplish great things.

1. IF I TAKE FULL RESPONSIBILITY FOR ALL OF MY ACTIONS . . .

2. IF I TAKE FULL RESPONSIBILITY FOR ALL OF MY THOUGHTS . . .

3. IF I TAKE FULL RESPONSIBILITY FOR ALL OF MY FEELINGS . . .

4. IF I TAKE FULL RESPONSIBILITY FOR MY EDUCATION . . .

5. IF I TAKE FULL RESPONSIBILITY FOR MY CAREER . . .

6. IF I TAKE FULL RESPONSIBILITY FOR MY RELATIONSHIPS . . .

7. IF I TAKE FULL RESPONSIBILITY FOR MY HEALTH . . .

8. IF I TAKE FULL RESPONSIBILITY FOR ALL THAT HAPPENS TO ME . . .

9. WHEN I AM ACTING FULLY RESPONSIBLE FOR MY LIFE . . .

10. IF I WERE TO CREATE MY VERY BEST SELF . . .

Whatever reason you had for not being somebody, there's somebody who had that same problem and overcame it.

Barbara Reynolds

2. **Write about what you have learned or relearned in this journal about personal responsibility and how you will use this knowledge to improve your life.** You might begin, *By reading and writing about personal responsibility, I have learned. . . .*

During my first semester in college, I was enrolled in a freshman English class. In high school I was usually able to pull off an A on my honors English papers without much work, and I thought I was a pretty good writer. So when I turned in my first college essay, I was expecting to get an A, or at worst a B. However, I was about to get a rude awakening. When we received our papers back a week later, I was shocked to see a C+ on my paper. I went to the instructor, and she said I just needed more practice and not to worry because I was in the class to learn. However, since I have high expectations for myself, those words weren't very comforting.

About that same time in my Strategies for College Success class, we were assigned to read a chapter in *On Course* about personal responsibility. The main idea is to adopt a "Creator" approach to problems, which I understood to mean basically seek solutions and not dwell on the negative. Then it clicked for me; I am responsible for my grades and I need to do whatever is necessary to get the ones I want. In high school, I could write one draft of an essay, turn it in, and I'd usually get an A, but that approach wasn't working in college. So, now I had to do something different. I started writing my papers before they were due and then meeting with my English teacher at least once a week to get her suggestions. Because I was a full-time student and also worked seventeen to twenty hours a week in the cashier's office, sometimes I had to see her during times that were inconvenient. But I had to be flexible if I wanted her critique. During English class, we'd do peer editing, and I found that helpful, too. When I was in high school, I only spent about an hour or two writing an essay. Now I was spending at least three to five hours.

To my surprise, after some not-so-great increases in grades, I received what I had been waiting for: my first A on an essay. Although my final grade in English was a B, I learned a number of important lessons. It's really important to take your time with writing, to have your instructor or someone else read a rough draft and give you some suggestions, and then to write a final draft. I also learned that nobody can make the grade for you; you have to be responsible for yourself. I may not always get an A, but I learned to face a challenge, and no matter what grade I receive, knowing that I took responsibility as a "Creator" was the greatest lesson of all.

ONE STUDENT'S STORY

Brian Moore
Glendale Community College, Arizona

Mastering Creator Language

? FOCUS QUESTION   How can you create greater success by changing your vocabulary?

The world of self-criticism on the one side and judgment toward others on the other side represents a major part of the dance of life.

Hal Stone and Sidra Stone

Have you ever noticed that there is almost always a conversation going on in your mind? Inner voices chatter away, offering commentary about you, other people, and the world. This self-talk is important because what you say to yourself determines the choices you make at each fork in the road. Victims typically listen to the voice of their Inner Critic or their Inner Defender.

The Inner Critic.   This is the internal voice that judges us as inadequate: *I'm so uncoordinated. I can't do math. I'm not someone she would want to date. I never say the right thing. My ears are too big. I'm a lousy writer.* The Inner Critic blames us for whatever goes wrong in our life: *It's all my fault. I always screw up. I knew I couldn't pass biology. I ruined the project. I ought to be ashamed. I blew it again.* This judgmental inner voice can find fault with anything about us: our appearance, our intellect, our performance, our personality, our abilities, how others see us, and, in severe cases, even our value as a human being: *I'm not good enough. I'm worthless, I don't deserve to live.* (While nearly everyone has a critical inner voice at times, if you often think toxic self-judgments like these last three, don't mess around. Get to your college's counseling office immediately and get help revising these noxious messages so you don't make self-destructive choices.)

Ironically, self-judgments have a positive intention. By criticizing ourselves, we hope to eliminate our flaws and win the approval of others, thus feeling more worthy. Occasionally when we bully ourselves to be perfect, we *do* create a positive outcome, though we make ourselves miserable in the effort. Often, though, self-judgments cause us to give up, as when I tell myself, *I can't pass math,* so I drop the course. What's positive about this? Well, at least I've escaped my problem. Freed from the pressures of passing math, my anxieties float away and I feel better than I have since the semester started. Of course, I still have to pass math to get my degree, so my relief is temporary.

Where does an Inner Critic come from? Here's one clue: Have you noticed that its self-criticisms often sound like judgmental adults we have known? It's as if our younger self recorded their judgments and, years later, our Inner Critic replays them over and over. Sometimes you can even trace a self-judgment back to a specific comment that someone made about you years ago. Regardless of its accuracy now, that judgment can affect the choices you make every day.

The Inner Defender.   The flip side of the Inner Critic is the Inner Defender. Instead of judging ourselves, the Inner Defender judges others: *What a boring teacher. My advisor screwed up my financial aid. My roommate made me late to class. No one knows what they're doing around here. It's all **their** fault!* Inner Defenders can find something to grumble about in virtually any situation. Their thoughts and conversations are full of blaming, complaining, accusing, judging, criticizing, and condemning others.

Like Inner Critics, Inner Defenders have a positive intention. They, too, want to protect us from discomfort and anxiety. They do so by blaming our problems on forces that seem beyond our control, such as other people, bad luck, the government, lack of money, uncaring parents, not enough time, or even too much time. My Inner Defender might say, *I can't pass math because my instructor is terrible. She couldn't teach math to Einstein. Besides that, the textbook stinks and the tutors in the math lab are rude and unhelpful. It's obvious this college doesn't really care what happens to its students.* Now I breathe a sigh of relief because I'm covered. If I drop the course, hey, it's not my fault. If I stay in the course and fail, it's not my fault either. And, if I stay in the course and somehow get a passing grade (despite my terrible instructor, lousy textbook, worthless tutors,

A loud, voluble critic is enormously toxic. He is more poisonous to your psychological health than almost any trauma or loss. That's because grief and pain wash away with time. But the critic is always with you—judging, blaming, finding fault.

Matthew McKay
and Patrick Fanning

What you're supposed to do when you don't like a thing is change it. If you can't change it, change the way you think about it. Don't complain.

Advice to Maya Angelou from
her grandmother

and uncaring college), well, then I have performed no less than a certified miracle! Regardless of how bad things may get, I can find comfort knowing that at least it's not my fault. It's *their* fault!

And where did this voice come from? Perhaps you've noticed that the Inner Defender's voice sounds suspiciously like our own voice when we were scared and defensive little kids trying to protect ourselves from criticism or punishment by powerful adults. Remember how we'd excuse ourselves from responsibility, shifting the blame for our poor choices onto someone or something else: *It's not my fault. He keeps poking me. My dog ate my homework. What else could I do? I didn't have any choice. My sister broke it. He made me do it. Why does everyone always pick on me? It's all their fault!*

We pay a high price for listening to either our Inner Critic or Inner Defender. By focusing on who's to blame, we distract ourselves from acting on what needs to be done to get back on course. To feel better in the moment, we sabotage creating a better future.

Fortunately, another voice exists within us all.

You must change the way you talk to yourself about your life situations so that you no longer imply that anything outside of you is the immediate cause of your unhappiness. Instead of saying, "Joe makes me mad," say, "I make myself mad when I'm around Joe."

Ken Keyes

The Inner Guide.   This is the wise inner voice that seeks to make the best of any situation. The Inner Guide knows that judgment doesn't improve difficult situations. So instead, the Inner Guide objectively observes each situation and asks, *Am I on course or off course? If I'm off course, what can I do to get back on course?* Inner Guides tell us the impartial truth (as best they know it at that time), allowing us to be more fully aware of the world around us, other people, and especially ourselves. With this knowledge, we can take actions that will get us back on course.

Some people say, "But my Inner Critic (or Inner Defender) is *right*!" Yes, it's true that the Inner Critic or Inner Defender can be just as "right" as the Inner Guide. Maybe you really are a lousy writer and the tutors in the math lab actually *are* rude and unhelpful. The difference is that Victims expend all their energy in judging themselves or others, while Creators use their energy to solve the problem. The voice we choose to occupy our thoughts determines our choices, and our choices determine the outcomes and experiences of our lives. So choose your thoughts carefully.

The language of responsibility

Translating Victim statements into the responsible language of Creators moves you from stagnant judgments to dynamic actions. In the chart below, the left-hand column presents the Victim thoughts of a student who is taking a challenging college course. Thinking this way, the student's future in this course is easy to predict . . . and it isn't pretty.

But, if she changes her inner conversation, as shown in the right-hand column, she'll also change her behaviors. She can learn more in the course and increase her likelihood of passing. More important, she can learn to reclaim control of her life from the judgmental, self-sabotaging thoughts of her Inner Critic and Inner Defender.

As you read these translations, notice two qualities that characterize Creator language. First, Creators accept responsibility for their situation. Second, they plan and take actions to improve their situation. So, when you hear **Ownership** and an **Action Plan**, you know you're talking to a Creator.

Excuses rob you of power and induce apathy
        Agnes Whistling Elk

Victims Focus on Their Weaknesses
I'm terrible in this subject.

Creators Focus on How to Improve
I find this course challenging, so I'll start a study group and ask more questions in class.

Victims Make Excuses
The instructor is so boring he puts me to sleep.

Creators Seek Solutions
I'm having difficulty staying awake in this class, so I'm going to ask permission to record the lectures. Then I'll listen to them a little at a time and take detailed notes.

Victims Complain
This course is a stupid requirement.

Creators Turn Complaints Into Requests
I don't understand why this course is required, so I'm going to ask my instructor to help me see how it will benefit me in the future.

Victims Compare Themselves Unfavorably to Others
I'll never do as well as John; he's a genius.

Creators Seek Help from Those More Skilled
I need help in this course, so I'm going to ask John if he'll help me study for the exams.

Victims Blame
The tests are ridiculous. The professor gave me an "F" on the first one.

Creators Accept Responsibility
I got an "F" on the first test because I didn't read the assignments carefully. From now on I'll take detailed notes on everything I read.

Victims See Problems as Permanent
I'll never understand this subject. It's a waste of time to study.

Creators Treat Problems as Temporary
Studying one night a week for this subject isn't working. I'll experiment with studying a little bit every day and see if I learn it better.

Victims Repeat Ineffective Behaviors
Going to the tutoring center is no help. There aren't enough tutors.

Creators Do Something New
I've been going to the tutoring center right after lunch when it's really busy. I'll start going in the morning to see if more tutors are available then.

Victims Try	Creators Do
I'll try to do better, but it's just no use.	To do better, I'll do the following: Attend class regularly, take good notes, ask questions in class, start a study group, and make an appointment with the teacher. If all that doesn't work, I'll think of something else.
Victims Predict Defeat and Give Up	**Creators Think Positively and Look for a Better Choice**
I'll probably fail. There's nothing I can do. I can't . . . I have to . . . I should . . . I quit. . .	I'll find a way. There's always something I can do. I can . . . I choose to . . . I will . . . I'll keep going. . .

I used to want the words "She tried" on my tombstone. Now I want, "She did it."
Katherine Dunham

When Victims complain, blame, and make excuses, they have little energy left over to solve their problems. As a result, they typically remain stuck where they are, telling their sad story over and over to any poor soul who will listen. (Ever hear of a "pity party"?) In this way, Victims exhaust not only their own energy but often drain the energy of the people around them.

By contrast, Creators use their words and thoughts to improve a bad situation. First, they accept responsibility for creating their present outcomes and experiences, and their words reflect that ownership. Next they plan and take positive actions to improve their lives. In this way, Creators energize themselves and the people around them.

Whenever you feel yourself slipping into Victim language, ask yourself: What do I want in my life—excuses or results? What could I think and say right now that would get me moving towards the outcomes and experiences that I want?

Journal Entry 4

In this activity you will practice the language of personal responsibility. By learning to translate Victim statements into Creator statements, you will master the language of successful people.

The way you use words has a tremendous impact on the quality of your life. Certain words are destructive; others are empowering.
Susan Jeffers

1. **Draw a line down the middle of a journal page. On the left side of the line, copy the ten Victim statements below.**

2. **On the right side of the line, translate the Victim statements into the words of a Creator.** The two keys to Creator language are taking ownership of a problem and taking positive actions to solve it. When you respond as if you are responsible for a bad situation, then you are empowered to do something about it (unlike Victims who must wait for someone else to solve their problems). Use the translations in the journal article on pages 33–34 as models.

3. **Write what you have learned or relearned about how you use language: Is it your habit to speak as a Victim or as a Creator? Do you find yourself more**

inclined to blame yourself, blame others, or seek solutions? Be sure to give examples. What is your goal for language usage from now on? How, specifically, will you accomplish this goal? Your paragraph might begin, *While reading about and practicing Creator language, I learned that I . . .*

Remember to DIVE DEEP!

VICTIM LANGUAGE	CREATOR LANGUAGE
1. If they'd do something about the parking on campus, I wouldn't be late so often.	
2. I'm failing because no one in my family is good at math. I think we've got defective math genes.	
3. I'm too shy to ask questions in class even when I'm confused.	
4. She's a lousy instructor. That's why I failed the first test.	
5. I hate group projects because people are lazy and I always end up doing most of the work.	
6. I wish I could write better, but I just can't.	
7. My friend got me so angry that I can't even study for the exam.	
8. I'll try to do my best this semester.	
9. The financial aid form is too complicated to fill out.	
10. I work nights so I didn't have time to do the assignment.	

If you are in shackles, "I can't" has relevance; otherwise, it is usually a roundabout way of saying "I don't want to," "I won't," or, "I have not learned how to." If you really mean "I don't want to," it is important to come out and say so. Saying "I can't" disowns responsibility.
Gay and Kathlyn Hendricks

Making Wise Decisions

 FOCUS QUESTION   How can you improve the quality of the decisions you make?

The end result of your life here on earth will always be the sum total of the choices you made while you were here.
Shad Helmstetter

Life is a journey with many opportunities and obstacles, and every one requires a choice. Whatever you are experiencing in your life today is the result of your past choices. More importantly, whatever you'll experience in the future will be fashioned by the choices you make from this moment on. This is an exciting thought. If we can make wiser choices, we can more likely create the future we want.

On the road to a college degree, you will face important choices such as these: Shall I . . .

- major in business, science, or creative writing?
- work full-time, part-time, or not at all?
- drop a course that bores me or stick it out?
- study for my exam or go out with friends?

My choice; my responsibility; win or lose, only I hold the key to my destiny.

Elaine Maxwell

The sum of these choices, plus thousands of others, will determine your degree of success in college and in life. Doesn't it seem wise, then, to develop an effective strategy for choice management?

The Wise Choice Process

In the face of any challenge, you can make a responsible decision by answering the six questions of the Wise Choice Process. This process is a variation of a decision-making process developed by Dr. William Glasser.

1. **WHAT'S MY PRESENT SITUATION:** The important information here is "What exists?" (not "Whose fault is it?"). Quiet your Inner Critic, that self-criticizing voice in your head. Ignore your Inner Defender, that judgmental voice that blames everyone else for your problems. Consider only the objective facts of your situation, including how you feel about them. Rely on your Inner Guide, your wise, impartial voice that tells the truth as best it can.

   For example: *I stayed up all night studying for my first history test. When I finished taking the test, I hoped for an A. At worst, I expected a B. When I got the test back, my grade was a D. Five other students got A's. I feel depressed and angry.*

I am the cause of my choices, decisions, and actions. It is I who chooses, decides, and acts. If I do so knowing my responsibility, I am more likely to proceed wisely and appropriately than if I make myself oblivious of my role as source.

Nathaniel Branden

2. **HOW WOULD I LIKE MY SITUATION TO BE?** You can't change the past, but if you could create an ideal outcome in the future, what would it look like?
   I would like to get A's on all of my future tests.

3. **DO I HAVE A CHOICE HERE?** The answer for a Creator is always "YES!" Don't fall into the Victim trap of believing you have no options. Instead, assume you can find a better choice; then you often will.

4. **WHAT ARE MY POSSIBLE CHOICES?** Create a list of possible choices that you *could* do, knowing that you aren't obligated to do any of them. Compile your list without judgment. Don't say, "Oh, that would never work." Don't even say, "That's a great idea." Judgment during brainstorming stops the creative flow. Move from judgments to possibilities, discovering as many creative options as you can. Give yourself time to ponder, explore, consider, think, discover, conceive, invent, imagine. Then dive even deeper. Your patience will often pay off with a helpful option that would have remained hidden had you merely dashed across the surface of your mind.

- *I could complain to my classmates and anyone else who will listen.*
- *I could drop the class and take it next semester with another instructor.*
- *I could complain to the department head that the instructor grades unfairly.*
- *I could ask my successful classmates for ideas.*
- *I could ask the instructor for suggestions about improving my grades.*
- *I could request an opportunity to retake the test.*
- *I could get a tutor.*

5. **WHAT'S THE LIKELY OUTCOME OF EACH POSSIBLE CHOICE?** Decide how you think each choice is likely to turn out. If you can't predict the outcome of one of your possible choices, stop this process and gather the information you need. For example, if you don't know the impact that dropping a course will have on your financial aid, find out now. Here are the possible choices from Step 4 and their likely outcomes:

A person defines and redefines who they are by the choices they make, minute to minute.

Joyce Chapman

- *Complain to classmates: I'd have the immediate pleasure of criticizing the instructor and maybe getting others' sympathy.*
- *Drop the class: I'd lose three credits this semester and have to make them up later.*
- *Complain to the department head: Probably he'd ask if I've seen my instructor first, so I wouldn't get much satisfaction.*
- *Ask successful classmates for ideas: I might learn how to improve my study habits; I might also make new friends.*
- *Ask the instructor for suggestions: I might learn what to do next time to improve my grade; at least the instructor would learn that I want to do well in this course.*
- *Request an opportunity to retake the test: My request might get approved and give me an opportunity to raise my grade. At the very least, I'd demonstrate how much I want to do well.*
- *Get a tutor: This action wouldn't help my grade on this test, but it would probably improve my next test score.*

Destiny is not a matter of chance; it is a matter of choice. It is not a thing to be waited for; it is a thing to be achieved.

William Jennings Bryant

6. **WHICH CHOICE(S) WILL I COMMIT TO DOING?** In this final step, decide which choices will likely create the most favorable outcome and commit to acting on them. If no favorable options exist, consider which choice leaves you no worse off than before. If no such option exists, then ask which choice creates the least unfavorable outcome.

I'll talk to my successful classmates, make an appointment with my instructor and have him explain what I could do to improve, and I'll request an opportunity to retake the test. If these choices don't raise my next test score to at least a B, I'll get a tutor.

Each situation will dictate the best options. In the example above, if the student had previously failed four tests instead of one, the best choice might be to drop the class. Or, if everyone in the class were receiving D's and F's, and if the student had already met with the instructor, a responsible option might be to see the department head about the instructor's grading policies.

Here's the bottom line: Our choices reveal what we *truly* believe and value, as opposed to what we *say* we believe and value. When I meekly wait for others to improve my life, I am being a Victim. When I passively wait for luck to go my way, I am being a Victim. When I make choices that take me off course from my future success just to increase my immediate pleasure (like partying instead of studying for an important test), I am being a Victim. When I make choices that sacrifice my goals and dreams just to reduce my immediate discomfort (like dropping a challenging course instead of spending extra hours working with a tutor), I am being a Victim.

The principle of choice describes the reality that I am in charge of my life. I choose it all. I always have, I always will.
Will Schutz

However, when I design a plan to craft my life as I want it, I am being a Creator. When I carry out my plan even in the face of obstacles (like, when my child's day-care provider gets sick and I exchange babysitting with a classmate for a week so I don't miss any classes), I am being a Creator. When I take positive risks to advance my goals (like asking a question in a large lecture class even though I am nervous), I am being a Creator. When I sacrifice immediate pleasure to stay on course to my dreams (like resisting the urge to buy a nifty new cell phone, allowing myself to cut back on my work hours to study more), I am being a Creator.

No matter what your final decision may be, the mere fact that you are defining and making your own choices is wonderfully empowering. By participating in the Wise Choice Process, you affirm your belief that you *can* change your life for the better. You reject the position that you are merely a Victim of outside forces, a pawn in the chess game of life. You insist on being the Creator of your own outcomes and experiences, shaping your destiny through the wisdom of your choices.

Journal Entry 5

In this activity you will apply the Wise Choice Process to improve a difficult situation in your life. Think about a current problem, one that you're comfortable sharing with your classmates and teacher. As a result of this problem, you may be angry, sad, frustrated, depressed, overwhelmed, or afraid.

Perhaps this situation has to do with a grade you received, a teacher's comment, or a classmate's action. Maybe the problem relates to a relationship, a job, or your health. The Wise Choice Process can help you make an empowering choice in any part of your life.

 Write the six questions of the Wise Choice Process, and answer each one as it relates to your situation.

The Wise Choice Process

1. WHAT'S MY PRESENT SITUATION? (Describe the problem objectively and completely.)

2. HOW WOULD I LIKE MY SITUATION TO BE? (What is your ideal future outcome?)

3. DO I HAVE A CHOICE HERE? (Yes!)

4. WHAT ARE MY POSSIBLE CHOICES? (Create a long list of specific choices that might create your preferred outcome.)

5. WHAT'S THE LIKELY OUTCOME OF EACH POSSIBLE CHOICE? (If you can't predict the likely outcome of an option, stop and gather more information.)

6. WHICH CHOICE(S) WILL I COMMIT TO DOING? (Pick from your list of choices in Step 4.)

2. **Write what you learned or relearned from doing the Wise Choice Process.** Be sure to Dive Deep. You might begin, *By doing the Wise Choice Process, I learned that I . . .*

Remember, you may wish to enliven your journal by adding pictures cut from magazines, drawings of your own, clip art, or quotations that appeal to you.

> *When I see all the choices I really have, it makes the world a whole lot brighter.*
> Debbie Scott, student

Personal Responsibility at Work

> *I found that the more I viewed myself as totally responsible for my life, the more in control I seemed to be of the goals I wanted to achieve.*
> Charles J. Givens,
> Entrepreneur and Self-Made
> Multimillionaire

A student once told me she'd had more than a dozen jobs in three years. "Why so many jobs?" I asked. "Bad luck," she replied. "I keep getting one lousy boss after another." Hmmmm, I wondered, twelve lousy bosses in a row? What are the odds of that?

Responsibility is about ownership. As long as I believe my career success belongs to someone else (like "lousy" bosses), I'm being a Victim, and my success is unlikely. Victims give little effort to choosing or preparing for a career. Instead, they allow influential others (like parents and teachers) or circumstances to determine their choice of work. They complain about the jobs they have, make excuses for why they haven't gotten the jobs they want, and blame others or their own unchangeable flaws for their occupational woes. By contrast, Creators know that the foundation of success at work (as in college) is accepting this truth: *By our choices, we are each the primary creators of the outcomes and experiences of our lives.*

Accepting responsibility in the work world begins with consciously choosing your career path. You alone can decide what career is right for you. That's why Creators explore their career options thoroughly, match career requirements with their own talents and interests, consider the consequences of choosing each career (such as how much education the career requires or what the employment outlook is), and they make informed choices. Choose your career wisely because few things in life are worse than spending eight hours a day, fifty weeks a year, working at a job you hate.

Taking responsibility for your work life also means planning your career path to keep your options open and your progress unobstructed. For example, you could keep your career options open in college by taking only general education courses while investigating several possible fields of work. Or you could eliminate a financial obstacle by getting enough education—such as a dental hygiene degree—to support yourself while pursuing your dream career—such as going to dental school.

In short, Creators make use of the power of wise choices. They believe that there is always an option that will lead them toward the careers they want, and they take responsibility for creating the employment they want. Instead of passively waiting for a job to come to them, they actively go out and look. One of my students lost a job when the company where she worked closed. She could have spent hours in the cafeteria complaining about her bad fortune and how she could no longer afford to stay in school. Instead she created employment for herself by going from store to store in a mall asking every manager for a part-time job until one said, "Yes." In the time she could have wasted in the cafeteria complaining about her money problems, she solved them with positive actions.

When it comes to finding a full-time career position, Creators continue to be proactive. They don't wait for the perfect job opening to appear in their local paper. They don't sit by the phone waiting for a call from an employment agency. They know that employers prefer to hire people they know and like, so Creators do all they can to get known and liked by employers in their career field. They start by researching companies that need their talents and for whom they might like to work. Then, they contact potential employers directly. They don't ask if the employer has a job opening. Instead, they seek an informational interview: "Hi, I've just gotten my degree in accounting, and I'd like to make an appointment to talk to you about your company. . . . What's that? You don't have any positions open at this time? No problem. I'm just gathering information at this point, looking for where my talents might make the most contributions. Would you have some time to meet with me this week? Or would next week be better?" Creators go to these information-gathering interviews prepared with knowledge about the company, good questions to ask, and a carefully prepared résumé. At the end of the meeting they ask if the interviewer knows of any other employers who might need their skills. They call all of the leads they get and use the referral as an opening for a job interview: "I was speaking with John Smith at the Ajax Company, and he suggested that I give you a call about a position you have open." A friend of mine got an information-gathering interview and wowed the personnel manager with her professionally prepared résumé and interviewing skills; even though the company "had no openings" when she called, two days after the interview, she was offered a position.

Accepting responsibility not only helps you *get* a great job, it makes it possible to *excel* on the job. Employers love responsible employees. Wouldn't you? Instead of complaining, blaming, making excuses, and thus creating an emotionally draining work environment, responsible employees create a positive workplace where absenteeism is low and work production is high. Instead of repeating ineffective solutions to problems, proactive employees seek solutions, take new actions, and try something new. They pursue alternative routes instead of complaining about dead ends. Creators show initiative instead of needing constant direction, and they do their best work even when the boss isn't looking. As someone once said, "There is no traffic jam on the extra mile." Creators are willing to go the extra mile, and this effort pays off handsomely.

If you run into a challenge while preparing for a career, seeking a job, or working in your career, don't complain, blame, or make excuses. Instead, ask yourself a Creator's favorite question: "What's my plan?"

Believing in Yourself: Change Your Inner Conversation

 FOCUS QUESTION How can you raise your self-esteem by changing your self-talk?

It is the mind that maketh good or ill, That maketh wretch or happy, rich or poor.
Edmund Spencer

Imagine this: Three students schedule an appointment with their instructor to discuss a project they're working on together. They go to the instructor's office at the scheduled time, but he isn't there. They wait forty-five minutes before finally giving up and leaving. As you learn what they do next, identify which student you think has the strongest self-esteem.

Student #1, feeling discouraged and depressed, spends the evening watching television while ignoring assignments in other subjects. Student #2, feeling insulted and furious, spends the evening complaining to friends about the inconsiderate, incompetent instructor who stood them up. Student #3, feeling puzzled about the mix-up, decides to call the instructor the next day to see what happened and to set up another meeting; meanwhile, this student spends the evening studying for a test in another class.

Which student has the strongest self-esteem?

The curse of stinkin' thinkin'

How is it that three people can have the same experience and respond to it so differently? According to psychologists like Albert Ellis, the answer lies in what each person believes caused the event. Ellis suggested that our different responses could be understood by realizing that the activating event (A) plus our beliefs (B) equal the consequences (C) (how we respond). In other words, A + B = C. For example:

Self-esteem can be defined as the state that exists when you are not arbitrarily haranguing and abusing yourself but choose to fight back against those automatic thoughts with meaningful rational responses.

Dr. Thomas Burns

Activating Event	+ **B**eliefs	= **C**onsequence
Student #1: Instructor didn't show up for a scheduled conference.	My instructor thinks I'm dumb. I'll never get a college degree. I'm a failure in life.	Got depressed and watched television all evening.
Student #2: Same.	My instructor won't help me. Teachers don't care about students. Life stinks.	Got angry and spent the night telling friends how horrible the instructor is.
Student #3: Same.	I'm not sure what went wrong. Sometimes things just don't turn out the way you plan. There's always tomorrow.	Studied for another class. Planned to call the instructor the next day to see what happened and set up a new appointment.

Ellis suggests that our upsets are caused not so much by our problems as by what we think about our problems. When our thinking is full of irrational beliefs, what Ellis calls "stinkin' thinkin'," we feel awful even when the circumstances don't warrant it. So, how we *think* about the issues in our lives is the real issue. Problems may come and go, but our "stinkin' thinkin'" stays with us. As the old saying goes, "Everywhere I go, there I am."

Stinkin' thinkin' isn't based on reality. Rather, these irrational thoughts are the automatic chatter of the Inner Critic (keeper of Negative Beliefs about myself) and the Inner Defender (keeper of Negative Beliefs about other people and the world).

So what about our three students and their self-esteem? It's not hard to see that student #1, who got depressed and wasted the evening watching television, has low self-esteem. This student is thrown far off course simply by the instructor's not showing up. A major cause of this self-defeating reaction is the Inner Critic's harsh self-judgments. Here are some common self-damning beliefs held by Inner Critics:

The Inner Critic keeps us feeling insecure and childlike. When it is operating, we feel like children who have done something wrong and probably will never be able to do anything right.

Hal Stone and Sidra Stone

I'm dumb.	I'm unattractive.
I'm selfish.	I'm lazy.

I'm a failure.

I'm incapable.

I'm not as good as other people.

I'm worthless.

I'm not college material.

I'm weak.

I'm a lousy parent.

I'm unlovable.

A person dominated by his Inner Critic misinterprets events, inventing criticism that isn't there. A friend says, "Something came up, and I can't meet you tonight." The Inner Critic responds, "What did I do wrong? I screwed up again, didn't I!"

The activating event doesn't cause the consequence; rather the judgmental chatter of the Inner Critic does. A strong Inner Critic is both a cause and an effect of low self-esteem.

Everyone has a critical inner voice. But people with low self-esteem tend to have a more vicious and vocal pathological critic.

Matthew McKay and Patrick Fanning

What about student #2, the one who spent the evening telling friends how horrible the instructor was? Though perhaps less apparent, this student also demonstrates low self-esteem. The finger-pointing Inner Defender is merely the Inner Critic turned outward and is just as effective at getting the student off course. Here are some examples of destructive beliefs held by an Inner Defender:

People don't treat me right, so they're rotten.

People don't act the way I want them to, so they're awful.

People don't live up to my expectations, so they're the enemy.

People don't do what I want, so they're against me.

Life is full of problems, so it's terrible.

Life is unfair, so I can't stand it.

Life doesn't always go my way, so I can't be happy.

Life doesn't provide me with everything I want, so it's unbearable.

A person dominated by her Inner Defender discovers personal insults and slights in neutral events. A classmate says, "Something came up, and I can't meet you tonight." The Inner Defender responds, "Who do you think you are, anyway? I can find someone a lot better to study with than you!"

The activating event doesn't cause the angry response; rather the judgmental chatter of the other-damning Inner Defender does. A strong Inner Defender is both a cause and an effect of low self-esteem.

Replacing a negative thought with a positive one changes more than just the passing thought—it changes the way you perceive and deal with the world.

Dr. Clair Douglas

Only student #3 demonstrates high self-esteem. This student realizes he doesn't know why the instructor missed the meeting. He doesn't blame himself, the instructor, or a rotten world. He considers alternatives: Perhaps the instructor got sick or was involved in a traffic accident. Until he can find out what happened and decide what to do next, this student turns his attention to an action that will keep him on course to another goal. The Inner Guide is concerned with positive results, not judging self or others. A strong Inner Guide is both a cause and an effect of high self-esteem.

Disputing irrational beliefs

How, then, can you raise your self-esteem?

First, you can become aware of the chatter of your Inner Critic and Inner Defender. Be especially alert when events in your life go wrong, when your desired outcomes and experiences are thwarted. That's when we are most likely to complain, blame, and excuse. That's when we substitute judgments of ourselves or others for the positive actions that would get us back on course.

Once you become familiar with your inner voices, you can begin a process of separating yourself from your Inner Critic and Inner Defender. To do this, practice disputing your irrational and self-sabotaging beliefs. Here are some effective ways to dispute:

- **Offer evidence that your judgments are incorrect**: *My instructor called me last week to see if I needed help with my project, so there's no rational reason to believe he won't help me now.*

- **Offer a positive explanation of the problem**: *Sure my instructor didn't show up, but he may have missed the appointment because of a last-minute crisis.*

- **Question the importance of the problem**: *Even if my instructor won't help me, I can still do well on this project, and if I don't, it won't be the end of the world.*

- **If you find that your judgments are true, instead of continuing to criticize yourself or someone else, offer a plan to improve the situation**: *If I'm honest, I have to admit that I haven't done well in this class so far, but from now on I'm going to attend every class, take good notes, read my assignments two or three times, and work with a study group before every test.*

According to psychologist Ellis, a key to correcting irrational thinking is changing a "must" into a preference. When we think "must," what follows in our thoughts is typically awful, terrible, and dreadful. For example, my Inner Defender's belief that an instructor "must" meet me for an appointment or he is an awful, terrible, dreadful person is irrational; I'd certainly "prefer" him to meet me for an appointment, but his not meeting me does not make him rotten—in fact, he may have a perfectly good reason for not meeting with me. As another example, my Inner Critic's belief that I "must" pass this course or I am an awful, terrible, dreadful person is irrational; I'd certainly "prefer" to pass this course, but not doing so does not make me worthless—in fact, not passing this course may lead me to something even better. Believing irrationally that I, another person, or the world "must" be a particular way, Ellis says, is a major cause of my distress and misery.

If all of the above ideas fail, you can always distract yourself from negative, judgmental thoughts. Simply tell yourself, "STOP!" and replace your blaming,

Does it help to change what you say to yourself? It most certainly does. . . . Tell yourself often enough that you'll succeed and you dramatically improve your chances of succeeding and of feeling good.

Drs. Bernie Zilbergeld and Arnold A. Lazarus

You mainly make yourself needlessly and neurotically miserable by strongly holding absolutist irrational Beliefs, especially by rigidly believing unconditional shoulds, oughts, and musts.

Albert Ellis

complaining, or excusing with something positive: Watch a funny movie, tell a joke, recall your goals and dreams, think about someone you love.

Wisely choose the thoughts that occupy your mind. Avoid letting automatic, negative thoughts undermine your self-esteem. Evict them and replace them, instead, with esteem-building thoughts.

Journal Entry 6

In this activity, you will practice disputing the judgments of your Inner Critic and your Inner Defender. As you become more skilled at seeing yourself, other people, and the world more objectively and without distracting judgments, your self-esteem will thrive.

1. **Write a sentence expressing a recent problem or event that upset you.** Think of something troubling that happened in school, at work, or in your personal life. For example, *I got a 62 on my math test.*

2. **Write a list of three or more criticisms your Inner Critic (IC) might level against you as a result of this situation. Have your Inner Guide (IG) dispute each one immediately.** Review the four methods of disputing described on page 43. You only need to use one of them for each criticism. For example,

IC: You failed that math test because you're terrible in math.
IG: It's true I failed the math test, but I'll study harder next time and do better. This was only the first test, and I now know what to expect next time.

3. **Write a list of three or more criticisms your Inner Defender (ID) might level against someone else or life as a result of this situation. Have your Inner Guide (IG) dispute each one immediately.** Again use one of the four methods for disputing. For example,

ID: You failed that math test because you've got the worst math instructor on campus.
IG: I have trouble understanding my math instructor, so I'm going to make an appointment to talk with him in private. John really liked him last semester, so I bet I'll like him, too, if I give him a chance.

4. **Write what you have learned or relearned about changing your inner conversation.** Your journal entry might begin, *In reading and writing about my inner conversations, I have discovered that. . . .* Wherever possible, offer personal experiences or examples to explain what you learned.

Enrolling in college at the age of twenty-eight was very intimidating to me. Having dropped out of high school at fifteen, I had a real problem with confidence. Even though I had a GED and was earning a decent living as a car salesman, I still doubted that I was smart enough to be successful in college. I finally took the leap and enrolled because I want a career where I don't have to work twelve hours a day, six days a week and never see my family. However, by the second week of the semester, I found myself falling back into old habits. I was sitting in the back of the classroom, asking what homework was due, and talking through most of the class. Negative thoughts constantly ran through my mind: *The teachers won't like me. I can't compete with the eighteen-year-olds right out of high school. I don't even remember what a "verb" is. I can't do this.*

Then in my College Success class, we read chapter two of *On Course* about becoming a Creator and disputing "stinking thinking." I realized I had taken on the role of the Victim almost my whole life, and I was continuing to do it now. One day I was on my porch

ONE STUDENT'S STORY

Dominic Grasseth
Lane Community College, Oregon

when I caught myself thinking my usual negative thoughts. It occurred to me that I was the only one holding me back, not the teachers, not the other students, not math, not English. If I wanted to be successful in college, I had to quit being scared. I had to change my thinking. So I made a deal with myself that any time I caught myself thinking negatively, I would rephrase the statement in a way that was more positive. I started to truly pay attention to the thoughts in my head and question the negative things I was telling myself. After that I began sitting up front in my classes and participating more. I've always been kind of scattered, so I started using a calendar and a dry erase board to keep track of what I had to do.

What amazes me is that I didn't really make that big a change, yet I finished the semester with a 4.0 average! All I did was realize that what I was saying to myself was my underlying problem. I am responsible for my thoughts, and the choice about whether or not to succeed is mine. These days when I have a ridiculous thought going through my mind and I change it, I smile. It's very empowering.

Why *Learn Study Skills?*

If you want to be successful in the work world, obviously you need to master the skills of your profession. Likewise, if you want to be successful in college, you need to master the skills of learning. What follows is the first of six sections throughout the book in which we'll look at effective study skills and how you can apply them to achieve greater academic success.

But first, let's address *why* you should learn and use these study skills. After all, you might be thinking, *I'm in college so I must have already developed some effective strategies for studying. Why do I need to waste time learning more of them?* Well, you might be right. But, be alerted that college raises the academic bar quite a few notches, and you may not have all of the skills necessary to meet your instructors' expectations. Or even your own. And it's a rare instructor, outside of a course like this one, who's going to take the time to teach you study skills when you're struggling. Then what? Psychologists who study student achievement have discovered that many students who struggle academically decide it's because they lack inborn ability. This belief leads to a sense of hopelessness: *If I wasn't born smart enough, there's nothing I can do about it.* Too often these students conclude they're not college material. Or they get discouraged about not doing as well in college as they had in high school. Then they stumble off course and quit.

By contrast, successful students typically attribute academic disappointments to their failure to use effective or appropriate strategies (rather than a lack of inborn intelligence). Their belief is, *I'm smart enough, so I must not be using the right approach. I need to become skilled at new study strategies so I can learn better.* They experiment with new approaches until they find what works for them, and soon they're back on course.

In each of the six study skills sections, you'll encounter practical answers to the question: "What do world-class learners do to get straight A's?" If you're willing to do what they do and you're willing to put in a reasonable and consistent effort, there's no reason you can't enjoy a successful journey to graduation. That's not saying you'll get straight A's or that your path will always be smooth. You'll probably hit a few bumps and take a few wrong turns. At times, your journey may seem like it will take forever. But, if you are a Creator, your chances of success are excellent!

One more thing before tackling our first study skill. When you see how I've presented each area of study skills—as a menu of strategies with only a brief explanation for each one, you may wonder about this format, especially if you have friends taking a similar course with a different book. Most likely their book will have long (maybe *very* long) chapters explaining the same study skills that you'll cover here in just a few pages. Actually, the first time I taught study skills many years ago, I used a book like that. One day we were going over note taking when a young man in my class said, "I guess note taking must be pretty complicated!" "Why do you say that?" I asked. "Well," he answered, "Look at how long this chapter is. If it takes that many pages to explain note taking, it must be like learning nuclear physics."

I had an "aha" that day: The way I was teaching study skills wasn't even close to the way I had learned to be an effective learner myself. In fact, as an undergraduate I never even read a book about study skills. At that time, my institution didn't offer a class like the one you're taking. Instead I learned my study skills "on the job." For example, one day I noticed a classmate's notes and they looked very different from mine. I asked about his notes and he offered a couple of sentences explaining how his system worked. That was it for instruction. His approach sounded appealing, so I tried it. Then, I adapted it to my own style, and tried it again. This new way helped me learn better and get better grades, so I kept doing it. No huge chapter to read. Just a quick explanation and lots of practice. After my student made his observation about note taking, I tried the abbreviated approach you're about to experience. My students started learning to use study skills more effectively and in less time. And that's what you can look forward to here.

Here's how it works: First, read the menu of suggestions. Next, pick the one strategy *you* think will help you the most. Then, *use* it. Modify it and use it again. And again. All the while, notice if your outcomes improve. With a reading strategy, for example, notice if it helps you read with greater understanding. Notice if you start reading faster with the same or greater comprehension. If so, add that strategy to your reading toolbox. Then try another strategy. And another. That's all there is to it. It's *not* nuclear physics! So let's get started.

Reading well is one of the most important skills for succeeding in college and in life. Yet, according to the American College Testing organization, about half (49 percent) of the 1.2 million students who took the ACT college entrance test in 2005 had scores indicating they were unready to handle college-level reading. A time-honored system for improving reading is called the SQ3R Method: Survey, Question, Read, Recite, and Review. In this section you'll learn these techniques and more. Experiment with these new reading strategies, and you'll soon find yourself reading faster and with greater understanding. That'll lead to deeper learning and higher grades.

Before Reading

1. Create a positive affirmation about reading. Do you have negative beliefs about your ability to understand and enjoy what you read? Create an affirming statement about reading, such as "*I enjoy reading books and articles of all kinds.*" Repeat this reading affirmation in order to revise any negative beliefs you may have about reading.

2. Create a reading plan. Make a plan to read often for short periods of time rather than in one marathon reading session. This approach keeps you current with your assignments and helps you remember more of what you read.

3. Do a survey of your reading assignment. Like observing a valley from a high mountain, a quick survey of your reading assignment gives you the big picture of what to expect. Thumb through the book taking in chapter titles, chapter objectives, focus questions, text headings, charts, graphs, illustrations, previews, and summaries. Especially note any words that are specially formatted, such as with CAPITALS, **bold**, *italics*, and so on. In a few minutes, you will have an overview of what you are about to read.

4. Identify the purpose of what you're reading. Keep asking yourself, "What's the point?" For example, the "point" of every section of *On Course* is to present you with beliefs or behaviors to add to

your toolbox for success in college and in life. By keeping this purpose in mind as you read, you can be on the lookout for a helpful belief or behavior, along with an explanation of how you can use it to enhance your success. (After that, of course, it's up to you to try them out!)

5. Turn text headings into questions. For example, suppose a computer book has a heading within the text that reads: **HTML Tags**. Turn this heading into one or more questions: *What is an HTML Tag? How are HTML Tags created?* (See additional examples in Wise Choices in College: Effective Studying in Chapter 5.) If you write your questions on notebook paper, leave room to insert answers. If you create your questions on 3″ x 5″ cards, write your answers on the backs.

During Reading

6. Read for the answers to your questions. Record the answers, the source, and page number. These questions and answers make terrific study materials. If you write the questions and answers on 3″ x 5″ cards, you can conveniently carry them with you to study during otherwise wasted time (such as when you're waiting in line somewhere).

7. Write questions in the margins. As you come across answers to your questions, write the questions in the margin. Later, while studying, you can ask yourself the questions in the margins and compare your answers to those found in the text.

8. Read in chunks. Poor readers read one word at a time, sometimes moving their lips while reading. Good readers don't read words; they read ideas, and ideas are found in groups of words. For example, try reading all of the words between the diamonds at once:

> ♦ *If you read* ♦ *the chunks* ♦ *you will increase* ♦ *your speed* ♦ *and your comprehension* ♦

Like any new habit, this method will initially feel awkward. As you practice, you'll find you can scan bigger and bigger chunks of information at increasingly faster rates of speed, like this:

♦ If you read the chunks ♦ you will increase your speed ♦ and your comprehension ♦

9. Concentrate on reading faster. In one experiment, students increased their reading speed up to 50 percent simply by concentrating on reading as fast as they could while still understanding what they were reading. You, too, can probably read faster by just *deciding* to.

10. Read for main ideas and supporting details. An essay or a chapter in a book usually has one main idea called the *thesis statement*. This statement typically appears in the first or last paragraph. The rest of the reading expands and supports the thesis. An individual paragraph usually has one main idea called the *topic sentence,* which is typically found in the first or last sentence of the paragraph. For each main idea, authors will usually offer support consisting of examples, experiences, explanations, and/or evidence.

11. Mark main ideas and supporting details. Create your own system for marking what you want to remember. Some readers use double underlining to indicate a thesis statement and single underlining to indicate a topic sentence. Others like to highlight main ideas with one color and supporting ideas with another. Read a whole paragraph before marking; it's easier to see what's important that way. Mark only 10 to 15 percent of your text, selecting only what is truly important.

12. Take notes. Paraphrase main ideas and supporting details in your notebook. Expressing the author's ideas in your own words anchors important ideas in your memory and allows you to add your own thoughts and questions.

13. Try to predict what's next. As you read, guess what the author will say in the next paragraph, page, or chapter. Making predictions keeps your mind alert and improves your comprehension.

14. Pause to recite. Have you ever finished reading something only to realize five minutes later that you can't remember a thing you read? Here's a remedy. At the end of a section, stop for a moment to recall what you have just been reading. Write or say aloud what you think are the main ideas and the most convincing support. State the answers to any questions you created earlier. This mini-review will help you clarify and remember the important ideas.

15. Look up the definition of key words. Use a dictionary when you don't know the meaning of a key word. Consider starting a vocabulary list in your journal. Or create a deck of 3" x 5" flash cards with new words on one side and definitions on the other. Use your new words in conversations to lock them in your memory. Developing an extensive and eloquent vocabulary is a great success strategy.

16. Read critically. Not all ideas in print are true. Learn to read critically by analyzing the validity of the text. Look for red flags that may suggest a credibility problem. Who is the author? What are his or her credentials? Is the support sufficient, or is the article mostly opinions and generalizations? Are the author's opinions supported by logic or by emotion? Are sources of information identified? Are they believable? Current? Does the author stand to gain (e.g., money, status, revenge) by your acceptance of his or her opinion? Are various sides of an issue presented or only one?

After Reading

17. Reread difficult passages or chapters. Some subjects are difficult to understand, and authors don't always write clearly. Reread challenging sections until the main ideas become clear. Trust yourself that, with enough effort, you will comprehend.

18. Review what you read. Ask yourself the following:

- What was the main idea?
- Why does the author think so? What are the reasons?
- How does the author know? What is the supporting evidence?
- What do you personally think of the author's main idea and support?
- What emotion (if any) does the reading stir in you?

19. Answer end-of-chapter questions. If the text provides review questions, see how well you can answer them. If one stumps you, skim the chapter for the answer. Review questions for chapters in *On Course* can be found on the Internet at *http://www.college.hmco.com/pic/downing5e.*

20. Reread the marked text. A great way to review is to reread the parts of the text you have underlined or highlighted.

21. Use a graphic organizer. A graphic organizer allows you to record information from your reading so that the relationship between the ideas is represented physically by their location on the page. The finished product turns mere information into a picture that allows you to see patterns and relationships. For example, after reading about inflation in an economics course, you might create a simple graphic organizer with two columns titled "Causes of Inflation" and "Effects of Inflation." The concept map on page 115 is a second example of a graphic organizer. For dozens of other graphic organizers, go to *http://www.eduplace.com/graphicorganizer.*

22. Read another book on the same subject. Sometimes another author will express the same idea in a way that makes more sense to you. Ask your instructor or a librarian to suggest supplemental reading.

23. Join classmates in quizzing each other on the reading. Ask classmates to create questions based on the reading. (See strategy #5 above.) Gather for a question and answer session.

24. Discuss or teach what you have read. Conversing about a reading assignment strengthens memory pathways that will help you remember key points. A powerful alternative is teaching the information to a friend or family member.

25. Seek assistance. If you continue to have difficulties understanding what you read, ask your instructor to explain the key points. For additional help, most colleges provide a reading center, a tutoring program, or both. If you continue to have problems understanding your reading assignments, see if your college has a diagnostician who can test you for a possible reading disability. Reading specialists may be able to help you improve your comprehension skills.

Reading Exercise

Experiment with one or more of these reading strategies and be prepared to discuss your results with classmates.

Embracing Change

Do one thing different this week

Many people resist change. It's easier to complain, blame, and make excuses. It's more challenging to experiment with new beliefs and behaviors, evaluate them, and then adopt the best ones permanently. But that is exactly what Creators do. Creators crave new methods for lifting the quality of their lives up a notch. And then another. And another. Creators embrace change because it's a great way—maybe the *only* way—to maximize their potential to live a rich, full life.

   In this chapter, you encountered a number of empowering beliefs and behaviors for taking maximum control of your life. Here's an opportunity to pick ONE of them and experiment with it more thoroughly. From the list below, choose one belief or behavior that you think might make the biggest improvement in your life. Then try it every day for one week. Put a check in the corresponding box each day that you take the action. After seven days, assess your results. If your outcomes and experiences improve, you now have a tool you can use for the rest of your life. As psychologist Carl Rogers observed, "The only person who is educated is the one who has learned how to learn and change."

Beliefs and Behaviors	Day 1	Day 2	Day 3	Day 4	Day 5	Day 6	Day 7
Think: "I accept responsibility for creating my life as I want it."							
Catch myself thinking or speaking Victim language and translate it into Creator language.							
Use the Wise Choice Process to make a decision.							
Catch myself using Stinkin' Thinkin' and dispute it.							
Demonstrate personal responsibility at my workplace.							
Use the following Reading Strategy (write your choice from pages 48–50):							

(*continued on page 52*)

During my seven-day experiment, what happened?
As a result of what happened, what did I learn or relearn?

Discovering Self-Motivation

Once I accept responsibility for creating my own life, I must choose the kind of life I want to create.

I am choosing all of the outcomes and experiences for my life.

SUCCESSFUL STUDENTS . . .	STRUGGLING STUDENTS . . .
■ **create inner motivation**, providing themselves with the passion to persist toward their goals and dreams, despite all obstacles.	▧ have little sense of passion and drive, often quitting when difficulties arise.
■ **design a compelling life plan**, complete with motivating goals and dreams.	▧ tend to invent their lives as they live them.
■ **commit to their goals and dreams**, visualizing the successful creation of their ideal future.	▧ wander aimlessly from one activity to another.

Popson's Dilemma

Fresh from graduate school, Assistant Professor Popson was midway through his first semester of college teaching when his depression started. Long gone was the excitement and promise of the first day of class. Now, only about two-thirds of his students were attending, and some of them were barely holding on. When Popson asked a question during class, the same few students answered every time. The rest stared off in bored silence. One student always wore a knit cap with a slender cord slithering from under it to an iPod in his shirt pocket. With ten or even fifteen minutes remaining in a class period, students would start stuffing notebooks noisily into their backpacks or book bags. Only one student had visited him during office hours, despite Popson's numerous invitations. And when he announced one day that he was canceling the next class to attend a professional conference, a group in the back of the room pumped their fists in the air and hooted with glee. It pained Popson to have aroused so little academic motivation in his students, and he began asking experienced professors what he should do.

Professor Assante said, "Research says that about 70 percent of students enroll in college because they see the degree as their ticket to a good job and fat paycheck. And they're right. College grads earn nearly a million dollars more in their lives than high school grads. Show them how your course will help them graduate and prosper in the work world. After that, most of them will be model students."

Professor Buckley said, "Everyone wants the freedom to make choices affecting their lives, so have your students design personal learning contracts. Let each one choose assignments from a list of options you provide. Let them add their own choices if they want. Even have them pick the dates they'll turn in their assignments. Give them coupons that allow them to miss any three classes without penalty. Do everything you can to give them choices and put them in charge of their own education. Once they see they're in control of their learning and you're here to help them, their motivation will soar."

Professor Chang said, "Deep down, everyone wants to make a difference. I just read a survey by the Higher Education Research Institute showing that two-thirds of entering freshmen believe it's essential or very important to help others. Find out what your students want to do to make a contribution. Tell them how your course will help them achieve those dreams. Even better, engage them in a service learning project. When they see how your course can help them live a life with real purpose, they'll be much more interested in what you're teaching."

Professor Donnelly said, "Let's be realistic. The best motivator for students is grades. It's the old carrot and stick. Start every class with a quiz and they'll get there on time. Take points off for absences and they'll attend regularly. Give extra points for getting assignments in on time. Reward every positive action with points and take off points when they screw up. When they realize they can get a good grade in your class by doing what's right, even the guy with the iPod will get involved."

Professor Egret said, "Most people work harder and learn better when they feel they're part of a team with a common goal, so help your students feel part of a community of learners. Give them interesting topics to talk about in pairs and small groups. Give them team assignments and group projects. Teach them how to work well in groups so everyone contributes their fair share. When your students start feeling like they belong and start caring about one another, you'll see their academic motivation go way up."

Professor Fanning said, "Your unmotivated students probably don't expect to pass your course, so they quit trying. Here's my suggestion:

Assign a modest challenge at which they can all succeed if they do it. And every student *has* to do it. No exceptions. Afterwards, give students specific feedback on what they did well and what they can do to improve. Then give them a slightly more challenging assignment and repeat the cycle again and again. Help them *expect* to be successful by *being* successful. At some point they're going to say, 'Hey, I can do this!' and then you'll see a whole different attitude."

Professor Gonzales said, "Learning should be active and fun. I'm not talking about a party; I'm talking engaging students in educational experiences that teach deep and important lessons about your subject. Your students should be thinking, 'I can't wait to get to class to see what we're going to do and learn today!' You can use debates, videos, field trips, group projects, case studies, learning games, simulations, role plays, guest speakers, visualizations . . . the possibilities are endless. When learning is engaging and enjoyable, motivation problems disappear."

Professor Harvey said, "I've been teaching for thirty years, and if there's one thing I've learned, it's this: You can't motivate someone else. Maybe you've heard the old saying, 'When the student is ready, the teacher will arrive.' You're just wasting your energy trying to make someone learn before they're ready. Maybe they'll be back in your class in five or ten years and they'll be motivated. But for now, just do the best you can for the students who *are* ready."

Listed below are the eight professors in this story. Based on your experience, rank the quality of their advice on the scale below. Give a different score to each professor. Be prepared to explain your choices.

Best Advice ←1 2 3 4 5 6 7 8 9 10 → Worst Advice

____ Professor Assante   ____ Professor Egret
____ Professor Buckley   ____ Professor Fanning
____ Professor Chang   ____ Professor Gonzales
____ Professor Donnelly   ____ Professor Harvey

DIVING DEEPER: Is there an approach not mentioned by one of the eight professors that would be even more motivating for you?

Creating Inner Motivation

 FOCUS QUESTIONS   How important do educators think motivation is to your academic success? What determines how motivated you are? What can you do to keep your motivation consistently high this semester . . . and beyond?

There are three things to remember about education. The first is motivation. The second is motivation. The third is motivation.

Terrell Bell, former US Secretary of Education

When embarking on an important journey, you're smart to prepare for major obstacles. Recently, two extensive surveys asked college and university educators to rank factors that hinder students' success and persistence. These surveys were done by American College Testing (ACT) and the Policy Center on the First Year of College. In both surveys, educators identified *lack of motivation* as the number one barrier to student success.

Lack of motivation has various symptoms: students arriving late to class or being absent; assignments turned in late or not at all; work done superficially or sloppily; appointments missed; offers of support ignored; and students not participating in class discussions or activities, to name just a few. But the most glaring symptom of all is the enormous number of students who vanish from college within their first year. According to ACT, in public four-year colleges in the United States, about one-third of students fail to return for their second year. And in public two-year colleges, it's even worse: Nearly *half* of first-year students don't make it to the second year. Despite these grim statistics, you can be among those who stay and thrive in higher education!

A formula for motivation

The study of human motivation—seeking to understand why we do what we do—is extensive and complex. However, one synthesis of a number of theories offers a practical understanding of academic motivation. It's represented by the formula: $V \times E = M$.

In this formula, "V" stands for "Value." In terms of your education, Value is determined by the benefits you believe you'll obtain from seeking and obtaining a college degree. The greater the benefits you assign to these experiences and outcomes, the greater will be your motivation. The greater your motivation, the higher the cost you'll be willing to pay in terms of time, money, effort, frustration, inconvenience, and sacrifice. Take a moment to identify the score that presently represents the personal Value you place on seeking and obtaining a college education. Choose a number from 0–10 (where "0" represents no perceived value and "10" represents an extremely high perceived value).

Today's theories about motivation emphasize the importance of factors within the individual, particularly the variables of expectancy and value. Students' motivations are strongly influenced by what they think is important (value) and what they believe they can accomplish (expectancy).

K. Patricia Cross

The "E" in this formula stands for "Expectation." In terms of your education, Expectation is determined by how likely you think it is that you can earn a college degree with a reasonable effort. Here, you need to weigh your abilities (how good a student you are and how strong your previous education is) against the difficulty of achieving your goal (how challenging the courses are that you will need to take and how much you are willing to sacrifice to be successful). Take a moment to identify the score that presently represents your personal Expectation of being able to complete a college degree with a reasonable effort. Choose a number from 0–10 (where "0" represents no expectation of success and "10" represents an extremely high expectation of success).

In a nutshell, this concept says that your level of Motivation in college is determined by multiplying your Value score by your Expectation score. For example, if the Value you place on a college degree is high (say, a 10) but your Expectation of success in college is low (say, a 1), then your Motivation score will be very low (10). Similarly, if your Expectation for success in college is high (say, a 9) but you put little value on a degree (say a 2), then once more, your Motivation score will be very low (18). In either case, your low score suggests that you probably won't do what's required to succeed in college: to make goal-directed choices consistently, to give a high-quality effort regularly, and to persist despite inevitable obstacles and challenges. Sadly, then, you'll join the multitude of students who exit college long before earning a degree.

Probably you see where all of this leads. To stay motivated in college, first, you have to find ways to raise (or keep high) the **Value** you place on college, including the academic degree you'll earn, the knowledge you'll gain, and the experiences you'll have while enrolled. Second, you have to find ways to raise (or keep high) the **Expectation** you have of being successful in college while making what you consider to be a reasonable effort. With our exploration of Effective Reading Skills in Chapter 2, we've already identified some important academic skills that, if mastered, will contribute to your high expectations for success in college. Throughout *On Course*, you'll encounter literally hundreds of other skills, both academic and otherwise, that can raise your realistic expectation of success in college even higher.

For now, however, we are going to focus on **Value**. Only you can determine how much value college holds for you, but let's look at some of the benefits that others have attributed to achieving a degree beyond high school.

Value of college outcomes

One of the most widely recognized benefits of a college degree is increased earning power. According to recent U.S. Census Bureau data, high school graduates earn an average of $1.2 million dollars during their working life. However, if you complete a two-year associate's degree, that lifetime total goes up $400,000 to $1.6 million dollars. If you complete a 4-year bachelor's degree, you can add another $500,000 for an average total of $2.1 million! Think what that additional money could do to help you and the people you love live a good life.

Not only does a college degree offer increased earnings, it also opens doors to employment in many desirable professions. Six out of every ten jobs now require some postsecondary education and training, according to data reported by the ERIC Clearinghouse on Higher Education. The U.S. Department of Labor predicts that by 2012 the number of jobs requiring advanced skills will grow at twice the rate of those requiring only basic skills.

A college degree confers many additional benefits. According to the Institute for Higher Education Policy and the Carnegie Foundation, college graduates enjoy higher savings levels, improved working conditions, increased personal and professional mobility, improved health and life expectancy, improved quality of life for offspring, better consumer decision making, increased personal status, more hobbies and leisure activities, a tendency to become more open-minded, more cultured, more rational, more consistent, and less authoritarian, and these benefits are passed on to their children.

Additionally, attaining a college degree can bring personal satisfaction and accomplishment. I once had a seventy-six-year-old student who inspired us all with her determination "to finally earn the college degree that I cheated myself

There is evidence that the time for learning various subjects would be cut to a fraction of the time currently allotted if the material were perceived by the learner as related to his own purposes.

Carl Rogers

For learning to take place with any kind of efficiency students must be motivated. To be motivated, they must become interested. And they become interested when they are actively working on projects which they can relate to their values and goals in life.

Gus Tuberville, former president, William Penn College

Table 3-1: One student's desired outcomes.

Desired Outcomes	Value
Earn a Grade Point Average (GPA) of 3.8 or better and make the Dean's list this semester.	A high GPA will look great on my transcript when I apply for a job. Also, it will give me a real boost of self-confidence.
In my English class, write at least one essay that contains no more than 2 non-standard grammar errors.	I want to be able to write anything without worrying that someone who reads it is going to think I'm stupid or illiterate.
In my student success class, learn at least three strategies for managing my time more effectively.	I feel overwhelmed and stressed with all I need to do, and learning how to manage my time better will lower my stress level.
Get an "A" in my accounting class.	I want a career in accounting, so doing well in this course is the first step towards success in my profession.
Make three or more new friends.	My friends from high school all went to other colleges or they're working. I want to make new friends here so I'll have people to hang out with and have fun on the weekends.

out of more than fifty years ago." Another valuable outcome of a college degree is the pride and esteem that many enjoy when they walk across the stage to receive their hard-earned diploma. And for some, a college degree is an essential step toward fulfilling a personal vision; such was true for one of my college roommates who, for as long as he can remember, dreamed of being a doctor (and today he is one).

Setting specific goals helps learners in at least three ways: The goals focus attention on important aspects of the task; they help motivate and sustain task mastery efforts; and they serve an information function by arming learners with criteria that they can use to assess and if necessary adjust their strategies as they work.

Jere Brophy

For some people, long-term goals are too distant to be motivating. They get fired up by the short-term goals they can nearly touch, such as outcomes they can create during this semester. Table 3-1 shows the short-term goals that one of my students chose for himself, along with his reasons why.

Value of college experiences

Value isn't found only in outcomes; it's also found in experiences. In fact, all human beings manage their emotions by doing their best to maximize positive experiences and minimize negative experiences. What, for example, is the value of playing an intramural sport, attending a movie, belonging to a fraternity or sorority, dancing, playing a video game, or hanging out with friends? Primarily, all are choices to manage our inner experiences. If done in excess, any one of them can get us off course from our desired outcomes. But done in moderation, all of these activities (and many others) can create a positive experience and contribute mightily to academic motivation. That's because, if you're enjoying the journey called college, you're much more likely to persist until you reach the destination called graduation.

So, what are your desired experiences in college? If someday in the future you were to tell someone that college was one of the best experiences you ever had, what specifically would you have experienced? Many will say "fun." Fair enough. Then make fun happen. Your challenge is to experience fun while staying on course to academic success. And you can do it! Consider these options for fun: What club could you join, what instructor could you get to know, what sport could you play, what classmate could you meet, what party could you attend, what new thing could you learn? By the way, for most college instructors, learning is high on their list of "fun," and they would love nothing more than to see you show joy in learning their subject. What if you made "joy in learning" one of your desired experiences? Would it make a difference in your overall experience of college?

So, think about it. What would you like to experience during this class or during this semester in college? Here are some additional experiences that my students desired: relaxation, mutual acceptance, respect, connection with others, self-confidence, an open mind, reflection about activities, passion for learning, total engagement, full-out participation, inspiration, excitement about this subject, synergy, courage, spirit of the group, calm acceptance of myself, joy, pride, and freedom. How about you?

Mohandas Gandhi said, "You must be the change you wish to see in the world." In other words, if you want to experience fun, *be* fun. If you want to experience total engagement, *be* totally engaged. If you want to experience connection with others, then *connect* with others. One of my students wanted to experience "creativity" in our student success class. To my delight, he proposed to *be* creative by asking to do an alternative to the final project. He proposed to write a rap song in which he promised to show that he had learned important success principles in our class. I told him he had my permission so long as he agreed to "rap" his project to our class on the last day of the semester. Little did I know that he was a professional rapper with a couple of CDs to his credit. As promised, he (and his whole group) showed up on the last day of the semester, handed out the words to "The College Success Rap," and treated us all to a rousing course finale. Best of all, he did a great job of demonstrating that he had learned many of the key principles of success, helping his classmates learn them even deeper. Afterwards he said, "Man, that was fun!"

Table 3-2 on page 60 lists the desired experiences that one of my students identified for herself, along with her reasons why.

German philosopher Friedrich Nietzsche once said, "He who has a why to live for can endure almost any how." He affirms that few obstacles can stop us when we understand the personal value we place on the outcomes and experiences of our journey. Discover your own motivation and your chances for success soar!

What ultimately counts most for each person is what happens in consciousness: the moments of joy, the times of despair added up through the years determine what life will be like. If we don't gain control over the contents of consciousness we can't live a fulfilling life.

Mihaly Csikszentmihaly

He who puts in four hours of "want to" will almost always outperform the person who puts in eight hours of "have to."

Roger von Oech

Table 3-2: One student's desired experiences.

Desired Experiences	Value
Fun	My brother dropped out of college because he said it was all work and no play. I know I'm going to have to work hard in college, but I want to have fun, too. I think if I'm enjoying myself, that'll make all assignments more bearable.
Academic confidence	I've never done particularly well in school although my teachers have always said I could be a good student if I applied myself more. I want to feel just as smart as any other student in my classes.
Excitement about learning	I didn't really like my classes in high school. I want to get excited about learning in at least one course, so I look forward to the homework and sometimes the class time goes so fast I can't believe when it's over.
Personal confidence	I have always been a shy person, and I want to become more outgoing so I can do well on future job interviews and be more assertive in my career so I get the promotions I deserve.

Journal Entry 7

In this journal entry, you'll identify your desired outcomes and experiences for this course and/or this semester. Developing clarity on what you want to create this semester will help you stay motivated and on course until the end. Use the student examples earlier in this section as models, but of course record your own desired outcomes, experiences, and reasons.

Success isn't a result of spontaneous combustion. You must set yourself on fire.
Arnold H. Glasow

1. In your journal, draw an empty table like Table 3-1. Fill in three or more of your own desired *outcomes* for this course and/or this semester. Next to each, explain why you value achieving that outcome. Remember, "outcomes" are those things you will take *away* with you at the end of the semester (like a grade or something you learn). At this point, you don't have to know HOW you will achieve these outcomes; you only need to know WHAT you want and WHY.

2. In your journal, place an empty table like Table 3-2. Fill in three or more of your desired *experiences* for this course and/or this semester. Next to each, explain

why you value having that experience. Remember, "experiences" are those things you will have *during* this semester (like fun or a sense of community). Once again, all that matters here is WHAT you would like to experience and WHY. Don't worry about HOW.

3. **Write about your level of motivation using the formula of V × E = M. Begin as follows:** *The Value I place on being a success in college is _____ [1–10] and my Expectation of being a success in college is _____ [1–10]. Multiplied together, this gives me an achievement motivation score of _____ [1–100].* Then continue by explaining your score and identifying specific actions you can do to raise it (or keep it high).

Remember, dive deep. When you explore your motivation at a deep level, you improve your chances of having an important insight that can change your life for the better. So dive deep and discover what really motivates you.

ONE STUDENT'S STORY
Chee Meng Vang
Inver Hills Community College, Minnesota

When I got to college, my biggest challenge was staying motivated. I was always going out clubbing with my friends, older sisters, and cousins. I was also shooting pool and hanging out with friends until late at night. I was lazy all the time and couldn't concentrate. I missed classes, fell behind in my homework, and tried to do everything at the last minute. This caused a lot of problems for me, like getting D's on my tests and quizzes. I felt like whatever happened to me was out of my control. I was feeling down and filled with dissatisfaction.

One night I was in a club, watching people drinking and dancing, and I thought, "This is getting boring. I'm tired and this isn't taking me anywhere at all." It was a good thing that College Success was part of my full-time student schedule. Our book was called *On Course*, and it helped me big time. It taught me to see myself as the primary cause of my outcomes and experiences and to find my desires that cause me to act. I was so stupid because my desire was right in front of me. There are so many reasons why it is important that I do well in college. My parents came to the United States from Laos, and all they ever wanted was a better life for their kids. It was hard for them in a new country, and we never had very much money. I realized I was being a loser and letting them down. Also, I am the first man in my family to go to college and my lovely five little brothers look up to me. I need to show them what a good role model their big brother can be. I want a career that will allow me to help my family, and when I have children, I don't want to be a dad working in McDonald's. My dream is to be a pharmacist, but I was headed in the wrong direction.

I come from a poor family, and I don't ever want to be like that in the future, so I had to make changes right away. I stopped going out to clubs and started taking responsibility. I became more outgoing in class. I studied two hours or more every day. I started getting A's and B's on my tests and quizzes. I finished the semester by raising my D grades to B's. As you can see, I've gone from being a lazy, unmotivated guy to a responsible, outgoing, I-control-my-destiny man. Now I don't feel like a victim any more. I've actually started to feel like a hero to my parents, my little brothers, and even to the small community where we live.

Designing a Compelling Life Plan

 FOCUS QUESTIONS If your life were as good as it could possibly be, what would it look like? What would you have, do, and be?

W hile growing up, Joan dreamed of becoming a famous singer. Following high school, she started performing in night clubs. She married her manager, and the two of them lived in a travel trailer, motoring from town to town in pursuit of singing jobs. After exhausting years on the road, Joan recorded a song. It didn't sell, and her dream began to unravel. Marital problems complicated her career. Career problems complicated her marriage. Joan grew tired of the financial and emotional uncertainty in her life. Finally, in frustration, she divorced her husband and gave up her dream of singing professionally.

Your goals are the road maps that guide you and show you what is possible for your life.
Les Brown

Although disappointed, Joan started setting new goals. She needed to earn a living, so she set a short-term goal to become a hairdresser. After graduating from cosmetology schools, Joan saved enough money to settle some debts, buy a car, and pay for a new long-term goal. She decided to go to a community college (where I met her) and major in dental hygiene.

Two years later, Joan graduated with honors and went to work in a dentist's office. Lacking a dream that excited her, Joan chose another long-term goal: earning her bachelor's degree. Joan worked days in the dentist's office and at night she attended classes. After a few years, she again graduated with honors.

Then, she set another long-term goal: earning her master's degree. Earlier in her life, Joan had doubted that she was "college material." With each academic success, her confidence grew. "One day I realized that, once I set a goal, it's a done deal," Joan said.

The most important thing about motivation is goal setting. You should always have a goal.
Francie Larrieu Smith

This awareness inspired her to begin dreaming again. As a child, Joan had always imagined herself as a teacher, but her doubts had always steered her in other directions. Masters degree now in hand, she returned to our college to teach dental hygiene. A year later, she was appointed department chairperson. In only seven years, Joan had gone from a self-doubting freshman to head of the college's dental hygiene department. Despite obstacles and setbacks, she continued to move in a positive direction, ever motivated by the promise of achieving personally valuable goals and dreams.

Roles and goals

According to psychologist Brian Tracy, many people resist setting life goals because they don't know how. Let's eliminate this barrier so you, like Joan, can experience the heightened motivation that accompanies personally meaningful goals.

CATHY by **Cathy Guisewite**

First, think about the roles you have chosen for your life. A life role is an activity to which we regularly devote large amounts of time and energy. For example, you're presently playing the role of college student. How many of the following roles are you also playing: friend, employee, employer, athlete, brother, sister, church member, son, daughter, roommate, husband, wife, partner, parent, grandparent, tutor, musician, neighbor, volunteer? Do you play other roles as well? Most people identify four to seven major life roles. If you have more than seven, you may be spreading yourself too thin. Consider combining or eliminating one or more of your roles while in college. If you have identified fewer than four roles, assess your life again. You may have overlooked a role or two.

Once you identify your life roles, think about your long-term goals for each one. Identify what you hope to accomplish in this role in the next two to five or even ten years. For example, in your role as a student, ten years from now will you have a two-year associate of arts (A.A.) degree? A four-year Bachelor of Arts (B.A.) or Bachelor of Science (B.S.) degree? Will you have attended graduate school to earn a Master of Arts (M.A.) or Master of Science (M.S.) degree? Or gone even farther to obtain a Doctor of Philosophy (Ph.D.) degree, a Medical Doctor (M.D.) degree, or a Doctor of Jurisprudence (J.D.) law degree? Any of these future academic goals could be yours.

One day Alice came to a fork in the road and saw a Cheshire cat in a tree. "Which road do I take?" she asked. "Where do you want to go?" was his response. "I don't know," Alice answered. "Then," said the cat, "it doesn't matter."

Lewis Carroll

How to set a goal

To be truly motivating, a goal needs five qualities. You can remember them by applying the DAPPS rule. "DAPPS" is an acronym, a memory device in which each letter of the word stands for one of five qualities: Dated, Achievable, Personal, Positive, and Specific.

Dated. Motivating goals have specific deadlines. A short-term goal usually has a deadline within a few months (like your semester's Desired Outcomes set in Journal Entry 7). A long-term goal generally has a deadline as far in the future as one year, five years, even ten years (like the goal you have for your most advanced academic degree). As your target deadline approaches, your motivation typically increases. This positive energy helps you finish strong. If you don't meet your deadline, you have an opportunity to examine what went wrong and create a new plan. Without a deadline, you might stretch the pursuit of a goal over your whole life, never reaching it.

Goals are dreams with a deadline.
Napoleon Hill

Achievable. Motivating goals are challenging but realistic. It's unrealistic to say you'll complete a marathon next week if your idea of a monster workout has been opening and closing the refrigerator. Still, if you're going to err, err on the side of optimism. When you set goals at the outer reaches of your present ability, stretching to reach them causes you to grow. Listen to other people's advice, but trust yourself to know what is achievable for you. Apply this guideline: "Is achieving this goal at least 50 percent believable to me?" If so and you *really* value it, go for it!

Personal. Motivating goals are *your* goals, not someone else's. You don't want to be lying on your deathbed some day and realize you have lived someone else's life. Trust that you know better than anyone else what *you* desire.

Positive. Motivating goals focus your energy on what you *do* want rather than on what you *don't* want. So translate negative goals into positive goals. For example, a negative goal to not fail a class becomes a positive goal to earn a grade of B or better. I recall a race car driver explaining how he miraculously kept his spinning car from smashing into the concrete racetrack wall: "I kept my eye on the track, not the wall." Likewise, focus your thoughts and actions on where you *do* want to go rather than where you *don't* want to go, and you, too, will stay on course.

Specific. Motivating goals state outcomes in specific, measurable terms. It's not enough to say, "My goal is to do better this semester" or "My goal is to work harder at my job." How will you know if you've achieved these goals? What specific, measurable evidence will you have? Revised, these goals become, "I will complete every college assignment this semester to the best of my ability" and "I will volunteer for all offerings of overtime at work." Being specific keeps you from fooling yourself into believing you've achieved a goal when, in fact, you haven't. It also helps you make choices that create positive results.

I always wanted to be somebody, but now I realize I should have been more specific.
Lily Tomlin

Through the years, I've had the joy of working with students who have had wonderful and motivating long-term goals: becoming an operating room nurse, writing and publishing a novel, traveling around the world, operating a refuge for homeless children, marrying and raising a beautiful family, playing professional baseball, starting a private school, composing songs for Aretha Franklin, becoming a college professor, swimming in the Olympics, managing an international mutual fund, having a one-woman art show, becoming a fashion model, getting elected state senator, owning a clothing boutique, and more. How about you? What do you *really* want?

Discover your dreams

Perhaps even more than goals do, dreams fuel our inner fire. They give our lives purpose and guide our choices. They provide motivating energy when we run headlong into an obstacle. Martin Luther King, Jr., had a dream that all people, regardless of differences, would live in a world of respect and harmony. When Candy Lightner's daughter was killed by a drunk driver, she transformed the tragedy into her dream to stop drunk driving, and her dream became the international organization, Mother's Against Drunk Driving (MADD). I found my dream only after twenty years of college teaching: My passion is empowering students with the beliefs and behaviors essential for living a rich and personally fulfilling life. While it's difficult to define a dream, they're big and they are often fueled by powerful emotions. Unlike goals, which usually fit into one of our life roles, dreams often take over our lives, inspire other people, and take on a life of their own. I sometimes wonder if people have dreams or if dreams have people.

The future belongs to those who believe in the beauty of their dreams.

Eleanor Roosevelt

If you presently have a big dream, you know how motivating it is. If you don't have a big dream, you're certainly in the majority. Most people have not found a guiding dream, yet they can still have a great life. College, though, offers a wonderful opportunity to discover or expand your dreams. You'll be exposed to hundreds, even thousands, of new people, ideas, and experiences. With each encounter, be aware of your energy. If you feel your voltage rise, pay attention. Something within you is getting inspired. If you're fortunate enough to find such a dream, consider the pithy advice of philosopher Joseph Campbell: "Follow your bliss."

Your Life Plan

What is significant about a life plan is that it can help us live our own lives (not someone else's) as well as possible.

Harriet Goldhor Lerner

Wise travelers use maps to locate their destination and identify the best route to get there. Similarly, Creators identify their goals and dreams and the most direct path there. In creating such a Life Plan, it helps to start with your destination in mind and work backwards. If you have a dream, accomplishing it becomes your ultimate destination. Or maybe your destination is the accomplishment of one or more long-term goals for your life roles. Since you can't complete a long journey in one step, your short-term goals become stepping stones, and each one completed brings you closer to the achievement of a long-term goal or dream.

Take a look at a page of a Life Plan that one student, Pilar, designed for herself. Although Pilar recorded her dream, not everyone will be able to do that. Her full Life Plan includes a page for each life role that she identified for herself, all of them with the same dream. Obviously, some life roles are going to make a more significant contribution to her dream than others. Notice that each long- and short-term goal adheres to the DAPPS Rule.

MY DREAM: I help families adopt older children (ten years old or older) and create home environments in which the children feel loved and supported to grow into healthy, productive adults.

MY LIFE ROLE: College student

MY LONG-TERM GOALS IN THIS ROLE:

1. I earn an Associate of Arts (A.A.) degree by June 2010.

2. I earn a Bachelor of Arts (B.A.) degree by June 2012.

3. I earn a Masters of Social Work (M.S.W.) degree by June 2014.

MY SHORT-TERM GOALS IN THIS ROLE (this semester)

1. I achieve an A in English 101, by December 18.

2. I write a research paper on the challenges of adopting older children, by November 20.

3. I achieve an A in Psychology 101 by December 18.

4. I learn and apply five or more psychological strategies that will help my family be happier and more loving by November 30.

5. I achieve an A in College Success by December 18.

6. I dive deep in every *On Course* journal entry, writing a minimum of 500 words for each one.

7. I learn five or more new success strategies and teach them to my younger brothers by November 30.

8. I take at least one page of notes in every class I attend this semester.

9. I turn in every assignment on time this semester.

10. I learn to use a computer well enough to prepare all of my written assignments, by October 15.

This is the first page of Pilar's six-page Life Plan. She wrote a similar page for each of her other five life roles: sister, daughter, friend, athlete, and employee at a group home for children.

We . . . believe that one reason so many high-school and college students have so much trouble focusing on their studies is because they don't have a goal, don't know what all this studying is leading to.

Muriel James and Dorothy Jongeward

Consciously designing your Life Plan, as Pilar did, has many advantages. A Life Plan defines your desired destinations in life and charts your best route for getting there. It gives your Inner Guide something positive to focus on when the chatter of your Inner Critic or Inner Defender attempts to distract you. And, like all maps, a Life Plan helps you get back on course if you get lost.

Perhaps most of all, a Life Plan is your personal definition of a life worth living. With it in mind, you'll be less dependent on someone else to motivate you. Your most compelling motivation will be found within.

Journal Entry 8

In this activity, you will design one or more parts of your Life Plan. To focus your thoughts, glance back at Pilar's Life Plan and use it as a model.

Many people fail in life, not for lack of ability or brains or even courage but simply because they have never organized their energies around a goal.

Elbert Hubbard

1. **Title a clean page in your journal: MY LIFE PLAN. Below the title, complete the part of your Life Plan for your role as a student.**

> **My Dream:** [If you have a compelling dream, describe it here. If you're not sure what your dream is, you can simply write, "I'm searching."]
>
> **My Life Role: Student**
>
> **My Long-Term Goals in this Role:** [These are the outcomes you plan to achieve as a student in the next two to ten years, or even longer if necessary.]
>
> **My Short-Term Goals in this Role:** [These are the outcomes you plan to achieve as a student this semester; each one accomplished brings you closer to your long-term goals as a student. To begin your list of short-term goals, you can write the same Desired Outcomes that you chose in Journal Entry 7; then add other short-terms goals as appropriate.]

Remember to apply the DAPPS rule, making sure that each long- and short-term goal is **D**ated, **A**chievable, **P**ersonal, **P**ositive, and **S**pecific. With this in mind, you may need to revise the Desired Outcomes that you transfer here from Journal Entry 7.

If you wish, repeat this process for one or more of your other life roles: career, parent, athlete, and so on. The more roles you plan, the more complete your vision of life will be. Taken together, these pages map your route to a rich, personally fulfilling life.

I started getting successful in school when I saw how college could help me achieve my dreams.

Bobby Marinelli, student

Importantly, at this time you don't have to know how to achieve your goals and dreams, so don't even think about the method. All you need to know is what you want. In the following chapters, you'll learn dozens of powerful strategies for turning your life plan into reality. For now, keep your eye on your destination!

Write about what you have learned or relearned by designing your life plan. In particular, identify any impact this effort has had on your level of motivation to do well in college this semester, or do well in any other parts of your life.

Committing to Your Goals and Dreams

 FOCUS QUESTIONS Do you start new projects (like college) with great enthusiasm, only to lose motivation along the way? How can you keep your motivation strong?

Always bear in mind that your own resolution to succeed is more important than any one thing.

Abraham Lincoln

Many people doubt they can achieve what they truly want. When a big, exciting goal or dream creeps into their thoughts, they shake their heads. "Oh, sure," they mumble to themselves, "how am *I* going to accomplish that?"

In truth, you don't need to know how to achieve a goal or dream when you first think of it. What you do need is an unwavering commitment, fueled by a strong desire. Once you promise yourself that you will do whatever it takes to accomplish your dream, you often discover the method for achieving it in the most unexpected ways.

Commitment creates method

A commitment is an unbending intention, a single-mindedness of purpose that promises to overcome all obstacles regardless of how you may feel at any particular moment. During the summer between my sophomore and junior years in college, I learned the power of commitment.

That summer, I used all of my savings to visit Hawaii. While there, I met a beautiful young woman, and we spent twelve blissful days together.

When you have a clear intention, methods for producing the desired results will present themselves.
Student Handbook, University of Santa Monica

One of my desires was to have a wonderful love relationship, so I promised to return to Hawaii during Christmas break. However, back in college six thousand miles away, my commitment was sorely tested. I had no idea how, in just three months, I could raise enough money to return to Hawaii. Committed to my dream, though, I spent weeks inventing and rejecting one scheme after another. (Though I didn't realize it at the time, I was actually using the Wise Choice Process to find my best option.)

Then one day, I happened upon a possible solution. I was glancing through *Sports Illustrated* magazine when I noticed an article written by a student-athlete from Yale University. Until that moment, all I'd had was a commitment. When I saw that article, I had a plan. A long shot, yes, but a plan, nonetheless: Maybe the editors of *Sports Illustrated* would buy an article about the sport I played, lightweight football. Driven by my commitment, I worked on an article every evening for weeks. Finally, I dropped it in the mail and crossed my fingers.

A few weeks later, my manuscript came back, rejected. On the printed rejection form, however, a kind editor had handwritten, "Want to try a rewrite? Here's how you might improve your article...."

Once a commitment is made without the option of backing out, the mind releases tremendous energy toward its achievement.

Ben Dominitz

I spent another week revising the article, mailed it directly to my encouraging editor, and waited anxiously. Christmas break was creeping closer. I had just about given up hope of returning to Hawaii in December.

Then one day my phone rang, and the caller identified himself as a photographer from *Sports Illustrated*. "I'll be taking photos at your football game this weekend. Where can I meet you?"

And that's how I learned that my article had been accepted. Better yet, *Sports Illustrated* paid me enough money to return to Hawaii. I spent Christmas on the beach at Waikiki, with my girlfriend on the blanket beside me.

Suppose I hadn't made a commitment to return to Hawaii? Would reading *Sports Illustrated* have sparked such an outrageous plan? Would I, at twenty years of age, have ever thought to earn money by writing a feature article for a national magazine? Doubtful!

What intrigues me as I recall my experience is that the solution for my problem was there all the time; I just couldn't see it until I made a commitment.

By committing to our dreams, we program our brains to look for solutions to our problems and to keep us going when the path gets rough. Whenever you're tempted to look for motivation outside yourself, remember this: Motivation surges up from a *commitment* to a passionately held purpose.

Visualize your ideal future

From my own experience, there is no question that the speed with which you are able to achieve your goals is directly related to how clearly and how often you are able to visualize your goals.

Charles J. Givens

Human beings seek to experience pleasure and avoid pain. Put this psychological truth to work for you by visualizing the pleasure you'll derive when you achieve your goals or dreams.

Cathy Turner explained how she visualized her way to winning two Olympic gold medals in speed skating: "As a little girl, I used to stand on a chair in front of the mirror and pretend I had won a gold medal. I'd imagine getting the medal, I'd see them superimposing the flag across my face just like they did on TV, and I would start to cry. When I really did stand on the podium, and they raised the American flag, it was incredible. I was there representing the United States, all of the United States. The flag was going up and the national anthem was being played, and there wasn't a mirror in front of me and it wasn't a chair

I was standing on. I had dreamt that for so long. All my life. And my dream was coming true right then and there."

To make or strengthen your commitment to achieve success in college, do what Cathy Turner did. Visualize yourself accomplishing your fondest goal and imagine the delight you'll experience when it actually happens. Let this desired outcome and the associated positive experiences draw you like a magnet toward a future of your own design.

Some years ago, I happened to glance at a three-ring notebook carried by one of my students. Taped to the cover was a photo showing her in a graduation cap and gown.

"Have you already graduated?" I asked.

"Not yet. But that's what I'll look like when I do."

"How did you get the photo?"

"My sister graduated from college a few years ago," she explained. "After the ceremony, I put on her cap and gown and had my mother take this picture. Whenever I get discouraged about school, I look at this photo and imagine myself walking across the stage to receive my diploma. I hear my family cheering for me, just like we did for my sister. Then I stop feeling sorry for myself and get back to work. This picture reminds me what all my efforts are for."

A few years later at her graduation, I remember thinking, "She looks just as happy today as she did in the photo. Maybe happier."

Life will test our commitments. To keep them strong in times of challenge, we need a clear picture of our desired results. We need a motivating mental image that, like a magnet, draws us steadily toward our ideal future.

The power of visualizing makes sense when you remember that getting anywhere is difficult if you don't know where you're going. A vivid mental image of your chosen destination keeps you on course even when life's adversities conspire against you.

How to visualize

Here are four keys to an effective visualization.

1. **RELAX.** Visualizing seems to have the most positive impact when experienced during deep relaxation. One way to accomplish deep relaxation is to breathe deeply while you tighten muscle groups one by one from the tip of your toes to the top of your head.

2. **USE PRESENT TENSE.** Imagine yourself experiencing success *now.* Therefore, use the present tense for all verbs: *I am walking across the stage to receive my diploma.* OR *I walk across the stage.* (Not past tense: *I was walking across the stage;* and not future tense: *I will be walking across the stage.*)

3. **USE ALL FIVE SENSES.** Imagine the scene concretely and specifically. Use all of your senses. What do you see, hear, smell, taste, touch?

I see a Chicago in which the neighborhoods are once again the center of our city, in which businesses boom and provide neighborhood jobs, in which neighbors join together to help govern their neighborhood and their city.
Harold Washington, Chicago's first black mayor

Visualization takes advantage of what almost might be called a 'weakness' of the body; it cannot distinguish between a vivid mental experience and an actual physical experience.
Dr. Bernie Siegel

4. **FEEL THE FEELINGS.** Events gain power to motivate us when accompanied by strong emotions. Imagine your accomplishment to be just as grand and magnificent as you wish it to be. Then feel the excitement of your success.

Psychologist Charles Garfield notes that athletes have used visualizations to win sports events; psychologist Brian Tracy writes about salespeople using visualizations to succeed in the business world; and Dr. Bernie Siegel, a cancer specialist, has even chronicled patients improving their health with visualizations.

Finally, consider this: the act of *keeping* your commitment may be as important, if not even *more* important than achieving a particular goal or dream. In this way, you raise your expectations for the success of future commitments, knowing that when you make a promise to yourself, you keep it.

So, create lofty goals and dreams. And, from deep within you, commit to their achievement.

Journal Entry 9

In this activity, you will visualize the accomplishment of one of your most important goals or dreams. Once you vividly picture this ideal outcome, you will have strengthened your commitment to achieve it, and you will know how to do the same thing with all of your goals and dreams.

Until one is committed there is hesitancy, the chance to draw back, always ineffectiveness. Concerning all acts of initiative (and creation), there is one elementary truth, the ignorance of which kills countless ideas and splendid plans: that the moment one definitely commits oneself, then Providence moves too. All sorts of things occur to help one that would never otherwise have occurred. A whole stream of events issues from the decision, raising in one's favour all manner of unforeseen incidents and meetings and material assistance, which no man could have dreamt would have come his way.
William Hutchison Murray,
Scottish mountaineer

 Write a visualization of the exact moment in the future when you are experiencing the accomplishment of your biggest goal or dream in your role as a student. Describe the scene of your success as if it is happening to you *now.* For example, if your desire is to graduate from a four-year university with a 4.0 average, you might write, *I am dressed in a long, blue robe, the tassel from my graduation cap tickling my face. I look out over the thousands of people in the audience, and I see my mother, a smile spreading across her face. I hear the announcer call my name. I feel a rush of adrenaline, and chills tingle on my back as I take my first step onto the stage. I see the college president smiling, reaching her hand out to me in congratulations. I hear the announcer repeat my name, adding that I am graduating with highest honors, having obtained a 4.0 average. I see my classmates standing to applaud me. Their cheers flow over me, filling me with pride and happiness. I walk . . .*

For visual appeal, consider also drawing a picture of your goal or dream in your journal. Or cut pictures from magazines and use them to illustrate your writing. If you are writing your journal on a computer, consider adding clip art that depicts your visualization. Allow your creativity to support your dream.

Remember the four keys to an effective visualization:

1. **Relax** to free your imagination.
2. Use **present tense verbs** . . . the experience is happening now!
3. Use **all five senses**. What do you see, hear, smell, taste, and feel (touch)?
4. Include **emotion.** Imagine yourself feeling great in this moment of grand accomplishment. You deserve to feel fantastic!

Read your visualizations often. Ideal times are right before you go to sleep and when you first awake in the morning. You may even wish to record your visualizations and listen to them often.

ONE STUDENT'S STORY

Amanda Schmeling
*Buena Vista University,
Iowa*

Coming to college hundreds of miles from home meant leaving behind my family and friends, but most importantly my identical twin sister. My eyes filled with tears as I hugged my sister goodbye. All our lives, we had done everything together, we relied on each other, and everyone knew us as a pair. In the first weeks of school without my sister, I felt homesick and lost. I was pulled in two directions, one half toward my familiar past and the other toward my unknown future. At college, all my energies went into acting like everything was okay, hiding my feelings from everyone. Despite this show on the outside, I was miserable on the inside. After weeks of struggling, I began to lose sight of why I had even come to college in the first place.

Just when I began thinking of quitting, we wrote a journal entry in my First-Year Seminar class. The directions asked us to visualize ourselves achieving an important goal or dream. In class we discussed the importance of seeing ourselves being successful and feeling the confidence we would gain. My professor asked us to draw a picture of the moment in our future when we were accomplishing our biggest dream after college. Some people drew sky scrapers and dollar signs; another drew a large family on a beautiful farm. After staring at the blank paper for a while, I began to draw the day when I achieve my dream of opening my own business. I sketched the unique colors of green, pink, blues, and purples that decorate the walls of my tea shop. I am preparing fragrant tea and baking delicious scones and cookies for my new customers. In the center of each table are gerbera daisies, tulips, and greens, each arrangement different from the next. My sister and mother are there to help me finish setting-up for the day. Everything around me is exactly how I want it, exactly how I dreamed it, and for now that is all that matters. Finally the day I have dreamed about since childhood has finally arrived.

Later that night as I was doing homework, my mind wandered back to my visualization. I could feel myself in that moment, I could see the doors opening, and I could hear the excitement. I thought to myself, *Maybe my future isn't so unclear, I know what I want, all I need to do is take hold of it.* My dreams had been there all along. I had just lost sight of them. My little "escape" to my future left me rejuvenated, and most importantly, I reconnected with my purpose for attending college—to earn my degree in business management. Since that day, my road continues to climb, twisting and turning, a new direction each day. I wake up not knowing how I will fare on my journey, but I know that no matter how hard the day may be, I still have my dream to look forward to. It's like a compass guiding me to my destination, my dream.

Self-Motivation at Work

Figure out what kind of job would make you happiest because the kind that would make you happiest is also the one where you will do your best and most effective work.

Richard Bolles, Career Expert, Author of *What Color is Your Parachute?*

One of the most important choices you will ever make is whether to seek a job or a career. When you have a job, you work for a paycheck. When you have a career, you work for the enjoyment and satisfaction you earn from your daily efforts...and you also get paid, possibly very well. I've had both, and I assure you, a career makes life a whole lot sweeter. If you want to feel motivated to get up and go to work fifty weeks a year, you'll definitely want to choose a career.

College is a great place to prepare for a career. But, to stay self-motivated, you'll want to match your career choice and college major with your unique interests, talents, and personality. I once had a student who was majoring in accounting because he'd heard that accountants make a lot of money. He saw no problem with the fact that he hated math. He thought he was preparing for a career when in fact he was preparing for a job.

Some of the most motivated students in higher education are those who see college as the next logical step on the path to their career goals. Sometimes these are younger students who are pursuing a lifelong dream of working in a particular profession. More often they are older students who've grown weary of working at uninspiring jobs and have come to college to prepare for rewarding careers. These self-motivated students are the ones who not only make the most of their education but who also enjoy the journey.

If you have a dream of a particular career, stay open to the possibility of finding something even more suited for you. If you're not yet sure what you want to do, keep exploring. The answer will probably reveal itself to you, and when it does, your life will change. One student I knew went from barely getting C's and D's to earning straight A's when she discovered her passion to be a kindergarten teacher.

Use your life-planning skills to design a motivating career path for yourself, identifying the long- and short-term goals that will act as stair-steps to your success. Using the DAPPS rule, you might create a career path like this:

2 years: I've received my A.A. degree in accounting with high honors and, by thoroughly researching accounting firms nationally, I've decided on five firms that look promising to work for after earning my B.A. degree.

5 years: I've earned my B.A. in accounting with high honors, and I'm employed in an entry-level accounting position in a firm of my choice earning $50,000 or more per year.

10 years: I own my own accounting firm, and I'm earning $150,000 or more per year, contributing to the financial prosperity and security of my clients.

Keep in mind that there is more to choosing an employer than how much money you're offered. Choosing an employer whose purpose and values are compatible with your own will assist you greatly to stay motivated. By reading a company's mission statement, you can find out what it claims are its purpose and values. For example, suppose you wanted to work in retail sales or marketing for one of the giant office products companies. Here is the mission statement for Staples:

Slashing the cost and hassle of running your office! Our vision is supported by our core values: C.A.R.E.

- *Customers*—Value every customer
- *Associates*—Support them as valuable resources
- *Real Communications*—share information with people when they need it
- *Execution*—achieve our business goals

Now, here is the mission statement for a major competitor, Office Depot:

Office Depot's mission is to be the most successful office products company in the world. Our success is driven by an uncompromising commitment to:

- *Superior Customer Satisfaction:* A company-wide attitude that recognizes that customer satisfaction is everything.
- *An Associate-Oriented Environment:* An acknowledgment that our associates are our most valuable resource. We are committed to fostering an environment where recognition, innovation, communication, and the entrepreneurial spirit are encouraged and rewarded.
- *Industry Leading Value, Selection, and Services:* A pledge to offer only the highest-quality merchandise available at everyday low prices, providing customers with an outstanding balance of value, selection, and services.
- *Ethical Business Conduct:* A responsibility to conduct our business with uncompromising honesty and integrity.
- *Shareholder Value:* A duty to provide our shareholders with superior Return-On-Investment.

Based on their mission statements, which company do you think has a purpose and value system that would create a more motivating work environment for you?

Once you actually begin your search for a position in your chosen career, your goal-setting abilities and visualizing skills will help you stay motivated. You can expect to make dozens of contacts with potential employers for each one that responds with interest to your inquiry. One way to keep yourself motivated during your search is to set a goal of making a specific number of contacts each week. *Goal: I will send a letter of inquiry and my résumé to ten or more potential employers each week.* In this way, you focus your energy on what you have control over—your own actions.

Additionally, take a few minutes each day to visualize yourself already in the career of your choice; see your office, your co-workers, and imagine yourself doing the daily activities of your career. This mental movie will reduce anxieties and remind you of the purpose for your hard work. Visualizing yourself in your ideal career will help keep you motivated when you encounter delays and disappointments on the path to your goal.

When you actually begin your career, self-motivation strategies will become extremely important to your success. You can't read many employment ads without noticing how many businesses are seeking employees who are "self-motivated." The ad might say "Must work well on own" or "Seeking a self-starter," but you know what such buzz words really mean. These employers want a worker who is able to take on a task and stick with it until completion despite obstacles or setbacks. Who wouldn't want a self-motivated worker? If you were an employer, wouldn't you?

Finally, your ability to set goals in your career is critical to your success. Goals and quotas are inevitable for those in sales positions, but many employers require all of their workers to set goals and create work plans. Your ability to set effective goals will not only help you excel at achieving goals for yourself, but also for your team, office, and company. As you move up in responsibility, your ability to coach others to set goals will be a great asset to the entire organization.

You will likely be working thirty, forty, or even more years. Your ability to discover inner motivation will have a great deal to do with the quality of the outcomes and experiences you create during all of these years.

Believing in Yourself: **Write a Personal Affirmation**

> **FOCUS QUESTIONS**   What personal qualities will you need to achieve your dreams? How can you strengthen these qualities?

We are what we imagine ourselves to be.
            Kurt Vonnegut, Jr.

Certain personal qualities will be necessary to achieve your goals and dreams. For example, if you desire a happy family life, you'll need to be loving, supportive, and communicative. To discover the cure for cancer, you'll need to be creative, persistent, and strong-willed.

Think of the short- and long-term goals you have for your education. What are the personal qualities you'll need to accomplish them? Will you need to be intelligent, optimistic, articulate, responsible, confident, goal-oriented, mature, focused, motivated, organized, hard-working, curious, honest, enthusiastic, self-nurturing?

The potential for developing all of these personal qualities, and more, exists in every healthy human being. Whether a particular person fulfills that potential is another matter.

During childhood, a person's judgment of his or her personal qualities seems to be based mostly on what others say. If your friends, family, or teachers told you as a child that you're smart, you probably internalized this quality and labeled yourself "smart." But if no one said you're smart, perhaps you never realized your own natural intelligence. Worse, someone important may have told you that you're dumb, thus starting the negative mind chatter of your Inner Critic.

We continue to be influenced by our earliest interactions with our parents. We hear their voices as our own internal self-talk. Those voices function like posthypnotic suggestions. They often govern our lives.

John Bradshaw

How we become the labels that others give us is illustrated by a mistake made at a school in England. A group of students at the school were labeled "slow" by their scores on an achievement test. Because of a computer error, however, their teachers were told these children were "bright." As a result, their teachers treated them as having high potential. By the time the error had been discovered, the academic scores of these "slow" students had risen significantly. Having been treated as if they were bright, the kids started to act bright. Perhaps, like these children, you have positive qualities waiting to blossom.

As adults, we can consciously choose what we believe. As one of my psychology professors used to say, "In your world, your word is law." In other words, my thoughts create my reality, and then I act according to that reality (regardless of its accuracy). For example, suppose I'm taking a large lecture class and I keep getting confused. Students sitting around me ask questions when they're confused, but I don't because, well, I've just never been comfortable asking questions in a large lecture hall—that's just the way I am. I'm shy. My Inner Defender is fine with this explanation because it protects me from doing something uncomfortable. The trouble is, the questions I don't ask keep popping up on tests, and I'm about to fail the course if I don't do something different.

I was saying "I'm the greatest" long before I believed it.

Muhammad Ali

Another part of me, my Inner Guide, knows I'd benefit from being bolder. In fact, if I want to pass this course, I *have* to be bolder! So I try an experiment. I start telling myself, *I am bold...I am bold...I am bold.* Of course, life keeps giving me chances to test my claim. A few class sessions later, I have another question, but I don't ask it. This time, though, I'm keenly aware of what I did: I took the wimpy way out. Undaunted, I continue my experiment, thinking, *I am bold...I am bold...I am bold.* The next time I have a question, I wait until after class and ask a fellow student. A little better, but still not *bold.* Then one day in class, I'm totally confused. *I am bold.* I shoot my hand in the air. Gulp. The professor calls on me, I ask my question, she answers, and, amazingly enough, I live to tell about it. Better yet, I get the answer correct on the next test. And best of all, my action finally corresponds with my claim. I came to a fork in the road (one I know so well), I consciously chose the bold path, I got the answer I needed, and I realize: My new thought generated new behaviors that, in turn, changed my outcomes and experiences for the better. And, if I did it once, I can do it again. Any time I need to. Any time I *choose* to!

Claiming your desired personal qualities

An effective way to strengthen desired qualities is to create a personal affirmation, a statement in which we claim desired qualities as if we already had them in abundance. Here are some examples:

- I am a bold, joyful, loveable man.
- I am a confident, creative, selective woman.
- I am a spiritual, wise, and curious man, finding happiness in all that I do.
- I am a supportive, organized, and secure woman, and I am creating harmony in my family.

Affirmations help us breathe life into personal qualities that we choose to strengthen. One of my colleagues recalls that whenever she made a mistake as a child, her father would say, "I guess that proves you're NTB." "NTB" was his shorthand for "not too bright." Imagine her challenge of feeling intelligent when she kept getting that message from her father! Today, she doesn't even need her father around; her Inner Critic is happy to remind her that she's NTB. She could benefit from an affirmation that says, "I am VB (very bright)."

What limiting messages did you receive as a child? Perhaps others said you were "homely," "stupid," "clumsy," or "always screwing up." If so, today you can create an affirmation that empowers your desired qualities. For example, you could say, "I am a beautiful, intelligent, graceful woman, turning any mistake into a powerful lesson."

Some people report that their positive affirmations seem like lies. The negative messages from their childhood (chanted today by their Inner Critics) feel more like the truth. If so, try thinking of your affirmation as prematurely telling the truth. You may not feel beautiful, intelligent, or graceful when you first begin claiming these qualities, but, just as the "slow" children at the English school responded to being treated as bright, with each passing day you can behave your way into believing the truth of your chosen qualities. Using affirmations is like becoming your own parent: You acknowledge the positive qualities that no one has thought to tell you about . . . until now. And then, most

"*Mother, am I poisonous?*"

importantly, you act on them, changing your outcomes and experiences in the process.

Living your affirmation

Of course, simply creating an affirmation is insufficient to offset years of negative programming. Affirmations need reinforcement to gain influence in your life. Here are three ways to empower your affirmation: Repeat...Dispute... Align.

Assume a virtue, if you have it not.
William Shakespeare

1. **Repeat your affirmation.** In this way you'll remember the qualities you have chosen to strengthen. One student repeated her affirmation during workouts on a rowing machine. The steady pace of the exercise provided the rhythm to which she repeated her affirmation. What would be a good occasion for you to repeat your affirmation?

2. **Dispute your Inner Critic.** Realize that you already possess the qualities you desire. You already *are* creative, persistent, loving, intelligent... whatever. These are your natural human qualities waiting to be re-empowered. To confirm this reality (and quiet your Inner Critic), simply recall a specific event in your past when you displayed a quality that is in your affirmation.

Affirmations have to be supported by the behavior that makes them happen.
Charles Garfield

3. **Align your words and deeds.** At each choice point, be what you affirm. If you say that you're "bold," make a bold choice. If you claim that you're "organized," do what an organized person does. If you assert that you're "persistent," keep going even when you don't feel like it. At some point, you'll have the evidence to assert, "Hey, I really am bold, organized, and persistent!" Your choices will prove the truth of your affirmation and your new outcomes and experiences will be the reward.

So, decide which personal qualities will help you stay on course to your goals and dreams and prepare to write a personal affirmation that will help you bring them forth!

Journal Entry 10

In this activity, you will create a personal affirmation. If you repeat your affirmation often, it will help you make choices that will strengthen the personal qualities needed to achieve your goals and dreams.

An affirmation is self-talk in its highest form.

Susan Jeffers

1. **Write a one-sentence statement of one of your most motivating goals or dreams in your role as a student.** You can simply copy one that you wrote in Journal Entry 8 (or create a new one if you prefer).

2. **Write a list of personal qualities that would help you achieve this educational goal or dream.** Use adjectives like *persistent, intelligent, hard-working, loving, articulate, organized, friendly, confident, relaxed,* and so on. Write as many qualities as possible.

3. **Circle the three qualities on your list that seem the most essential for you to achieve your goal or dream as a student (from Step 1).**

4. **Write three versions of your personal affirmation.** Do this by filling in the blanks in sentence formats A, B, and C below. Fill the blanks with the three personal qualities you circled in Step 3 above. NOTE: Use the same three personal qualities in each of the three formats.

    Format A: I am a ___, ___, ___ man/woman.
    Example: I am a strong, intelligent, persistent woman.

    Format B: I am a ___, ___, ___ man/woman, ___ing _____.
    Example: I am a strong, intelligent, persistent woman, creating my dreams.

    Format C: I am a ___, ___, ___ man/woman, and I _____.
    Example: I am a strong, intelligent, persistent woman, and I love life.

    Don't copy the examples; create your own unique affirmation.

5. **Choose the one sentence from Step 4 that you like best and write that sentence five or more times.** This repetition helps you to begin taking ownership of your affirmation and desired qualities.

6. **Write three paragraphs—one for each of the three qualities in your affirmation.** In each of these paragraphs, write about a specific experience when you displayed your desired quality. For example, if one of your desired qualities is persistence, tell a story about a time in your life when you were persistent (even a little bit!). Write the story like a scene from a book, with enough specific details that readers will feel as though they are seeing what you experienced. Your paragraph might begin, *The first quality from my affirmation is . . . A specific experience in my life when I demonstrated that quality was . . .*

The practice of doing affirmations allows us to begin replacing some of our stale, worn out, or negative mind chatter with more positive ideas and concepts. It is a powerful technique, one which can in a short time completely transform our attitudes and expectations about life, and thereby totally change what we create for ourselves.

Shakti Gawain

You can add creativity to your journal by writing your affirmation with colors, maybe adding pictures or key words cut from magazines, drawings of your own, clip art, or quotations that appeal to you.

ONE STUDENT'S STORY

Donna Ludwick
*Carteret Community
College, Virginia*

Twenty-three years after dropping out of high school, I finally enrolled in college. In between, I got married, worked as a waitress, had three children, and adopted a fourth. My first baby got cancer and had three serious operations between the ages of two and five. What she and the other kids in the hospital went through touched my heart, and I knew I wanted to help kids who were dealing with serious illnesses. I had always thought that school was useless and that I didn't have the smarts to finish, but I started to see that the only way I was going to make something of myself was to go to college. When I was in my thirties, I got my GED and became a certified nursing assistant. A few years later, I took the big step and came to college.

It was scary sitting in classes with people my daughter's age. They had such young minds and it all came so natural to them. One day while trying to do my math homework, I found myself saying, "I can't do this. I'm too stupid." Then I remembered my affirmation. We were reading *On Course* in my developmental English class, and the affirmation I wrote was, "I am a persistent, confident, hardworking woman, and I love to learn new things; I will be successful." At that moment, I felt like a boulder had been lifted off my shoulders. It took me four hours to finish that assignment, but I wouldn't quit. I passed the next math test, and that made me feel more confident and work even harder. I applied my affirmation qualities in English, too. I knew what I wanted to say, but I couldn't put it on paper. I'd write, revise, tear it up, and start all over. But I wouldn't quit! I swear I worked more than 100 hours on some of those essays, and pretty soon I started to turn my thoughts into what I really mean.

Sometimes it's a real struggle to work thirty-five hours a week, raise my kids, and go to school, too. Then I think, "This is going to get me what I want in life." I want to become a Licensed Practical Nurse, then go on for my RN degree and work in a hospital with those kids. I keep my affirmation on my refrigerator so I see it every day. With my affirmation staring me in the face, it reminds me I've come this far, and I'm not going to give up now. I really am a persistent, confident, hardworking woman, and I do love to learn new things. I *will* be successful!

Effective note taking is your memory's good friend and will go a long way toward raising your expectations of success in your studies. Taking notes promotes thorough reading in your text books and active listening in your classes, greatly increasing what you recall later. Well-organized notes also allow you to review what you read and heard, as well as decide what to study and remember. Successful college students take notes in nearly every class. Successful professionals use note taking to record important meetings, agreements, projects, results, and concerns. The following strategies will help you take better notes in both academic and professional settings. No single method of note taking is best for everyone, so experiment with the strategies below and personalize a system that works well for you.

Before Note Taking

1. Create a positive affirmation about taking notes. Many students hold negative beliefs about their ability to take good notes or the value of doing so. Create an affirming statement about taking notes, such as, *I take notes that capture all of the important concepts, making learning easy and fun.* Along with your personal affirmation, repeat this note-taking affirmation to motivate new learning behaviors.

2. Get note-taking supplies that fit your style. Experiment and decide on your best note-taking supplies. Do you prefer pens or pencils? Do you like one-color ink or the rainbow look? Do you prefer three-ring binders, composition books, spiral binders, 3"x 5" cards, or laptop computer for in-class notes?

3. Read and take notes on homework assignments before class. By doing so, you are better prepared to decide what information from the lecture or class discussion belongs in your notes.

4. Prepare a list of questions based on homework assignments. After reading homework assignments, write questions you would like answered in class. If you write them on binder paper, leave space after each question to write the answer. If you write them on 3" x 5" cards, put answers on the back to create great study cards. Bring the questions with you to class.

5. Bring note-taking supplies to every class and use them. As obvious as this suggestion is, some students don't take notes simply because they don't have a pen or paper with them. That's like a carpenter showing up for work without a hammer and screw driver. It should never happen!

During Note Taking

6. Use the outline method: An outline (depicted on page 82) shows the relationship of various ideas. Ideas that reach to the left-hand margin are major topics and are usually numbered. Subtopics are indented about one-half inch. Sub-subtopics are indented about one inch. Outlining is a good method when the information presented is well organized.

7. Use a concept map. A concept map (see example on page 115) graphically shows the relationships between main ideas and supporting elements in a complex lecture or reading assignment. Write the key idea in the center of a page; then, by placing satellites around the center, add sub-ideas, and sub-sub-ideas. Concept maps are especially helpful for taking notes when the instructor leaps from idea to idea. When the instructor returns to an idea already mentioned, you can add these new thoughts to the concept map in their proper relationship to ideas already recorded.

8. Use the Cornell Method: This method divides the page into three sections (depicted on page 83). The largest section (A) on the right is for taking notes during class or while reading. You can use your preferred note-taking method here: an outline, a concept map, or your own invention. Fill in Section B later, writing questions that are answered in Section A. When reviewing, simply cover your notes with your hand and quiz yourself with the questions in the left margin. The third section (C) allows space for summarizing the main points on that page of notes. As a variation, using a spiral binder for each subject, you can take class notes on the right page and write notes from your corresponding reading on the left (facing) page.

Course: Psychology 101
Date: October 5
Topic: Abraham Maslow

1. Abraham Maslow (1908–1970)
   — Family immigrated to Brooklyn
      — One of seven children
      — Unhappy, neurotic child
   — Taught at Teachers College, Brooklyn College, Brandeis
   — Sought to understand human motivations
   — Became leader of humanistic psychology movement of the
      1950's and 1960's

2. Maslow's Hierarchy: Theory of Human Motivation (like a pyramid)
   — Physiological needs (the foundation)
      — Food, rest, shelter, etc.
   — Safety needs
      — Security, stability, freedom from fear
   — Psychological needs
      — Belonging, love, affiliation, acceptance, esteem, approval,
         recognition
   — Self-actualization (top of the pyramid)
      — Need to fulfill oneself
         — Maslow: "to become everything that one is capable of
            becoming."

3. Humanistic psychology
   — Maslow led the "Third Force" in psychology
      — Alternative to…
         — Freudian psychoanalysis
         — Behaviorist psychology
   — Stressed the power of a person to choose how to behave
      — As opposed to…
         — Freudians: Choices controlled by childhood influences
         — Behaviorists: Choices controlled by conditioning
   — Appealed to the individualistic, rebellious college students of the
      1960's

9. Record only important ideas in your notes. Some students try to write everything an instructor says. Don't. Become skilled at ignoring digressions and recording only important points. The ideas that follow will help you perfect this skill.

10. Listen and look for cues. Instructors may *tell* you what information belongs in your notes. If you hear your instructor say any of the following phrases, start taking notes: *"The main point here is . . . , In other words . . . , In conclusion . . . , Obviously . . . ,*

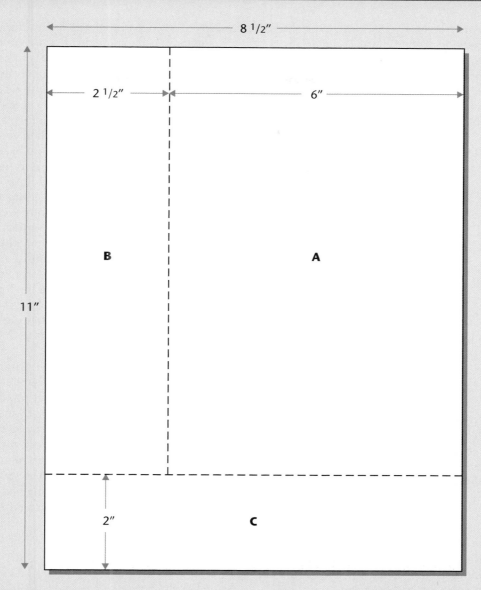

Most importantly..., To summarize..., The key here is..., This will definitely be on the final exam." Instructors will also *show* you nonverbally what is important. Start writing if you see your instructors do any of the following: Write on the blackboard, show a PowerPoint slide or transparency, emphasize an idea on a handout, read or point out a passage in your textbook, look carefully at lecture notes before speaking, become emotionally excited about an idea, lavishly praise a student's question or answer.

11. Listen for answers to your prepared questions. You've brought questions to class about your reading assignments. Now listen to the lecture or class discussion through the filter of those questions.

When you hear an answer, jot it down. If the class is ending without one of your questions being answered, ask it, adding the answer to your notes. If you don't get all of your questions answered, schedule an appointment with your instructor to get the answers.

12. Use abbreviations: Create your own personal abbreviations to make note taking go faster. For example:

ex	example
&	and
con't	continued
dept	department
imp	important
→	leads to
#	number
=	equals
1st	first
vs	versus
w/	with
w/o	without
nec	necessary
etc.	and other things

13. If you can't keep up, leave spaces. Some instructors talk with the speed of a freight train. Don't panic. Leave space in your notes. After class, confer with a classmate or the instructor to fill in the blanks.

14. Record the class. If your instructor's primary teaching style is lecture, ask him or her for permission to record it. You can listen to the lecture as many times as you wish to fill in gaps in your notes or review difficult concepts. However, don't procrastinate until you have forty-five hours of lecture to listen to but only twenty-four hours until the final exam. Instead, listen often to short segments of these recordings.

After Note Taking

15. Review your notes. As soon after a class as possible, read over your notes and fill in any missing information. If there is something you don't understand, ask a classmate, tutor, or the instructor to clarify your confusion. Make sure you understand everything

you wrote down. As you design your semester schedule, you may wish to provide breaks between classes to allow for an immediate review of your notes.

16. Talk about your notes. Thoroughly explain to someone else the key points you have recorded from a book or class. By verbalizing your understanding, you better organize the information in your memory for later retrieval. When you uncover areas of confusion, you can follow up by reviewing the reading or asking questions of your instructor.

17. Compare notes. Compare your notes with those of a competent classmate or study group members. Not only will you have an opportunity to correct errors and resolve any blanks in your notes, but reciting your notes will also help you remember them.

18. Revise your notes as appropriate. As you review your notes, make necessary revisions. Eliminate notes that seem unnecessary or off the topic. Add notes to further clarify a point. If you use the Cornell Method of note taking, this is the time to add questions in the margin next to your notes and summaries in the bottom section.

19. Review your notes periodically. Studies of learning suggest that we lose up to 80 percent of what we learned within twenty-four hours. Strengthen your memory pathways by frequently reviewing your notes during the semester. Try quickly reading over your notes every day for a week, then once a week thereafter. When the exam date approaches, you'll be amazed at how much you recall without painful cramming sessions.

20. Rehearse your notes aloud. By reading your notes aloud, you engage multiple senses and, especially for auditory learners, increase the amount of information you remember.

Note-Taking Exercise

In an upcoming class, take notes in a new way. Besides the option mentioned in this chapter, explore other methods at http://www.eduplace.com/graphicorganizer. Compare your experimental notes with those of a classmate, seeing which of you has recorded more comprehensive information for later studying.

Embracing Change

Do one thing different this week

You can wait until someone else (like your instructor) motivates you . . . or you can be a Creator and do it for yourself. From the list below, pick ONE new belief or behavior that you will experiment with for one week. Check off each day that you do the action. See if this new choice increases the **value** you place on your academic efforts, increases your **expectations** that you will be successful in your academic efforts, or both. After seven days, assess your results. If your outcomes and experiences improve, you now have a tool you can use for the rest of your life.

Beliefs and Behaviors	Day 1	Day 2	Day 3	Day 4	Day 5	Day 6	Day 7
Think: "I am choosing all of the outcomes and experiences for my life."							
Review and, if appropriate, revise my desired outcomes and desired experiences for this semester (recorded in Journal Entry 7).							
Set a goal using the DAPPS rule.							
Review my Life Plan (recorded in Journal Entry 8).							
Focusing on an additional role in my life, write another page of my Life Plan.							
Reread my Visualization of achieving my goal or dream as a student (recorded in Journal Entry 9).							
Write a visualization in which I am achieving a goal or dream in another life role.							
Demonstrate self-motivation at my workplace.							
Say my affirmation ____ times every day (recorded in Journal Entry 10).							
Use the following Note-Taking Strategy (write your choice from pages 81–84):							

(continued on page 86)

During my seven-day experiment, what happened?
As a result of what happened, what did I learn or relearn?

Mastering Self-Management

4

Once I accept responsibility for choosing and creating the life I want, the next step is taking purposeful actions that will turn my desires into reality.

I am taking all of the actions necessary to achieve my goals and dreams.

SUCCESSFUL STUDENTS . . .	STRUGGLING STUDENTS . . .
■ **act on purpose,** choosing deeds that move them on course to their goals and dreams.	■ wait passively or wander from one unpurposeful activity to another.
■ **employ self-management tools,** regularly planning and carrying out purposeful actions.	■ live disorganized, unplanned lives, constantly responding to whims of the moment.
■ **develop self-discipline,** showing commitment, focus, and persistence in pursuing their goals and dreams.	■ quit or change course when their actions don't lead to immediate success.

The Procrastinators

Two students from Professor Hallengren's English composition class sat in the cafeteria discussing the approaching deadline for their fourth essay.

"There's no way I can get this essay done on time," **Tracy** said. "I've turned in every essay late, and I still owe him a rewrite on the second one. Professor Hallengren is going to be furious!"

"You think you're in trouble!" **Ricardo** said. "I haven't even turned in the last essay. Now I'm going to be two essays behind."

"How come?" Tracy asked. "I would have thought a young guy right out of high school would have all the time in the world."

"Don't ask me where my time goes," Ricardo answered, shrugging. "Deadlines keep sneaking up on me, and before I know it, I'm weeks behind. I live on campus, and I don't even have to commute. But something always comes up. Last weekend I was going to write that other essay and study for my sociology test, but I had to go to a wedding out of state on Saturday. I was having such a good time, I didn't drive back until Monday morning. Now I'm even further behind."

"So that's why you missed English class on Monday," Tracy said. "Professor Hallengren lectured us because so many students were absent."

"I know I miss too many classes. One time I stayed home because I didn't have my essay ready. And sometimes I stay up late talking to my girl-friend on the phone or playing video games. Then I can't get up in the morning."

"My situation is different," Tracy said. "I'm in my thirties and I'm a single mother. I have three kids: five, seven, and eight. I work twenty hours a week, and I'm taking four courses. I just can't keep up with it all! Every time I think I'm about to catch up, something goes wrong. Last week one of my kids got sick. Then my refrigerator broke, and I had to work overtime for money to get it fixed. Two weeks ago they changed my schedule at work, and I had to find new day care. Every professor acts like his class is all I have to do. I wish! The only way I could do everything is give up sleeping, and I'm only getting about five hours a night as it is."

"What are you going to do?" Ricardo asked.

"I don't think I can make it this semester. I'm considering dropping all of my classes."

"Maybe I should drop out, too."

1. Who do you think has the more challenging self-management problem, Ricardo or Tracy? Be prepared to explain your choice.

2. If this person asked for your advice on how to do better in college, what specific self-management strategies would you recommend that he or she adopt?

DIVING DEEPER: Which person's situation, Ricardo's or Tracy's, is more like yours? Explain the similarity and identify what you do to keep up with all of the things you need to do.

Acting on Purpose

 FOCUS QUESTIONS   Have you ever noticed how much highly successful people accomplish? How do they make such effective use of their time?

reators do more than dream. They make a plan and then take one step after another . . . even when they don't *feel* like it . . . until they achieve their objective. Goals and dreams set your destination, but only persistent purposeful actions will get you there.

Thomas Edison did more than dream of inventing the light bulb; he performed more than ten thousand experiments before achieving his goal. Martin Luther King Jr. did more than dream of justice and equality for people of all races; he spoke and organized and marched and wrote. College graduates did more than dream of their diplomas; they attended classes, read books, wrote essays, conferred with instructors, rewrote essays, formed study groups, did library research, asked questions, went to support labs, sought out tutors, and more!

When we consider the accomplishments of successful people, we may forget that they weren't born successful. Most achieved their success through the persistent repetition of purposeful actions. Creators apply a powerful strategy for turning dreams into reality: **Do important actions first, *before* they become urgent**.

Do not confuse a creator with a dreamer. Dreamers only dream, but creators bring their dreams into reality.
Robert Fritz

Harness the power of Quadrant II

The significance of **importance** and **urgency** in choosing our actions is illustrated in the chart of the Quadrant II Time Management System® on the next page (from Stephen Covey's book *The 7 Habits of Highly Effective People*). This chart shows that our actions fall into one of four quadrants, depending on their importance and urgency.

Only you can determine the Importance of your actions. Sure, others (like friends and relatives) will have their opinions, but they don't really know what you value. If an action will help you achieve what you value, then it's *Important* and you'd be crazy not to do it. Sadly, though, many people fill their time with unimportant actions, thus sabotaging their goals and dreams.

Likewise, only you can determine the Urgency of your actions. Sure, others (like instructors and counselors) will set deadlines for you, but these external finish lines won't be motivating unless you make them personally important. If meeting an approaching deadline will help you achieve something you value, it's *Urgent* and you'd be crazy not to meet that deadline. Sadly, though, many people miss urgent deadlines, thus sabotaging their goals and dreams.

I've heard all sorts of excuses for why students "couldn't" get an assignment in on time. However, when I asked if they could have met the deadline if it was

I am personally persuaded that the essence of the best thinking in the area of time management can be captured in a single phrase: organize and execute around priorities.
Stephen Covey

Not all of your daily activities are of equal importance, and your mission is to organize and prioritize all activities into a working plan.

Charles J. Givens

worth one million dollars, their answer was almost always, "Sure, but it wasn't." So now we know the real problem. It wasn't that they "couldn't" meet the deadline. They just didn't make the deadline valuable enough to do what needed to be done. Creators choose their own goals and meet deadlines (even those set by others) because it's what *they* want, because it's important to creating the life *they* desire.

As you read on about the four quadrants, ask yourself, "In which quadrant am I choosing to spend most of my time?" No quadrant is "better" than others, but the choice you make will dramatically affect the outcomes and experiences you create.

QUADRANT I ACTIONS (Important and Urgent) are important activities done under the pressure of nearing deadlines. One of my college roommates began his junior paper (the equivalent of two courses) just three days before it was due. He claimed that success in college was *important* to him, and the impending deadline certainly made this assignment *urgent.* He worked on the paper for seventy-two hours straight, finally turning it in without time even to proofread. Although he squeaked by this time, he fell deeper and deeper into this pattern of procrastination, until in our senior year he failed out of college. People who spend their lives in Quadrant I are constantly dashing about putting out brush fires in their lives. They frantically create modest achievements in the present while sacrificing extraordinary success in the future. Worse, Quadrant I is the quadrant in which people experience stress, develop ulcers, and flirt with nervous breakdowns.

It is not enough to be busy . . . the question is: What are we busy about?

Henry David Thoreau

QUADRANT II ACTIONS (Important and Not Urgent) are important activities done *without* the pressure of looming deadlines. When you engage in an important activity with time enough to do it well, you can create your greatest

	Urgent	**Not Urgent**
Important	**Quadrant I** *Example:* Staying up all night cramming for an 8:00 A.M. test.	**Quadrant II** *Example:* Creating a study group in the first week of the semester.
Not Important	**Quadrant III** *Example:* Attending a hastily called meeting that has nothing to do with your goals.	**Quadrant IV** *Example:* Mindlessly watching television until 4:00 A.M.

dreams. Lacking urgency, Quadrant II actions are easily postponed. Almost all of the suggestions in this book belong in Quadrant II. For example, you could postpone forever keeping a journal, using the Wise Choice Process, adopting the language of Creators, discovering and visualizing your dreams, designing a life plan, and creating personal affirmations. However, when you do take purposeful actions such as these, you create a rich, full life. Quadrant II is where you will find Creators.

QUADRANT III ACTIONS (Not Important and Urgent) are unimportant activities done with a sense of urgency. How often have you responded to the demand of your ringing phone only to be trapped in long, unwanted conversations? Or you agree to do something only because you can't bring yourself to say "no"? Anytime we allow someone else's urgency to talk us into an activity unimportant to our own goals and dreams, we have chosen to be in Quadrant III.

QUADRANT IV ACTIONS (Not Important and Not Urgent) are simply time wasters. Everyone wastes some time, so it's not something to judge yourself for, though your Inner Critic will probably try. Instead, listen to your Inner Guide, become more conscious of your choices, and minimize wasting the irreplaceable hours of each day. A college professor I know surveyed his classes and found that many of his students regularly watch more than forty hours of television per week. That's the equivalent of a full-time job without pay or benefits!

What to do in Quadrant II

Creators spend as much time as possible in Quadrant II. In college, Creators schedule conferences with their instructors. They organize study groups. They rewrite their notes on graphic organizers and study them for short periods nearly every day. They predict questions on upcoming tests and carry the answers on 3″ × 5″ study cards. No external urgency motivates them to take these purposeful actions. They create their own urgency by a strong commitment to their valued goals and dreams.

By contrast, Victims spend much of their time in Quadrants III and IV, where they repeat unproductive actions like complaining, excusing, blaming, and wasting time. Not surprisingly, they move farther and farther off course.

If you want to know which quadrant you are in at any moment, ask yourself this question: "Will what I'm doing now positively affect my life one year from today?" If the answer is "yes," you are in Quadrant I or II. If the answer is "no," you are probably in Quadrant III or IV.

Creators say "no" to Quadrant III and Quadrant IV activities. Sometimes the choice requires saying "no" to other people: *No, I'm not going to be on your committee this semester. Thank you for asking.* Sometimes this choice requires saying "no" to themselves: *No, I'm not going to sleep late Saturday morning. I'm going to get up early and study for the math test. Then I can go to the movies with my friends without getting off course.*

While it is true that without a vision the people perish, it is doubly true that without action the people and their vision perish as well.

Johnetta B. Cole, president, Spelman College

A vision without a task is but a dream, a task without a vision is drudgery, a vision and a task is the hope of the world.

From a church in Sussex, England ca. 1730

When we say "no" to Quadrants III and IV, we free up time to say "yes" to Quadrants I and II. Imagine if you spent just thirty additional minutes each day taking purposeful actions. Think how dramatically that one small choice could change the outcome of your life!

Journal Entry 11

In this activity, you will assess the degree to which you are acting on purpose. *Your* purpose! As you spend more time in Quadrants I and II, you will notice a dramatic improvement in the results you are creating.

Remember to reread the visualization of your dream (Journal Entry 9) often to help you stay motivated. Also, remember to say your affirmation (Journal Entry 10) each day to enhance the personal qualities that will keep you on course to your dreams! These are both great Quadrant II actions.

1. Write a list of fifteen or more specific actions you have taken in the past two days. (The actions will be *specific* if someone could have recorded you doing them with a camcorder.)

2. Using an entire journal page, draw a four-quadrant chart like the example on page 90.

3. Write each action from your list in Step 1 in the appropriate quadrant on your chart. After each action, put the approximate amount of time you spent in the activity. For example, Quadrant IV might be filled with actions such as these:

1. Watched TV (2 hours)
2. Phone call to Terry (1 hour)
3. Watched TV (3 hours)
4. Went to the mall and wandered around (2 hours)
5. Hung out in the cafeteria (2 hours)
6. Played video game (2 hours)

4. Write about what you have learned or relearned concerning your use of time. Effective writing anticipates questions that a reader may have and answers these questions clearly. To dive deep in this journal entry, answer questions such as the following:

- What exactly did you discover after analyzing your time?
- In which quadrant do you spend the most time?
- What specific evidence did you use to draw this conclusion?
- If you continue using your time in this way, are you likely to reach your goals and dreams? Why or why not?

- What most often keeps you from taking purposeful actions?
- How do you feel about your discoveries?
- What different choices, if any, do you intend to make about how you use time?

Employing Self-Management Tools

 FOCUS QUESTION   How can you devote more time to creating the outcomes and experiences that matter most to you?

At the beginning of a class, I asked my students to pass in their assignments. A look of panic came over one man's face. "What assignment?" he moaned. "You mean we had an *assignment* due today?" On another day, I overheard one student ask a friend: "Did you study for the math test today?" "No," the friend replied, "I didn't have time." Not long ago, a student told me, "I'm doing fine in my classes, but that's because I'm letting the rest of my life go down the drain."

Time is the coin of your life. It is the only coin you have, and only you can determine how it will be spent.

Carl Sandburg

Do these situations sound familiar? Do you sometimes give a half-hearted effort on important tasks . . . or finish them late . . . or not even do them at all? Do you neglect one important role in your life to do well in another? It's no easy matter getting everything done, especially if you're adding college to an already demanding life. But there are proven tools that can help you work more effectively and efficiently.

Typically these are called "Time Management" tools, but the term's misleading because no one can actually manage time. No matter what we mortals do, time just keeps on ticking. What we *can* manage, however, is ourselves. More specifically, we can manage the choices we make daily. **The secret to effective self-management is making choices that maximize the time you spend in Quadrants I and II.** These are the quadrants, you'll recall, where all of your actions are important to achieving your goals and dreams.

I think that learning about and using time is a very complicated kind of learning. Many adults still have difficulty with it.

Virginia Satir

Understand that there's no "right" self-management tool that you *have* to use. Rather, there are many tools to experiment with until you find the combination that works best for you. How will you know when you've found your best self-management system? You'll start achieving more of your desired outcomes and experiences with less stress. As a bonus, when you find the self-management approach that feels right for you, your expectations of success in college (and elsewhere) will go up because now you'll be confident you can get the required work done. Here are three of the best tools for making sure that you spend most of your time creating a great future.

Monthly Calendars

The first self-management tool, a **Monthly Calendar** (page 98), provides an overview of your upcoming Quadrant I and II commitments, appointments, and assignments. Use it to record classes, labs, work hours, doctor's appointments, family responsibilities, parties, job interviews, and conferences with instructors. Also put on your calendar the due dates of tests, research papers, final exams, projects, lab reports, and quizzes. A monthly planner is an easy and effective self-management tool to use all by itself. In a glance, you can see what you're scheduled to do in the days, weeks, even months to come.

Scheduling purposeful actions is one thing; actually doing them is quite another. Once you have chosen your priorities, let nothing keep you from completing them except a rare emergency or special opportunity. Make a habit of saying "no" to unscheduled, low-priority alternatives found in Quadrants III and IV.

In addition to paper calendars, many people today keep their appointment schedule on a personal digital assistant (PDA). PDAs, which cost between $60 and $750, are tiny, handheld computers that can do a lot more than merely store your calendar. Depending on the model, a PDA can also record your important contact information (address and phone book), play music, take digital pictures, surf the Internet, and allow you to download and respond to email. A free electronic alternative is an online calendar hosted by a number of Internet sites (simply do an Internet search for "online calendar"). A unique advantage of these services is that most allow you to create calendars that can be accessed and updated by members of a group. So, if you have a project group, a study team, or a large family, an online calendar service might be just the right tool for managing your collective schedules.

Next Actions Lists

A **Next Actions List** (page 99) records everything you need to do "next" (as opposed to a calendar where you schedule actions on a particular day or at a particular time). Whenever you have some free time that you might otherwise waste, your Next Actions List provides Quadrant I or II actions to complete. Here's how to use one:

1. Write your life roles and corresponding goals, which you defined in Chapter 3, in the shaded boxes. This first step makes your Next Actions List more effective than a mere to-do list by ensuring that your actions are directed at the accomplishment of one or more of your important goals.

2. List Quadrant I (Important and Urgent) actions for each of your goals. For example, if your short-term goal for Math 107 is to earn an A, your list might contain actions like these:

   Role: Math 107 student

Goal: Grade A

- *Attend classes on time (MWF).*
- *Read pages 29–41 and do problems 1–10 on page 40.*
- *Study 2 hours or more for Friday's test on Ch's 1–3.*

Each of these three actions is **important,** and each is relatively **urgent.** Notice that each action is written to heed the DAPPS rule, just as your goals are. Each action is Dated, Achievable, Personal, Positive, and Specific. Especially be specific. Vague items such as *Do homework* provide little help when the time comes to take action. Much more helpful are specifics, such as *Read pages 29–41 and do problems 1–10 on page 40.*

3. List Quadrant II (Important and Not Urgent) actions under each of your goals. For example, your list for Math 107 might continue with actions like these:

- *Make appointment with Prof. Finucci and ask her advice on preparing for Friday's test.*
- *Attend appointment with math lab tutor.*
- *Meet with study group and compare answers on practice problems.*

These Quadrant II behaviors are the sorts of activities that struggling students seldom do. You could go through the entire semester without doing any of these purposeful actions because none of them is urgent. But when you consistently choose Quadrant II actions, this decision makes a big difference in the results you create.

Whenever you have free time during the day, instead of slipping unconsciously into Quadrants III or IV, check your Next Actions List for purposeful actions. As you complete an action, cross if off your list. As you think of new important actions, add them to your list under the appropriate role. A bonus of keeping a Next Actions List is that it eliminates the burden of remembering numerous small tasks, freeing your brain to do more creative and critical thinking.

Tracking Forms

The third self-management tool, a **Tracking Form** (on page 100), is a variation of an old friend. You've already used a version of a Tracking Form in the Embracing Change experiment at the end of each chapter. As demonstrated there, a Tracking Form is ideal for scheduling actions that you decide are important to reach a personal goal. Elite athletes typically use some form of this tool to plan and monitor their training. A Tracking Form helps you coordinate many actions all directed at a common goal.

Suppose, for example, you decide to use a Tracking Form to help you gain a deep understanding of sociology and earn an A in the course. One helpful outer (physical) action might be "Read the textbook one or more hours." A possible inner (mental) action is "Say my affirmation five or more times." So, you write these two actions in the appropriate left-hand column, and put the dates of the next fourteen days at the top of the check-box columns.

Each day that you take these actions, you check the appropriate box, and at the end of fourteen days, you'll see exactly what you have (or have not) done to achieve your goal. One of my students commented, "Before I used the Tracking Form, I thought I was studying a lot. Now I realize I'm not studying enough." She started studying more, and her grades improved dramatically. A Tracking Form keeps your Inner Defender from fooling you into thinking you're doing what's necessary to stay on course when, in fact, you're not.

The rewards of effective self-management

Some people resist using a written self-management system. "These forms and charts are for the anally retentive," one student objected. "Everything I need to do, I keep right here in my head." I know this argument well, because I used to make it myself. Then one day, one of my mentors replied, "If you can remember everything you need to do, I guess you're not doing very much." Ouch. Then he whomped me again, "I guess some people would rather be right than successful."

I decided it wouldn't kill me to experiment with written self-management tools. Over time, I came up with my own combination of the tools we've been examining. In the process I became aware of how I had been wasting precious time. With my old self-management system (mostly depending on my memory, with an occasional "note to self") the best I did was remember to do what was important and urgent. The worst I did was forget something vital, then waste time cleaning up the mess I had made. With my new system, I not only complete my Quadrant I actions now, I also spend large chunks of time in Quadrant II, where I take important actions before they become urgent. I'm better at keeping commitments to myself and others. I'm less tempted to go off course. Relieved of remembering every important task I need to do, my mind is free to think more creatively and boldly. And, most of all, my written self-management system helps me carry out the persistent, purposeful actions necessary to achieve my goals and dreams.

If you're already achieving all of your greatest goals and dreams, then keep using your present self-management system because it's working! However, if your Inner Guide knows you could be more successful than you are now, then maybe it's time to implement a new approach to managing your choices. You'll rarely meet a successful person who doesn't use some sort of written self-management system, whether in the world of work or in college. In fact, researchers at the University of Georgia found that students' self-management skills and attitudes are even better predictors of their grades in college than their Scholastic Aptitude Test (SAT) scores.

Consistently using a written self-management system is a habit that takes time to establish. You may begin with great energy, only to find later that a week has gone by without using it. Avoiding self-judgment, simply examine where you went astray and begin your plan anew. Experiment until you find the system that works best for your personality and creates the outcomes and experiences you desire. In time, your skills in using your personally designed written self-management system will excel. And then watch how much more you accomplish!

Journal Entry 12

In this activity, you'll explore how you could improve your present self-management system. By becoming more effective and efficient in the use of time, you'll complete a greater number of important actions and maximize your chances of attaining your goals and dreams.

I used to wonder how other students got so much done. Now that I'm using a planner, I wonder how I settled for doing so little.
John Simmons, student

1. **Write about the system (or lack of system) that you presently use to decide what you will do each day.** There is no "wrong" answer, so don't let your Inner Critic or Inner Defender get involved. Consider questions such as how you know what homework to do, when to prepare for tests, what classes to attend, and what instructor conferences to go to? How do you track what you need to do in other roles, such as your social or work life? Why do you currently use this approach? How well is your system working (giving examples wherever possible)? How do you *feel* while using this approach to self-management (e.g., stressed, calm, energized, frantic, etc.)?

2. **Write about how you *could* use or adapt the three self-management tools in this chapter to improve your outcomes and experiences. Or, if you do not want to use or adapt any of these tools, explain why.** Consider the Monthly Calendar, the Next Actions List, and the Tracking Form. How might you use them separately or in combination? How could you use computers or other technology in your self-management approach? How might you use written self-management tools not mentioned here that you may know about? In short, invent your own system for managing your choices that you think will maximize the quality of your outcomes and experiences. Should you need them, copies of a Monthly Calendar, a Next Actions List, and Tracking Form can be found on the Internet at *college.hmco.com/pic/ downing5e.*

Monthly Calendar

Monday	Tuesday	Wednesday	Thursday	Friday	Saturday	Sunday

Month _____

Next Actions List

Role:
Goal:

Role:
Goal:

Role:
Goal:

Role:
Goal:

Role:
Goal:

Role:
Goal:

Telephone calls

Miscellaneous actions

Tracking Form

Role:

Dream:

Long-term goal:

Short-term goals (to be accomplished this semester):

1.

2.

3.

4.

OUTER (Physical) Action Steps

Dates:

INNER (Mental) Action Steps

Dates:

When the fall semester began, I wasn't sure how I was going to fit everything into my schedule. In addition to taking three college courses, I was waitressing twenty-four hours a week, taking dance classes, teaching dance classes to kids, spending time with my boyfriend, doing housework and errands, hanging out with friends from three different groups (high school, college, and church), and rehearsing two evenings a week for an annual December musical at Memorial Auditorium that draws thousands of people. I'd stay up late to get my homework done, then wake up exhausted. I was struggling in math, and in my heart I knew I could be doing better in my other classes. I'd forget to turn in homework, I was skimping on preparation for my dance classes, I wasn't calling friends back, and I'd forget to bring costumes and makeup to rehearsals for the musical. I was sick all the time with colds and headaches. I was seriously stressed and not doing full justice to anything.

Before I lost all hope, my Human Career Development class went over self-management tools. I developed my own system and started writing down everything I needed to do. I keep a big calendar by my bed so I see it in the morning, and I carry a smaller calendar in my purse. My favorite tool is a list of everything I have to do put into categories. I make a new list every day and put important things at the top so it's okay if I don't get to the ones on the bottom. My system helps me see what my priorities are and get them done first so I don't feel so scattered.

By doing important things first, I began having more focus, not rushing as much, and getting more done. Of course I had to let a few lower priority things go for a while, like doing housework and spending as much time with some of my friends. I started getting more sleep, completing my homework, and getting A's on all of my tests while doing everything else that I needed to do. After a while, I began to accomplish so much more and I realized that I *do* have enough time to fit all of the important things into my schedule. In fact, every once in a while now I actually find myself with a luxury I haven't had in a long while—free time.

ONE STUDENT'S STORY

Allysa LePage
*Sacramento City
College, California*

Developing Self-Discipline

? FOCUS QUESTIONS Do you find yourself procrastinating, even on projects that mean a great deal to you? How can you keep taking purposeful actions even when you don't feel like it?

Self-discipline is self-caring.
Dr. M. Scott Peck

Every semester perfectly capable students abandon their goals and dreams. Somewhere along the path, they get distracted and stop or they wander off in another direction.

"Hey," their instructors want to shout, "the goals and dreams you say you want are over here! Keep coming this way. You can do it!"

Maybe these students believe college is a sprint, over in a flash. Not so. Like most grand victories, college is a marathon. It may take only thirty seconds to stride proudly across the stage to receive your college diploma, but it will have taken you thousands of persistent small steps taken over years to get there.

In a word, success takes self-discipline—the willingness to do whatever has to be done, whether you feel like it or not, until you reach your goals and dreams. Every January, athletic clubs are wall-to-wall with people who made New Year's resolutions to get in shape. You know what happens. A month later, the crowds are gone, reminding us that getting and staying in shape takes commitment, focus, and persistence.

So it goes with every important goal we set. Our actions reveal whether we have the self-discipline to stay on course in the face of tempting alternatives. Most students want to be successful, but *wanting* and *doing* are worlds apart. Partying with friends is easier than going to class . . . day after day. Talking on the phone is easier than reading a challenging textbook . . . hour after hour. Watching television is easier than doing research at the library . . . night after night.

To be disciplined or nondisciplined is a choice you make every minute and every hour of your life. Discipline is nothing more than the process of focusing on any chosen activity without interruption until that activity is complete.

Charles J. Givens

Many people choose instant gratification. Few choose the far-off rewards of persistent and purposeful actions. Many begin the journey to their dreams; few finish. Yet all we need to do is put one foot in front of the other . . . again and again and again. A journey of a thousand miles may begin with a single step, but many more better follow.

Self-discipline has three essential ingredients: **commitment, focus,** and **persistence.** In Journal Entry 9, you explored how to strengthen your commitment. Now take a look at focus and persistence.

Staying focused

Distractions constantly tug at our minds, and, like an unruly child, the unfocused mind dashes from one distraction to another. Everyone has experienced losing focus for a minute, an hour, even a day. But struggling students lose focus

Calvin and Hobbes   by Bill Watterson

for weeks and months at a time. They start arriving late, skipping classes, doing sloppy work, ignoring assignments. They take their eyes off of the prize and forget why they are in college.

For many students, the time to beware losing focus is at midterm. The excitement of the new semester has been replaced by the never-ending list of assignments. That's when Inner Defenders start offering great excuses to quit: *I've got boring teachers, my schedule stinks, I'm still getting over the flu, next semester I could start all over.* And Inner Critics chime in with practiced self-judgments: *I never could do math, I'm not as smart as my classmates, I'm too old, I'm too young, I'm not really college material.*

Your Inner Guide, however, knows that winners stay focused and finish strong. They complete the semester with a bang, not a snivel. Their efforts go up as the semester winds down. Your Inner guide can help you regain focus by addressing one question: *What are my goals and dreams?* If you need a reminder, revisit your life plan in Journal Entry 8 and the visualization of your biggest academic goals or dream in Journal Entry 9. If your goals and dreams don't motivate you to keep taking purposeful actions right to the finish line, then perhaps you need to rethink where you want to go in life.

Being persistent

If focus is self-discipline in thought, then persistence is self-discipline in action. Here's the question your Inner Guide can ask when you slow down or quit: "Do I love myself enough to keep going?" You are the one who'll benefit most from the accomplishment of your goals and dreams . . . and you're the one who will pay the price of disappointment if you fail.

Here's the thing, though. Although failure is certain if you quit, success isn't guaranteed simply because you persist. Sometimes wisdom requires more than simply repeating the same thing over and over expecting a better result. If Plan A isn't working, don't quit. But also don't keep doing what isn't working! Change your approach. Move on to Plan B. Or C or D if necessary. One of my students learned just how powerful persistence and a willingness to try something different can be.

When Luanne enrolled in my English 101 class, she had taken and failed the course three times before. She had actually developed some good writing skills, but she definitely needed to master Standard English to pass the course. "I know," she said, "that's what all my other teachers told me." She paused, took a deep breath and added, "At least I'm not a quitter."

I asked Luanne why she was going to college. As she told me about her dream to work in television, her eyes sparkled. I asked if mastering standard grammar would help her achieve her dream. She hesitated, perhaps nervous about where her answer might lead.

Finally she said, "Yes."

You always have to focus in life on what you want to achieve.

Michael Jordan

Perhaps the most valuable result of all education is the ability to make yourself do the thing you have to do, when it ought to be done, whether you like it or not; it is the first lesson that ought to be learned; and however early a man's training begins, it is probably the last lesson that he learns thoroughly.

Thomas Henry Huxley

"Great! So, what's one action that, if repeated every day for a month or more, would improve your grammar?" She needed to discover a Quadrant II activity and make it a new habit.

"Probably studying my grammar book."

I handed her a **32-Day Commitment Form** (see page 106). "Okay, then, I'm inviting you to make a commitment to study your grammar book for thirty-two days in a row. You can put a check on this form each day that you keep your promise to yourself. Will you do it?"

"I'll try."

"C'mon, Luanne. You've been *trying* for six semesters. My question is, 'Will you commit to studying grammar for thirty minutes every day for the next thirty-two days?'"

She paused again. Her choice at this moment would surely affect her success in college, and probably the outcome of her life.

"Okay," she said, "I'll do it."

And she did. Each time I passed the writing lab, I saw Luanne working on grammar. The tutors joked that they were going to start charging her rent.

But that's not all Luanne did. She attended every English class. She completed every writing assignment. She met with me to discuss her essays. She created flash cards, writing problem sentences on one side and corrections on the other. In short, Luanne was taking the persistent actions of a self-disciplined student.

As mentioned earlier, to receive a passing grade in English 101, students had to pass one of two exit exam essays graded by other instructors. The first exam that semester brought Luanne some good news: She had gotten her highest score ever. But there was the usual bad news as well: Both exam graders said her grammar errors kept them from passing her.

Luanne was at another important choice point. Did she have the self-discipline to persist in the face of discouraging news? Would she quit or finish strong?

"Okay," she said finally, "show me how to correct my errors." We reviewed her essay, sentence by sentence. The next day she went to the writing lab earlier; she left later. She rewrote the exam essay for practice, and we went over it again. Applying self-discipline, Luanne's mastery of standard grammar continued to improve.

That semester, the second exam was given on the Friday before Christmas. In order to finalize grades, all of the English 101 instructors met that evening to grade the essays. I promised to call Luanne with her results.

The room was quiet except for rustling papers as two dozen English instructors read one essay after another. At about ten o'clock that night, I received my students' graded essays. I looked quickly through the pile and found Luanne's. She had passed! As I dialed the phone to call her, Luanne's previous instructors told others about her success.

"Merry Christmas, Luanne," I said into the phone, "you passed!"

I heard her delight, and at that moment, two dozen instructors in the room began to applaud.

The major difference I've found between the highly successful and the least successful is that the highly successful stick to it. They have staying power. Everybody fails. Everybody takes his knocks, but the highly successful keep coming back.

Sherry Lansing, chairman, Paramount Pictures

A dream doesn't become reality through magic; it takes sweat, determination, and hard work.

Colin Powell

Journal Entry 13

In this activity, you will apply self-discipline by planning and carrying out a thirty-two day commitment. Some behavioral psychologists suggest that breaking an old habit or starting a new one requires about thirty-two days.

1. From your life plan in Journal Entry 8, copy one of your most important and challenging short-term goals from your role as a *student*.

2. Write and complete the following sentence stem five or more times: I WOULD MOVE STEADILY TOWARD THIS GOAL IF EVERY DAY I . . .

Write five or more different physical actions that *others can see you do* and that you can do every day of the week, including weekends. So you wouldn't write, "be motivated" or "attend class." Others cannot see your motivation, and you can't attend class every day for thirty-two days straight. Instead, if your short-term goal is to earn an "A" in English, you might complete the sentence with specific actions such as these:

1. **I WOULD MOVE STEADILY TOWARD THIS GOAL IF EVERY DAY I** *spend at least fifteen minutes doing exercises in my grammar book.*

2. **I WOULD MOVE STEADILY TOWARD THIS GOAL IF EVERY DAY I** *write at least two hundred words in my journal.*

3. **I WOULD MOVE STEADILY TOWARD THIS GOAL IF EVERY DAY I** *revise one of my previous essays, correcting the grammar errors that my teacher marked.*

Chances are, all of these actions will fall in Quadrant II.

3. On a separate page in your journal, create a 32-Day Commitment Form or attach a photocopy of the one on page 106. Complete the sentence at the top of the form ("Because I know . . . ") with ONE action from your list in Step 2. For the next thirty-two days, put a check beside each day that you keep your commitment.

4. Write your thoughts and feelings as you begin your 32-day commitment. Develop your journal paragraphs by asking and answering readers' questions, such as, How self-disciplined have you been in the past? What is your goal? What were some possible actions you considered? What action did you choose for your 32-Day Commitment? How will this action, when performed consistently, help you reach your goal? What challenges might you experience in keeping your commitment? How will you overcome these challenges? How do you feel about undertaking this commitment? What is your prediction about whether or not you will succeed in keeping your 32-Day Commitment?

IMPORTANT: If you miss a day on your 32-Day Commitment, don't judge yourself or offer excuses. Simply ask your Inner Guide what got you off course, renew your commitment to yourself, and start over at Day 1.

> *My Daddy used to ask us whether the teacher had given us any homework. If we said no, he'd say, "Well, assign yourself." Don't wait around to be told what to do. Hard work, initiative, and persistence are still the nonmagic carpets to success.*
> Marian Wright Edelman

> *Becoming a world-class figure skater meant long hours of practice while sometimes tolerating painful injuries. It meant being totally exhausted sometimes, and not being able to do all the things I wanted to do when I wanted to do them.*
> Debi Thomas

32-Day Commitment

Because I know that this commitment will keep me on course to my goals, I promise myself that every day for the next 32 days I will take the following action: _____

_____

_____

Day 1		Day 17	
Day 2		Day 18	
Day 3		Day 19	
Day 4		Day 20	
Day 5		Day 21	
Day 6		Day 22	
Day 7		Day 23	
Day 8		Day 24	
Day 9		Day 25	
Day 10		Day 26	
Day 11		Day 27	
Day 12		Day 28	
Day 13		Day 29	
Day 14		Day 30	
Day 15		Day 31	
Day 16		Day 32	

I was a first-year student and enjoying college, but I was having a hard time in my electronics class. The teacher lectured about things like current, watts, volts, and resistance, and even though I read the book, took notes in class, and asked questions, I still wasn't understanding what I needed to. When I got back my first test, I didn't fail but I did pretty badly. I was scared because, if this is what the first test was like, how hard would the rest of them be? This was a new experience for me because I never had to study much to do well in school. I knew that I had to try something different if I was going to pass electronics.

In my Student Learning and Success class, I read about the 32-day commitment, and I decided to give it a try. I decided to read one section from my electronics book twice every day for thirty-two days. I figured that if I read the section twice, maybe I would understand it better the second time around. However, as the semester went on, I still wasn't doing so hot. At times I felt like quitting my commitment because, even though I was reading every section twice, I still

wasn't getting it. By midterm, I was ahead of the class in the book, and when the instructor taught the section, it was all review for me. Then one day he was putting examples on the board, and I realized, "Hey, I know this stuff." Since I already understood most of the material, I had time to focus on the things that I didn't understand. Everything that was still blurry to me he made clear. On the next chapter test, I got a 93, and in the end I passed the class with a B.

It's amazing what doing one little thing for thirty-two days can do for you. I never would have thought committing thirty-two days to reading a section from my book twice would help so much. Before, I'd say, "Yeah, I read it," but I was only skimming. When I read it a second time, I picked up things that I missed the first time through and I really understood what I was reading. In the end the 32-day commitment was able to help me pass my electronics class, but even more important, this experience gave me a lot more confidence. Now I know that I can pass all of the challenging classes on the way to my degree.

ONE STUDENT'S STORY

Holt Boggs
Belmont Technical College, Ohio

Self-Management at Work

Success in business requires training and discipline and hard work. But if you're not frightened by these things, the opportunities are just as great today as they ever were.

David Rockefeller, Former Chairman, The Chase Manhattan Bank

As it is in college, success in the workplace means converting your goals into a step-by-step plan and having the self-discipline to spend the majority of your time doing what is important, preferably before it becomes urgent. Here in the realm of action, doers separate themselves from dreamers. Folks in business often refer to this aspect of success as "doing diligence."

In college, "doing diligence" is wise because the effort usually nets you good grades, and a high GPA impresses potential employers with both your intelligence and your work ethic. But getting good grades isn't all you can do in college to stand out in a job interview. Here are some other Quadrant II actions that will look great on your résumé: gain experience in your career field through part-time jobs, volunteer work, internships, or cooperative-education experiences; demonstrate leadership qualities through your involvement with the student government; create a portfolio of your best college work; or join clubs or activities that relate to your future career. Wise choices like these offer employers something that distinguishes you from all the other applicants for the job.

When it comes time to search for a position in your field, your effective self-management skills will once more serve you well. Consider using the **Tracking Form** to direct your outer and inner action steps toward your employment goal. The **Next Actions List** is a great tool for keeping track of essential one-time actions like returning calls or sending thank-you notes after an interview. **Monthly Calendars** help you avoid the embarrassment of arriving late or having to cancel a job interview because of a scheduling conflict. All of these tools will allow you to monitor your use of time, assuring that you spend the bulk of your time productively in Quadrants I and II.

As you begin your career search, consider doing the following outer action steps. Develop a list of careers that interest you. Make a list of potential employers in each career. Attend a résumé-writing workshop. Write a résumé and cover letter to showcase the talents and experiences you offer an employer. Personalize each cover letter to fit the job you're applying for. Develop your telephone skills. Participate in mock interviews where others ask you likely questions. Your college career center or a career development course can help you take these job-search actions effectively.

Searching for employment can get discouraging, and you would be wise to take some inner actions to maintain a positive attitude. You could create an affirmation as a mental pick-me-up. For example, "I am enthusiastically taking all of the actions necessary to find the ideal position to start my career." Or "I optimistically send out ten job inquiries each week." If you find an important action difficult to do (like calling employers to see if they have unadvertised openings), you could visualize yourself doing it and having the experience go extraordinarily well.

Once you move into your career, your self-management skills will become essential for accomplishing all you have to do. Notice how many people at your workplace carry planners, either paper or electronic. If you don't already have a planner that works for you, experiment to see if one will help you to manage the avalanche of tasks that will come your way in a new position. There's no one-size-fits-all self-management system for everyone, but there is one self-management system that will fit you. And it's your responsibility to find or invent it.

At the beginning of your career, tasks will likely take you twice as long to do as they will after a few years of practice. So not only do you need to manage your next actions list, you'll also need to make some sacrifices to get them all done. People with a "job" mentality sometimes stop short of getting all of their work done because work inevitably leaks into their personal time. They work only until their "shift" is over. On the other hand, people with a "career" mentality know that sometimes they'll need to stay late or take work home. They have the discipline to work until the task is done. Of course, these folks have to find a balance that allows them to have a personal life as well. The important thing to know is that the workload is always heavy at the beginning of a career, and this is the time when you establish your reputation as someone who can be counted on to get the job done.

Believing in Yourself: **Develop Self-Confidence**

 FOCUS QUESTIONS In which life roles do you feel most confident? In which do you experience self-doubt? What can you do to increase your overall self-confidence?

If people don't feel good about themselves and believe that they'll win a championship, they never will.

Tara VanDerveer, head coach of the 1990 NCAA Championship Stanford women's basketball team

O n the first day of one semester, a woman intercepted me at the classroom door.

"Can I ask you something?" she said. "How do I know if I'm cut out for college?"

"What's your opinion?" I asked.

"I think I'll do okay."

"Great," I said.

She stood there, still looking doubtful. "But . . . my high school counselor said. . . ." She paused.

"Let me guess. Your counselor said you wouldn't do well in college? Is that it?"

She nodded. "I think he was wrong. But how do I know for sure?"

Indeed! How *do* we know? There will always be others who don't believe in us. What matters, however, is that we have confidence in ourselves. Self-confidence is the core belief that *I CAN*, the unwavering trust that I can successfully do whatever is necessary to achieve my goals and dreams.

Ultimately, it matters little whether someone else thinks you can do something. It matters greatly whether *you* believe you can. Luck aside, you'll probably accomplish just about what you believe you can. In this section we'll explore three effective ways to develop greater self-confidence.

Create a success identity

Are you confident that you can tie your shoes? Of course. And yet there was a time when you weren't. So how did you move from doubt to confidence? Wasn't it by practicing over and over? You built your self-confidence by stacking one small victory upon another. As a result, today you have confidence that you can tie your shoes every time you try. By the same method, you can build a success identity in virtually any endeavor.

The life of Nathan McCall illustrates the creation of a success identity under difficult circumstances. McCall grew up in a Portsmouth, Virginia, ghetto where his involvement with crimes and violence led to imprisonment. After his release, McCall attended college and studied journalism. As you might imagine, one of his greatest challenges was self-doubt. But he persevered, taking each challenge as it came—one more test passed, one more course completed. After graduation, he got a job with a newspaper, and over the years he steadily rose to the position of bureau chief. Recalling his accumulated successes, McCall wrote in his journal, "These experiences solidify my belief that I can do anything I set my mind to do. The possibilities are boundless." Boundless indeed! McCall went from street-gang member and prison inmate to successful and respected reporter for the *Washington Post,* and his book, *Makes Me Wanna Holler,* climbed to the *New York Times* bestseller's list.

Genuine self-confidence results from a history of success, and a history of success results from persistently taking purposeful actions. That's why a 32-day commitment (Journal Entry 13) is not only an effective self-management tool but also a great way to start building a success identity. After we experience success in one area of our life, self-confidence begins to seep into every corner of our being, and we begin to believe *I CAN.*

Celebrate your successes and talents

A friend showed me a school assignment that his eight-year-old daughter had brought home. At the top of the page was written: *Nice job, Lauren. Your spelling is very good. I am proud of you.* What made the comments remarkable is this: The teacher had merely put a check on the page; Lauren had added the compliments herself.

At the age of eight, Lauren has much to teach us about building self-confidence. It's great when someone else tells us how wonderful our successes and talents are. But it's even more important that we tell ourselves.

One way to acknowledge your success is to create a deck of victory cards: Every day, write at least one success (big or small) on a 3″ × 5″ card. Add it to your growing deck of victory cards and read through the deck every day. Or post the cards on a wall where you'll be reminded often of your accomplishments: *Got an 86 on history test . . . Attended every class on time this week . . . Exercised for two hours at gym.* In addition to acknowledging your successes, you can celebrate them by rewarding yourself with something special—a favorite dinner, a movie, a night out with friends.

Visualize purposeful actions

We can also strengthen our self-confidence by visualizing purposeful actions done well, especially actions outside our comfort zone. Psychologist Charles Garfield once performed an experiment to determine the impact of visualizations on a group of people who were afraid of public speaking. These nervous speakers were divided into three subgroups:

Group 1 read and studied how to give public speeches, but they delivered no actual speeches.

Group 2 read about speechmaking and also gave two talks each week to small audiences of classmates and friends.

Group 3 read about effective speaking and gave one talk each week to small groups. This group also watched videotapes of effective speakers and, twice a day, *mentally rehearsed* giving effective speeches of their own.

Experts on public speaking, unaware of the experiment, evaluated the effectiveness of these speakers both before and after their preparation. Group 1 did not improve at all. Group 2 improved significantly. Group 3, the group that had visualized themselves giving excellent speeches, improved the most.

Mentally rehearsing purposeful actions will not only help you improve your ability to do the action but will also reduce associated fears. Suppose you're feeling anxious about an upcoming test. Your Inner Critic is probably visualizing a disaster: *As soon as I walk into the exam room, my pulse starts racing, I start sweating, I start feeling weak, and my mind goes totally blank. I fail!*

What if you visualized a more positive experience? You could imagine yourself taking the test confidently, creating an ideal outcome. Your revised mental movie might look like this: *I walk into the exam fully prepared. I've attended all of my classes on time, done my very best work on all my assignments, and studied effectively. Feeling confident, I find a comfortable seat and take a few moments to breathe deeply, relax, and focus myself. I concentrate on the subject matter of this test. I release all my other cares and worries, feeling excited about the opportunity to show how much I have learned. The instructor walks into the room and begins handing out the exams. I know that any question the instructor asks will be easy for me to answer. I glance at the test and see questions that my study group and I have prepared for all semester. Alert and aware, I begin to write. Every answer I write flows easily from the storehouse of knowledge I have in my mind. I work steadily and efficiently, and, after finishing, I check my answers thoroughly. I hand in the exam with a comfortable amount of time remaining, and as I leave the room, I feel a pleasant weariness. I am confident that I have done my very best.*

Since you choose the movies that play in your mind, why not choose to star in a movie in which you successfully complete purposeful actions?

Creators know there are many choices that will strengthen self-confidence. When we consciously choose options like creating a success identity, celebrating our successes and talents, and visualizing the successful completion of purposeful actions, we will soon be able to say with supreme confidence: *I CAN.*

Peak performers develop powerful mental images of the behavior that will lead to the desired results. They see in their mind's eye the result they want, and the actions leading to it.

Charles Garfield

If we picture ourselves functioning in specific situations, it is nearly the same as the actual performance. Mental practice helps one to perform better in real life.

Dr. Maxwell Maltz

Journal Entry 14

I n this activity, you will practice ways to increase your self-confidence. Self-confident people *expect* success which, in turn, strengthens their motivation and fuels their energy. If what they are doing isn't working, they don't quit. Instead, they switch to Plan B (or C or D) and persist. Then they finish strong, consistently giving their best to achieve their goals and dreams! In this way, the very success they expect often becomes a reality.

I wanted to be the best dentist that ever lived. People said, "But she's a woman; she's colored," and I said, "Ha! Just you wait and see."
Bessie Delany, Dentist and Author

1. **List the successes you have created in your life.** The more successes you list, the more you will strengthen your self-confidence. Include small victories as well as big ones.

2. **List your personal skills and talents.** Again, the longer your list, the more you will strengthen your self-confidence. What are you good at doing? Don't overlook talents that you use daily. No talent is too insignificant to acknowledge.

3. **List positive risks that you have taken in your life.** When did you stretch your comfort zone and do something despite your fear?

4. **List important actions that you presently have some resistance about doing.** What purposeful actions cause anxious rumblings in the pit of your stomach? Maybe you fear asking a question in your biology lecture or you're nervous about going to a scheduled job interview.

If you have no confidence in self, you are twice defeated in the race of life. With confidence, you have won even before you have started.
Marcus Garvey

5. **Write a visualization of yourself successfully doing one of the actions you listed in Step 4.** Remember to use the four keys to effective visualizing discussed in Journal Entry 9:

   1. **Relax.**
   2. **Use present tense verbs.**
   3. **Be specific** and use many senses.
   4. **Feel the feelings.**

As a model for your writing, reread the positive visualization on page 111.

Few abilities will do more to raise your realistic expectations of being successful in college than effective writing skills. In almost every college course, you'll be asked to write essays, journals, research papers, or lab reports. Many tests will require writing, too. In your career you'll probably write more than you can now imagine. Even to apply for most jobs, you'll need to write a cover letter and résumé. As you probably know, much writing today is done on computers because they simplify revising and editing your work. You can add, delete, and move any number of words, easily printing out drafts as you go along. A combination of good writing skills and the ability to edit effectively on your computer will enable you to demonstrate your best thinking to professors and employers alike. Here, then, are some great strategies to help you write better in college and on your job.

Before Writing

1. Create a positive affirmation about writing. Create an affirming statement such as, *"I write well, clearly expressing the important ideas I have to say."* Along with your personal affirmation, repeat this writing affirmation to revise your beliefs about your ability to write well.

2. If you get to choose the topic, pick one that truly interests you. You'll enjoy researching and writing about something meaningful to you, and your grades will probably improve as well. Even if you are assigned a topic, look for an angle on the topic that appeals to you.

3. Begin immediately. Even if you only think of a few ideas, write something to get your mind focused on the topic. Your unconscious mind will then begin mulling over the issues even when you're engaged in something else. Along with the next five suggestions, this step will prepare you for a productive brainstorming session (described in #9 below).

4. Create intriguing focus questions. Continue your initial exploration by deciding what questions you have about your topic. For example, suppose you're

assigned to write about financial aid. You could ask, "What mistakes keep students from getting all of the financial aid they are entitled to?" "Is there a way to legally avoid repaying student loans?" and "What are the secrets of getting the most in scholarship money?" If a question truly intrigues you, the focus of your inquiry will be clear, you'll be more likely to enjoy the experience of writing, and your final product will probably represent your best writing skills.

5. Seek answers to your questions in the library. If your topic calls for research, go to your library and search for sources of information that answer your focus questions. Learn to use the computer catalog to find books, periodicals, journals, and other reference material. Don't forget about electronic sources, such as CD-ROMS. Be sure to write down the source of your information for later inclusion in your essay and your list of references. Cards ($3'' \times 5''$) are convenient for recording these sources.

6. Search for answers to your questions on the Internet. Internet search engines are computer programs that search out Web pages containing information of interest to you. One of the most popular search engines on the Internet is Yahoo.com. I have heard that Yahoo stands for You Always Have Other Options, which suggests it was developed by Creators who know the value of having many choices. Another popular search engine is Google.com.

7. Ask other people to answer your questions. Say, "I was wondering how you'd answer this question . . ." Engage anyone who'll talk to you, including participants of computer listservs (online discussion groups) to which you belong. At the least, having a conversation about your topic will get your creative juices flowing. At best, you may get fascinating answers that will suggest a whole new slant on your topic. If you know of experts, seek them out for an interview. In the example above regarding an essay about financial aid, you'd surely benefit from a chat with someone in your college's financial aid office.

8. Carry and use 3" × 5" cards for notes. Once you begin thinking about a subject, ideas will come to you at the strangest times. You may be ordering French fries in the cafeteria when a great idea hits you. Don't think you'll remember it later. Pull out a 3" × 5" card and make a note. Keep your cards clipped together for organizing later.

9. Brainstorm. After you have taken the previous steps, your mind should be overflowing with ideas. Set aside a special time to brainstorm in depth about your topic. Some people call this a "brain dump." You can brainstorm on paper, but using a computer is even better because you can later delete or rearrange ideas easily. Record every idea that comes into your head with no attempt to evaluate its worth—such judgment stifles creativity. If you have notes on 3" × 5" cards, add them as well.

10. Organize your thoughts. Use an organizing strategy that feels right to you. The following two strategies offer ways to create a blueprint for your writing.

    Outline. The table of contents of this book is an outline that shows the major (flush left) and supporting (indented) topics of *On Course*. An additional outline can be seen on page 82. An outline is a great organizing strategy if your preferred way of learning requires a linear, left-brained approach. In Journal Entry 24 you will discover if this is how you prefer to learn or if your natural learning style would prefer a concept map.

    Concept map. A concept map (p.115) shows the connections between key elements in a complex idea. Suppose you were going to write an essay about your long-term goal as a student and how you planned to achieve it. You would write the key idea or question in the center of a page and add subideas (or subquestions) branching off from the center. This is a great brainstorming and organizing strategy if your preferred way of learning is holistic and right-brained (which you'll explore in Journal Entry 24).

If you find that one of these methods works well for you, look for computer programs designed specifically to help you create outlines and concept maps.

11. Incubate your ideas. Let your ideas grow without conscious intervention. As you work on other things, your conscious and unconscious minds will transform your ideas into concepts you might never have thought of. Again, have 3" × 5" cards or note paper ready to capture ideas as they come to your awareness.

During Writing

12. Create a thesis that expresses your main idea. This sentence or group of sentences states the main idea you most want your readers to remember. Everything else you write exists to expand and explain your thesis. You may need to write for a while before your thesis emerges. It may even change as you write farther. But eventually you'll need a clearly stated thesis, because an essay without one is like a body without a spine—nothing holds it together. If you're composing on a computer, you will appreciate the ease with which you can revise and move your thesis where it fits best.

13. Write a hook. The first few sentences or paragraphs should hook your readers' attention. You can capture your reader with strategies such as an intriguing story (anecdote), question, humor, quotation, or shocking statement. A good hook grabs your reader because it makes a promise about what you will deliver and the style with which you will write it. You don't have to write the hook first. In fact, the best hook may become apparent only after you've written the first draft of your essay.

14. Use transitions. A transition is a bridge between ideas. Help your reader follow your flow of ideas by using transitional words or phrases. When you offer support, signal with phrases such as *for example, as an illustration,* or *for instance.* When you point out similarities, signal with *likewise* or s*imilarly.* When you point out differences, signal with *by contrast, but, however,* or *on the contrary.* When you summarize or conclude, signal with *in other words, in summary, in conclusion,* or *finally.* Treat your readers like tourists in a strange land. As their guide, you don't want to lose or confuse them.

CONCEPT MAP

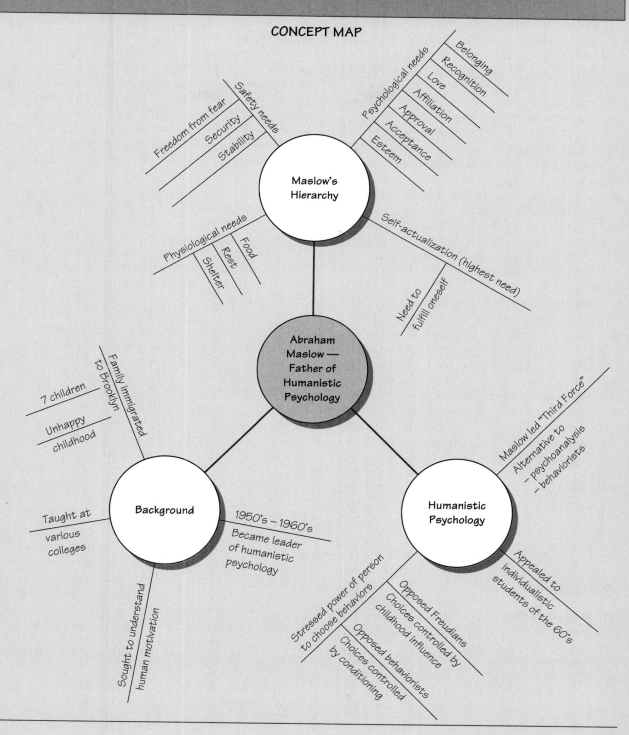

Maslow's Hierarchy

- Safety needs
  - Freedom from fear
  - Security
  - Stability
- Psychological needs
  - Belonging
  - Recognition
  - Love
  - Affiliation
  - Approval
  - Acceptance
  - Esteem
- Physiological needs
  - Food
  - Rest
  - Shelter
- Self-actualization (highest need)
  - Need to fulfill oneself

Abraham Maslow — Father of Humanistic Psychology

Background

- Family immigrated to Brooklyn
- 7 children
- Unhappy childhood
- Taught at various colleges
- 1950's – 1960's Became leader of humanistic psychology
- Sought to understand human motivation

Humanistic Psychology

- Maslow led "Third Force"
  - Alternative to
    - psychoanalysis
    - behaviorists
- Appealed to individualistic students of the 60's
- Stressed power of person to choose behaviors
- Opposed Freudians
  - Choices controlled by childhood influence
- Opposed behaviorists
  - Choices controlled by conditioning

115

15. Answer reader questions. Good writing anticipates and answers questions that an interested reader would ask. Even if you created questions before you began writing, be alert for new questions that emerge as you write. Two questions that almost always need answering are "*Why?*" and "*How do you know?*" Other important questions begin with *What? When? Who? Where? How?* and *What if?*

16. Use the 4 E's to generate specific and sufficient support. The 4 E's represent four questions that almost always need answering as you write: Can you give an EXAMPLE of that? Can you give an EXPERIENCE to illustrate that? Can you EXPLAIN that further? Can you give EVIDENCE to support that? If you fully answer one or more of the questions represented by the 4 E's, your writing will be more effective.

17. Cite your sources. If for support you quote or paraphrase an idea that belongs to someone else, identify your source. Not to do so is plagiarism, which is intellectual theft. In a research paper, add a bibliography of works cited. For an example, see the bibliography at the end of this book (page 255).

18. Write a satisfying conclusion. One easy way to conclude is to summarize the main points you have made. For a more sophisticated conclusion, end with an echo of something you wrote earlier in your essay. For example, suppose your hook was "Do you realize that college graduates earn nearly a million dollars more in their lives than do nongrads?" You might echo this thought in your conclusion: "So, if you want to raise your lifetime earnings by nearly a million dollars, learn the beliefs and behaviors of successful students and earn your college degree."

After Writing

19. Incubate again. Set your writing aside. When you return to revise your writing, you'll often find that you have a new perspective on what you wrote.

20. Revise your writing. Re-vision means to "see again." When you revise, look for major changes that will improve the quality of your communication: a new thesis statement, better organization,

additional support (examples, experience, explanation, evidence), improved transitions, a catchier beginning, a stronger conclusion.

21. Edit carefully. Writing filled with errors is distracting to readers. At best, they're likely to think less of what you have to say because of the errors. At worst, they may misunderstand your meaning. Here's a trick to improve your proofreading: Begin at the end of your essay and read one sentence at a time backwards. By reading from the end to the beginning, you can focus on the details of grammar, spelling, and punctuation rather than the thoughts. If writing on a computer, do a spellcheck. Remember that a computer's spellcheck will not pick up words incorrectly used but correctly spelled (like *there* for *their*). Your computer may also help you identify possible grammar errors that need to be corrected.

22. Seek help. Ask your instructor if it's okay to get help before turning in your writing. If so, take advantage of various options. Some instructors provide class time for peer editing, during which classmates exchange papers and provide each other suggestions for improvement. Be sure to bring your rough draft with you to class to benefit from peer editing. A second option is to create your own peer editing opportunity by getting a classmate or friend to read your essay and suggest areas for improvement. Another option is to take your essay to your campus tutoring center and seek help. Be aware that a tutor's job is not to write or even rewrite your paper for you. A good tutor will help you organize your thoughts, suggest areas of your essay that need revision, and help you identify materials for grammar or punctuation issues that you need to study. Finally, a great option is to take a rough draft to an appointment with your instructor and ask for feedback before you write your final draft.

23. Read aloud. Where you stumble over your own words, you can be sure your reader will, too. Smooth out these final rough spots before turning in your paper.

24. Learn from errors. Most instructors will provide feedback on problems in the logic and development of your ideas. Some, especially English instructors, will mark grammar and punctuation errors as well. When you get your assignment back, study and learn to correct every problem in your writing. Everyone makes errors, but Creators make them only once.

25. Revise your writing. Use the feedback you get to revise and improve your assignment. Impressed with your initiative, most instructors will be glad to meet with you to discuss your revision. Some will even raise your grade if your revision shows improvement. Regardless of how your instructor responds to your revisions, realize that there is as much or more learning available to you in revising as there was in writing what you turned in.

Writing Exercise

Compare the quality of your writing in Journal Entries 1–2 with the quality of your writing in Journal Entries 13–14. Be prepared to explore the following questions:

- Even though you are writing your journals primarily for yourself, has the quality of your writing improved? If so, how? Offer examples.

- If your writing has not improved, why do you suppose it hasn't?

- Which of your journal entries do you think is the best written?

- What could you do to improve the writing in your remaining journal entries?

- How did you feel about writing when you began this course?

- Have your feelings about writing changed while keeping your journal? If so, how? And why?

Embracing Change

Do one thing different this week

Creators take Important actions daily, both URGENT (Quadrant I) and NOT URGENT (Quadrant II). From the actions below, pick ONE new belief or behavior and experiment with it for one week. See if this new choice helps you create more positive outcomes and experiences. After seven days, assess your results. If your outcomes and experiences improve, you now have a tool you can use for the rest of your life.

Beliefs and Behaviors	Day 1	Day 2	Day 3	Day 4	Day 5	Day 6	Day 7
Think: "I am taking all of the actions necessary to acheive my goals and dreams."							
Pause, look at what I am doing, and decide what Quadrant I am in at that moment.							
Use a Monthly Calendar.							
Use a Next Actions List.							
Use a Tracking Form.							
Make and keep a 32-Day Commitment.							
Demonstrate effective self-management skills at my work place.							
Celebrate a success, big or small.							
Visualize myself taking a purposeful action.							
Use the following writing strategy (write your choice from pages 113–117):							

(continued on page 119)

During my seven-day experiment, what happened?

As a result of what happened, what did I learn or relearn?

Employing Interdependence

Once I accept responsibility for taking purposeful actions to achieve my goals and dreams, I then develop mutually supportive relationships that make the journey easier and more enjoyable.

I am giving and receiving help.

SUCCESSFUL STUDENTS . . .	STRUGGLING STUDENTS . . .
■ **develop mutually supportive relationships,** recognizing that life is richer when giving to and receiving from others.	▨ remain dependent, co-dependent, or independent in relation to others.
■ **create a support network,** using an interactive team approach to success.	▨ work alone, seldom cooperating with others for the common good of all.
■ **strengthen relationships with active listening,** showing their concern for the other person's thoughts and feelings.	▨ listen poorly, demonstrating little desire to understand another person's perspective.

Professor Rogers' Trial

Professor Rogers thought her Speech 101 students would enjoy role-playing a real court trial as their last speech for the semester. She also hoped the experience would teach them to work well in teams, a skill much sought after by employers. So, she divided her students into groups of six—a team of three defense attorneys and a team of three prosecuting attorneys—providing each group with court transcripts of a real murder case. Using evidence from the trial, each team would present closing arguments for the case, after which a jury of classmates would render a verdict. Each team was allowed a maximum of twenty-four minutes to present its case, and all three team members would receive the same grade.

After class, **Anthony** told his teammates, **Silvie** and **Donald,** "We'll meet tomorrow at 4:00 in the library and plan a defense for this guy." Silvie felt angry about Anthony's bossy tone, but she just nodded. Donald said, "Whatever," put his earphones on, and strolled away singing louder than he probably realized.

"Look," Anthony said to Silvie at 4:15 the next day, "we're not waiting for Donald any more. Here's what we'll do. You go first and take about ten minutes to prove that our defendant had no motive. I'll take the rest of the time to show how it could have been the victim's brother who shot him. I want an A out of this."

Silvie was furious. "You can't just decide to leave Donald out. Plus, what about the defendant's fingerprints on the murder weapon! We have to dispute that evidence or we'll never win. I'll do that. And I'll go last so I can wrap up all the loose ends. I want to win this trial."

The defense team met twice more before the trial. Donald came to only one of the meetings and spent the entire time reading the case. He said

he wasn't sure what he was going to say, but he'd have it figured out by the day of the trial. Anthony and Silvie argued about which evidence was most important and who would speak last. At one point, the college librarian had to "shush" them when Silvie lost her temper and started shouting at Anthony that no one had elected him the leader.

The day before the trial, Anthony went to Professor Rogers. "It's not fair that my grade depends on my teammates. Donald could care less what happens, and Silvie is always looking for a fight. I'll present alone, but not with them." "If you were an actual lawyer," Professor Rogers replied, "do you think you could go to the judge and complain that you aren't getting along with your partners? You'll have to figure out how to work as a team. The trial goes on as scheduled, and all three of you will get the same grade."

On the day of the trial, the three student prosecutors presented one seamless and persuasive closing argument. Then Anthony leapt up, saying, "I'll go first for my team." He spoke for twenty-one minutes, talking as fast as he could to present the entire case, including an explanation of how the defendant's fingerprints had gotten on the murder weapon. Silvie, greatly flustered, followed with a seven-minute presentation in which she also explained how the defendant's fingerprints had gotten on the murder weapon. At that point, Professor Rogers announced that the defense was already four minutes over their time limit. Donald promised to be brief. He assured the jury that the defendant was innocent and then read three unconnected passages from the transcript as "proof." His presentation took seventy-five seconds. The jury deliberated for five minutes and unanimously found the defendant guilty. Professor Rogers gave all members of the defense team a D for their speeches.

Listed below are the characters in this story. Rank them in the order of their responsibility for the group's grade of D. Give a different score to each character. Be prepared to explain your answer.

Most responsible ← 1 2 3 4 → Least responsible

____ Professor Rogers   ____ Silvie
____ Anthony   ____ Donald

DIVING DEEPER: Imagine that you have been assigned to a group project in one of your college courses and that the student whom you scored above as most responsible for the group's grade of D (Anthony, Silvie, or Donald) is in your group. What positive actions could you take to help your group be a success despite this person?

Developing Mutually Supportive Relationships

 FOCUS QUESTION How could you make accomplishing your success a little easier and a lot more fun?

No man is an island, entire of itself; every man is a piece of the continent, a part of the main.

John Donne

One semester, in the eleventh week, Martha made an announcement. "This is the last time I'll be in class. I'm withdrawing from college. I just wanted to say how much I'll miss you all."

A concerned silence followed Martha's announcement. Her quiet, solid presence had made her a favorite with classmates.

"My babysitter just moved," Martha explained, "and I've been trying to find someone I trust to look after my one-year-old... with no luck. My husband took his vacation this week to take care of her, but he has to go back to work. I have to drop out of school to be with my baby. Don't worry," she added weakly, "I'll be back next semester. Really, I will."

"But there are only a few more weeks in the semester. You can't drop out now!" someone said. Martha merely shrugged her shoulders, clearly defeated.

Then one of the other women in the class said, "My kids are grown and out of the house, and this is the only class I'm taking this semester. I'd be willing to watch your child for the next few weeks if that would help you get through the semester. The only thing is, you'll need to bring your baby to my house because I don't have a car."

"I don't have a car either," Martha said. "Thanks anyway."

"Wait a minute," a young man in the class said. "Not so fast. Aren't we learning that we're all in this together? I have a car. I'll drive you and your child back and forth until the semester's over."

Martha sat for a moment, stunned. "Really? You'd do that for me?" In three minutes Martha's fate had changed from dropping out of school to finishing her courses with the help of two classmates.

All of us decide whether we'll go for our dreams alone or if we'll seek and accept assistance from others along the way. In Western culture we often glorify the solitary hero, the strong individual who stands alone against all odds. This script makes good cinema, but does it help us stay on course to our dreams?

After all, who of us actually goes unaided by others? We eat food grown *by others*. We wear clothes sewn *by others*. We live in houses built *by others*. We work at businesses owned *by others*. And so it goes.

Nobody but nobody can make it out here alone.
Maya Angelou

Ways to relate

When it comes to relating to others, we generally choose one of four paths, depending on the beliefs we hold about ourselves and other people:

- When I believe, *I can't achieve my goals by myself*, I choose **Dependence**.
- When I believe, *I have to help other people get their goals before I can pursue my goals*, I choose **Codependence**.
- When I believe, *By working hard, I can get some of what I want all by myself*, I choose **Independence**.
- When I believe, *I know I can get some of what I want by working alone, but I'll accomplish more and have more fun if I give and receive help*, I choose **Interdependence.**

Which belief do you hold? More important, which belief will best help you stay on course to your goals and dreams?

We are all interdependent. Do things for others—tribe, family, community—rather than just for yourself.
Chief Wilma Mankiller

A sign of maturity

Moving from dependence or codependence to independence is a major step toward maturity. However, Creators know that life can be easier and more enjoyable when people cooperate. They know that moving from independence to *inter*dependence demonstrates the greatest maturity of all.

Interdependent students maximize their results in college by seeking assistance from instructors, study partners, librarians, academic advisors, counselors, community services, and family members. Interdependent students know that it's a lot easier getting to graduation with a supportive team than it is by themselves.

Interdependence will help you stay on course in college and support your success in ways you can't even imagine now. A friend of mine who buys old houses, remodels them, and resells them for a tidy profit ran into difficult times. His renovated houses weren't selling, he was short of money to begin new projects, and bankers were unwilling to lend him additional money. Creditors

Don't be fooled into thinking you are alone on your journey. You're not. Your struggle is everyone's struggle. Your pain is everyone's pain. Your power is everyone's power. It is simply that we take different paths along our collective journey toward the same destination.
Benjamin Shield

began to harass him, and for a few weeks he considered declaring bankruptcy. Then he created an ingenious plan to raise capital: He asked friends to contribute money to his "investment fund," agreeing to pay them higher interest rates than banks were paying at the time. Within two weeks, he had accumulated enough money not only to sustain himself until his properties sold, but also to buy two new houses to remodel. With the help of friends, he was back in business.

Among the most destructive relationships are those based on codependence. Codependent people are motivated not by their own successes, but by someone else's approval or dependence upon them. *I am worthwhile*, the codependent believes, *only if someone else can't get along without me*. Codependent people abandon their own dreams and even endure abuse to keep the approval of others.

John was a bright fellow who had been in college for seven years without graduating. During a class discussion, he related an experience that he said was typical of him: He had been studying for a midterm test in history when a friend called and asked for help with a test in biology, a course John had already passed. John set aside his own studies and spent the evening tutoring his friend. The next day John failed his history exam. In his journal, he wrote, "I've learned that in order to be successful, I need to make my dreams more important than other people's approval. I have to learn to say 'no.'" Codependent people like John often spend time in Quadrant III, engaged in activities that are urgent to someone else but unimportant to their own goals and dreams.

With codependence, dependence, and independence, giving and receiving are out of balance. The codependent person *gives* too much. The dependent person *takes* too much. The independent person seldom gives or receives. By contrast, the interdependent person finds a healthy balance of giving and receiving, and everyone benefits. That's why building mutually supportive relationships is one of the most important Quadrant II behaviors you'll ever undertake.

Giving and receiving

A story is told of a man who prayed to know the difference between heaven and hell. An angel came to take the man to see for himself. In hell, the man saw a huge banquet table overflowing with beautifully prepared meats, vegetables, drinks, and desserts. Despite this bounty, the prisoners of hell had withered, sunken looks. Then the man saw why. The poor souls in hell could pick up all the food they wanted, but their elbows would not bend, so they could not place the food into their mouths. Living amidst all that abundance, the citizens of hell were starving.

Then the angel whisked the man to heaven where he saw another endless banquet table heaped with a similar bounty of splendid food. Amazingly, just as in hell, the citizens of heaven could not bend their elbows to feed themselves.

"I don't understand," the man said. "Is heaven the same as hell?"

The angel only pointed. The residents of heaven were healthy, laughing, and obviously happy as they sat together at the banquet tables. Then the man saw the difference.

The citizens of heaven were feeding each other.

Journal Entry 15

In this activity, you will explore your beliefs and behaviors regarding giving and receiving.

1. **Write and complete the following ten sentence stems:**

1. A specific situation when someone assisted me was . . .
2. A specific situation when I assisted someone else was . . .
3. A specific situation when I made assisting someone else more important than my own success and happiness was . . .
4. When someone asks me for assistance I usually feel . . .
5. When I think of asking someone else for assistance I usually feel . . .
6. What usually gets in the way of my asking for help is . . .
7. If I often asked other people for assistance . . .
8. If I joyfully gave assistance to others . . .
9. If I gratefully accepted assistance from others . . .
10. One goal that I could use assistance with today is . . .

No matter what accomplishments you make, somebody helps you.
Althea Gibson Darben

2. **Write about what you discovered by completing the sentence stems in Step 1: Is your typical relationship to others (1) dependent, (2) codependent, (3) independent, or (4) interdependent?** Describe how you have most often related to others in the past and how you intend to relate to others in the future.

Here's a reminder from the section on effective writing strategies (p. 116). To dive deeper: **Use the 4 E's**. The 4 E's represent four questions that readers often wanted answered:

- Can you give an **EXAMPLE** of that?
- Can you give an **EXPERIENCE** to illustrate that?
- Can you **EXPLAIN** that further?
- Can you give **EVIDENCE** to support that?

As you fully answer one or more of these questions, you will begin writing more effectively.

During my first semester in college, I struggled in my Calculus class. I didn't understand anything my instructor taught, and his mathematical terms bounced off me like a foreign language. I dreaded going to class and frequently zoned out when I did. After class, I attempted to teach myself the material, but I couldn't understand the confusing terms. I started turning in my homework late and incomplete, and my first two test grades were in the low sixties. I knew I needed help, but I was too independent to admit it.

One day, in my freshman seminar class, my instructor began discussing independent individuals. He informed us that it takes a strong person to be independent, but what he went on to say hit me like a brick: "It takes a stronger individual to be *inter*dependent." I stared at him for a while, pondering his last few words. That night, I cracked open the *On Course* textbook and began to read through Chapter 5. It stressed that people who are interdependent (rely on others as well as themselves) are happier and have greater success in life than those who are independent (rely only on themselves). Persuaded by the readings, I met with

ONE STUDENT'S STORY
Jason Matthew Loden
Avila University,
Missouri

my Calculus instructor and arranged twice-a-week tutoring sessions. I also formed a Calculus study group with my friends Joey and Amy, and we began meeting every Friday.

At the beginning of each tutoring session, my instructor gave me a quiz. Then we would focus on one specific element of Calculus, such as derivatives as they relate to velocity. In my study group, we dove into our homework, sharing our answers along with the processes we used to solve them. At first, I was very frustrated, but after a month of hard work and interdependent studying, I started to grasp the whole idea of Calculus. By the end of the semester, I had become a Quadrant II student in Calculus. I no longer worried about my homework or stressed over class because I prepared a little each day with the help of my instructor and friends. My grade steadily improved throughout the semester leading to a fabulous 94 on my final, which allowed me to achieve an A for the course. Before this experience, I knew that I had a good chance of success in life as an independent individual. Now that I know the power of a support group, there's no stopping me!

Creating a Support Network

? **FOCUS QUESTION**   How could you create and sustain an effective support network to help achieve your greatest dreams in college and in life?

I not only use all the brains that I have, but all that I can borrow.

Woodrow Wilson

For solving most problems, ten brains are better than one and twenty hands are better than two. Although Victims typically struggle alone, Creators know the incredible power of a network of mutually supportive people.

This ingredient of success has been called **OPB: Other People's Brains** or **Other People's Brawn**. College provides a great place to develop the habit of using OPB to achieve maximum success. Let's consider some choices you could make to create a support network, one that will help you not only achieve your goals in college but enjoy the experience as well.

Seek help from your instructors

Building positive relationships with your college instructors is a powerful Quadrant II action that can pay off handsomely. Your instructors have years of specialized training. You've already paid for their help with your tuition, and all you have to do is ask.

Find out your professors' office hours and make appointments. Come to your conferences prepared with questions or requests. You'll likely get very good help. As a bonus, by getting to know your instructors, you may find a mentor who will help you in college and beyond.

Get help from college resources

Nearly every college spends a chunk of tuition money to provide support services for students, but these services go to waste unless you use them. Do you know what support services your college offers, where they are, and how to use them?

Confused about future courses to take?   Get help from your advisor or someone in the counseling center. They can help you decide on a major and create an academic plan that includes all of your required courses and their prerequisites.

Academic problems?   Get help at one of your college's tutoring labs. Many colleges have a writing lab, a reading lab, and a math lab. Other sources of academic assistance might include a science learning center or a computer lab. Your college may also have a diagnostician who tests students for learning disabilities and suggests ways of overcoming them.

Money problems?   Get help from your college's financial aid office. Money is available in grants and scholarships (which you don't pay back), loans (which you do pay back, usually at low interest rates), and student work programs (which offer jobs on campus). Your college may also have a service that can locate an off-campus job, perhaps one in the very career field you want to enter after graduation. In Chapter 8, you'll find detailed information about addressing your money problems (see pages 235–241).

Personal problems?   Get help from your college's counseling office. Trained counselors are available at many colleges to help students through times of emotional upset. It's not unusual for students to experience some sort of personal difficulty during college; Creators seek assistance.

Health problems?   Get aid from your college's health service. Many colleges have doctors who see students at little or no cost. Health-related products may be available inexpensively or even for free. Your college may even offer special health insurance for students.

Problems deciding on a career?   Get help from your college's career office. There you can take aptitude tests, discover job opportunities, learn to write or improve your résumé, and practice effective interviewing skills.

To reach your goals you need to become a team player.
Zig Ziglar

Problems getting involved socially at your college?   Request assistance from your college's student activities office. Here you'll discover athletic teams, trips, choirs, dances, service projects, student professional organizations, the college newspaper and literary magazine, clubs, and more, just waiting for you to get involved.

Create a project team

If you're tackling a big project, why not create a team to help? A project team accomplishes one particular task. In business, when a project needs attention, an ad hoc committee is formed. *Ad hoc* in Latin means "toward this." In other words, an ad hoc committee comes together for the sole purpose of solving one problem. Once the task is complete, the committee disbands.

One of my students created a project team to help her move. More than a dozen classmates volunteered, including a fellow who provided a truck. In one Saturday morning, the team packed and delivered her possessions to a new apartment.

What big project do you have that would benefit from the assistance of a group? The only barrier standing between you and a project team is your willingness to ask for help.

Start a study group

Love thy neighbor as thyself, but choose your neighborhood.
Louise Beal

One of the very best strategies for success in college is forming a study group. A study group differs from a project team in two ways. First, a study group is created to help everyone on the team excel in a particular course. Second, a study group meets many times throughout a semester. Occasionally a study group is so helpful that its members stay together throughout college. Here are three suggestions for maximizing the value of your study group:

1. **Choose only Creators.** As the semester begins, make a list of potential members: classmates who attend regularly, come prepared, and participate actively. Also watch for that quiet student who doesn't say much but whose occasional comments reveal a special understanding of the subject. After the first test or essay, find out how the students on your list performed and

©ED ARNO / *SCIENCE 80*

invite three or four of the most successful to study with you.

2. **Choose group goals.** Regardless of potential, a study group is only as effective as you make it. Everyone should agree upon common goals. You might say to prospective study group members, "My goal in our math class is to master the subject and earn an A. Is that what you want, too?" Team up with students whose goals match or exceed your own.

3. **Choose group rules.** The last step is establishing team rules. Pat Riley, one of the most successful professional basketball coaches ever, has his players create a "team covenant." Before the season, they agree on the rules they will follow to stay on course to their goal of a championship. Your team should do the same. Decide where, how often, and what time you'll meet. Most important, agree on what will happen during the meetings. Many study groups fail because they turn into social gatherings. Yours will succeed if you adopt rules like these:

Rule 1: *We meet in the library every Thursday afternoon from one o'clock to three o'clock.*

Rule 2: *Each member brings twenty new questions with answers, including the source (e.g., textbook page or class notes).*

Rule 3: *All written questions are asked, answered, and understood before any socializing.*

If people around you aren't going anywhere, if their dreams are no bigger than hanging out on the corner, or if they're dragging you down, get rid of them. Negative people can sap your energy so fast, and they can take your dreams away from you, too.
Earvin (Magic) Johnson

One student I know took this advice and started a study group in his anatomy and physiology class, a course with a notoriously high failure rate. At the end of the semester, he proudly showed me a thank-you card signed by the other four members of his group. "We couldn't have done it without you," they wrote. "Thanks for *making* us get together!" Everyone in the group had passed the course.

Who you spend time with will dramatically affect your outcomes and experiences in college. If you hang out with people who place little value on learning or a college degree, it's challenging to resist their negative influence. However, if you associate with highly committed, hard-working students, their encouragement can motivate you to stay on course to graduation even when the road gets rough. One of my students actually moved to a new apartment when he realized that "friends" from his old neighborhood spent most of their time putting down his efforts to get a college degree. When it comes to selecting your "group" in college, be sure to choose people who want what you do out of life.

Many people collaborate only with others who are like them. One of the greatest benefits of your college experience is meeting people of diverse backgrounds, with different ideas, skills, experiences, abilities, and resources. Be sure to network with those who are older or younger than you, who are from different states or countries, who are of different races or cultures, and who have different religions or political preferences.

Start a contact list of the people you meet in college. You might even want to write a few notes about them: their major or career field, names of family members, hobbies, interests, and especially their strengths. Keep in touch with these people during and after college.

Creators develop mutually supportive relationships in college that continue to support them for years—even for a lifetime. Don't get so bogged down with the daily demands of college that you fail to create an empowering support network.

Journal Entry 16

In this activity, you will explore the creation of a support network. Afterward, you may decide to start networking more, using OPB to help you achieve your greatest goals and dreams.

1. **Write and complete the following sentence stems:**

1. An outer obstacle that stands between me and my success in college is... [Examples might be a lack of time to study or a teacher you don't understand.]

2. Someone besides me who could help me overcome this outer obstacle is...

3. How this person could help me is by...

4. An inner obstacle that stands between me and my success in college is... [Examples might be shyness or a tendency to procrastinate.]

5. Someone besides me who could help me overcome this inner obstacle is...

6. How this person could help me is by...

7. The most challenging course I'm taking in college this semester is...

8. This course is challenging for me because...

9. Someone besides me who could help me overcome this challenge is...

10. How this person could help me is by...

2. **Write about two (or more) choices you could make to create a stronger support network for yourself in college.** Consider the choices you could make to overcome the challenges and obstacles to your success that you identified in Step 1. Consider also any resistance you may have about taking steps to create a support network. Dive deep as you explore each choice fully.

In the first semester in my freshmen year, one of the most challenging things for me was my sociology class. It was a lecture class, and all the teacher did was talk for the whole hour while we took notes. I wasn't used to that way of learning, and from the first day most of it went right over my head. In high school, teachers usually gave us some leeway on assignments and tests, but my sociology instructor expected everything explained in depth. After I did horribly on the first test, I went to see the teacher during his office hours to get some help.

He gave me some ideas about how to study for his class, and then he suggested that I meet with some other students in the class who were getting it. I hadn't been in a study group before, but it made sense to study with people in my class who understood sociology better than I did. There were three of us, a girl who knew about as much as I did and a guy who really understood the class. When we ran into each other in the library, we'd meet to get ready for the next test. The guy in our group would ask questions about what the teacher went over to see how much we already knew. Then he would explain what we didn't know. I felt that I was getting a better understanding of the class and my test scores started to improve little by little.

I wound up getting a C in sociology, but without my study group I probably would have gotten a D or an F. Next semester, I'm going to join a study group for my hardest subjects, but this time I'm going to use more of what I learned from my experience with the sociology study group and also from the *On Course* book in my student success seminar. I'll start the study group earlier in the semester before I fall behind. I think a study group should be made up of people you know and get along with so there aren't problems that get you away from studying. I'll also make sure that my next group is a little more organized, with scheduled times to meet. And finally, we'll have a plan of what we're going to do so we won't meet for a long time without accomplishing anything. It's good to talk to a teacher, but sometimes you need another student to explain ideas in layman's terms so you can really understand them.

ONE STUDENT'S STORY

Neal Benjamin
Barton County Community College, Kansas

Strengthening Relationships with Active Listening

? **FOCUS QUESTIONS** Do you know how to strengthen a relationship with active listening? What are the essential skills of being a good listener?

When people talk, listen completely. Most people never listen.

Ernest Hemingway

Once we have begun a mutually supportive relationship, we naturally want the relationship to grow. Books on relationships abound, suggesting untold ways to strengthen a relationship. At the heart of all of these suggestions is a theme: We must show that we value the other person professionally, personally, or both.

For the lack of listening, billions of losses accumulate: retyped letters, rescheduled appointments, rerouted shipments, breakdowns in labor management relations, misunderstood sales presentations, and job interviews that never really get off the ground.

Michael Ray and
Rochelle Myers

Many ways exist to demonstrate another's value to us. Some of the most powerful methods include keeping promises, giving honest appreciation and approval, resolving conflicts so that both people win, staying in touch, and speaking well of someone when talking to others. However, for demonstrating the high esteem with which you value another person, there may be no better way than active listening.

Few people are truly good listeners. Too often, we're thinking what we want to say next. Or our thoughts dash off to our own problems, and we ignore what the other person is saying. Or we hear what we *thought* the person was going to say rather than what he actually said.

Good listeners, by contrast, clear their minds and listen for the entire message, including words, tone of voice, gestures, and facial expressions. No matter how well one person communicates, unless someone else listens actively, both the communication and the relationship are likely to go astray. Imagine the potential problems created if good listening skills are absent when an instructor says to a class, "I need to change the date of the final exam from Monday to the previous Friday. I just found out that I need to turn in my final grades on Monday." Suppose a student assumes that the instructor said the exam will be moved to the *following* Friday (instead of the *previous* Friday). When that student shows up on the "following" Friday, not only will the exam be long over, but the instructor will have turned in the final course grades as well. Talk about an unpleasant surprise!

Listening actively means accepting 100 percent responsibility for receiving the same message that the speaker sent, uncontaminated by your own thoughts or feelings. That's why active listening begins with empathy, the ability to understand the other person as if, for that moment, you *are* the other person. To empathize doesn't mean that you necessarily agree. Empathy means understanding what the other person is thinking and feeling. And you actively reveal this understanding.

With empathetic listening, you send this message: *I value you so much that I am doing my very best to see the world through your eyes.*

Active listening, sometimes called reflective listening, involves giving verbal feedback of the content of what was said or done along with a guess at the feeling underneath the spoken words or acts.

Muriel James and
Dorothy Jongeward

How to listen actively

Active listening is a learned skill. You will become an excellent listener if you master the following four steps:

Step 1: Listen to understand.   Listening isn't effective when you're simply waiting for the first opportunity to insert your own opinion. Instead, focus fully on the speaker, activate your empathy, and listen with the intention of fully understanding what the other person thinks and feels.

Step 2: Clear your mind and remain silent.   Don't be distracted by judgmental chatter from your Inner Critic and Inner Defender. Clear your mind, stay focused, and be quiet. Let your mind listen for thoughts. Let your heart listen for the undercurrent of emotions. Let your intuition listen for a deeper message hidden beneath the words. Let your companion know that you are actively listening. Sit forward. Nod your head when appropriate. Offer verbal feedback that shows you are actively listening: "Mmmmm...I see...Uh huh..."

If I were to summarize in one sentence the single most important principle I have learned in the field of interpersonal relations, it would be this: Seek first to understand, then to be understood.

Stephen Covey

Step 3: Ask the person to expand or clarify.   Don't make assumptions or fill in the blanks with your own experience. Invite the speaker to share additional information and feelings.

- *Tell me more about that.*
- *Could you give me an example?*
- *Can you explain that a different way?*
- *How did you feel when that happened?*
- *What happened next?*

Step 4: Reflect the other person's thoughts and feelings.   Don't assume you understand. In your own words, restate what you heard, both the ideas and the emotions. Then verify the accuracy of your understanding.

- To a classmate: *Sounds like you're really angry about the instructor's feedback on your research paper. To you, his comments seem more sarcastic than helpful. Is that it?*
- To a professor: *I want to be clear about the new date for the final exam. You're postponing the exam from Monday to the following Friday. Have I got it right?*

Notice that reflecting adds nothing new to the conversation. Don't offer advice or tell your own experience. Your goal is merely to understand.

What few people realize is that failure to be a good listener prevents us from hearing and retaining vital information, becoming a roadblock to personal and professional success.

Jean Marie Stine

Use active listening in your college classes

Active listening not only strengthens relationships with people, it strengthens our understanding of new concepts. In class, successful students clear their minds and prepare to hear something of value. They reflect the instructor's ideas, confirming the accuracy of what they heard. When confused, they ask the instructor to expand or clarify, either in class or during the instructor's conference hours. As Creators, these students actively listen to understand.

Choose today to master active listening. You'll be amazed at how much this choice will improve your relationships and your life.

Journal Entry 17

In this activity, you will practice the skill of active listening by writing out a conversation with your Inner Guide. As discussed earlier, thoughts are dashing through our minds much of the time. Writing a conversation with your Inner Guide applies this knowledge in a new and powerful way. First, it helps us become more aware of the thoughts that are guiding our choices, both those that keep us on course and especially those that push us off course. Second, writing this conversation encourages us to explore our thoughts in more depth, much as we would help a friend dig deeper into a problem in order to find a positive solution. Third, it reminds us that we are not our thoughts and we can change them when we realize that doing so would benefit us. And, finally, writing this conversation with our Inner Guide gives us practice with an important mental skill used by highly intelligent and adaptive people: *metacognition*. Metacognition is the skill of thinking about our thinking. Developing metacognition allows us to see where our thinking is flawed and allows us to change it to achieve better outcomes and experiences. If you've ever talked out loud to yourself while working on a problem, you were probably using metacognition. You may find writing this dialogue to be a new (and perhaps unusual) experience, but the more you practice, the more you'll see what a valuable success skill it is to have a conversation with yourself as an active listener. And, of course, becoming an active listener with others will strengthen those relationships immeasurably.

If there is any one secret of success, it lies in the ability to get the other person's point of view and see things from his angle as well as your own.

Henry Ford

1. **Write a conversation between you (ME) and your Inner Guide (IG) about a problem you are facing in college. Label each of your IG's responses with the listening skill it uses: silence, expansion, clarification, reflection (be sure to reflect feelings as well as thoughts). Let your IG demonstrate the skills of active listening without giving advice.**

Here's an example of such a conversation:

ME: I've been realizing what a difficult time I have asking for assistance.

IG: Would you like to say more about that? **(Expansion)**

ME: Well, I've been having trouble in math. I know I should be asking more questions in class, but . . . I don't know, I guess I feel dumb because I can't do the problems myself.

IG: You seem frustrated that you can't solve the math problems without help. **(Reflection)**

ME: That's right. I've always resisted that sort of thing.

IG: What do you mean by "that sort of thing?" **(Clarification)**

ME: I mean that ever since I can remember, I've had to do everything on my own. When I was a kid, I used to play alone all the time.

Dr. Eliot's listening was not mere silence, but a form of activity. Sitting very erect on the end of his spine with hands joined in his lap, making no movement except that he revolved his thumbs around each other faster or slower, he faced his interlocutor and seemed to be hearing with his eyes as well as his ears. He listened with his mind and attentively considered what you had to say while you said it. . . . At the end of an interview the person who had talked to him felt that he had his say.

Henry James about Charles W. Eliot, former president of Harvard

IG: Uh huh . . . **(Silence)**

ME: I never had anyone to help me as a kid. And I don't have anyone to help me now.

IG: So, no one is available to help you? Is that how it seems? **(Reflection)**

ME: Well, I guess I could ask Robert for help. He seems really good in math, but I'm kind of scared to ask him.

IG: What scares you about asking him? **(Expansion)** . . . etc.

Imagine that the conversation you create here is taking place over the phone. Don't hang up until you've addressed all aspects of the problem and know what your next action step will be. Let your Inner Guide demonstrate how much it values you by being a great listener.

2. Write what you learned or relearned about active listening during this conversation with your Inner Guide. Remember to dive deep to discover a powerful insight. When you think you have written all you can, see if you can write at least one more paragraph.

Interdependence at Work

Over 90 percent of us who work for a living do so in organizations, and the ability to function effectively as a member of a team is usually an imperative of success.

Nathaniel Branden, Psychologist

You may have noticed that many employment ads say, "Looking for a team player" or "Must relate well to others." Few abilities have more impact on your success at work than your ability to interact well with supervisors, peers, subordinates, suppliers, and customers. And enhancing this ability starts now.

Someday you'll probably ask a former professor or employer to write you a letter of recommendation. What they write on that future day will depend on the relationships you're building with them now. Are you someone who works well with others? Someone who completes assignments and does them with excellence? Attends classes regularly and on time? Is respectful of others? Self-aware? Responsible? A former student called me with a request that I write her a recommendation. After much thought, I said no. Based on her performance in my class, I could not honestly write anything that would help her chances of getting hired. Sadly, when she was "blowing off" my course, she hadn't anticipated the day when she would need me to speak well of her to a potential employer.

In the work world, most people must interact well with others to keep their jobs or to advance. In college, one way to continue developing effective interdependence is by participating actively in study groups. Learning to work collaboratively now will contribute to your success tomorrow (not to mention that your grades will likely be higher).

As you begin a search for your ideal job, one of the best sources of information about what a career is *really* like is someone who is doing it now. By conducting information-gathering interviews with enough people who are working in your chosen profession, you'll learn about qualifications, employment outlook, work conditions, and salaries. If you don't know anyone in the career of your choice, be a Creator and ask people you know for referrals. If that fails, try the Yellow Pages. Call a company you find there, ask for the Public Information Office, and explain the information you're seeking. Besides the information you may uncover, who knows who might be impressed with your professional approach to job hunting?

The same information-gathering strategy is helpful when it comes to learning important information about a particular employer you may be considering. Talk to people who work at the company and find out from the inside what it's really like. For example, if you find the company's mission statement appealing, ask employees if the company backs up those words with actions. Of course, it's important to talk to a number of people to avoid being swayed by one or two biased opinions.

Many people limit their job search to employment agencies and advertised positions, jobs listed in the "visible" marketplace. However, some career specialists estimate that as many as 85–90 percent of the available jobs are unlisted and found only by uncovering them in the "invisible" marketplace. Creators discover these unpublished openings by networking. Do that by seeking informational interviews with possible employers, and ask them if they know of others who might have a job for which you'd qualify. Additionally, you can ask friends and acquaintances if they know of positions that are available where they work. Ask professors if they've heard of job openings. Ask at church and club meetings. Ask all of these folks to spread the word that you're looking for a position. You never know who might help you discover an opening that would be ideal for you. A great job might become visible only because you asked a friend who asked a co-worker who asked his sister who asked her boss who said, "Sure, we've got a job like that. Have the person call me."

Another great strategy during a job search is to develop a support group, especially one made up of other job seekers. Support groups not only provide emotional support when disappointments (and your Inner Critic) strike, they can also give you helpful suggestions and practice at essential skills. For example, support groups can critique your résumé and cover letters. They can help you practice your interviewing skills. Someone in your support group may share an experience that can teach you a valuable lesson. For instance, if someone reports going blank when an interviewer asked, "Do you have any questions for me?" you'll learn to prepare questions to ask at your own interviews.

Okay, you've gotten your dream position in the company you wanted. Teamwork continues to have a big impact on your work life. The *Harvard Business Review* reported a study that discovered why some scientists at Bell Labs in New Jersey were considered "stars" by their colleagues. Interestingly, the stars had done no better academically than their less successful colleagues. In fact, the study found that the stars and their co-workers were very similar when measured on IQ and personality tests. What distinguished the stars was their strong networks of important colleagues. When problems struck, the stars always had someone to call on for advice, and their requests for help were responded to quickly. Interdependence transformed good scientists into stars.

I once asked a very successful investment banker (he retired at the age of thirty-five) how important networking was in his profession. "Well, there's networking up here," he said, holding his hand as high in the air as he could reach, "and then there's everything else down here." He dropped his hand to within inches of the floor. "In this business, you either build relationships or you die."

One last suggestion about interdependence could apply anywhere on your career path, but is particularly important once you are in your job. Find a mentor. A mentor is someone further along in his or her career development and willing to guide and help newer employees like you. Keep your eyes open for someone successful whose qualities you admire. You can create an informal mentoring relationship by making choices that put you into frequent contact with this person, or you can create a formal relationship by actually asking the person to be your mentor. With the wisdom of experience, a mentor can help keep you on course to career success.

Believing in Yourself: **Be Assertive**

 FOCUS QUESTION How can you communicate in a style that strengthens relationships, creates better results, and builds strong self-esteem?

Occasionally, we encounter someone who doesn't want us to achieve our goals and dreams. More often, though, we run across folks who are too busy, too preoccupied, or couldn't care less about helping us. Meeting such people is especially likely in a bureaucracy like a college or university. How we communicate our desires to them has a profound impact not only on the quality of the relationships and results we create, but on our self-esteem as well.

According to family therapist Virginia Satir, the two most common patterns of ineffective communication are **placating** and **blaming**. Both perpetuate low self-esteem.

Once a human being has arrived on this earth, communication is the largest single factor determining what kinds of relationships she or he makes with others and what happens to each in the world.

Virginia Satir

Placating   Victims who placate are dominated by their Inner Critic. They place themselves below others, protecting themselves from the sting of criticism and rejection by saying whatever they think will gain approval. Picture placators on their knees, looking up with a pained smile, nodding and agreeing on the outside, while fearfully hiding their true thoughts and feelings within. "*Please, please approve of me,*" they beg as their own Inner Critic judges them unworthy. To gain this approval, placators often spend time in Quadrant III doing what is urgent to others but unimportant to their own goals and dreams. Satir estimated that about 50 percent of people use placating as their major communication style.

Blaming   Victims who blame are dominated by their Inner Defender. They place themselves above others, protecting themselves from disappointment and failure by making others fully responsible for their problems. Picture them sneering down, a finger jabbing judgmentally at those below. Their Inner Defender snarls, "*You never. . . . Why do you always. . . ? Why don't you ever. . . ? It's your fault that. . . .*" Satir estimated that about 30 percent of people use blaming as their major communication style.

Either passively placating or aggressively blaming keeps Victims from developing mutually supportive relationships, making the accomplishment of their dreams more difficult. The inner result is damaged self-esteem.

Leveling

What, then, is the communication style of Creators? Some have called this style assertiveness: boldly putting forth opinions and requests. Satir calls this communication style *leveling*. Leveling is characterized by a simple, yet profound, communication strategy: asserting the truth as you see it.

Learning to perceive the truth within ourselves and speak it clearly to others is a delicate skill, certainly as complex as multiplication or long division, but very little time is spent on it in school.

Gay and Kathlyn Hendricks

Creators boldly express their personal truth without false apology or excuse, without harsh criticism or blame. Leveling requires a strong Inner Guide and a commitment to honesty. Here are three strategies that promote leveling:

1. Communicate purposefully.   Creators express a clear purpose even in times of emotional upset. If a Creator goes to a professor to discuss a disappointing grade, she will be clear whether her purpose is to (1) increase her understanding of the subject, (2) seek a higher grade, (3) criticize the instructor's grading ability, or accomplish some other option. By knowing her purpose, she has a way to evaluate the success of her communication. The Creator states purposefully, *When I saw my grade on this lab report, I was very disappointed. I'd like to go over it with you and learn how to improve my next one.*

2. Communicate honestly.   Creators candidly express unpopular thoughts and upset feelings in the service of building mutually supportive relationships. The Creator says honestly, *I'm angry that you didn't meet me in the library to study for the sociology test as you agreed.*

We should replace our alienating, criticizing words with "I" language. Instead of, "You are a liar and no one can trust you," say, "I don't like it when I can't rely on your words—it is difficult for us to do things together."

Ken Keyes

3. Communicate responsibly.   Because responsibility lies within, Creators express their personal responsibility with I-messages. An I-message allows Creators to take full responsibility for their reaction to anything another person may have said or done. An effective I-message has four elements:

A statement of the situation:	*When you . . .*
A statement of your reaction:	*I felt/thought/decided . . .*
A request:	*I'd like to ask that you . . .*
An invitation to respond:	*Will you agree to that?*

Let's compare Victim and Creator responses to the same situation. Imagine that you feel sick one day and decide not to go to your history class. You phone a classmate, and she agrees to call you after class with what you missed. But she never calls. At the next history class, the instructor gives a test that was announced the day you were absent. Afterward, your classmate apologizes: "Sorry I didn't call. I was swamped with work." What response do you choose?

Placating: *Oh, don't worry about it. I know you had a lot on your mind. I probably would have failed the test anyway.*

Blaming: *You're the lousiest friend I've ever had! After making me fail that test, you have some nerve even talking to me!*

> *I speak straight and do not wish to deceive or be deceived.*
>
> Cochise

Leveling: *I'm angry that you didn't call. I realize that I could have called you, but I thought I could count on you to keep your word. If we're going to be friends, I need to know if you're going to keep your promises to me in the future. Will you?*

Notice that the leveling response is the only one of the three that positively addresses the issue, nurtures a relationship of equals, and demonstrates high self-esteem.

Making requests

Making effective requests is another demonstration of both assertiveness and high self-esteem. Creators know they can't reach their greatest goals and dreams alone, so they ask for help. The key to making effective requests is applying the DAPPS rule. Whenever possible, make your requests <u>D</u>ated, <u>A</u>chievable, <u>P</u>ersonal, <u>P</u>ositive, and (above all) <u>S</u>pecific. Here are some translations of vague Victim requests to specific, clear Creator requests:

> *If you go to somebody and say, "I need help," they'll say, "Sure, honey, I wish I could," but if you say, "I need you to call so-and-so on Tuesday, will you do that?" they either will say yes or they'll say no. If they say no, you thank them and say, "Do you know someone who will?" If they say yes, you call on Wednesday to see if they did it. You wouldn't believe how good I've gotten at this, and I never knew how to ask anybody for anything before.*
>
> Barbara Sher

Victim Requests	Creator Requests
1. I'm going to be absent next Friday. It sure would be nice if someone would let me know if I miss anything.	1. John, I'm going to be absent next Friday. Would you be willing to call me Friday night and tell me what I missed?
2. I don't suppose you'd consider giving me a few more days to complete this research paper?	2. I'd like to request an extension on my research paper. I promise to hand it in by noon on Thursday. Would that be acceptable?

When you make specific requests, the other person can respond with a clear "yes" or "no." If the person says "no," all is not lost. Try negotiating:

1. *If you can't call me Friday night, could I call you Saturday morning to find out what I missed?*

2. *If Thursday noon isn't acceptable to you, could I turn my paper in
   on Wednesday by 5:00?*

A Creator seeks definite yes or no answers. Victims often accept "maybe" or "I'll try" for fear of getting a "no," but it's better to hear a specific "no" and be free to move on to someone who will say "yes."

One of my mentors offered a valuable piece of advice: "If you go through a whole day without getting at least a couple of 'no's,' you aren't asking for enough help in your life."

Saying "no"

Saying "no" is another tool of the assertive Creator. When I think of the power of saying "no," I think of Monique. One day after class she took a deep breath, sighed, and told me she was exhausted. She complained that everyone at her job kept bringing her tasks to do. As a result, she had virtually no social life, and she was falling behind in college. She wanted advice on how to manage her time better.

"Sounds like you're working 60 hours a week and doing the work of two people," I observed. She nodded modestly. "Here's an outrageous thought: The next time someone at work brings you more to do, say 'no'."

"That sounds so rude."

"Okay then, say, 'I'm sorry, but my schedule is full, and I won't be able to do that.'"

"What if my boss asks? I can't say 'no' to her."

"You can say, 'I'll be glad to take that on. But since I have so many projects already, I'll need you to give one of them to someone else. That way I'll have time to do a good job on this new project.'"

Monique agreed to experiment with saying "no." The next time I saw her, she was excited. "I sent my boss a memo telling her I had too much work and I couldn't take on the latest project she had assigned me. Before I'd even talked to her about the memo, one of my co-workers came by. He said our boss had sent him to take over some of my projects. Not only didn't I get the new project, I got rid of two others. I just might be able to finish this semester after all."

Monique's voice had a power that hadn't been there before. With one "no" she had transformed herself from exhausted to exhilarated. That's the power of a Creator being assertive.

When two people are relating maturely, each will be able to ask the other for what he or she wants or needs, fully trusting that the other will say "no" if he or she does not want to give it.

Edward Deci

Journal Entry 18

In this activity, you will explore assertiveness. This powerful way of being creates great results, strengthens relationships, and builds self-esteem.

 1. **Write three different responses to the instructor described in the following situation.** Respond to the instructor by (1) placating, (2) blaming, and (3)

leveling. For an example of this exercise, refer to the journal article on page 139.

Situation: You register for a course required in your major. It is the last course you need to graduate. When you go to the first class meeting, the instructor tells you that your name is NOT on the roster. The course is full, and no other sections of the course are being offered. You've been shut out of the class. The instructor tells you that you'll have to postpone graduation and return next semester to complete this required course.

Remember, in each of your three responses, you are writing what you would actually say to the instructor—first as a placator, second as a blamer, and third as a leveler.

2. **Now, think about one of your most challenging academic goals. Decide who could help you with this goal. Write a letter to this person and request assistance.** You can decide later if you actually want to send the letter.

When things really get difficult, all I can say is, ask for help.

Dr. Bernie Siegel

Here are some possibilities to include in your letter:

- Tell the person your most challenging academic goal for this semester.
- Explain how this goal is a steppingstone to your dream.
- Describe your dream and explain its importance to you.
- Identify your obstacle, explaining it fully.
- Discuss how you believe this person can help you overcome your obstacle.
- Admit any reluctance or fear you have about asking for assistance.
- Request *exactly* what you would like this person to do for you and persuade him or her to give you helpful assistance.

Remember, for effective requests, use the DAPPS rule.

3. **Write what you have learned or relearned about being assertive.** How assertive have you been in the pursuit of your goals and dreams? How has this choice affected your self-esteem? What changes do you intend to make in communicating (placating, blaming, leveling), making requests, and saying "no"? Be sure to use the 4 E's (Experiences, Examples, Explanation, and Evidence) to support what you say.

Developing effective study skills is obviously a key to success in college. But studying doesn't end with graduation. Employees in today's fast-changing world must know both how to earn a living and how to "learn" a living. To excel in a challenging career after college, you'll need to learn even more than you ever learned in college. This section offers some effective strategies for learning effectively in college and beyond. Experiment and see which ones appeal to you.

Before Studying

1. Create a positive affirmation about studying. You may hold negative beliefs about studying that will sabotage your success. If so, create an affirming statement about studying, like, *"I love learning new things."* Along with your personal affirmation, repeat this study affirmation in order to make new choices about studying.

2. Create an ideal study space. Having one comfortable place where you always study has many advantages. You have the study materials you need close at hand. You aren't distracted by unfamiliar sights or sounds. And your mind becomes accustomed to shifting into study gear whenever you enter your study area. Design your study area so you always enjoy being there. Minimum requirements include a comfortable chair, plenty of light, room to spread out your materials, and space to store your books and supplies. Personalize your study area to make it even more inviting. For example, display pictures of loved ones or add plants. Do whatever it takes to create a space you look forward to entering.

3. Make a list of important assignments. The Next Actions List on page 99 is ideal for this purpose. Put the most urgent assignments on the top of your Next Actions List. As you study, check off each completed item; then go to the next one. This method allows you to use your valuable study time efficiently.

4. Study your challenging subjects first. Tackle difficult subjects when your mind is alert and more receptive to new information. Save your easier subjects for dessert.

5. Arrange to be undisturbed. Do whatever is necessary to minimize interruptions. Tell friends and relatives not to contact you during your regular study hours. Put a Do-Not-Disturb sign on your door. Let your answering machine take telephone calls. If necessary, study where no one can easily disturb you, such as at your college library. Protect the sanctity of your study time.

6. Tell yourself "I will remember what I'm about to study." Simply telling yourself to remember what you are studying can increase your ability to recall the information later.

7. Do a data dump. Write down everything you already know about the subject you're preparing to study. This activity starts your brain thinking about the subject at hand. It's the mental equivalent of stretching your muscles and warming up before playing a sport.

8. Form a study group. Studying with other Creators is a great way to improve your study efficiency. Follow the suggestions on pages 128–129 to ensure that your study group functions at top form.

During Studying

9. Play soft, instrumental music in the background. Studies show that listening to instrumental music with about sixty beats per minute induces *alpha* brain waves and therefore enhances learning for some people. Classical music of the baroque period is ideally suited for this purpose.

10. Change subjects after forty-five to sixty minutes. Studies of learning reveal that we recall the most from the beginning of a study session, next most from the end of a study session, and least from the middle. This is called the "Primacy-Recency" effect. Changing tasks periodically provides more beginnings and endings, so you'll typically learn more from three one-hour sessions, each on a different subject, than you will with one three-hour session on the same subject.

11. Take a short break every thirty minutes or so. Get up and stretch. Walk around. Get a drink of water. Stretch and walk around a little more. Now return to your studying refreshed.

12. Study during your prime learning times. Some people are most alert in the morning, whereas others learn best in the evening. Still others come alive in the middle of the day. Investing one hour of studying in your prime time is probably worth two (or more) hours of studying in your off times. Schedule your day to use your peak learning times for studying.

13. Create Q & A cards. On one side of a 3" × 5" card, write a question (Q) that your instructor might ask on a test. Create questions from both class discussions and readings. Remember, you can create questions by simply turning textbook headings and key terms into questions. On the back of the Q & A cards, write the answers (A). Show these questions to your instructor, confirming that they'll lead you to important answers in the course. Carry Q & A cards with you everywhere. Pull them out for a quick review whenever you have a few extra minutes. If you study them only twenty minutes per day, that's over two hours of extra studying each week. See examples on page 144.

14. Use graphic organizers. A graphic organizer is great for visual learners because it clearly pictures the relationship of ideas to one another. For example, each chapter in *On Course* begins with a graphic organizer: a chart comparing Victims and Creators. A concept map (see page 115) is another kind of graphic organizer. You'll find many more examples of graphic organizers at *http://www.eduplace.com/graphicorganizer*.

15. Create study sheets containing key math and science formulas. Use the study sheets to solve practice problems, being sure you understand each step.

16. Review briefly every day. Repetition strengthens memory, so set aside a minimum of ten to fifteen minutes daily for reviewing your courses. Review your Q & A cards, graphic organizers, study sheets, or class notes regularly, and you'll be pleased to see how easily you recall the information later. Ideal times to review are right before going to sleep or directly upon waking in the morning.

17. Use the postage stamp method. Here's one of my personal favorites. Seven days before a test, write a summary of the information you need to know on one side of a full sheet of paper (8.5 " by 11"). Every couple of hours, read and study the summarized information. Every day until the test, copy your notes onto a sheet of paper half as large—condensing ideas as necessary—and study the information for several thirty-minute sessions that day. As your page of notes gets smaller by half each day, you'll soon need to use abbreviations, acronyms, and symbols to get all the information recorded. When your notes are finally on a piece of paper about the size of a postage stamp, study them right up to the exam. On the way to the exam, roll your postage stamp into a tiny ball and toss it in the trash. You are ready for the test.

After Studying

18. Review, Review, Review. The key to retaining information is moving it from short-term memory to long-term memory. Repetition is the key. Shortly after your study period, spend ten minutes reviewing the key concepts or terms you learned. Two hours later review again. Review once more before going to sleep. For the next three days, review these same concepts or terms daily. Next, review them weekly. This repeated review takes little effort but creates much learning.

19. Create an instant replay of your study session. Run a movie in your mind of your entire study session. For example, mentally reconstruct conversations with your study partner(s), picture your Q & A cards, visualize your graphic organizers. Best of all, do this mental review at times that would otherwise be wasted, such as when commuting or standing in a line.

20. Discuss concepts often. Conversation solidifies learning. Whenever possible, talk about new concepts with study partners and your instructors.

21. Have someone quiz you. This is a great activity to do in your study group. Or, provide a friend with your Question & Answer cards, and have her quiz you.

Front

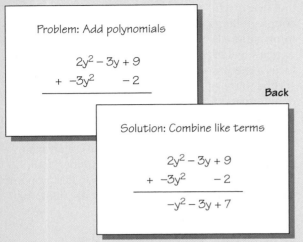

Sample Problem-Solution Note Cards

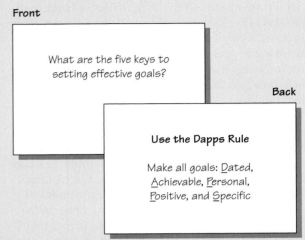

A Question-and-Answer Card

22. Teach what you learn. Find people who will assume the role of your students. Tell them, "I learned something new in class today, and I'd like to see if I can explain it clearly enough for you to understand." One student I knew put her children to bed each night in a most creative way; she donned hand puppets and delivered animated lectures to her children about what she had learned that day.

23. Seek tutoring. If you don't understand something you're studying or need more one-on-one ex- planations, go to the tutoring center on your campus to get help. If the first tutor you see isn't much help, ask for a different tutor the next time.

Studying Exercise

Interview successful students and ask for their favorite study strategies. See if you can discover additional strategies not on the list above.

Embracing Change

Do one thing different this week

Creators create mutually supportive relationships, giving and receiving help. Experiment with being more interdependent by picking ONE new belief or behavior and trying it for one week. Put a check next to each day that you take the action. As before, assess your results after a week. See if this new choice helps you create more positive outcomes and experiences. If your outcomes and experiences improve, you now have a strategy you can use for the rest of your life.

Beliefs and Behaviors	Day 1	Day 2	Day 3	Day 4	Day 5	Day 6	Day 7
Think: "I am giving and receiving help."							
Ask an instructor for help.							
Seek help from a college resource.							
Find and work with a study partner.							
Create and meet with a study group.							
Have a meaningful conversation with someone very different from myself.							
Use an "I" statement in assertively expressing something that upsets me.							
Make a request for help with a problem.							
Offer help to someone with a problem.							
Say "no" to a request of me.							
Use the following study strategy (write your choice from pages 142–144):							

(continued on page 146)

During my seven-day experiment, what happened?
As a result of what happened, what did I learn or relearn?

Gaining Self-Awareness

6

Despite all of my efforts to create success in college and in life, I may still find myself off course. Now is the perfect time to identify and revise the inner obstacles to my success.

I am choosing habit patterns and core beliefs that support my success.

SUCCESSFUL STUDENTS . . .	STRUGGLING STUDENTS . . .
■ **recognize when they are off course.**	▓ unconsciously wander through life unaware of being off course.
■ **identify their self-defeating patterns** of thought, emotion, and behavior.	▓ remain unaware of their self-defeating patterns of thought, emotion, and behavior.
■ **rewrite their outdated Scripts,** revising limited core beliefs and self-defeating patterns.	▓ unconsciously persist in making choices based on outdated Scripts, finding themselves farther and farther off course with each passing year.

Strange Choices

"Do your students make really strange choices?" Professor Assante asked.

The other professors looked up from their lunches. "What do you mean?" one asked.

"At the beginning of each class, I give short quizzes that count 50 percent of the final grade," **Professor Assante** replied. "One of my students comes late to every class, even though I keep telling her there's no way she can pass the course if she keeps missing the quizzes. But she still keeps coming late! What is she thinking?"

"That's nothing," **Professor Buckley** said. "I've got a really bright student who attends every class and offers great comments during discussions. But the semester is almost over, and he still hasn't turned in any assignments. At this point, he's too far behind to pass. Now that's what I call a strange choice."

"You think that's strange," **Professor Chen** said, "I'm teaching composition in the computer lab. Last week I sat down next to a woman who was working on her essay, and I suggested a way she could improve her introduction. I couldn't believe what she did. She swore at me, stormed out of the room, and slammed the door."

Professor Donnelly chimed in. "Well, I can top all of you. In my philosophy class, participation counts one-third of the final grade. I've got a student this semester who hasn't said a word in twelve weeks. Even when I call on him, he just shakes his head and says something under his breath that I can't hear. One day after class, I asked him if he realized that if he didn't participate in class discussions, the best grade he could earn is a D. He just mumbled, 'I know.' Now there's a choice I don't get!"

"How about this!" **Professor Egret** said. "I had a student last semester with a B average going into the final two weeks. Then he disappeared. This semester, I ran into him on campus, and I asked what happened. 'Oh,' he said, 'I got burned out and stopped going to my classes.' 'But you only had two more weeks to go. You threw away thirteen weeks of work,' I said. You know what he did? He shrugged his shoulders and walked away. I wanted to shake him and say, 'What is wrong with you?'"

Professor Fanning said, "Talk about strange choices. Last week I had four business owners visit my marketing class to talk about how they promote their businesses. Near the end of the period, a student asked if the business owners had ever had problems with procrastination. While the panelists were deciding who was going to answer, I joked, 'Maybe they'd rather answer later.' Okay, it was weak humor, but most of the students chuckled, and then one panelist answered the question. The next day I got a call from the dean. The student who'd asked about procrastination told him I'd mocked her in front of the whole class, and now she's going to drop out of college. I had videotaped the class, so I asked her if she'd be willing to watch the tape. Later she admitted I hadn't said what she thought I had, but she still dropped out of school. What is it with students today and their bizarre choices?"

Listed below are all of the professors' students. Choose the one you think made the strangest choice and speculate why this student made the choice. Dive deeper than obvious answers such as "He's probably just shy." Why do you suppose he is shy? What past experiences might have made him this way? What might the inner conversation of his Inner Critic and Inner Defender sound like? What emotions might he often feel? What beliefs might he have about himself, other people or the world? In what other circumstances (e.g., work, relationship, health) might a similar choice sabotage his success?

_____ Professor Assante's student
_____ Professor Buckley's student
_____ Professor Chen's student
_____ Professor Donnelly's student
_____ Professor Egret's student
_____ Professor Fanning's student

DIVING DEEPER: Recall a course you once took in which you made a choice that your instructor might describe as "strange." Explain why you made that choice. Dive deep, exploring what _really_ caused your choice.

Recognizing When You Are Off Course

 FOCUS QUESTIONS In which of your life roles are you off course? Do you know how you got there? More important, do you know how to get back on course to your desired outcomes and experiences?

Take a deep breath, relax, and consider your journey so far.

You began by accepting personal responsibility for creating your life as you want it. Then you chose personally motivating goals and dreams that give purpose and direction to your life.

Consider this: If at first you don't succeed, something is blocking your way.

Michael Ray and
Rochelle Myers

Next, you created a self-management plan and began taking effective actions. Most recently, you developed mutually supportive relationships to help you on your journey. Throughout, you have examined how to believe in yourself.

Despite all these efforts, you may still be off course—in college, in a relationship, in your job, or somewhere else in your life. You just aren't achieving your desired outcomes and experiences. Once again, you have an important choice to make. You can listen to the blaming, complaining, and excusing of your Inner Critic and Inner Defender. Or you can ask your Inner Guide to find answers to important questions such as . . .

- _What habits do I have that sabotage my success?_
- _What beliefs do I have that get me off course?_
- _How can I consistently make wise choices that will create a rich, personally fulfilling life?_

The mystery of self-sabotage

Self-sabotage has probably happened to everyone who's set off on a journey to a better life. Consider Jerome. Fresh from high school, Jerome said his dream was to start his own accounting firm by his thirtieth birthday. He set long-term goals of getting his college degree and passing the C.P.A. (certified public accountant) exam. He set short-term goals of earning A's in every class he took during his first semester. He developed a written self-management system and demonstrated interdependence by starting a study group. But at semester's end, the unthinkable happened: Jerome failed Accounting 101!

Wait a minute, though. Jerome's Inner Guide has more information. You see, Jerome made some strange choices during his first semester. He skipped his accounting class three times to work at a part-time job. On another day, he didn't attend class because he was angry with his girlfriend. Then he missed two Monday classes when he was hung-over from weekend parties. He was late five times because parking was difficult to find. Jerome regularly put off doing homework until the last minute because he was so busy. He didn't hand in an important assignment because he found it confusing. And he stopped going to his study group after the first meeting because . . . well, he wasn't quite sure why. As the semester progressed, Jerome's anxiety about the final exam grew. The night before, he stayed up late cramming, then went to the exam exhausted. During the test, his mind went blank.

Haven't you, too, made choices that worked against your goals and dreams? Haven't we all! We take our eyes off the path for just a moment, and some invisible force comes along and pulls us off course. By the time we realize what's happened—if, in fact, we ever do—we can be miles off course and feeling miserable.

What's going on around here, anyway?

Unconscious forces

One of the most important discoveries in psychology is the existence and power of unconscious forces in our lives. We now know that experiences from our past linger in our unconscious minds long after our conscious minds have forgotten them. As a result, we're being influenced in our daily choices by old experiences we don't even recall.

Experiments by Dr. Wilder Penfield of the Montreal Neurological Institute offer evidence that our brains may record nearly every experience we have ever had. Dr. Penfield performed brain surgery on patients who had local anesthesia but were otherwise fully awake. During the operation, he stimulated brain cells using a weak electric current. At that moment his patients reported re-experiencing long-forgotten events in vivid detail.

Further research by Joseph LeDoux, a neuroscientist at the Center for Neural Science at New York University, suggests that a part of our brain called the amygdala stores emotionally charged but now unconscious memories. The amygdala, like a nervous watchman, examines every present experience and compares it to what happened to us in the past. When a key feature of a present event is similar to a distressing event from the past, it declares a match. Then, *without our conscious knowledge*, the alarmed amygdala hijacks our rational thought processes and demands that we respond to the present event as we learned to respond to the similar past event. The problem is, the outdated response is often totally inappropriate in our present situation. By the time the amygdala loosens its grip on our decision-making power, we may have made some very bad choices.

Progressively we discover that there are levels of experience beneath the surface, beneath our consciousness, and we realize that these may hold the key both to the problems and the potentialities of our life.

Ira Progoff

We know from surgical experiences that electrical stimulation delivered to the temporal area of the brain elicits images of events that occurred in the patient's past. This is confirmation that such memories are "stored," but in most instances they cannot be voluntarily recollected. Thus, all of us "know" more than we are aware that we know.

Richard Restak, M.D.

If many of the forces that get us off course are unconscious, how can we spot their sabotaging influence? By analogy, the answer appears in a fascinating discovery in astronomy. Years ago, astronomers developed a mathematical formula to predict the orbit of any planet around the sun. Only one planet, Uranus, failed to follow its predicted orbit. Astronomers were baffled as to why Uranus was "off course" until the French astronomer Leverrier proposed an ingenious explanation: The gravitational pull of an invisible planet was getting Uranus off course. Sure enough, when stronger telescopes were created, the planet Neptune was discovered, and Leverrier was proven correct.

Here's the point: Like planets, we all have invisible Neptunes tugging at us every day. For us, these invisible forces are not in outer space; they exist in inner space, in our unconscious minds. As with Uranus, the first clue to spotting the existence of these unconscious forces is recognizing that we are off course. So, be candid. Where are you off course in your life today? What desired outcomes and experiences are you moving away from instead of toward? What goals and dreams seem to be slipping away? Self-awareness like this allows you to identify the self-sabotaging choices that got you off course and replace them with wiser choices that will get you back on course to the life you want to create.

In the entire history of science, it is hard to find a discovery of comparable consequence to the discovery of the power of unconscious belief as a gateway—or an obstacle—to the hidden mind, and its untapped potentialities.

Willis Harman

Journal Entry 19

In this activity, you will recall times in your life when you were off course and took effective actions to get back on course. Everyone gets off course at times, but only those who are self-aware can consistently make positive changes to improve their lives.

 1. **Write about a time when you made a positive change in your life.** Examples include ending an unhealthy relationship, entering college years after high school, changing careers, stopping an addiction, choosing to be more assertive, or changing a negative belief you held about yourself, other people, or the world. Dive deep in your journal entry by asking and answering questions such as the following:

I learned that I could not look to my exterior self to do anything for me. If I was going to accomplish anything in life I had to start from within.

Oprah Winfrey

- In what area of my life was I off course?
- What choices had I made to get off course?
- What changes did I make to get on course?
- What challenges did I face while making this change?
- What personal strengths helped me make this change?
- What benefits did I experience as a result of my change?
- If I hadn't made this change, what would my life be like today?

The truth is that our finest moments are most likely to occur when we are feeling deeply uncomfortable, unhappy, or unfulfilled. For it is only in such moments, propelled by our discomfort, that we are likely to step out of our ruts and start searching for different ways or truer answers.

M. Scott Peck, M.D.

 2. **Write about an area of your life in which you are off course today.** If you need help in identifying an area, review your desired outcomes and experiences from Journal Entry 7 and your goals and dreams from Journal Entry 8. Explain which area of your life is furthest from the way you would like it to be. What choices have you made that got you off course? What will be the effect on your life if you continue to stay off course?

The fact that you've made positive changes in the past is a good reminder that you have the personal strengths to make similar changes whenever you wish. All you need is the awareness that you're off course and the motivation to make new choices.

Identifying Your Scripts

 FOCUS QUESTIONS   What habit patterns in your life get you off course? How did these habit patterns develop?

What lies behind us and what lies before us are tiny matters compared to what lies within us.

Oliver Wendell Holmes

Once you realize you're off course, you need to figure out how to get back on course. Unfortunately, the forces pulling us off course are often just as invisible to us as the planet Neptune was to Leverrier and his fellow observers of outer space.

As observers of inner space, psychologists seek to identify what they can't actually see: the internal forces that divert human potential into disappointment. In various psychological theories, these unconscious inner forces have been called names such as ego defenses, conditioned responses, programs, mental tapes, blind spots, schemas, and life-traps.

The term we'll use to describe our internal forces was coined by psychologist Eric Berne: **Scripts.** In the world of theater, a script tells an actor what words, actions, and emotions to perform onstage. When the actor gets a cue from others in the play, he doesn't make a choice about his response. He responds automatically as his script directs. Performance after performance, he reacts the same way to the same cues.

Responding automatically from a dramatic script is one sure way to succeed as an actor. However, responding automatically from a *life* Script is one sure way to struggle as a human being.

© 1990 by S. Gross

Anatomy of a Script

Everyone has scripts. I do, your instructor does, your classmates do, you do. Some scripts have helped us achieve our present success. Other scripts may be getting us off course from our goals and dreams. Becoming aware of our unique personal scripts helps us make wise choices at each fork in the road, choices that help us create the life we want.

Scripts are composed of two parts. Closest to the surface of our consciousness reside the directions for how we are to think, feel, and behave. **Thought patterns** include habitual self-talk such as *I'm too busy, I'm good at math, I always screw up, I can't write.* **Emotional patterns** include habitual feelings such as anger, excitement, anxiety, sadness, or joy. **Behavior patterns** include habitual actions such as smoking cigarettes, always arriving on time, never asking for help, exercising regularly. When people know us well, they can often predict what we will say, feel, or do in a given situation. This ability reveals their recognition of our patterns.

Deeper in our unconscious mind lies the second, and more elusive, part of our Scripts, our **core beliefs.** Early in life, we form core beliefs about the world (e.g., *The world is safe* or *The world is dangerous*), about other people (e.g., *People can be trusted* or *People can't be trusted*), and about ourselves (e.g., *I'm worthy* or *I'm unworthy*). Though we're seldom aware of our core beliefs, these unconscious judgments dictate what we consistently think, feel, and do. These beliefs become the lenses through which we see the world. Whether accurate or distorted, our beliefs dictate the choices we make at each fork in the road. What do you believe that causes you to make choices that other people think are strange? More important, what do

A psychological script is a person's ongoing program for his life drama which dictates where he is going with his life and how he is to get there. It is a drama he compulsively acts out, though his awareness of it may be vague.

Muriel James and
Dorothy Jongeward

The grooves of mindlessness run deep. We know our scripts by heart.

Ellen J. Langer

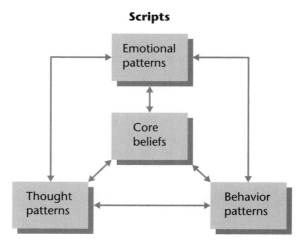

you believe that keeps you from creating the outcomes and experiences you want?

How we wrote our Scripts

Though no one knows exactly how we wrote our life Scripts as children, reasonable explanations exist. One factor seems to be **how others responded to us.** Imagine this scene: You're two years old. You're feeling lonely and hungry, and you begin to cry. Your mother hurries in to pick you up. "There, there," she croons. "It's all right." She hugs you, feeds you, sings to you. You fall asleep full and content. If this happens often enough, what do you suppose you'd decide about the world, about other people, about yourself? Probably you'd believe *The world is kind, People will help me, I am lovable.* In turn, these beliefs would dictate your thoughts, emotions, and behaviors. With positive beliefs such as these at the core of your Scripts, very likely you'd develop optimistic thought patterns (e.g., *If I ask, I'll get help*), positive emotional patterns (e.g., joy and harmony), and empowering behavior patterns (e.g., asking for what you want).

The hearts of small children are delicate organs. A cruel beginning in this world can twist them into curious shapes. The heart of a hurt child can shrink so that forever afterward it is hard and pitted as the seed of a peach.

Carson McCullers

Now imagine the same childhood scene with a different response. You cry but no one comes. You scream louder, but still no one comes. Finally you abandon hope that anyone will respond. Imagine also that being ignored happens often. You'd probably develop core beliefs such as *The world doesn't care about me, People won't help me, I'm not important.* You could very well develop pessimistic thought patterns (e.g., *I'm alone*), negative emotional patterns (e.g., anxiety and anger), and passive behavior patterns (e.g., not asking for what you want).

Now, imagine this scene one more time. As you're crying for attention and food, an adult storms into your room, screams "Shut up!" and slaps your face. After a few wounding experiences like this, you may decide *The world is a dangerous and painful place, People will hurt me, I'm unlovable!* These beliefs may lead to defensive thought patterns (e.g., *People are out to get me*), defensive emotional patterns (e.g., fear and rage), and defensive behavior patterns (e.g., immediately fighting or fleeing at the first sign of danger). Imagine how easily these patterns could get you off course later in life.

A second factor that seems to shape our Scripts is **what significant adults said to us.** What did they say about the world: Is it safe or dangerous? What did they say about other people: Can they be trusted or not? And, perhaps most important, what did important adults say about us? Psychologists have a term for qualities that tell us how we "are" or "should be": **attributions.** Common attributions tell us to be *good, quiet, rebellious, devoted, helpful, athletic, sexy, tough, independent, dependent, invisible, macho, dominant, competitive, smart, shy,* or *confident.*

Parents, deliberately or unaware, teach their children from birth how to behave, think, feel, and perceive. Liberation from these influences is no easy matter.

Eric Berne

Psychologists also have a term for the qualities that tell us what we "are not" or "should not be": **injunctions.** Common injunctions include *don't be yourself,* *don't talk back, don't feel, don't think, don't be intimate, don't say no, don't say yes, don't get angry, don't trust, don't love yourself, don't be happy, don't be weak, don't believe in yourself, don't exist.*

We first make our habits, and then our habits make us.
John Dryden

A third way we seem to write our Scripts is by **observing the behavior of significant adults.** Children notice, *What did important adults do? If it's right for them, it's right for me.* When children play, we see them trying on adult behaviors, conversations, and emotions. It doesn't take a detective to figure out where they learned them. From significant adults we learn not only our unique personal scripts but also our cultural scripts. For example, some cultures encourage individuality while others place family and community above all other concerns. Each belief is deeply imbedded in the culture and becomes the lens through which its members see the world, influencing their choices whether they are aware of the beliefs or not.

In these ways we develop our unique Scripts comprised of core beliefs and their resulting patterns of thoughts, feelings, and behaviors. At critical choice points, especially when we are under stress, we unconsciously refer to our Scripts for guidance: *What similar experience have I had in the past? What thoughts, emotions, or actions did I choose back then? Did that choice increase or decrease my pain or pleasure? Oh, look, here's a response that seemed to work back then. I'll use it again now.*

The good news about our unconscious Scripts is that their intention is always positive—always to minimize our pain, always to maximize our pleasure. Many of us made it through the mental, emotional, and physical challenges of growing up with the help of our childhood Scripts. Some of us would not have survived without them.

But, as you might guess, there is bad news as well: When we make unconscious, Script-guided choices as adults, we often get off course. That's because the Scripts we developed in childhood seldom apply to the situations of our present lives. Imagine an actor in a Broadway show who can't stop playing a role from his grade school play! Many of us do the equivalent of this in our daily lives.

To others, a choice I make may seem strange. To me, it makes perfect sense. The important issue, though, is: Do my habitual choices help or hinder me in the pursuit of the life I want to create?

Self-defeating habits

The more you are keenly aware of your misery-creating thoughts, feelings, and behaviors, the greater your chances are of ridding yourself of them.
Albert Ellis

Though our unconscious Scripts are as invisible to us as the planet Neptune was to early astronomers, we can often see their influence in our lives. Put a check next to any of the following patterns of thought, emotion, and behavior that are often true of you. These habits may reveal the presence of outdated Scripts that get you off course. In particular, see if you can identify any habits that may have gotten you off course in the area you wrote about in Journal Entry 19.

☐ 1. I waste a lot of time doing unimportant things (e.g., television, video games).

☐ 2. I wonder if I'm "college material."

☐ 3. I easily get upset (e.g., angry, sad, anxious, depressed, guilty, frustrated).

☐ 4. I hang out with people who don't support my academic goals.

☐ 5. I believe that most people don't like me.

☐ 6. I often turn in college assignments late.

☐ 7. I get nervous around my instructors.

☐ 8. I worry excessively about doing things perfectly.

☐ 9. I think most of my classmates are smarter than I am.

☐ 10. I quit on things that are important to me.

☐ 11. I allow a person in my life to treat me badly.

☐ 12. I don't believe I deserve success as much as other people do.

☐ 13. I miss more college classes than I should.

☐ 14. I'm very critical of myself.

☐ 15. I wait until the last minute to do important college assignments.

☐ 16. I don't ask questions in class or participate in class discussions.

☐ 17. I often break promises I have made to myself or others.

☐ 18. I am addicted to something (e.g., caffeine, alcohol, cigarettes, soft drinks, drugs).

☐ 19. I experience severe test anxiety.

☐ 20. I feel uncomfortable about asking for help.

☐ 21. I don't get along with one or more people with whom I live.

☐ 22. I often side-talk or daydream in my college classes.

☐ 23. I seldom do my best work on college assignments.

☐ 24. I am very critical of other people.

☐ 25. I get extremely nervous when I speak to a group.

☐ 26. I keep promising to study more in college, but I don't.

☐ 27. I get my feelings hurt easily.

☐ 28. I am a loner.

☐ 29. I . . . _____

☐ 30. I . . . _____

It is not true that life is one damn thing after another— it's one damn thing over and over.

Edna St. Vincent Millay, American Poet

Are you aware of any other of your patterns—mental, emotional, or behavioral? If so, add them to the list above.

Journal Entry 20

In this activity, you will explore self-defeating patterns in your life that may reveal unconscious Scripts. You're about to embark on an exciting journey into your inner world! There you can discover—and later revise—the invisible forces that have gotten you off course from your goals and dreams.

All serious daring starts from within.

Eudora Welty

1. **Write about one of your self-defeating *behavior* patterns.** Choose a behavior pattern that you checked on the list above or identify a self-defeating behavior that isn't on the list but which you do often. Remember to develop your journal paragraphs by anticipating questions that someone reading it might have about this behavior pattern. (Even you might have questions when you read your journal ten years from now.) For example,

- What exactly is your self-defeating behavior pattern?
- What are some specific examples of when you did this behavior?
- What may have caused this habit?
- What undesirable effects has it had on your life?
- How would your life be improved if you changed it?

One student began by writing, *One of my self-defeating behaviors is that I seldom do my best work on college assignments. For example, in my biology lab . . .*

2. **Repeat Step 1 for one of your self-defeating *thought* patterns or for one of your self-defeating *emotional* patterns.** Once again, choose a pattern that you checked on the list above or identify a habit that isn't on the list but that you often think or feel. You might begin, *One of my self-defeating thought patterns is that I often wonder if I am smart enough to be successful in college. I especially think this during exams. For example, last Thursday I . . . Or . . . One of my self-defeating emotional patterns is that I often feel frustrated. For example . . .*

At different points in my life I've given up when I ran into a challenge. As a child, I loved baseball, but when I got hit in the face with a ball, I stopped playing. In school, I started having problems with my writing skills, and I was diagnosed with a learning disability. I got all kinds of accommodations, even more than I deserved, and I started goofing off. I convinced myself that success was getting the best grades possible with the least amount of work. After high school, college didn't seem like a viable option, so I joined the Marine Corps Reserve. Boot camp was even harder than I thought it would be. Once again, I used the minimum amount of effort necessary to complete each task, and I failed to achieve the level of success in the Marines that I could have. When I left the Marines to get a civilian job, I defined success as getting maximum compensation for minimum effort.

I got a job at the phone company and at first it seemed perfect. I'm very well paid for very little effort. However, this situation isn't as rewarding as I thought it would be. After a few years I began to want a greater challenge. I knew I needed an education to advance in the workplace, so I started taking college courses part-time. For the first year I avoided classes that involved a lot of writing as I was still intimidated by past failures in this area. But when poor writing began to affect my grades in other courses, I decided to take a composition class. In that class we read *On Course*, and in the chapter about self-awareness, I began to see how negative scripts could cause problems. I started wondering if there was a script contributing to the frustration I was feeling in my life.

ONE STUDENT'S STORY
James Floriolli
*Foothill College,
California*

An idea kept coming up that at first I was unwilling to accept. I had always thought of myself as a hard worker, but looking back on my life I could not deny there were challenges I had run away from. When baseball had required extra work to get past my fear of the ball, I quit. When school stopped coming easily to me, I quit. When I realized how hard I'd have to work to be a success in the Marines, I quit. Seeing this pattern was powerful for me. Finally, I felt like I understood how I ended up in the situation I am in. I realized that I'll do anything to avoid feeling bad. If I feel down in any way, I'm willing to throw everything out the window to feel better. In the past, I have doubted myself and been afraid to take risks. I overvalued security and undervalued me. I need to believe I am capable of accomplishing anything I want to.

Soon I have to pick my college major. One option is to get a computer science degree and continue working at the phone company. This would probably lead to the greatest profit and security. Or, I could choose a major that would prepare me for my dream job working in the front office of a professional baseball team. Obviously, going for my dream would be very difficult and call for a large initial pay cut. Knowing I have an issue with not following through on my most challenging commitments, I need to set my goals very carefully. No matter what I choose, I hope that when everything is said and done I will be proud of what I have accomplished. This will mean I have successfully revised my negative script of running from important challenges in my life.

Rewriting Your Outdated Scripts

Once in a writing class, I was explaining how to organize an essay when a student named Diana told me she didn't understand. She asked if I'd write an explanation on the blackboard.

Earlier in the class, we'd been talking about the differences between left-brain and right-brain thinking. We'd discussed how the left side of our brain deals with logical, organized information, while the right side deals with more creative, intuitive concepts. "No problem," I said to Diana, "I hear your left brain crying out for some order. Let's see if I can help."

As I turned to write on the blackboard, she screamed, "You have no right to talk to me that way!"

I was stunned. Talk about a strange response! I took a deep breath to compose myself. "Maybe we could talk about this after class," I said.

We don't see things as they are, we see them as we are.

Anaïs Nin

The impact of outdated beliefs

Diana and I did talk, and I learned that she was in her late thirties, a single mother of an eight-year-old daughter. Our conversation wandered for a while; then Diana mentioned that she had always disliked school. In elementary school, she had consistently gotten low grades. One day, when Diana was about twelve, she overheard her father and mother talking. "I don't know what we're going to do with Diana," her father said. "She's the *half-brain* of the family."

Diana accepted as a fact other people's belief that she couldn't think or learn. She developed patterns of thoughts, emotions, and behaviors that supported this belief. She decided that school was a waste of time (thought), she exploded when anyone questioned her about schoolwork (emotion), and she was often absent (behavior). Diana barely graduated from high school, then got a menial job that bored her.

We are what we think.
All that we are arises
With our thoughts.
With our thoughts,
We make the world.

The Buddha

For nearly twenty years, Diana heard her Inner Critic (sounding much like her father) telling her that something was wrong with her brain. Finally, another inner voice began to whisper, *Maybe—just maybe . . . .* Then one day she took a big risk and enrolled in college.

"So what happens?" she said, getting angry again. "I get a teacher who calls me a *half-brain*! I knew this would happen. I ought to just quit."

I used my best active listening skills: I listened to understand, not to respond. I reflected both her thoughts and her anger. I asked her to clarify and expand. I allowed long periods of silence.

Finally, her emotional storm subsided. She took a deep breath and sat back.

I waited a few moments. "Diana, I know you think I called you a 'half-brain.' But what I actually said was *left* brain. Remember we had been talking in class about the difference between left-brain and right-brain thinking? Two different approaches to planning your essay? I was talking about that."

"But I *heard* you!"

We are, each of us, our own prisoner. We are locked up in our own story.

Maxine Kumin

"I know that's what you *heard*. But that isn't what I *said*. I've read two of your essays, and I know your brain works just fine. What really matters, though, is what *you* think! You need to believe in your own intelligence. Otherwise, you'll always be ready to hear people call you a 'half-brain' no matter what they really said."

Diana had come within an inch of dropping out of college, of abandoning her dreams of a college degree. And all because of her childhood Script.

Doing the rewrite

Until we revise our limiting Scripts, we're less likely to achieve some of our most cherished goals and dreams. That's why realizing we're off course can be a blessing in disguise. By identifying the self-defeating patterns of thought, emotion, and behavior that got us off course, we may be able to discover and revise the underlying core beliefs that are sabotaging our success.

Diana stuck it out and passed English 101. She persevered and graduated with an Associate of Arts degree in early childhood education. When I spoke to her last, she was working at a nursery school and talking about returning to college to finish her bachelor's degree. Like most of us, she'll probably be in a tug of war with her Scripts for the rest of her life. But now, at least, she knows that she, and not her Scripts, can be in charge of making her choices.

It is a marvelous faculty of the human mind that we are also able to stop old programming from holding us back, anytime we choose to. That gift is called conscious choice.

Shad Helmstetter

One of the great discoveries about the human condition is this: We are not stuck with our Scripts. We can re-create ourselves. By revising our outdated Scripts, we can get back on course and dramatically change the outcomes of our lives for the better.

Journal Entry 21

In this activity, you'll practice revising your Scripts, thus taking greater control of your life. As in Journal Entry 17, you'll once again be writing a conversation with your Inner Guide, a critical thinking skill that empowers you to become your own best coach, counselor, mentor, and guide through challenging times. This practical application of critical thinking greatly enhances your self-awareness, helping you make the wise choices necessary to create your desired outcomes and experiences.

1. **Write a dialogue with your Inner Guide that will help you revise your self-sabotaging Scripts.**

Have your Inner Guide ask you the ten questions below. After answering each question, let your Inner Guide use the active listening skills that will help you dive deep:

1. **Silence**
2. **Reflection** (of your thoughts and feelings)
3. **Expansion** (by asking for examples, evidence, and experience)
4. **Clarification** (by asking for an explanation)

Ten questions from your Inner Guide:

1. In what area of your life are you off course?
2. What self-defeating **thought patterns** of yours may have contributed to this situation?
3. What different thoughts could you choose to get back on course?
4. What self-defeating **emotional patterns** of yours may have contributed to this situation?
5. What different emotions could you choose to get back on course?
6. What self-defeating **behavior patterns** of yours may have contributed to this situation?
7. What different behaviors could you choose to get back on course?
8. What limiting **core beliefs** of yours (about the world, other people, or yourself) may have led you to adopt the self-defeating patterns that we've been discussing?
9. What different beliefs could you choose to get back on course?
10. As a result of what you've learned here, what new behaviors, thoughts, emotions, or core beliefs will you adopt?

A sample dialogue appears below.

Sample dialogue with your Inner Guide

IG: In what area of your life are you off course? [Question 1]
ME: My grades are terrible this semester.
IG: Would you say more about that? [Expansion]
ME: In high school I got mostly A's and B's even though I played three sports. My goal this semester is to have at least a 3.5 grade point average, but the way things are going, I'll be lucky if I even get a 2.0.
IG: What self-defeating **thought patterns** of yours may have contributed to this situation? [Question 2]
ME: I guess I tell myself I shouldn't have to work hard to get good grades in college.

In developing our own self-awareness many of us discover ineffective scripts, deeply embedded habits that are totally unworthy of us, totally incongruent with the things we really value in life.
Stephen Covey

IG: Why do you think that? Is there a deeper meaning? [Clarification]

ME: If I have to study hard, then I must not be very smart.

IG: That's a good awareness! What different thoughts could you choose to get back on course to your goal of getting at least a 3.5 average? [Question 3]

ME: I could remind myself that going to college is like moving from the minor leagues to the major leagues. The challenge is a lot greater, and I better start studying like a major league student or I'm not going to succeed.

IG: What self-defeating **emotional patterns** of yours may have contributed to this situation? [Question 4]

ME: I get really frustrated when I don't understand something right away.

IG: So you want to understand it immediately. [Reflection]

ME: Absolutely. When I don't get it right away, I switch to something else.

IG: That's understandable since everything came so easy to you in high school. What different emotion could you choose to get you back on course to your goal of a 3.5 G.P.A.? [Question 5]

ME: I could do the same thing I do in basketball when the coach asks me to shut down the other team's top scorer. I can psych myself up and push myself to study harder. My college degree is worth a lot more to me than winning a basketball game.

IG: What self-defeating **behavior patterns** of yours may have contributed to this situation? [Question 6]

ME: Like I said before, I get frustrated when I don't understand something right away, and then I put it aside. I always plan to come back to it later, but usually I don't.

IG: Are there any other self-defeating behaviors you can think of? [Expansion]

ME: I don't ask my teachers for help or go to the tutoring center either. I guess I hate asking for help. It's like admitting that I'm not very smart.

IG: There's that concern again about not being smart enough. [Reflection]

ME: I hadn't realized my Inner Critic is so loud!

IG: Now you can prove your Inner Critic wrong. What different behaviors could you choose to get back on course to your goal? [Question 7]

ME: I could ask my teachers for more help and go to the tutoring center. Also, when I set homework aside, I could write on my calendar when I'm going to work on it again. I'm really good about doing things that I write down.

IG: I like it! What limiting **core beliefs** of yours (about the world, other people, or yourself) may have led you to adopt the self-defeating patterns that we've been discussing? [Question 8]

ME: This conversation has made me realize I have some doubts about whether I'm as smart as I think I am. Maybe I don't believe I can really succeed in college unless studying comes easy for me. Maybe I got a little spoiled and lazy in high school.

Whatever we believe about ourselves and our ability comes true for us.
Susan L. Taylor, Editor-in-chief, *Essence Magazine*

IG: What different core belief could you choose to get back on course to your goal? [Question 9]

ME: I can succeed in college if I'm willing to do the work . . . and give it my best.

IG: That's great!! Do the work and do your best! As a result of what you've learned here, what new behaviors, thoughts, emotions, or core beliefs will you commit to? [Question 10]

ME: When I feel like putting an assignment aside, I'll work on it at least fifteen more minutes. Then, if I stop before I'm finished, I'll write on my calendar when I'm going to work on it again and I'll go back and finish later. If I'm still having trouble with the assignment, I'll ask my professor for help. And I'll keep reminding myself, "Do the work and do my best." If that doesn't help, I'll be back to talk to you some more. I *will* get a 3.5 average! Thanks for listening.

Self-Awareness at Work

Many people spend more time choosing a movie than choosing their career. As a result, the unlucky ones later dread going to work, perhaps for the rest of their lives! Creators, by contrast, devote time and effort to one of life's most important Quadrant II activities: conscious career planning. As a result, many of them actually enjoy going to work.

Conscious career planning requires self-awareness. How else can you find a match between you and the thousands of career possibilities open to you? A place to start your planning is taking an inventory of your **hard skills**. Hard skills are the special-knowledge skills that you've learned to do throughout your life. They include such abilities as swimming, writing, programming computers, playing racquetball, solving mathematics problems, building a house, creating a budget, giving a speech, drawing blood, writing a business plan, designing a garden, cooking lasagna, backpacking, playing chess, and reading. You probably learned many of your hard skills from a teacher, coach, mentor, or book. These skills can typically be filmed on a camcorder, and they tend to be applicable only in limited and specific situations; for example, writing a business plan isn't a skill of much value when you're programming computers. To begin your inventory of hard skills, ask yourself, "What talents have gotten me compliments, recognition, or awards? In which school courses have I received good grades? When did I feel fully alive, extremely capable, or very smart, and what skills was I using at the time?" Finding a match between your hard skills and the requirements of a career is essential for success.

Continue your self-assessment with an inventory of your **soft skills**. Soft skills are the ones you have developed to cope with life. They include the ones you're exploring in this book: making choices as a Creator, motivating yourself, being industrious, developing relationships, demonstrating self-awareness, finding lessons in every experience, managing your emotions, and believing in yourself. Many of these soft skills you learned unconsciously as you faced life's challenges. Usually, they are attitudes and beliefs, so they can't be filmed for playback. They are as invisible as oxygen but just as important to the quality of your life. Unlike hard skills, soft skills tend to be helpful in any career; for example, feeling confident is valuable whether you are an accountant, computer programmer, or nurse. To create an inventory of your soft skills, ask yourself, "What personal qualities have earned me compliments? What accomplishments am I proud of and what inner qualities helped me achieve them?" Finding a match between your soft skills and the demands of a career further increases your chances of rising to the top of your profession.

To create a third component of your self-assessment, identify your **personal preferences**. To do so, go to your college's career center and ask to take one of the well-known interest inventories: the *Strong Interest Inventories* (SII), the *Self-Directed Search* (SDS) or the *Myers-Briggs Type Indicator*® (MBTI®) instrument.

These tools help you discover personal preferences and suggest possible college majors and career choices that will match your interests. An additional tool, the *Holland Code*, places you in one of six personality types and suggests possible careers for each. Which of the following personality types sounds most like you?

1. **Realistic** personalities prefer activities involving objects, tools, and machines. Possible Careers: mechanic, electrician, computer repair, civil engineer, forester, industrial arts teacher, dental technician, farmer, carpenter.

2. **Investigative** personalities prefer activities involving abstract problem solving and the exploration of physical, biological, and cultural phenomena for the purpose of understanding and controlling them. Possible Careers: chemist, economist, detective, computer analyst, doctor, astronomer, mathematician.

3. **Artistic** personalities prefer activities involving self-expression, using words, ideas, or materials to create art forms or new concepts. Possible Careers: writer, advertising manager, public relations specialist, artist, musician, graphic designer, interior decorator, inventor.

4. **Social** personalities prefer activities involving interaction with other people to inform, train, develop, help, or enlighten them. Possible Careers: nurse, massage therapist, teacher, counselor, social worker, day-care provider, physical therapist.

5. **Enterprising** personalities prefer activities involving the persuasion and management of others to attain organizational goals or economic gain. Possible Careers: salesperson, television newscaster, bank manager, lawyer, travel agent, personnel manager, entrepreneur.

6. **Conventional** personalities prefer activities involving the application of data to bring order out of confusion and develop a prescribed plan. Possible Careers: accountant, computer operator, secretary, credit manager, financial planner.

The research of Dr. John Holland, creator of the Holland Code, shows that people tend to be satisfied in careers that are compatible with their personality type, and people are less satisfied when the match isn't there. Becoming aware of your interest preferences and personality type improves your chances of finding a satisfying career match.

Another important area of self-knowledge is your Scripts, those that support your success and especially those that don't. For example, what beliefs do you hold that might keep you from pursuing or succeeding in your chosen career? If one of your Scripts is to distrust other people, then it will be difficult for you to develop the support systems that will enhance your success. This awareness allows you to make a conscious choice about revising the Script. Remember, since you wrote your script originally, you can rewrite it in the service of a successful career.

Self-awareness in the workplace will also help you notice when your self-sabotaging habits get you off course. For example, you'll stop arriving at meetings late; instead, you'll arrive a few minutes early. You'll stop interrupting when others are talking; instead, you'll listen actively. You'll stop acting as if you know all the answers; instead, you'll ask others for their opinions. In short, you'll become conscious of converting your destructive behavior into constructive behavior. If you've ever had bosses or co-workers who demonstrate any of these negative behaviors, you'll know how you wished they would become aware of what they were doing and change.

To summarize, cultivating the soft skill of self-awareness will help you choose a career that you will enjoy and bring out the behaviors, beliefs, and attitudes that will help you to excel in that profession.

Believing in Yourself: **Write Your Own Rules**

 FOCUS QUESTIONS What personal rules do you have that dictate the choices you make daily? Which of these rules helps you create high self-esteem?

Few things affect self-esteem more than our sense of personal power. When we feel like mere passengers, with no apparent choice in where we're going in life, self-esteem shrivels. When we feel like the pilots of our lives, with the power to choose wisely and reach our destinations, self-esteem grows.

I think you're going to be very surprised to discover that you may be living by rules of which you're not even aware.
Virginia Satir

Outdated Scripts can steal our sense of personal power and drag down our self-esteem. When these unconscious programs take over, we essentially turn over the controls of our lives to the scared and confused child of our past. Then we make those strange choices that push us far off course and leave us wondering, "How the heck did I get way over here?" If we want to reclaim our personal power and increase self-esteem, we need to choose wise rules to live by.

As an example, former first lady Eleanor Roosevelt chose these life rules: *Do whatever comes your way as well as you can. Think as little as possible about yourself; think as much as possible about other people. Since you get more joy out of giving joy to others, you should put a good deal of thought in the happiness that you are able to give.*

According to psychologist Virginia Satir, we are all living by rules; the important question is *Are we aware of our rules?* You'll want to become conscious of and revise any self-defeating rules that are holding you back. You'll want to identify and preserve any empowering rules that are keeping you on course. Finally, you'll want to write new rules that will support you in achieving even greater victories.

Three success rules

The most important thing is to have a code of life, to know how to live.

Hans Selye, M.D.

I have polled thousands of college instructors, and they consistently identify three behaviors that their most successful students demonstrate. As you'll see, these rules apply just as well to creating great outcomes in other life roles such as your career and relationships. Consider, then, these three rules as the foundation of your personal code of conduct.

Rule 1: I show up. Commit to attending every class from beginning to end. Someone once said that 90 percent of success is simply showing up. Makes sense, doesn't it? How can you be successful at something if you're not there? Studies show a direct correlation between attendance and grades (as one measure of success). At Baltimore City Community College, a study found that, on average, the more classes students missed, the lower their grades were, especially in introductory courses. A study by a business professor at Arizona State University showed that, on average, his students' grades went down one full grade for every two classes they missed. If you can't get motivated to show up, maybe you need new goals and dreams.

People who lead a satisfying life, who are in tune with their past and with their future—in short, people whom we would call "happy"—are generally individuals who have lived their lives according to rules they themselves created.

Mihaly Csikszentmihalyi

Rule 2: I do my best work. Commit to doing your best work on all assignments, including turning them in on time. You'd be amazed at how many sloppy assignments instructors see. But it isn't just students who are guilty. A friend in business has shown me hundreds of job applications so sloppily prepared that they begged to be tossed in the trash. Doing your best work on assignments is a rule that will propel you to success in all you do.

Rule 3: I participate actively. Commit to getting involved. College, like life, isn't a spectator sport. Come to class prepared. Listen attentively. Take notes. Think deeply about what's being said. Ask yourself how you can apply your course work to achieve your goals and dreams. Read ahead. Start a study group. Ask questions. Answer questions. If you participate at this high level of involvement, you couldn't keep yourself from learning even if you wanted to.

Some students resist adopting these three basic rules of success. They say, "But what if I get sick? What if my car breaks down on the way to class? What if . . . ?" I trust that by now you recognize the voice of the Inner Defender, the internal excuse maker.

I'll give you the Four Rules of Success:

1. Decide what you want.

2. Decide what you want to give up in order to get what you want.

3. Associate with successful people.

4. Plan your work and work your plan.

Blair Underwood, Actor

Of course something may happen to keep you from following your rules. Each rule is simply your *intention*. Each rule identifies an action you believe will help you achieve your desired outcomes and experiences. So you *intend* to be at every class from beginning to end. You *intend* to do your very best work and turn assignments in on time. You *intend* to participate actively. Your promise is never to break your own rules for a frivolous reason. However, you'll always break your own rules if something of a higher value (like your health) demands it. At each fork in the road, the key to your success is being aware of which choice leads to the future you want. When you are a Creator, you make each choice uncontaminated by the past (your scripts), informed by your own rules of conduct, and ultimately determined by which option, in that moment, will best support the achievement of your goals and dreams.

Changing your habits

Exceptional students follow not only these three basic rules of success; they also add their own for college and life. By choosing personal rules, they commit to replacing their scripts with consciously chosen habits. Here are a few of my own life rules:

What is hateful to you do not to your fellowman. That is the entire Law; all the rest is commentary.

        The Talmud

- I keep promises to myself and others.
- I seek feedback and make course corrections when appropriate.
- I arrive on time.
- I do my very best work on all projects important to me.
- I play and create joy.
- I care for my body with exercise, healthy food, and good medical care.

Do I follow these rules every day of my life? Unfortunately, no. And when I don't, I soon see myself getting off course. Then I can re-elect to follow my self-chosen rules and avoid sabotaging the life I want to create.

Once we follow our own rules long enough, they're no longer simply rules. They become habits. And once our positive actions, thoughts, and feelings become habits, few obstacles can block the path to our success.

Journal Entry 22

In this activity, you will write your own rules for success in college and in life. By following your own code of conduct, you will more likely stay on course toward your greatest dreams.

    To focus your mind, ask yourself, "What do successful people do consistently? What are their thoughts, attitudes, behaviors, and beliefs?"

Sow a thought, reap an act; Sow an act, reap a habit; Sow a habit, reap a character; Sow a character, reap a destiny.

        Anonymous

1. Title a clean journal page "MY PERSONAL RULES FOR SUCCESS IN COLLEGE AND IN LIFE." Below that, write a list of your own rules for achieving your goals in college. List only those actions to which you're willing to commit to do consistently. You might want to print your rules on certificate paper and post them where you can see them daily (perhaps right next to your affirmation). Consider adopting the following as your first three rules:

1. I show up.
2. I do my very best work.
3. I participate actively.

2. **Write your thoughts and feelings about your personal rules.** As you write your response, consider answering questions such as the following:

- Which of my rules is the most important? Why?
- What experiences have I had that suggest the value of these rules?
- With which rule(s) will I most easily cooperate? Why?
- Which rule(s) will challenge me the most to keep? Why?

What if one of your rules was: I dive deep! How much would that rule improve your results in college and in life? Use the 4 E's—Examples, Experiences, Explanation, and Evidence—to dive deep in your writing.

I was never a drinker in high school, but when I turned twenty-one, I started going out to bars with my friends. I found that "liquor courage" made me feel better about myself. When I was drinking, I was funny, had a great time, and I was happy. Then I started having blackouts. One time I woke up in my truck, surrounded by policemen, and I had no idea how I had gotten there or where I had been. Another time, I woke up in my bed and there were traffic citations all over the place. I found out later that I had spent the night in jail and the police had sent me home in a cab, but what made it worse was that I didn't remember a second of it. I had always gotten good grades before, but now I started missing my college classes. I wasn't doing as well as I wanted, especially in my nursing classes, like microbiology. I felt crappy and started putting even more pressure on myself. Then I would drink and it made me feel better, almost like a good friend. Trouble was, I'd wake up the next day and my life was falling apart. People were telling me that I could get a medical withdrawal, and I started thinking about dropping out of college.

Looking back on it now, I realize that I had completely lost control of my inner core. I've never been a quitter, though, and I started using my journal entries for this course to figure out my challenges and how to fix them. My entries would run on for five or six pages as I poured myself emotionally into my writing. I was excited because it was a way to express myself positively. About half way through the semester, I made a

ONE STUDENT'S STORY
Brandeé Huigens
Northeast Iowa Community College, Iowa

new rule for myself and told my class about it: *I will abstain from drinking alcohol.* From day one, it was a rule that took over my life, and I decided to track it with a 32-day commitment. To support my change, I started going to AA meetings and I got a counselor at the Substance Abuse Services Center. I reread my journals for inspiration, and every day in this class we'd share how we were doing on our commitments. Of course there were times I was tempted to drink, but I successfully completed my thirty-two days, and then I just kept going. In the last six months, I have abstained from drinking every day but one.

Today, I think about how powerful it was to write that little sentence and make a new rule for myself. It set so many other things in motion. Some are obvious, like I got sober and stopped having blackouts. My final grades were awesome, and I even got a B in micro, the hardest course I ever took. I also got a new perspective on grades. I always wanted to be perfect so I could get approval from my family, but now I see a B as a success instead of a failure. Perhaps most of all, I learned that in trying to please everyone else but me, I had lost focus on what is important to me and all I want to accomplish. Now I've created an assertiveness rule. I've starting speaking up for myself and saying "no," and I can feel my confidence and self-esteem getting stronger. From this class and from the people I shared it with, I have learned how to stand up for myself. My inner core is not fully complete, but the seed has been planted and it is definitely starting to grow.

Tests offer a great opportunity for heightened self-awareness. They provide you with essential feedback about whether or not you are on course in a particular subject. A test is simply a feedback mechanism, so there's no benefit to letting your Inner Critic ("I'm so stupid") or Inner Defender ("My instructor is so lousy") get involved. Here's what your Inner Guide knows: If a test score reveals that you're exactly on course, you can confidently keep doing whatever you've been doing because it's working. However, if a test score reveals that you are off course, it's time to change tactics.

Three factors determine how well you score on tests. The first is how well you have prepared. The second is how well you take tests. The third is how much you have learned from previous tests. The strategies below will enable you to maximize your scores on various kinds of tests.

Before a Test

1. Create a positive affirmation about taking tests. Create an affirming statement such as, "I prepare thoroughly for all tests and love showing how much I've learned." Along with your personal affirmation, repeat this test-taking affirmation to revise your beliefs about your ability to succeed on tests.

2. Find out what will be covered on the test. Ask your instructor questions such as *Will the test cover everything from the beginning of the course or only since the midterm? Will the test cover only material covered in lecture or from the readings as well?* You can plan your studying better when you understand what you are responsible for knowing.

3. Find out how you will be tested. The way you prepare for a test depends on the kind of questions you will be asked: multiple-choice, true-false, fill-in-the-blank, matching, short-answer, skill demonstration, problem-solving, essay, or some other format. To find out, ask your professor. Better yet, if your professor schedules special study sessions, be there. Such sessions provide a perfect opportunity for discovering both what will be on the test and how you will be tested. You may even get valuable practice by taking a test that was given in a previous semester.

4. Set a study schedule. To maximize your learning efficiency, spread your study sessions over time. Avoid cramming! Use your self-management tools from Chapter 4 to schedule and track your studying. Use the effective study strategies you learned in Chapter 5.

5. Take a practice test. Either by yourself or with a study group, create and take a practice test. If you've created Q & A cards, these become your test. Besides readying yourself mentally, a practice test also prepares you emotionally. Having a dress rehearsal helps calm nerves and reduce test anxiety.

6. Visualize success. Create a mental movie of yourself taking the exam with confidence, understanding every question, finishing on time, and receiving your test back with a high grade. Play this positive movie in your mind often.

7. Get to the exam room early and find a comfortable place. Set up your supplies (pens, pencils, paper, white-out, allowed books, calculator, and so on). Have a clock or watch so you can keep track of time. You might even bring a picture that inspires you, like a photo of your family or a picture of you in a graduation gown. If it's a long exam, you might want to bring water and snacks, if they are allowed.

During a Test

8. Right before the exam is handed out, relax, say your affirmation(s), and visualize your success once more. If you have read your assignments, studied regularly, attended classes, and done everything that successful students do, this last-minute mental preparation will enable you to do your best work on the test. Take a deep breath and begin.

9. Skim the test. Get an immediate overview of the whole test. Discover where the easy and difficult questions are. Understand the point value of each question and each section of the test. This information allows you to make strategic choices about how to take the test. While skimming, you may even notice the answer to one question revealed in another question.

10. Read and follow the directions carefully. If you give a great answer to a question that wasn't asked, you won't do well. Likewise, if the directions allow you the option of marking two or more multiple-choice answers and you mark only one, you'll probably lose points. Be sure you understand exactly what you are being asked to do, and do it.

11. Do easy questions first. Easy points build confidence for the rest of the test. Return to the unanswered questions later, doing the ones with higher point values first. By following this plan, if you run out of time, you've earned the most points possible.

12. For multiple-choice questions: 1. Read the question and decide on an answer first; then look for that answer in the list of choices. 2. If you aren't sure, eliminate obvious incorrect answers and choose from those remaining. 3. When eliminating unlikely answers, often you can cross out answers with qualifiers like *all, always, never, must,* or *every.* 4. When eliminating, also look for grammatical clues to cross out an answer (e.g., the subject in the question doesn't agree with the verb in a possible answer). 5. If two answers are similar (e.g., have similar words like *independent* and *interdependent*), one of them is likely the correct answer.

6. Look for answers contained in other questions.

7. If the question is based on a reading passage, read the questions before reading the passage; look for answers as you read the passage.

13. For true-false questions: 1. Answer questions you know first. 2. If any part of the statement is false, the entire statement is false. 3. If the question contains a qualifier like *all, every, never,* or *always,* the answer is probably false. 4. If the question contains a qualifier like *some, a few, occasionally,* or *sometimes,* the answer is probably true.

14. For fill-in-the-blank questions: 1. Make sure your answer fits grammatically into the sentence (e.g., don't insert a noun if the space in the sentence requires a verb). 2. See if the answer is revealed in another question on the test. 3. Always write something in the blank.

15. For short-answer questions: 1. Begin your answer with the key part of the question. Suppose the question is "What are the advantages of using a tracking form?" Begin your answer, "The advantages of using a tracking form include . . ." 2. Plan your answer to fit in the space provided whenever possible. 3. Always write something in response to the question.

16. For matching questions: 1. Match the pairs you know. 2. Cross out pairs as you match them so you

For Better or For Worse®   by Lynn Johnston

can see which choices remain. 3. Match all remaining pairs as best you can.

17. For essay questions: 1. Underline key words in the question. Words like *compare and contrast, describe*, and *explain the cause* require different sorts of responses. Be sure to do what is requested. 2. Brainstorm by jotting down ideas related to the question. 3. Organize your ideas into a logical order. Creating a clear organization not only helps you write an effective essay; it also allows your professor to follow your ideas easily and give you maximum points for your ideas. 4. Reword the question and make it the first sentence of your answer. See suggestion 15 above for an example. 5. Answer questions your reader may have about your ideas. For example, readers often want to know "Why?" and "How do you know?" 6. Offer specific support for your ideas. As you know, the 4 E's (Examples, Experiences, Explanation, and Evidence) are ideal for adding powerful support. 7. Write a conclusion that summarizes the main points you have made. 8. Proofread carefully for grammar, spelling, and punctuation errors. 9. If your handwriting is difficult to read, recopy for neatness. For further neatness, consider printing, writing on every other line, and writing on one side of the paper only.

18. For mathematics tests: 1. Jot down on the test any formulas necessary to solve the problem. 2. Estimate the answer. When finished, compare your answer with your estimate. If they are very different, check your computations. 3. Write out every step of your solution; even if you get the final answer wrong, the instructor may give you partial credit. 4. Revisit each question and confirm that you have done all that was asked. 5. Double-check all calculations.

19. Review your answers. If you finish with time to spare, don't leave yet. Return to the parts with the most points available and check your answers. Check other parts in descending order of points available. Bring white-out to the exam for making corrections neatly. Remain at the exam until you've thoroughly reviewed each question and every answer.

20. Offer an answer for every question. Unless there's a penalty for wrong answers, guess at any questions that remain blank. Even for an essay question, write something. You might pick up a few more points.

21. Match questions to the answer sheet. If the test has a separate answer sheet (as many standardized tests do), confirm that your answers are correctly matched to the appropriate question.

After a Test

22. Reward yourself. No matter how you did on the test, treat yourself for your efforts in preparing for and taking the test. Go out to dinner, take a bubble bath, rent a movie.

23. Get the correct answers to all questions you missed and study them. Ask the instructor for the correct answers. If you don't get the answers from the instructor, ask classmates. Creators may miss a question once, but they never miss it twice. This action is absolutely essential for courses that build directly on previous knowledge, such as mathematics and foreign languages.

24. Analyze your errors. Remember, a test merely provides feedback about whether or not you are on course in a class. Make a careful analysis to maximize the value of this feedback. How many points did you miss because of inadequate preparation (you didn't understand the material)? How many points did you lose because of carelessness (you got the plus and minus signs reversed in a math problem)? How many points did you miss because of poor time management (you ran out of time and lost points on questions you could have answered)? How many points did you miss because of anxiety (your mind went blank)? With this information you'll be able to make a study plan that will create a better grade next time.

Test-Taking Exercise

Create a twenty-five-question test for a course you are now taking; write out your answers to each question. Include five questions each of the following kinds: (1) true-false, (2) matching, (3) fill-in-the-blank, (4) multiple-choice, and (5) short-answer or essay questions. Or, for a mathematics or science course, prepare problems like the ones you have been studying. Design your questions so that a student who answers correctly will be demonstrating the essential knowledge/skills covered in this course. Have a meeting with your instructor and ask for feedback on the quality of your questions and answers. Revise them based on what you discover in the conversation with your instructor.

Embracing Change

Do one thing different this week

Creators make choices with minimal contamination from the past. They do all they can to become aware of the habits of thought, emotion, and behavior that sabotage their success. Additionally, they identify limiting beliefs they have about themselves, other people or the world. With this awareness of their Scripts, they take steps to revise any self-sabotaging habit patterns or beliefs, empowering them to create greater success. From the actions below, pick ONE new belief or behavior and experiment with it for one week, seeing if this new choice helps you create more positive outcomes and experiences. After seven days, assess your results. If your outcomes and experiences improve, you now have a tool that will help you stay on course for the rest of your life.

Beliefs and Behaviors	Day 1	Day 2	Day 3	Day 4	Day 5	Day 6	Day 7
Think: "I am choosing habit patterns and core beliefs that support my success."							
Identify a "strange choice" that someone else makes and speculate about what belief about themselves, other people or life would generate such a choice.							
Identify a choice I make that someone else might think is "strange" and speculate about what belief about myself, other people or life would cause me to make such a choice.							
Identify an area of my life in which I am off course (even a little).							
Identify a **behavior** that gets me off course and replace it with one that is more self-supporting.							
Identify a **thought** that gets me off course and replace it with one that is more self-supporting.							
Identify an **emotion** that gets me off course and replace it with one that is more self-supporting.							
Identify a **belief** that gets me off course and replace it with one that is more self-supporting.							
Identify the experience that I most enjoyed this week and identify careers that would provide similar experiences on a regular basis.							
Review my personal rules (Journal Entry 22) and identify which ones I kept that day.							
Use the following test-taking strategy (write your choice from pages 170–172):							

(continued on page 175)

During my seven-day experiment, what happened?

As a result of what happened, what did I learn or relearn?

Adopting Lifelong Learning

7

As a Creator, I take personal responsibility for learning all of the information, skills, and life lessons necessary to achieve my goals and dreams.

I learn something valuable from every experience I have.

SUCCESSFUL STUDENTS . . .	STRUGGLING STUDENTS . . .
become active learners, implementing a variety of deep-processing strategies, distributing them frequently over time, and spending a significant amount of time on each one.	learn superficially, forgetting much of what they learn shortly after being tested.
discover their preferred learning style, utilizing strategies that allow them to maximize their learning of valuable new information and skills.	often experience frustration, boredom, or resistance when their instructors don't teach the way they prefer to learn.
learn to make course corrections, giving them the flexibility to change their approach, improve their results, and learn powerful life lessons.	keep doing what they are doing in college and in life even when it isn't working.

A Fish Story

One September morning, on their first day of college, two dozen first-year students made their way into the biology laboratory. They sat down six at a lab table and glanced about for the professor. Because this was their first college class, most of the students were a bit nervous. A few introduced themselves. Others kept checking their watches.

At exactly nine o'clock, the professor, wearing a crisply pressed white lab coat, entered the room. "Good morning," he said. He set a white plate in the middle of each table. On each plate lay a small fish.

"Please observe the fish," the professor said. "Then write down your observations." He turned and left the room.

The students looked at each other, puzzled. This was *bizarre!* Oh, well. They took out scrap paper and wrote notes such as, *I see a small fish.* One student added, *It's on a white plate.*

Satisfied, they set their pens down and waited. And waited. For the entire class period, they waited. A couple of students whispered that it was a trick. They said the professor was probably testing them to see if they'd do something wrong. Time crawled by. Still they waited, trying to do nothing that would get them in trouble. Finally, one student mumbled that she was going to be late for her next class. She picked up her books and stood. She paused. Others rose as well and began filing out of the room. Some looked cautiously over their shoulders as they left.

When the students entered the biology lab for their second class, they found the same white plates with the same small fish already waiting on their laboratory tables. At exactly nine o'clock, the professor entered the room. "Good morning. Please take out your observations of the fish," he said.

Students dug into their notebooks or book bags. Many could not find their notes. Those few who could held them up for the professor to see as he walked from table to table.

After visiting each student, the professor said, "Please observe the fish. Write down all of your observations."

"Will there be a test on this?" one student asked. But the professor had already left the room, closing the door behind him. Frustrated, the student blurted, "Why doesn't he just tell us what he wants us to know?"

The students looked at one another, more puzzled. They peered at the fish. Those few who had found their notes glanced from the fish to their notes and back again. Was the professor crazy? What else were they supposed to notice? It was only a stupid fish.

About then, one student spied a book on the professor's desk. It was a book for identifying fish, and she snatched it up. Using the book, she quickly discovered what kind of fish was lying on her plate. She read eagerly, recording in her notes all of the facts she found about her fish. Others saw her and asked to use the book, too. She passed the book to other tables, and her classmates soon found descriptions of their fish. After about fifteen minutes the students sat back, very pleased with themselves. Chatter died down. They waited. But the professor didn't return. As the period ended, all of the students carefully put their notes away.

The same fish on the same white plate greeted each student in the third class. The professor entered at nine o'clock. "Good morning," he said. "Please hold up your observations." All of the students held up their notes immediately. They looked at each other, smiling, as the professor walked from table to table, looking at their work. Once again, he walked toward the door. "Please . . . *observe* the fish. Write down *all* of your observations," he said. And then he left.

The students couldn't believe it. They grumbled and complained. *This guy is nuts. When is he going to teach us something? What are we paying tuition for, anyway?* Students at one table, however, began observing their fish more closely. Other tables followed their example.

The first thing all of the students noticed was the biting odor of aging fish. A few students recorded details about the fish's color that they had failed to observe in the previous two classes. They wondered if the colors had been there originally or if the colors had appeared as the fish aged. Each group measured its fish. They poked it and described its texture. One student looked in its mouth and found that he could see light through its gills. Another student found a small balance beam, and each group weighed its fish. They passed around someone's pocket knife. With it, they sliced open the fish and examined its insides. In the stomach of one fish they found a smaller fish. They wrote quickly, and their notes soon overflowed onto three and four sheets of paper. Finally someone shouted, "Hey, class was over ten minutes ago." They carefully placed their notes in three-ring binders. They said good-bye to their fish, wondering if their finny friends would be there on Monday.

They were, and a vile smell filled the laboratory. The professor strode into the room at exactly nine o'clock. The students immediately thrust their notes in the air. "Good morning," the professor said cheerfully, making his way from student to student. He took longer than ever to examine their notes. The students shifted anxiously in their chairs as the professor edged ever closer to the door. How could they endure the smell for another class period? At the door, the professor turned to the students.

"All right," he said. "Now we can begin."
—Inspired by Samuel J. Scudder, "Take This Fish and Look at It" (1874)

- If you had been in this biology lab class, what lessons about college and life would you have learned from the experience?

DIVING DEEPER: When you think you have discovered one life lesson, dive deeper and find another even more powerful lesson. And then another and another.

Becoming an Active Learner

FOCUS QUESTIONS How does the human brain learn? How can you use this knowledge to become a highly effective learner?

Successful athletes understand how to get the most out of their physical abilities. Likewise, if you want to be a successful learner, you need to understand how to get the most out of your mental abilities. Much has been discovered, especially in the last few decades, about how human beings learn. To benefit from these discoveries, let's take a quick peek into our brains.

How the human brain learns

The human brain, weighing in at about three pounds, is composed of trillions of cells. About 100 billion of them are neurons, and here's where much of our learning takes place. When a potential learning stimulus occurs (such as reading this sentence), some neurons send out spikes of electrical activity that cause nearby neurons to generate their own electrical impulses, creating a pattern of neurons that fire together. I like to picture a bunch of neurons joining hands in my brain, jumping up and down, and having a learning party. If this particular party happens only once, the stimulus that caused it is likely to be lost (such as a joke you heard yesterday but can't remember today). However, if you cause the same collection of neurons to fire repeatedly (such as telling the joke to ten different people), the result is a long-term memory. According to David Sousa, author of *How the Brain Learns*, "Eventually, repeated firing of the pattern binds the neurons together so that if one fires, they all fire, ultimately forming a new memory trace."

In other words, if you want learning to stick, you need to create networks of neurons that fire together. In this way, learning literally changes the structure of your brain. Neuroscientist Robert Jacobs and his colleagues found in autopsy studies that graduate students actually had 40 percent more neural connections than those of high school dropouts. Jacobs' research joins many other brain studies to reveal an important fact: **To excel as a learner, create as many neural connections in your brain as possible.**

> *The human brain has the largest area of uncommitted cortex (no particular required function) of any species on earth. This gives humans extraordinary flexibility and capacity for learning.*
>
> Eric Jensen

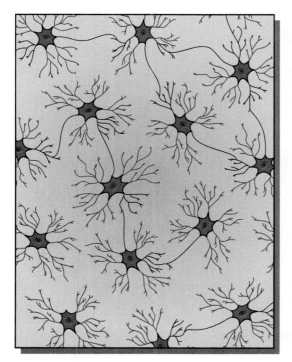

Neurons Before Learning

Neurons After Learning

Three keys to deep and lasting learning

With this brief exposure to what goes on in our brains, let's explore how highly effective learners maximize their learning potential. Whether they know it or not, they have figured out how to create many strong neural connections in their brain. And you can, too.

The short answer is: Become an active learner. Learning is not a spectator sport. You don't create deep and lasting learning by passively listening to a lecture, or casually skimming your texts, or having a tutor solve math problems for you. In order to create strong neural networks, you've got to participate actively in the learning process. Here are three keys to help you do that.

In a time of drastic change, it is the learners who inherit the future.

Eric Hoffer

1. Prior Learning: Past learning success enhances present learning in two ways. First, as we learned in Chapter 3, past success increases your expectations of present success so your achievement motivation stays high. Second, brain research reveals that when you can connect what you are learning now to previously stored information (e.g., already formed neural networks), you learn the information or skill faster and more deeply. For example, the first word processing program I learned was Word Perfect. It took me a long time to learn because I had no past knowledge about word processing (meaning my brain contained no neural networks relevant to my present learning). First I had to learn what word processing can do (such as delete whole paragraphs) and then I had to learn how to do that function with Word Perfect. Later, when I was learning another word processing program, Microsoft Word, I had a great advantage. Not only did I have my previous success to give me confidence, I already knew what word processing can do, so I was able to learn this new program in a fraction of the time. Put another way, I already had neural networks in my brain related to word processing, and learning Microsoft Word got those neurons partying.

The contribution of prior learning to new learning helps explain why some learners have difficulty with academic skills such as math, reading, and writing. If their earlier learning was shaky, they're going to have difficulty with new learning. They don't have strong neural networks on which to attach the new learning. It's like trying to construct a house on a weak foundation. In such a situation, the best option is to go back and strengthen the foundation, which is exactly the purpose of developmental courses. However, there's no point trying to learn these foundational skills the same way you learned them before. After all, how you learned them before didn't make the learning stick. So this time you need to employ different, more effective learning strategies, ones that will create the needed neural networks. If that's your situation, this time you'll have the advantage of employing the more effective strategies described below.

2. Quality of Processing. How I exercise affects my physical strength, and likewise how I study affects the strength of my neural networks and, therefore, the quality of my learning. Some information (such as medical terms or multiplication tables) must be recalled exactly as presented. For such learning tasks, memorization strategies (like those in the Wise Choices in College section later in this chapter) are the type of processing that will help most. However, much of what you'll be asked to learn in college is too complex for mere memorization (though many struggling students try). For mastering complex information and skills, you'll want to use what learning experts call **deep processing** (or "elaborative rehearsal"). The Wise Choices in College sections in Chapters 2–7 offer many examples of deep-processing strategies (e.g., creating graphic organizers, generating important questions, summarizing information in your own words). These are the types of processing activities that successful learners actively employ in their studies. These efforts are what make the learning stick for months, years, and even a lifetime.

Almost everyone has had occasion to look back upon his school days and wonder what has become of the knowledge he was supposed to have amassed during his days of schooling.

John Dewey

Successful athletes know the value of varied training activities, often called cross training. Similarly, successful learners know the value of using *varied* **deep-processing** strategies. That's because the more different ways you deep-process new learning, the stronger your neural networks will become. For example, to effectively learn the information you're presently reading, active learners might do many (perhaps all) of the following deep-processing strategies:

1. Underline or highlight key ideas.
2. Create a concept map or outline of this information.
3. Make a list of ten favorite deep-processing strategies from Chapters 2–7.
4. Discuss this information with a classmate.
5. Create a two-column chart comparing effective learners and ineffective learners.
6. List questions about learning and ask them in class.
7. Read the book mentioned in this section, *How the Brain Learns*.
8. Dive deep while writing Journal Entry 23.
9. Draw a diagram showing how human brains learn.
10. Participate fully in the related in-class activity.
11. Create a test based on the information in this section.
12. Teach this information to someone not reading *On Course*.

When you actively study any information or skill using numerous and varied deep-processing strategies, you create and strengthen related neural networks and your learning soars.

Quantity of Processing. The quality of your learning is significantly affected by how often and how long you engage in varied deep processing. The most effective approach is called "distributed practice." As the name implies, the human brain learns best when learning efforts are distributed over time. No successful athlete waits until the night before a competition to begin training.

Why, then, do struggling students think they can start studying the night before a test? An all-night cram session may make a deposit in their short-term memory, perhaps even allowing them to pass a test the next day. However, most students have experienced the ineffectiveness of cramming when they encounter "summer amnesia"—forgetting in the fall much of what they learned during the previous school year. That's the result of not creating strong neural networks that make learning endure. To create strong neural networks, process the target information or skill with varied deep-processing strategies and do it ***frequently***. As an example, on each of the next twelve days you could do one of the dozen deep-processing strategies listed above. Doing so will cause your related neural networks to fire often, become stronger, and create more deep and lasting learning. A Tracking Form (see page 100) would be ideal for managing this learning plan.

Also important in building strong neural networks is the *length* of time you spend each time you process the target information or skills. Clearly, deep processing for only five minutes generates less learning than deep processing for sixty minutes. So, highly effective learners put in **sufficient time on task.** The traditional guideline is two hours of study time for every hour of class time. Many struggling students, however, not only don't study very often, they don't study very long. Their minds wander. They get distracted. They get up to answer the phone and the next thing they know, it's time to go to bed. Some students may have a chemical imbalance that prevents them from focusing for long periods of time. If you think this may be true for you, make an appointment with your college's disability counselor to begin finding a remedy. But for most students, the more likely cause is a lack of perceived value in their studies. As discussed in Chapter 3, motivation drops when we don't perceive value in the effort. If this is true for you, get clear on how mastering this subject will *benefit* you. Sometimes the course content is essential in a chosen career. Or the value could be having a desired experience, such as the mental challenge of solving math problems. Or maybe you just accept that this course is a necessary (if undesired) step toward your valued degree. In this case, just grind it out and do what is needed to pass the course, knowing that afterwards you'll be one step closer to your valued goal of a college degree.

But what if you *are* studying for many hours and still struggling? When it comes to time on task, struggling students can fool themselves. They study for a long time, then wonder why their grades are poor. Their Inner Defender may blame the instructor: *Her tests are so unfair. I studied for hours and she still failed me.* Or, their Inner Critic may point the finger of blame inward: *It doesn't matter how long I study, I'll never get it.* More likely, they weren't using deep-processing techniques. Remember those times when you read a whole chapter of a book and later couldn't recall a thing? Sure you put in the time, but since it wasn't quality time (deep processing), no change took place in the neurons in your brain. So make your study time pay off by using varied deep-processing strategies.

Your learning choices

Learning. . . . should be a joy and full of excitement. It is life's greatest adventure; it is an illustrated excursion into the minds of noble and learned men, not a conducted tour through a jail.

Taylor Caldwell

With what you now know about how the human brain learns, you have choices that most struggling students don't even know exist. You can improve your efforts by connecting new learning to what you learned in the past, or move to a lower level course and strengthen your foundation. You can implement a variety of the deep-processing strategies found in the Wise Choices in College sections of Chapters 2–6 or, for remembering factual information, use the effective memory strategies found in the Wise Choices section later in this chapter. And you can use self-management tools like the Tracking Form and 32-Day Commitment Form to help you distribute your learning over time and put in sufficient time on task.

These are the strategies that active learners use to build strong neural networks in their brain. They will work for you, too.

Journal Entry 23

In this activity, you'll explore how you learned something (anything) using the approach of an active learner. Then you'll plan how you might use this same approach to improve your learning outcomes and experiences in college.

 1. Write about something you have learned simply because you loved learning it. It can be something you learned in school or anywhere else. What are you good at? What do you know more about than most people? What are your hobbies? What have you spent a lot of time doing? After identifying what you learned, discuss the following questions (and anything else you wish to explore):

- What was the most helpful thing you did to learn this (deep processing)?
- What else did you do to learn this (variety of approaches)?
- How often did you engage in learning this (frequency)?
- When you engaged in learning this, how long did you usually spend (duration)?
- How did you feel when you engaged in learning this (experiences)?
- What were the rewards for learning this (outcomes)?

Your journal entry might begin, "One thing I enjoyed learning is . . .

 2. Write about a course you are now taking from the point of view of an active learner. Here's how: Imagine that it is a year from now. You passed the course with an A. In fact, you are the most successful and skilled learner your instructor has ever taught. That's why your instructor has invited you back to speak to the present class, asking you to tell them exactly what you did to learn so effectively in the course. Discuss the same seven questions from Step 1 (and anything else you want to tell the present class of students).

Remember, you are not limited to what you are presently doing in the course you choose to write about. You are visualizing yourself as the most highly effective learner you can imagine doing all of the things that outstanding learners do. Your journal entry might begin, *I'm grateful for this opportunity to share with you exactly what I did that helped me be such a successful learner when I took this class . . .*

Remember, diving deep changes the neurons in your brain and leads to deep and lasting learning. You can practice diving deep and being an active learner right here in this journal entry. As you may have realized by now, writing a journal is a very powerful way to deep-process your experiences!

Discovering Your Preferred Learning Style

 FOCUS QUESTIONS What is your preferred way of learning? What can you do when your instructor doesn't teach the way you prefer to learn?

Education is our passport to the future, for tomorrow belongs to the people who prepare for it today. . . . Give your brain as much attention as you do your hair and you'll be a thousand times better off.

Malcolm X

Especially today, well into the information age, staying on course to our goals and dreams requires us to learn vast amounts of information, facts, theories, and skills. Now that you know how the human brain learns best, all that learning shouldn't be a problem for an effective learner. But further research on how the human brain learns reveals a complication. Each of us has our own preferred way of taking in and deeply processing our learning experiences. Each of us has a preferred way of creating meaning from the jumble and rush of information we encounter in college, at work, at home, and everywhere else in life. Knowing how you personally prefer to learn gives you a great advantage everywhere in life, but especially in college when you encounter an instructor who doesn't teach the way you prefer to learn.

Self-Assessment: How I prefer to learn

Before reading on, take a self-assessment inventory. It will give you insights about how your brain, with its unique set of past learning experiences, prefers to gather and process information.

In each group below, rank all four answers (A, B, C, D) from the *least* true of you to the *most* true of you. Give each possible answer a different score. There are no right or wrong answers; your opinion is all that matters. Remember, items that are MOST TRUE OF YOU get a 4. You can also take this self-assessment on the Internet at *college.hmco.com/pic/downing5e.*

Least true of you ← 1 2 3 4 → Most true of your

1. I would prefer to take a college course

——— A. in science.

——— B. in business management.

——— C. in group dynamics.

——— D. as an independent study that I design.

2. I solve problems by

——— A. standing back, thinking, and analyzing what is wrong.

——— B. doing something practical and seeing how it works.

——— C. leaping in and doing what feels right at the time.

——— D. trusting my intuition.

3. Career groups that appeal to me are

——— A. engineer, researcher, financial planner.

——— B. administrator, city manager, military officer.

——— C. teacher, social worker, physical therapist.

——— D. entrepreneur, artist, inventor.

4. Before I make a decision, I need to be sure that

——— A. I understand all of the relevant ideas and facts.

——— B. I'm confident my solution will work.

——— C. I know how my decision will affect others.

——— D. I haven't overlooked a more creative solution.

5. I believe that

——— A. life today needs more logical thinking and less emotion.

——— B. life rewards the practical, hard-working, down-to-earth person.

——— C. life must be lived with enthusiasm and passion.

——— D. life, like music, is best composed by creative inspiration, not by rules.

6. I would enjoy reading a book titled

_____ A. *Great Theories and Ideas of the Twentieth Century.*

_____ B. *How to Organize Your Life and Accomplish More.*

_____ C. *The Keys to Developing Better Relationships.*

_____ D. *Tapping into Your Creative Genius.*

7. I believe the most valuable information for making decisions comes from

_____ A. logical analysis of facts.

_____ B. what has worked in the past.

_____ C. gut feelings.

_____ D. my imagination.

Knowledge of our brain dominance empowers us as individuals and groups to achieve more of our full potential.
        Ned Herrmann

8. I am persuaded by an argument that

_____ A. offers statistical or factual proof.

_____ B. presents the findings of recognized experts.

_____ C. is passionately presented by someone I admire.

_____ D. explores innovative possibilities for future change.

9. I prefer a teacher who

_____ A. lectures knowledgeably about the important facts and theories of the subject.

_____ B. provides practical, step-by-step, hands-on activities with clear learning objectives.

_____ C. stimulates exciting class discussions and group projects.

_____ D. challenges me to think for myself and explore the subject in my own way.

10. People who know me would describe me as

_____ A. logical.

_____ B. practical.

_____ C. emotional.

_____ D. creative.

Total your ten scores for each letter and record them below:

_____ A. THINKING   _____ B. DOING

_____ C. FEELING   _____ D. INNOVATING

Your scores suggest the following:

30–40 = You have a strong preference to learn this way.

20–29 = You are capable of learning this way when necessary.

10–19 = You avoid this way of learning.

Discoveries about learning styles can help us maximize what we learn. These discoveries suggest that each of us develops a preferred way of learning, a style that requires less effort from our brain, and that style produces more learning than a less preferred style of learning. For a quick understanding of learning preferences, sign your name twice, once with each hand. Notice that your preferred hand allows you to write quickly, easily, effectively, much as your preferred learning style allows you to learn. Your non-preferred hand usually writes more slowly, painstakingly, less effectively, much the way you learn with your less preferred style(s) of learning. You are able to sign your name with either hand, but you *prefer* one over the other.

Although there is no preferred way for everyone to learn, there is a preferred way for *you* to learn, and the self-assessment you just took begins your understanding of what that way is. Your scores indicate your order of preference for four different learning approaches: THINKING, DOING, FEELING, and INNOVATING. More specifically, your scores suggest what types of questions motivate you, how you prefer to gather relevant information, and how you prefer to process information to discover meaningful answers.

It is very natural to teach in the same way we learn. It may be difficult for us to believe that others could learn in a way that is foreign and difficult for us.

Carolyn Mamchur

Traditional college teaching—characterized by lectures and textbook assignments—typically favors the learning preference of THINKERS, and, to a somewhat lesser degree, DOERS. As more instructors discover the importance of individual learning styles, however, many are adapting their teaching methods to help all learners maximize their academic potential.

However, if you encounter an instructor who doesn't teach all of the time the way you prefer to learn (and most won't), take responsibility for your learning and experiment with some of the suggestions below. Perhaps most important of all, develop flexibility in how you learn. The more choices you have, the richer will be your learning experience and the greater your success.

In the following paragraphs, you'll discover how Thinkers, Doers, Feelers, and Innovators prefer to learn. You may want to start by reading the section about your own learning preference (based on your self-assessment score). There you'll find options to use when your instructors don't teach as you prefer to learn. By looking at the other learning styles as well, you'll see additional ways to expand your menu of effective learning strategies. Your goal here is to find deep-processing strategies that are compatible with and supportive of your preferred way of learning.

A. Thinking learners

Motivating questions: Thinking learners are energized by questions that begin with "What?" *What theory supports that claim? What does a statistical analysis show? What is the logic here? What facts do you have? What experts have written about this?*

Preferred ways of gathering information: Thinkers enjoy pondering facts and theories. They learn well from instructors who present information with lectures, visual aids, PowerPoint slides, instructor-modeled problem solving, textbook readings, independent library research, and activities that call upon logical skills, such as debates. Thinkers benefit from time to reflect on what they are learning.

Preferred ways of processing information: Thinkers respect logical argument supported by documented facts and data. They are uncomfortable with answers that depend on tradition, emotion, personal considerations, or intuition. They excel at analyzing, dissecting, figuring out, and using logic to arrive at reasoned answers. Thinkers like well-organized and well-documented information, and they benefit from deep-processing strategies that bring order to complex information, such as creating outlines or comparison charts.

When your instructor doesn't teach to your preferred style:
What you can do:

- Construct important "What?" questions and search for their answers in class sessions and homework assignments.
- Construct and answer other types of questions your instructor might ask: How? Who? Why? What if?
- Read all of your textbook assignments carefully, creating well-organized notes that identify the key points.
- Resist getting upset if your instructor asks you to work in groups or has students do some of the teaching.
- Organize your lecture and reading notes in a logical fashion, using outlines and comparison charts wherever appropriate.
- Study with classmates who have different preferred ways of learning from your own as they may provide insights about how to learn best from your instructor's teaching style.

Ask your instructor to do the following:

- Answer your important "What?" questions in class or in a conference.
- List important points on the blackboard or on handouts.
- Provide handouts of PowerPoint presentations.
- Allow students time to answer discussion questions in writing before answering them aloud.
- Suggest additional readings, especially those written by recognized authorities in the subject.
- Provide examples of past test questions.
- Demonstrate the step-by-step solution of a math or science problem.
- Provide data or other objective evidence that supports theories presented.

B. Doing learners

Motivating questions: Doing learners are energized by questions that begin with "How?" *How does this work? How can I use this? How will this help me or others? How did this work in the past? How can I do this more efficiently? How do experts do this?*

Preferred ways of gathering information: Doers enjoy taking action. They learn well from instructors who present factual information and practical skills in a step-by-step, logical manner; who then present models or examples from experts in the field; and who allow students to do hands-on work in guided labs or practice applications. Doers benefit from the opportunity to dive right in and do the work.

Preferred ways of processing information: Doers honor objective testing of an idea or theory, whether their own or an expert's. They are uncomfortable with answers based on abstract theories, emotion, personal considerations, or intuition. They excel at being unbiased, taking action and observing outcomes, following procedures, and using confirmed facts to arrive at reasoned answers. Doers, like thinkers, appreciate well-organized and well-documented information. They benefit from deep-processing strategies that bring order to complex information, such as creating flow charts or a model of the concepts to be learned.

When your instructor doesn't teach to your preferred style:
What you can do:

The important thing is not to stop questioning. . . . Never lose a holy curiosity.
Albert Einstein

- Construct important "How?" questions and search for their answers.
- Construct and answer other types of questions your instructor might ask: What? Who? Why? What if?
- Practice using the course information or skills outside of class.
- Find someone who uses the course information or skills in their work and shadow them for a day or more.
- Resist getting upset if your instructor seems more interested in theories than in application.
- Organize your lecture and reading notes in a step-by-step fashion, using outlines and study charts wherever appropriate.
- Study with classmates who have preferred ways of learning different from your own as they may provide insights into how to learn best from your instructor's teaching style.

Ask your instructor to do the following:

- Answer your important "How?" questions in class or in a conference.
- Explain practical applications for theories taught in the course.
- Provide a visual model of the concept (such as the Scripts Model in Chapter 6)

- List important steps on the blackboard or on handouts.
- Demonstrate the information or skill in a step-by-step manner.
- Invite guest speakers who can explain real-world application of the course information or skill in their daily work.
- Observe and give corrective feedback as you demonstrate your hands-on understanding of the subject.

C. Feeling learners

Motivating questions: Feeling learners are energized by questions that begin with "Why?" or "Who?" *Why do I want or need to know this subject? Who is going to teach me? Who is going to learn this with me? Why do they want to know this information? Who here cares about me? Who here do I care about?*

Preferred ways of gathering information: Feeling learners enjoy personal connections and an emotionally supportive environment. They learn well from instructors who are warm and caring; who value feelings as well as thoughts; and who create a safe, accepting classroom atmosphere with activities like group work, role playing, and sharing of individual experiences. Feeling learners benefit from an opportunity to relate personally with both their instructors and classmates.

Preferred ways of processing information: Feeling learners honor their emotions and seek answers that are personally meaningful. They are uncomfortable with answers based on abstract theories or dispassionate facts and data. They excel at responding to emotional currents in groups, empathizing with others, considering others' feelings in making decisions, and using empathy and gut feelings to arrive at personally relevant answers.

When your instructor doesn't teach to your preferred style:
What you can do:

It is only an education that liberates. Education helps one cease being intimidated by strange situations. Once you have it in your mind, you can go anywhere.

Maya Angelou

- Construct important "Who?" and "Why?" questions and search for their answers.
- Construct and answer other types of questions your instructor might ask: What? How? What if?
- Discover the value of this subject for you personally.
- Organize your notes and study materials using concept maps.
- Resist feeling upset if your instructor seems distant or aloof.
- Practice using the course information or skill with people in your life.
- Make friends with classmates and discuss the subject with them outside of class.

- Record class sessions (with permission) and listen to recordings during free time.
- Study with classmates who have different preferred ways of learning from your own as they may provide insights into how to learn best from your instructor's teaching style.
- Teach what you are learning to someone else.

Ask your instructor to do the following:

- Answer your important "Who?" and "Why?" questions in class or in a conference.
- Explain how you might make a personal application of the course information.
- Meet with you outside of class, perhaps for tutoring, so you can get to know one another better and feel more comfortable in the class.
- Provide occasional opportunities for small-group activities within the classroom.
- Tell stories about how he or she (or someone else) has personally used the information or skills taught in the course.
- Let you do some of the course assignments with a partner or in a group.
- Allow students time to talk in pairs about discussion questions before answering them in front of the whole class.

D. Innovating learners

Motivating questions: Innovating learners are energized by questions that begin with "What if?" or "What else?" *What if I tried doing this another way? What else could I do with this? What if the situation were different?*

Preferred ways of gathering information: Innovators enjoy seeking new possibilities, imagining unseen futures. They learn well from instructors who encourage students to discover new and innovative applications; who allow students to use their intuition to create something new; and who use approaches such as independent projects, flexible rules and deadlines, a menu of optional assignments, metaphors, art projects, and visual aids. Innovators benefit from the freedom to work independently and let their imaginations run free.

Preferred ways of processing information: Innovators honor personal imagination and intuition. They are uncomfortable with answers based on abstract theories, cold facts, hard data, emotion, or personal considerations. They excel at trusting their inner vision, their intuitive sense of exciting future possibilities, and their imaginations.

Since we can't know what knowledge will be most needed in the future, it is senseless to try to teach it in advance. Instead, we should try to turn out people who love learning so much and learn so well that they will be able to learn whatever needs to be learned.

John Holt

When your instructor doesn't teach to your preferred style:

What you can do:

- Construct important "What if?" and "What else?" questions and search for their answers.
- Construct and answer other types of questions your instructor might ask: What? How? Who? Why?
- Resist feeling upset when your instructor or classmates don't immediately see something as you do.
- Organize your notes and study materials using concept maps and personally meaningful symbols or pictures.
- Think about the content creatively (how could I adapt this?) and metaphorically (what is this like?)
- Study with classmates who have different preferred ways of learning from your own as they may provide insights into how to learn best from your instructor's teaching style.

Ask your instructor to do the following:

- Answer your important "What if?" and "What else?" questions in class or in a conference.
- Allow you to design some of your own assignments for the course.
- Use visual aids to explain concepts in class.
- Recommend a book for you to read by the most innovative or rebellious thinker in the field.
- Evaluate your learning with essays and independent projects rather than with objective tests.

Highly effective learners realize that not all instructors will teach to their preferred way of learning. They take responsibility for not only *what* they learn in every class but also *how* they learn it. They discover deep-processing methods that maximize their learning regardless of the subject or the way the instructor teaches.

Journal Entry 24

In this activity, you'll apply what you have learned about your preferred ways of learning to improve your results in a challenging course.

 Write about the most challenging course you are taking this semester. Using what you just learned about how you prefer to learn, explain why the course may be difficult for you: Consider the subject matter, the teaching methods of the instructor, the textbook, and any other factors that may contribute to making this course difficult for someone with your preferred way(s) of

Young cat, if you keep your eyes open enough, oh, the stuff you would learn! The most wonderful stuff!

Dr. Seuss

learning. (If you are not taking a challenging course this semester, write about the most challenging course you have taken any time in your education.)

2. **Using what you now know about the way you prefer to learn, write about choices you can make that will help you learn this challenging subject more easily.** Refer to pages 187–192 for possible choices.

By choosing different ways of learning in a challenging course, you can avoid the excusing, blaming, and complaining of a Victim and apply the solution-orientation of a Creator.

The challenge for me was chemistry. In lecture, the words were coming at me but the material wasn't sticking. The teacher was dry, standoffish and intimidating, and he never joked around. I could read the book, reread it, and still wonder what I had just read. I was so frustrated because I needed to pass chemistry to get into my major. Realizing this, I was spending ten to twelve hours a week studying, and I even started a study group and got a tutor. With all this help, I was doing fine on the assignments, but the tests were killing me. I would take one look at them and my mind would go blank. I was stressed and so tempted to drop the course.

About that time I took the self-assessment in *On Course* about how I prefer to learn. I scored highest as a *feeling* learner, with *doing* learner second. I learned it's important for me to relate well personally with my instructors and classmates. Also, I want to see and touch what I'm learning, and I'm not comfortable with abstract theories and dispassionate facts. BINGO!! The light went on. My favorite subjects in high school were classes like art and English where I could be creative and hands on. My favorite teacher was my art teacher who is a kind, caring person who told lots of stories that related art to lessons in life. Now I'm in chemistry which is exactly the type of subject I'm uncomfortable with and I have a professor who is distant and intimidating.

ONE STUDENT'S STORY
Melissa Thompson
Madison Area Technical College, Wisconsin

I knew what I had to do, and I probably wouldn't have done it before taking my College Success class.

I asked my chemistry instructor if I could stay after class to talk with him. I explained what I had discovered about my learning preference and why I was so challenged by chemistry. He agreed to meet with me after every class. During lecture, I'd write questions in the margins of my notes or leave a space wherever I got lost. I'd also highlight things in my book that I didn't understand. Going over my questions with him after class was helpful because everything was fresh in my mind. He would take my questions and answer them in different ways than he had in class. Then I would tell him what I thought he was saying and he would coach me until I had it right. Once I got to know him, I realized he was actually very friendly and helpful. He's a quiet person, but I could tell how much he loves chemistry. Before, when I walked into class, I felt intimidated, but before long I felt more comfortable.

Soon after these meetings started, my grades began to come up. I was retaining the information and it showed. I worked hard, and in the end I did pass chemistry. If I hadn't found out about my learning preference and done something different, I don't think I would have passed. My professor is definitely a "thinker," and he handles things so differently than I do. Once I understood the situation, though, I knew I had to step up and be in control of my life, and I did.

Learning to Make Course Corrections

 FOCUS QUESTIONS   How can you recognize when you are off course? More important, how can you get back on course?

Here's a little problem for you: Draw *one straight line* that touches all three of the stars below:

The capacity to correct course is the capacity to reduce the differences between the path you are on now and the optimal path to your objective . . . .

Charles Garfield

Notice how your Scripts and preferred learning style dictate the way you go about solving this problem:

- **What are you thinking?** Do you think, *This is great, I love intellectual challenges,* or *I was never any good at puzzles,* or *This is impossible,* or *Oh, I already know the answer,* or *Who cares?*

- **What are you feeling?** Do you feel excited by the challenge, or overwhelmed by the difficulty, or irritated by the request, or bored by your disinterest, or depressed by your inability to solve it immediately?

- **What are you doing?** Do you immediately begin drawing lines to seek a solution, or sit back trying to think of a solution, or turn the page to look for the answer, or ask a friend, or keep reading without attempting to solve the puzzle?

- **What are your unconscious core beliefs?** This puzzle is easy to solve, but most people have unconscious beliefs that keep them from seeing the answer. What belief is keeping you from solving this simple problem?

If your present habit patterns and beliefs aren't working to solve the puzzle, you'll have to change your approach. The same is true in life. When you face a problem and your present choices aren't working, you need to learn to do, think, feel, or believe something different. In other words, you need to make a course correction.

All human beings are periodically tested by the power of the universe . . . how one performs under pressure is the true measure of one's spirit, heart, and desire.

Spike Lee

Change requires self-awareness and courage

Before we can make a course correction, we need to be aware that we are off course. Luckily, the world bombards us with helpful feedback every day. Sadly, many ignore it. At first, feedback taps us politely on the shoulder. If we pay no heed, feedback shakes us vigorously. If we continue to ignore it, feedback may knock us to our knees, creating havoc in our lives. This havoc might look like failing out of school or getting fired from a job. There's usually plenty of feedback long before the failure or firing if we will only heed its message.

In college, think of yourself as an airplane pilot and your instructors as your personal air traffic controllers. When they correct you in class or write a comment on an assignment or give you a grade on a test, what they are really saying is, *You're on course, on course . . . whoops, now you're off course, off course . . . okay, that's right, now you're back on course.* Airplane pilots appreciate such feedback. Without it they might not get to their destination. Likewise, effective learners welcome their instructors' feedback and use it to stay on course. They heed every suggestion instructors offer on assignments; they understand the message in their test scores; they request clarification of any feedback they don't understand; and they ask for additional feedback. Maybe the idea of paying attention to feedback sounds obvious to you, but I can't tell you how many students I've had who made the same mistakes over and over, ignoring both my feedback and the reality that when you keep doing what you've been doing, you'll keep getting what you've been getting.

Everywhere in life, heeding feedback is critical to creating the life you want. The feedback may be something said by friends, lovers, spouses, parents, children, neighbors, bosses, co-workers, and even strangers. Or it may be more subtle, coming in the form of an unsatisfying relationship, a boring job or runaway credit card debt. Any areas of discomfort or distress are red flags of warning: *Hey, wake up! You're headed away from your desired outcomes and experiences. You need to make a change!*

You see, it's one thing to be aware that you are off course. It's quite another to do something about it. Something different. Something uncomfortable. Maybe even something frightening. Course correction is not for the disempowered. It requires courage to admit that what you are doing isn't working, to abandon the familiar, and to walk into the unknown. Victims stay stuck. Creators change.

Change and lifelong learning

When we make a course correction, we hope the change improves the quality of our lives. Sometimes it does. Sometimes it doesn't. But change *always* presents an opportunity for learning. That's the way the University of Life works, and you're enrolled whether you know it or not. Courses in the University of Life are a little different from those in a regular college. These courses are often offered by the Department of Adversities and they include subjects such as Problems 101, Obstacles 203, Mistakes 305, Failures 410, and, for some, a graduate course called Catastrophes 599. Tests are given often, and there are no answers in the back of the book. In fact, there is no textbook in these courses, only your experiences from which to learn and, hopefully, grow wiser. Following are some examples of the kind of wisdom that the University of Life can teach.

One of my off-course students was feeling overwhelmed by all she had to do, and then she made a course correction, changing the way she tackled large projects. In her journal she wrote, "When I break a huge task into chunks and do a little bit every day, I can accomplish great things."

©TED GOFF

Another off-course student discovered he was an expert at blaming his failures in college on other people: his boss, his teachers, his parents, his girlfriend. He decided to change and hold himself more responsible. He learned, "In the past I have spent more energy on getting people to feel sorry for me than I have on accomplishing something worthwhile."

A third off-course student was filled with hate for her father who she felt had abandoned her, and then she decided to change. She forgave him and moved on with her life. She wrote, "Spending all of my time hating someone leaves me little time to love myself."

And one more off-course student realized how little effort and care he put into everything he did, including his college assignments. He discovered, "I'm always looking for ways to cut corners, to get out of doing what's necessary. It doesn't work. I have to do my best in order to be successful."

We seldom move toward our goals and dreams in a straight line. With constant course corrections, however, we improve the chances that we will get there eventually. And along the way, the University of Life offers us exactly the lessons we need to develop our full potential. We only have to listen and learn as a Creator.

If we don't change direction soon, we'll end up where we're going.

Professor Irwin Corey

Journal Entry 25

In this activity, you will explore making course corrections to improve your outcomes and experiences.

Did you figure out how to connect the three stars with one straight line? If you were stumped, what limiting belief kept you from solving this problem? Did you assume that you were restricted to a pen or pencil with a narrow

Write about where you are presently off course in your role as a student and offer a plan for making a course correction. In your journal entry, address the following:

1. Examine each of your college classes to see in which one you are most off course. Write about your desired outcomes and / or experiences for

point? You weren't. In fact, the solution is to use a writing implement (such as a large crayon) with a point wide enough to cover all three stars in one straight line. Once you change your limiting belief, solving the problem is easy! How many other problems could you solve in your life if you mastered the creative art of course correction?

the course and where you actually are in the pursuit of these goal(s). If you believe that you are on course in all of your college classes, write about where you are off course in another role in your life.

2. Write about any feedback (from inside or outside of you) informing you that you're off course. What does this feedback tell you is the cause of your problem? Is it your present ways of thinking, feeling, doing, or believing? If you need more feedback, ask your instructor or your Inner Guide.

3. Write about new ways of thinking, feeling, doing, and/or believing that will replace your old ways and move you back on course. What will you do differently? Design a concrete plan to change.

4. Explain the lesson that you believe the University of Life wants you to learn from this situation.

ONE STUDENT'S STORY

Jessie Maggard
*Urbana University,
Ohio*

The first friends I made in college were my teammates on the soccer team. After practice we started riding around, shopping, and going to parties. We almost never talked about school or personal problems. To them, play time was more important. I wasn't getting much sleep and I was exhausted all the time. I didn't feel like studying and when I went to class, I wasn't learning much. Then a couple of things happened that shook me up. First, my English teacher handed back a paper and told me it wasn't very good. I thought all day about what she said and it really bothered me. I'm the first person in my family to go to college, and I started worrying about whether I was going to make it. If I was doing poorly in a class that I thought was easy, what would happen in more difficult classes? Second, I learned that my parents were getting divorced. I tried talking about my feelings with some of my teammates, but they just listened and didn't say anything. I might as well have been talking to a wall, and I realized they weren't really interested in my problems.

The *On Course* book talks about how easy it is to get off course even when you want to be successful. That is so true. By the time soccer season ended, I was *way* off course and I knew I had to make some serious changes. At first I spent more time by myself. I wrote out a schedule and started to get more organized. Then I slowly began spending more time with people in my dorm, and over time I developed friendships with six amazing people who have really touched me. Doing well in school is important to them, too. We started studying together, and my grades began to improve. I even got comments from my teachers about how I had changed. Still, I felt weighed down by my parents' divorce and it was a huge distraction from my schoolwork. One of my new friends had gone through her parents' divorce, and she gave me tips on how she had gotten through it. She encouraged me to sit down with my parents and talk about my feelings. I did, and it helped so much to talk with them and understand why they had fallen out of love with each other.

Through all of this, I've learned that when you get off course, you have to do something different. My soccer friends had different goals. I'm not trying to put them down. Their goals weren't bad, they just weren't my goals. My goal is to get my degree and teach kindergarten, and when I was hanging out with my soccer friends, I was headed in the wrong direction. I totally changed my peer group, and now I am back on course. I know I'm the only person who can change my life. I just need the courage to stand up for myself. At the time, changing seemed so difficult, but now in the big picture, it seems so easy.

Lifelong Learning at Work

The intellectual equipment needed for the job of the future is an ability to define problems, quickly assimilate relevant data, conceptualize and reorganize the information, make deductive and inductive leaps with it, ask hard questions about it, discuss findings with colleagues, work collaboratively to find solutions and then convince others.

Robert B. Reich, former U.S. Secretary of Labor

Some students believe that once they graduate from college they'll finally be finished with studying and learning. In fact, a college diploma is merely a ticket into the huge University of Work. In one year recently, U.S. employers spent more than 55 billion dollars for employee training, according to the American Society for Training and Development.

Continuing education in the workplace includes instruction in hard skills, such as mastering a new product line, a computer system, or government regulations. Companies also offer their employees instruction in many of the same soft skills that you're learning in this book, skills such as listening, setting goals, and managing your time and work projects. In fact, soft skills are in such demand in the workplace today that top training consultants charge many thousands of dollars *per day* to teach these skills to employees of American businesses.

Smart workers take full advantage of the formal classes provided by their employers. They also take full advantage of the informal classes provided by the University of Life. In this university, you have the opportunity to learn from every experience you have, especially those on the job. Lifelong learners aren't devastated by a setback, such as having a project crumble or even losing their job. They learn from their experiences and come back stronger and wiser than ever. A report by the Center for Creative Leadership compared executives whose careers got off course with those who did well. Although both groups had weaknesses, the critical difference was this: Executives who did *not* learn from their mistakes and shortcomings tended to fail at work. By contrast, those executives who *did* learn the hard lessons taught by their mistakes and failures tended to rebound and resume successful careers.

Your work-world learning begins as soon as you get serious about finding your ideal job. Unless you're sure about your career path, you'll have much research to do. Even if you do feel sure about your career choice, further research might lead to something even better. More than 20,000 occupations and 40,000 job titles exist today, and you'll want to identify careers that match the personal talents and interests you identified in your self-assessment.

Your college's library or career center probably has a number of great resources to learn about careers. For example, computerized programs such as DISCOVER, SIGI PLUS, CHOICES, and CIS may be available to explore thousands of career possibilities. Helpful books include the *Dictionary of Occupational Titles* (DOT), which offers brief descriptions of several thousand occupations; *The Guide for Occupational Exploration* (GOE), another source of occupational options; and the latest edition of the *Occupational Outlook Handbook* (OOH), which provides information about the demand for various occupations. With these resources, you can learn important facts about careers you may never have heard of, including the nature of the work, places of employment, training and qualifications required, earnings, working conditions, and employment outlook. Keep in mind that in today's fast-paced world, occupations will be available when you graduate that don't even exist today.

Ned Herrmann, creator of the Brain Dominance Inventory, wrote, "Experience has shown that alignment of a person's mental preferences with his or her work is predictive of success and satisfaction while nonalignment usually results in poor performance and dissatisfaction." So use your discoveries in this chapter about your preferred thinking styles to help you choose a compatible career. See Figure 1 below for some examples.

When you have narrowed your career choices, you may want to learn even more before committing yourself. To get the inside scoop on how a career may fit you, get some hands-on experience. Find part-time or temporary work in the field, apply for an internship, or even do volunteer work. At one time I thought I

Figure 1: Learning Preferences and Compatible Careers

A. Thinking Learner: biologist, stock broker, engineer, city manager, science teacher, computer designer/programmer, computer technician, detective, educational administrator, radiologist, electrical engineer, financial planner, lawyer, chemist, mathematician, medical researcher, physician, statistician, veterinarian

B. Doing Learner: reporter, accountant, librarian, bookkeeper, clinical psychologist, credit advisor, historian, environmental scientist, farmer, hotel/motel manager, marketing director, military personnel, police officer, realtor, school principal, technical writer

C. Feeling Learner: actor, social worker, clergy, sociologist, counseling psychologist, human resource manager, public relations specialist, journalist, musician, teacher, nurse, occupational therapist, organizational development consultant, recreational therapist, sales, writer

D. Innovating Learner: dancer, poet, advertising designer, florist, psychiatrist, artist, creative writer, entrepreneur, fashion artist, playwright, film maker, graphics designer, humorist, inventor, landscape architect, nutritionist, photographer, editor, program developer

"Even though you're exceptionally well qualified, Kate, I'd say that 'victim' is not a good career choice."

wanted to be a veterinarian, but one summer of working in a veterinary hospital quickly taught me that it was a poor career match for me. I'm sure glad I found out *before* I went through many years of veterinary school!

Now it's time for your job interviews. Keep in mind that most employers are looking for someone who can learn the new position and keep learning new skills for years to come. In fact, a recent U.S. Department of Labor study found that employers of entry-level workers considered specific technical skills less important than the ability to learn on the job. So, how can you present yourself in the interview as a lifelong learner? First, of course, have a transcript with good grades to demonstrate your ability to learn in college. Be ready for questions like, "How do you keep up with advancements in your field? What workshops or seminars have you attended? What kind of reading do you do?" Go to the interview prepared to ask good questions of your own. And demonstrate that one of the things you're looking for in a particular job is its ability to help you keep learning your profession.

Today's work world is marked by downsizing and rightsizing. Companies are operating with leaner staffs, and this means that every employee is critical to the success of the business. It also means that someone who can't keep up with inevitable changes is expendable. One powerful way to give yourself a competitive advantage is to continually learn new skills and knowledge, even before you need them on your job. When your supervisor says, "Does anyone here know how to use a desk-top publishing program?" you'll be able to say, "Sure, I can do that." Another way to keep learning on the job is to seek out feedback. Superior performers want to hear what others think of their work, realizing that this is a great way to learn to do it even better.

According to Anthony J. D'Angelo, author of the *College Blue Book*, world knowledge doubles every fourteen months. Suppose he's way off, and knowledge actually doubles only every five years as others claim. That still means we'll have to keep learning a little every day just to keep pace and a lot every day to get ahead. Educator Marshall McLuhan once said, "The future of work consists of *learning* a living (rather than *earning* a living)." His observation becomes truer with each passing day. Future success at work belongs to the lifelong learners.

Believing in Yourself: **Develop Self-Respect**

 FOCUS QUESTIONS   What is your present level of self-respect? How can you raise your self-respect, and therefore your self-esteem, even higher?

Self-respect is the core belief that I AM AN ADMIRABLE PERSON. If self-confidence is the result of **what** I do, then self-respect is the result of **how** I do it.

Two crucial choices that build up or tear down my self-respect are whether or not I live with integrity and whether or not I keep my commitments.

Live with integrity

Always aim at complete harmony of thought and word and deed.
Mohandas K. Gandhi

The foundation of integrity is my personal value system. What is important to me? What experiences do I want to have? What experiences do I want others to have? Do I prize outer rewards such as cars, clothes, compliments, travel, fame, or money? Do I cherish inner experiences such as love, respect, excellence, security, honesty, wisdom, or compassion?

Integrity derives from the root word *integer*, meaning "one" or "whole." Thus we create integrity by choosing words and deeds that are one with our values. Many students say they value their education, but their actions indicate otherwise. They leave assignments undone; they do less than their best work; they miss classes; they come late. In short, their choices contradict what they say they value. Choices that lack integrity tear at a conscious person's self-respect.

One of my greatest integrity tests occurred years ago when I left teaching to find a more lucrative career. I was excited when hired as a management trainee at a high-powered sales company. Graduates of this company's five-year training program were earning more than thirty times what I had earned as a teacher. I couldn't wait!

This above all; to thine own self be true
And it must follow, as the night the day
Thou canst not then be false to any man
Polonius, in Shakespeare's *Hamlet*

My first assignment was to hire new members of the company's sales force. I gave applicants an aptitude test that revealed whether they had what it took to succeed in sales. When the scores came back to the sales manager, he would tell me whether or not the applicants had qualified. If so, I'd offer them a sales position. Lured by dreams of wealth, many of them left the security of a steady salary for the uncertainty of a commission check. Unfortunately, few of them lasted more than a few months. They sold to their friends. They struggled. They disappeared.

Before long, I noticed an unsettling fact: No applicant ever failed the aptitude test. Right after this realization, I interviewed a very shy man who was a lineman for the local telephone company. He was only a year from early retirement, but he was willing to give up his retirement benefits for the promise of big commissions. If ever someone was wrong for sales, I thought, this was the person. I knew he'd be making a terrible mistake to abandon his security for the seductive promise of wealth. Surely here was one person who wouldn't pass the aptitude test. But he did.

"In fact," the sales manager told him in person, "you received one of the highest scores ever. How soon can you start?"

"Errr . . . well, let's see. It's Friday. I guess next week? If that's okay?"

That night, after the sales manager had left, I went into his office and located the lineman's folder. I opened it and found the test results. His score was zero. The man had not even scored!

All weekend, my stomach felt as though I had swallowed acid. My self-respect sank lower and lower. My Inner Defender kept telling me it was the lineman's choice, not mine. It was his life. Maybe he'd prove the aptitude test wrong. Maybe he would make a fortune in sales. My Inner Guide just shook his head in disgust.

On Monday, I phoned the lineman and told him his actual score.

He was furious. "Do you realize what I almost did?"

I thought, *Do you realize what I almost did?* Two weeks later I quit. Soon after, my stomach felt fine.

Each time you contradict your own values, you make a withdrawal from your self-respect account. Each time you live true to your values, you make a deposit. Here's a quick way to discover what you value and whether you are living with integrity: Ask yourself, *What qualities and behaviors do I admire in others? Do I ever allow myself to be less than what I admire?*

When you find that your choices are out of alignment with your values, you need to revise your dreams, goals, thoughts, feelings, actions, or beliefs. You can't abandon what you hold sacred and still retain your self-respect.

> *You will always be in fashion if you are true to yourself, and only if you are true to yourself.*
> Maya Angelou

Keep commitments

Now let's consider another choice that influences your self-respect. Imagine that someone has made a promise to you but doesn't keep it. Then he makes and breaks a second promise. And then another and another. Wouldn't you lose respect for this person? What do you suppose happens when the person making and breaking all of these promises is YOU?

True, your Inner Defender would quickly send out a smoke screen of excuses. But the truth would not be lost on your Inner Guide. The fact remains: You made commitments and broke them. This violation of your word makes a major withdrawal from your self-respect account.

To make a deposit in your self-respect account, keep commitments, especially to yourself. Here's how:

- **Make your agreements consciously**. Understand exactly what you're committing to. Say "no" to requests that will get you off course; don't commit to more than you can handle just to placate others.
- **Use Creator language**. Don't say, *I'll* try *to do it.* Say, *I* **will** *do it.*
- **Make your agreements important**. Write them down. Tell others about them.
- **Create a plan; then do everything in your power to carry out your plan**.
- **If a problem arises or you change your mind, renegotiate** (don't just abandon your promise).

The person we break commitments with the most is, ironically, ourselves. How are you doing in this regard? Here's some evidence: How are you doing with the commitment you made to your goals and dream in Journal Entry 8? How are you doing with your 32-Day Commitment from Journal Entry 13?

If you haven't kept these commitments (or others), ask your Inner Guide, *What did I make more important than keeping my commitment to myself?* A part of you wanted to keep your agreement. But another, stronger part of you obviously resisted. Pursue your exploration of this inner conflict with total honesty and you may uncover a self-defeating pattern or limiting core belief that is crying out for a change. Our choices reveal what we truly value.

Keeping commitments often requires overcoming enormous obstacles. That was the case with one of my students. Rosalie had postponed her dream of becoming a nurse for eighteen years while raising her two children alone. Shortly after enrolling in college, her new husband asked her to drop out to take care of his two sons from a former marriage. Rosalie agreed, postponing her dream once more. Now back in college ten years later, she made what she called a "sacred vow" to attend every class on time, to do her very best on all work, and to participate actively. This time she was committed to getting her nursing degree. Finally her time had come.

Then, one night she got a call from one of her sons who was now married and had a two-year-old baby girl. He had a serious problem: His wife was on drugs. Worse, that day she had bought two hundred dollars worth of drugs on credit, and the drug dealers were holding Rosalie's granddaughter until they got paid. Rosalie spent the early evening gathering cash from every source she could. All night she lay awake, waiting to hear if her grandchild would be returned safely.

At six in the morning, Rosalie got good news when her son brought the baby to her house. He asked Rosalie to watch the child while he and his wife had a serious talk. Hours passed, and still Rosalie cared for the baby. Closer and closer crept the hour when her college classes would begin. She started to get angrier and angrier as she realized that once again she was allowing others to pull her off course. And then she remembered that she had a choice. She could stay home and feel sorry for herself, or she could do something to get back on course.

At about nine o'clock, Rosalie called her sister who lived on the other side of town. She asked her sister to take a cab to Rosalie's house, promised to pay the cab fare, and even offered to pay her sister a bonus to watch the baby.

"I didn't get to class on time," Rosalie said. "But I got there. And when I did, I just wanted to walk into the middle of the room and yell, 'YEEAAH!! I MADE IT!!'"

If you could have seen her face when she told the class about her ordeal and her victory, you would have seen a woman who had just learned one of life's great lessons: When we break a commitment to ourselves, something inside of us dies. When we keep a commitment to ourselves, something inside of us thrives. That something is self-respect.

Journal Entry 26

In this activity, you will explore strengthening your self-respect. People with self-respect honor and admire themselves not just for *what* they do but for *how* they do it.

Character, simply stated, is doing what you say you're going to do. A more formal definition is: Character is the ability to carry out a worthy decision after the emotion of making that decision has passed.

Hyrum W. Smith

1. **Write about a time when you passed a personal integrity test.** Tell about an experience when you were greatly tempted to abandon one of your important values. Describe how you decided to "do the right thing" instead of giving in to the temptation.

2. **Write about a time when you kept a commitment that was difficult to keep.** Fully explain the commitment you made to yourself or to someone else, and discuss the challenges—both inner and outer—that made it difficult for you to keep this promise. Explain how you were able to keep the commitment despite these challenges.

Remember, asking motivating questions leads to meaningful answers. Anticipate questions a curious reader might ask you about your stories . . . and answer them.

Especially in introductory college courses, you will be asked to memorize many details, including definitions, names, facts, and formulas. Some people have a knack for remembering such things. Fortunately for others, memory can be improved by employing a process. Before memorizing, we encode the information; during memorizing, we store it for later use; after memorizing, we attempt to retrieve what we have stored. By using the following strategies, you will find that recalling information will become easier. You'll notice that many of these strategies are compatible with what we know about how the human brain learns, including employing a variety of memory techniques and distributing them over time. In this way you are forming strong new neural networks that help your brain recall the information when it is needed later.

Before Memorizing

1. Create a positive affirmation about memorizing. Many students hold negative beliefs about their ability to memorize. Create an affirming statement about your memory, such as, "I easily recall everything I memorize." Along with your personal affirmation, repeat this memory affirmation in order to reprogram your beliefs about your ability to memorize.

2. Choose to remember. You've used this strategy when you put your keys down and said to yourself, "Be sure to remember that the keys are on the kitchen table." Likewise, tell yourself to remember what you're memorizing in college. Intention is powerful.

3. Post memory cards. Create cards with words, diagrams, formulas, or concepts you want to memorize. Post these cards where you'll see them often (on your mirror, refrigerator, and so on). Then go about your daily life. Over the next week or two, you will unconsciously absorb some or all of the posted information.

4. Plan more than one session. Research shows that memorizing over several short sessions rather than one long session aids recall. In other words, you'll probably remember more after six half-hour sessions than you will after one three-hour session. This is called "distributed practice."

5. Relax. Research also shows that *alpha* states, induced by relaxation, enhance memory. Before memorizing, do some deep, rhythmic breathing or another relaxation activity.

During Memorizing

6. Organize the information in a meaningful way. Which is easier to remember: Four random numbers (8, 9, 1, 2) or a date (1982)? Organizing the four unrelated numbers into a date allows your memory to store and recall them more easily. If the date is particularly meaningful (e.g., 1982 is the year your brother was born), it will be even easier to recall. Many of the strategies that follow are techniques for organizing information in a meaningful way.

7. Create associations. When you associate something new with something you already know, the new information is easier to recall. Suppose you want to remember the name of your new mathematics teacher, Professor Getty; you could associate his name with the Battle of Gettysburg that you studied in American history. You might even visualize him wearing a uniform and carrying a musket. Now you'll remember his name.

8. Use the loci technique. The loci technique is a variation of association. *Loci* is Latin for "place," so with this strategy, you associate a new item you want to memorize with a familiar place. Suppose you're studying parts of the brain and you need to remember the *amygdala*. Think of a familiar place, like your living room. Picture your television turned to your favorite talk show and the host introducing a woman wearing a bright red dress. The host is saying, "Please welcome Amy G. Dala." Review this mental image several times a day for two or three days. When you need to recall the *amygdala*, mentally visit your living room, turn on the television, and there's Amy G. Dala waiting to be introduced. You can now associate other parts of the brain with additional items in your living room. Say, isn't that a neo-cortex sitting on your couch?

9. Invent word acronyms. A word acronym uses the first letter of a group of words to create a new word. If you want to memorize the names of the Great

Lakes, you can use the acronym HOMES: Huron, Ontario, Michigan, Erie, Superior. In this book, you encountered the DAPPS Rule, an acronym that helps you remember the important features of a goal: Dated, Achievable, Personal, Positive, Specific. To create an acronym, simply take the first letters of the words you want to recall and rearrange them to spell a real (HOMES) or made-up (DAPPS) word.

10. Invent sentence acronyms. A sentence acronym uses the first letters of a group of words and creates a sentence. For example, music students recall the notes on the lines of a musical staff (E-G-B-D-F) by the sentence "Every Good Boy Does Fine." If you wanted to memorize the four qualities of effective visualizing (Relax, use Present tense verbs, use all five Senses, include your Feelings), you could invent the acronym sentence "Real People Seek Freedom."

11. Assign a number. When memorizing a specific number of items, identify how many there are. This number will help you know when you have forgotten one or more. For example, in Wise Choices in College: Effective Writing, you learned about the 4 E's (Examples, Experiences, Explanations, and Evidence) as ways to dive deeper as you write. Remembering that there are *four* E's (not three or five) helps you realize if you've forgotten any of them.

12. Visualize. Suppose you're trying to memorize the bones in a human hand. Look at a picture of a hand in your textbook; then close your eyes and visualize the same picture in your mind, including the name of each bone. Go back and forth between the picture in the book and the picture in your mind until they are identical.

13. Create a concept map. A concept map shows the connections between key elements in a complex idea. It combines key advantages of visualizing and associating. Creating concept maps helps memorizing by combining the left brain's verbal and analytical skills with the right brain's spatial and creative abilities. (See example on page 115.)

14. Recite. Do you ever have trouble recalling someone's name two minutes after being introduced? Try saying the person's name immediately after being introduced. "It's nice to meet you, *Bob*." Say his name again a few moments later. "Where do you live, *Bob*?" Reciting the name aloud firmly implants it in your memory. Try the same recitation strategy when memorizing course material.

15. Create and listen to audio recordings. Record questions, leave a ten-to fifteen-second silence, then record the answer. The pause gives you time to fill in the answer as you listen. ("Three tools for improved self-management are . . . *fifteen-second pause* . . . a Monthly Calendar, Next Actions List, and Tracking Form.") You can listen to the recordings while commuting or waiting, helping you make the most of your time each day. Self-made study recordings are especially helpful for auditory learners, people who remember best what they hear.

16. Use several senses. Studies reveal that we recall information better when several senses are engaged during the learning process. Look at the item to be remembered (visual). Recite it aloud (auditory). Write it (kinesthetic).

After Memorizing

17. Repeat, Repeat, Repeat. When trying to remember a new phone number, you probably say it over and over until it sticks in your memory. So you already know the importance of *repetition* in creating a strong memory. Whatever you want to memorize, repeat it over and over to yourself.

18. Revisit visualizations. Throughout your day, recall the image (such as the bones of a human hand) that you committed to memory. Return to the original picture to fill in missing information.

19. Have others quiz you. Give friends or study group members the information you have memorized and have them test your recall. Have them ask the questions in random order so you don't become dependent on the sequence of questions for remembering the answers.

20. Go to sleep. Review what you want to memorize right before going to bed. Your brain will continue to process the information while you sleep, helping you remember it better. A quick review in the morning will solidify what you memorized the night before.

Memorizing Exercise

Suppose you were asked to memorize all of the memory strategies you just read about. How would you go about it? Fully describe your methods.

Embracing Change

Do one thing different this week

Being a lifelong learner will enhance the quality of your outcomes and experiences through your years in higher education and for the rest of your life. Victims handicap their future success by focusing on "getting out" of college. Consequently, they either don't graduate or, if they do earn a degree, their learning experience is so superficial that they haven't created a strong foundation on which to build their success. Creators, on the other hand, participate actively in the learning process and, thus, have the information and skills (not to mention the neural networks) that will enhance their success for years to come. Here's your chance to develop one lifelong learning strategy. From the actions below, pick ONE new belief or behavior and experiment with it for one week, seeing if this new choice helps you create more positive outcomes and experiences. After seven days, assess your results. If your outcomes and experiences improve, you now have a learning tool that will help you stay on course for the rest of your life.

Beliefs and Behaviors	Day 1	Day 2	Day 3	Day 4	Day 5	Day 6	Day 7
Think: "I learn valuable lessons from every experience I have."							
Use the following deep processing strategy chosen from the Wise Choices in College section in Chapters 2–6:							
Study my most challenging subject for a minimum of ____ minutes, using a variety of deep processing strategies.							
Find someone in my class with the same learning preference as my own and ask about his/her most effective learning strategy.							
Make an educated guess about the learning preference of one of my present or past instructors, based on the way s/he teaches.							
Identify one piece of feedback received that day and determine what change, if any, I will make as a result of that feedback.							
Change one behavior, thought, feeling or belief and identify the life lesson it provides.							
Use the following memory strategy (write your choices from pages 205–207):							

(continued on page 209)

During my seven-day experiment, what happened?

As a result of what happened, what did I learn or relearn?

Developing Emotional Intelligence

8

Creating worldly success is meaningless if I am unhappy. That means I must accept responsibility for creating the quality of not only my outcomes but also my inner experiences.

I create my own happiness and peace of mind.

SUCCESSFUL STUDENTS . . .	STRUGGLING STUDENTS . . .
■ **demonstrate emotional intelligence,** using feelings as a compass for staying on course to their goals and dreams.	■ allow themselves to be hijacked by emotions, making unwise choices that get them off course.
■ **effectively reduce stress,** managing and soothing emotions of upset such as overwhelm, anger, fear, and sadness.	■ take no responsibility for managing their emotions, instead acting irrationally on impulses of the moment.
■ **create flow,** feeling fully and positively engaged in college and the rest of their lives.	■ frequently experience boredom or anxiety in their lives.

After Math

When **Professor Bishop** returned midterm exams, he said, "In twenty years of teaching math, I've never seen such low scores. Can anyone tell me what the problem is?" He ran a hand through his graying hair and waited. No one spoke. "Don't you people even care how you do?" Students fiddled with their test papers. They looked out of the window. No one spoke.

Finally, Professor Bishop said, "Okay, Scott, we'll start with you. What's going on? You got a 35 on the test. Did you even *study?*" **Scott**, age eighteen, mumbled, "Yeah, I studied. But I just don't understand math." Other students in the class nodded their heads. One student muttered, "Amen, brother."

Professor Bishop looked around the classroom. "How about you, Amelia? You didn't even show up for the test." **Amelia**, age thirty-one, sighed. "I'm sorry, but I have a lot of other things besides this class to worry about. My job keeps changing my schedule, I broke a tooth last week, my roommate won't pay me the money she owes me, my car broke down, and I haven't been able to find my math book for three weeks. I think my boyfriend hid it. If one more thing goes wrong in my life, I'm going to scream!"

Professor Bishop shook his head slowly back and forth. "Well, that's quite a story. What about the rest of you?" Silence reigned for a full minute. Suddenly **Michael**, age twenty-three, stood up and snarled, "You're a damn joke, man. You can't teach, and you want to blame the problem on us. Well, I've had it. I'm dropping this stupid course. Then I'm filing a grievance. You better start looking for a new job!" He stormed out of the room, slamming the door behind him.

"Okay, I can see this isn't going anywhere productive," Professor Bishop said. "I want you all to go home and think about why you're doing so poorly. And don't come back until you're prepared to answer that question honestly." He picked up his books and left the room. Amelia checked her watch and then dashed out of the room. She still had time to catch her favorite television show in the student lounge.

An hour later, Michael was sitting alone in the cafeteria when his classmates Scott and **Kia**, age twenty, joined him. Scott said, "Geez, Michael, you really went off on Bishop! You're not really going to drop his class, are you?" "Already did!" Michael snapped as his classmates sat down. "I went right from class to the registrar's office. I'm outta there!"

I might as well drop the class myself, Kia thought. Ever since her fiancé had called off their engagement sixteen months before, she'd been too depressed to do her homework. Familiar tears blurred her vision.

Scott said, "I don't know what it is about math. I study for hours, but when I get to the test, I get so freaked it's like I never studied at all. My mind just goes blank." Thinking about math, Scott started craving something to eat.

"Where do you file a grievance against a professor around here, anyway?" Michael asked.

"I have no idea," Scott said.

"What?" Kia answered.

Michael stood and stomped off to file a grievance. Scott went to buy some French fries. Kia put her head down on the cafeteria table and tried to swallow the burning sensation in her throat.

Listed below are the five characters in this story. Rank them in order of their emotional intelligence. Give a different score to each character. Be prepared to explain your choices.

Most emotionally ← 1 2 3 4 5 → Least emotionally
intelligent   intelligent

___ Professor Bishop   ___ Amelia   ___ Scott
___ Michael   ___ Kia

DIVING DEEPER: Imagine that you have been asked to mentor the person whom you ranked number 5 (least emotionally intelligent). Other than recommending a counselor, how would you suggest that this person handle his or her upset in a more emotionally intelligent manner?

Understanding Emotional Intelligence

 FOCUS QUESTIONS   What is emotional intelligence? How can you use your emotions as a compass to stay on course to a rich, fulfilling life?

In the realm of emotions, many people are functioning at a kindergarten level. There is no need for self-blame. After all, in your formal education, how many courses did you take in dealing with feelings?
Gay and Kathlyn
Hendricks

I know it is hard to accept, but an upset in your life is beneficial, in that it tells you that you are off course in some way and you need to find your way back to your particular path of clarity once again.

Susan Jeffers

During final exam period one semester, I heard a shriek from the nursing education office. Seconds later, a student charged out of the office, screaming, scattering papers in the air, and stumbling down the hall. A cluster of concerned classmates caught up to her and desperately tried to offer comfort. "It's all right. You can take the exam again next semester. It's okay. Really." She leaned against the wall, eyes closed. She slid down the wall until she sat in a limp heap, surrounded by sympathetic voices. Later, I heard that she dropped out of school.

At the end of another semester, I had the unpleasant task of telling one of my hardest-working students that she had failed the proficiency exams. Her mother had died during the semester, so I was particularly worried about how she would handle more bad news. We had a conference, and upon telling her the news, I began consoling her. For about a minute, she listened quietly and then said, "You're taking my failure pretty hard. Do you need a hug?" Before I could respond, she plucked me out of my chair and gave me a hug. "Don't worry," she said, patting my back. "I'll pass next semester," and sure enough, she did.

For most of us, life presents a bumpy road now and then. We fail a college course. The job we want goes to someone else. The person we love doesn't return our affections. Our health gives way to sickness. How we handle these distressing experiences is critical to the outcomes of and experiences of our lives.

Success depends on much more than high IQs and academic success. Karen Arnold and Terry Denny at the University of Illinois studied eighty-one valedictorians and salutatorians. They found that ten years after graduation, only 25 percent of these academic stars were at the highest level of their professions when compared with others their age. Actually, many were doing poorly. What seems to be missing for them is **emotional intelligence**.

An experiment during the 1960s shows just how important emotional control is to success. Four-year-old children at a preschool were told they could have one marshmallow immediately, or if they could wait for about twenty minutes, they could have two. More than a dozen years later, experimenters examined the differences in the lives of the one-marshmallow (emotionally impulsive) children and the two-marshmallow (emotionally intelligent) children. The adolescents who as children were able to delay gratification were found to be superior to their counterparts as high school students and to score an average of 210 points higher on their SAT's (Scholastic Aptitude Tests). Additionally, the two-marshmallow teenagers had borne fewer children while unmarried and had experienced fewer problems with the law. Clearly the ability to endure some emotional discomfort in the present in exchange for greater rewards in the future is a key to success.

Four components of emotional intelligence

As a relatively new field of study, emotional intelligence is still being defined. However, Daniel Goleman, author of the book *Emotional Intelligence*, identifies four components that contribute to emotional effectiveness. The first two qualities are personal and have to do with recognizing and effectively managing one's own emotions. The second two are social and have to do with recognizing and effectively managing emotions in relationships with others.

1. **EMOTIONAL SELF-AWARENESS: Knowing your feelings in the moment.** Self-awareness of one's own feelings as they occur is the foundation of emotional intelligence and is fundamental to effective decision making. Thus, people who are keenly aware of their changing moods are better pilots of their lives. For example, emotional self-awareness helps you deal effectively with feelings of overwhelm instead of using television (or some other distraction) as a temporary escape.

Every great, successful person I know shares the capacity to remain centered, clear and powerful in the midst of emotional "storms."
Anthony Robbins

2. **EMOTIONAL SELF-MANAGEMENT: Managing strong feelings.** Emotional Self-Management enables people to make wise choices despite the pull of powerful emotions. People who excel at this skill avoid making critical decisions during times of high drama; instead they wait until their inner storm has calmed and then make considered choices that contribute to their desired outcomes and experiences. For example, emotional self-management helps you resist dropping an important class simply because you got angry at the teacher. It also helps you make a choice that offers delayed benefits (e.g., writing a term paper) in place of a choice that promises instant gratification (e.g., attending a party).

3. **SOCIAL AWARENESS: Empathizing accurately with other people's emotions.** Empathy is the fundamental "people skill." Those with empathy and compassion are more attuned to the subtle social signals

that reveal what others need or want. For example, social awareness helps you notice and offer comfort when someone is consumed by anxiety or sadness.

4. **RELATIONSHIP MANAGEMENT: Handling emotions in relationships with skill and harmony.** The art of relationships depends, in large part, upon the skill of managing emotions in others. People who excel at skills such as listening, resolving conflicts, cooperating, and articulating the pulse of a group do well at anything that relies on interacting smoothly with others. For example, relationship management helps a person resist saying something that might publicly embarrass someone else.

Knowing your own emotions

The foundation of emotional intelligence is a keen awareness of our own emotions as they rise and fall. None of the other abilities can exist without this one. Here are some steps toward becoming more attuned to your emotions:

Academic intelligence has little to do with emotional life. The brightest among us can founder on the shoals of unbridled passions and unruly impulses; people with high IQ's can be stunningly poor pilots of their private lives.

Daniel Goleman

Build a vocabulary of feelings.   Learn the names of emotions you might experience. There are dozens. How many can you name beyond anger, fear, sadness, and happiness?

Be mindful of emotions as they are happening.   Learn to identify and express emotions in the moment. Be aware of the subtleties of emotion, learning to make fine distinctions between feelings that are similar such as sadness and depression.

Understand what is causing your emotion.   Look behind the emotion. See when anger is caused by hurt feelings. Notice when anxiety is caused by irrational thoughts. Realize when sadness is caused by disappointments. Identify when happiness is caused by immediate gratification that gets you off course from your long-term goals.

Recognize the difference between a feeling and resulting actions.   Feeling an emotion is one thing; acting on the emotion is quite another. Emotions and behaviors are separate experiences, one internal, one external. Note when you tend to confuse the two, as a student did who said, "My teacher made me so angry I had to drop the class." You can be angry with a teacher and still remain enrolled in a class that is important to your goals and dreams.

You will never reach your full potential without emotional intelligence. No matter how academically bright you may be, emotional illiteracy will limit your achievements. Developing emotional wisdom will fuel your motivation, help you successfully negotiate emotional storms (yours and others'), and enhance your chances of creating your greatest goals and dreams.

Journal Entry 27

In this activity, you will explore your ability to understand your own emotions and recognize them as they are occurring. This ability is the foundation for all other abilities constituting emotional intelligence.

It made me feel better sometimes to get something down on paper just like I felt it. It brought a kind of relief to be able to describe my pain. It was like, if I could describe it, it lost some of its power over me. I jotted down innermost thoughts I couldn't verbalize to anyone else, recorded what I saw around me, and expressed feelings inspired by things I read.

Nathan McCall

1. **Write about an experience when you felt one of the following emotions: FRUSTRATION or ANGER, FEAR or ANXIETY, SADNESS or DEPRESSION.** Describe fully what happened and your emotional reaction. Because emotions are difficult to describe, you may want to try a comparison like this: *Anger spread through me like a fire in a pile of dry hay . . .* or *I trembled in fear as though I was the next person to stand before a firing squad,* or *For weeks, depression wrapped me in a profound darkness.* Of course, you will compose your own comparison. Your journal entry might begin, *Last week was one of the most frustrating times of my entire life. It all began when . . .* Importantly, be aware of any emotions that you may feel *as* you are writing.

2. **Write about an experience when you felt HAPPINESS or JOY.** Once again, describe fully what happened and your emotional reaction. A possible comparison: *Joy bubbled like champagne in my soul, and I laughed uncontrollably.* Importantly, be aware of any emotions that you may feel *as* you are writing.

3. **Write about any emotional changes you experienced *as you described* each of these two emotions. What did you learn or relearn about how you can affect your emotions?** If you weren't aware of any changes in your present emotions as you described past emotions, write as best you can about why that might be so. Were you not experiencing any emotions at all? Or could you have been unaware of the emotions you were feeling?

Reducing Stress

 FOCUS QUESTION   How can you soothe stressful feelings that make life unpleasant and threaten to get you off course?

Changes and challenges are inevitable in our lives; thus, so is the potential for stress. Maybe you waited until the last minute to print your essay for English class and the printer wouldn't work. Stress. Or you bounced a six-dollar check and the bank charged you a $25 penalty. Stress! Or you've got a test coming up in history and you're two chapters behind in your reading. STRESS!

When I started college, I had been in an abusive relationship for almost three years. I was terrified to leave this man (I'll call him Henry) because we have a child together and he had convinced me that I had no worth as a human being without him. At 6'4" Henry is a foot taller and weighs twice as much as I do. He would punch or kick me until I was in so much pain I couldn't go to my classes. When I did go, I'd often leave early because he became convinced I was cheating on him and I didn't want to give him another reason to beat me. I have a fair amount of academic ability and I did well in high school, but I started allowing my emotions to overrun my intelligence. It was like I had a bunch of emotions in a bowl and I'd just pull one out at random when something happened. One day when my mother expressed concern about my bruises, I got furious at her, but instead of getting angry at Henry for beating me, I'd feel afraid, confused, and depressed. Rather than stepping back and thinking logically about what was going on, I allowed my emotions to control me.

Studying became my escape. In my freshman year experience course, I loved expressing myself in my journals. In Chapter 8, I started writing about my emotions, and for the first time in years, I wasn't ashamed of my feelings. I decided to be totally honest, and I wrote down exactly what was going on and

ONE STUDENT'S STORY

Lindsey Beck
*Three Rivers Community
College, Connecticut*

how I *really* felt about it (not how Henry told me I felt about it). Writing the journals really made me look at myself and ask, *What am I doing in this relationship?* When I read about all of the positive ways I could manage my emotions, I started looking at things as though I wasn't going to take it any more. I got stronger every day, and then one day I made the decision to leave Henry.

I've always done well at writing papers, studying, and taking tests, but I've never really taken responsibility for my emotions before. I learned that I need to get my emotional life under control if I want the rest of my life to work. I now realize that how I feel at one moment isn't necessarily how I'll feel ten minutes later. Emotions change. Why let things control me that are so temporary? By growing emotionally, I'm able to control my emotions instead of letting them control me. I am finally starting to picture a positive life for myself without Henry, and I am growing more confident every day. My dream is to earn a degree in microbiology and make a difference by working for the World Health Organization. Enrolling in this course was the best life decision I will probably ever make. If I hadn't, ten years from now, I might not have wanted to change my life. However, I have been able to do that, and now I have my whole life ahead of me.

Even life's pleasant events, like a new relationship or a weekend trip, can bring on a positive form of stress called *eustress*. If we're not careful, stress of one kind or another can bump us off course.

What is stress?

The American Medical Association defines stress as any interference that disturbs a person's mental or physical well-being. However, most of us know stress simply as the "wear and tear" that our minds and bodies experience as we attempt to cope with the changes and challenges of life. Our body's response to a stressor is much the same today as it was for our ancestors thousands of years ago. As soon as we perceive a threat, our brain releases the stress hormones cortisol and epinephrine (also known as adrenaline), and instantly our bodies respond with an increase in heart rate, metabolism, breathing, muscle tension, and blood pressure. We're ready for "fight or flight."

To our ancestors, this stress response literally meant the difference between life and death. After they'd survived a threat (a saber-toothed tiger, perhaps), the stress hormones were gone from their bodies within minutes. In modern life, however, much of our stress comes from worrying about past events, agonizing about present challenges, and fretting about future changes. Instead of stress hormones being active in our bodies for only minutes, they may persist for months or even years at a time. For many of us, then, stress is a constant and toxic companion.

What happens when stress persists?

Ongoing stress is bad news for our health, damaging almost every bodily system. It inhibits digestion, reproduction, growth, tissue repair, and the responses of our immune system. As just one example of the impact of long-term stress on our health, Carnegie Mellon University researchers exposed four hundred volunteers to cold viruses and found that people with high stress in their lives were twice as likely to develop colds as those with low stress.

In fact, the National Institute for Mental Health estimates that 70 to 80 percent of all doctor visits are for stress-related illnesses. Physical symptoms of stress can be as varied as high blood pressure, muscle tension, headaches, backaches, indigestion, irritable bowel, ulcers, chronic constipation or diarrhea, muscle spasms, tics, tremors, sexual dysfunction, fatigue, insomnia, physical weakness, and emotional upsets.

Immediately relevant to college students is the discovery that stress has a negative impact on memory and other mental skills such as creativity, concentration, and attention to details. When you're feeling stressed, you can't do your best academic work, let alone enjoy doing it. So, when you feel stressed, what are your choices?

Unhealthy stress reduction

When stressed, Victims' greatest concern is escaping the discomfort as fast as possible. To do so, they often make unwise choices: drinking alcohol to excess, going numb for hours in front of a television or computer, working obsessively, fighting, taking numbing drugs, going on shopping binges, eating too much or too little, smoking excessively, gulping caffeine, or gambling more than they can afford to lose. When confronted with the damage of their self-sabotaging behavior, they typically blame, complain, and make excuses. *Stress made me do it!*

The process of living is the process of reacting to stress.
Stanley J. Sarnoff, M.D.

Every stress leaves an indelible scar, and the organism pays for its survival after a stressful situation by becoming a little older.
Hans Selye, M.D.

Of all the drugs and the compulsive behaviors that I have seen in the past twenty-five years, be it cocaine, heroin, alcohol, nicotine, gambling, sexual addiction, food addiction, all have one common thread. That is the covering up, or the masking, or the unwillingness on the part of the human being to confront and be with his or her human feelings.
Richard Miller, M.D.

Like the impulsive children of the marshmallow experiment, Victims seek instant gratification but give little thought to the impact of these choices on their futures. By making one impulsive and ill-considered choice after another, Victims are at high risk for moving farther and farther off course.

Healthy stress reduction

There's a better way to reduce stress. Creators realize that managing emotions intelligently means making wise choices that release the grip of stress, not just mask it. Effective at identifying their distressing feelings early, Creators take positive actions to avoid being hijacked by emotional upset. Here's a menu of healthy and effective strategies for managing four of the most common symptoms of stress.

A special note to the highly stressed: Your Inner Defender may take one look at the list of strategies to follow and say something like, "I can't deal with this right now. It's just going to make me even *more* stressed out!" If that's really the case, consider making an appointment at your campus counseling office to get some caring, professional help for your stress.

To reduce your stress on your own, here's a simple, two-step plan. First, read the section below that addresses your most pressing symptoms of stress: Overwhelm, Anger, Depression, or Anxiety. In that section, pick one stress reduction strategy and make a 32-day commitment (page 106) to do it. In little more than a month, you'll likely feel less stressed. Better yet, you'll have proven that *you*, and not stress, are in charge of your life.

Overwhelm: Overwhelm is probably the most common stressor for college students. Its message, if heeded, is valuable: Your life has gotten too complicated, your commitments too many. Overwhelm warns us that we've lost control of our lives. Creators often notice overwhelm when it shows up as a tightness or pain in their jaw, shoulders, or lower back. Or they may notice themselves thinking, "If one more thing goes wrong, I'm going to scream!" Or, maybe they *do* scream! With this awareness, Creators understand it's time to take action. Many positive strategies exist for rescuing your life from the distress of overwhelm.

Choose new behaviors: Here are some actions you can take when you feel that your life is stretched a mile wide and an inch thin. As you'll see, many of them are variations of self-management strategies you learned in Chapter 4:

- *Separate from an external stressor.* Perhaps the external stressor is a neighbor's loud music or a demanding job. You can choose to study in the library where it's quiet and find a new job with fewer demands.
- *List and prioritize everything you need to do.* Using a Next Actions List (page 99), record all of your incomplete tasks according to life roles.

When you take full responsibility here and now for all of your feelings and for everything that happens to you, you never again blame the people and situations in the world outside of you for any unhappy feelings that you have.

Ken Keyes

THE FAR SIDE BY GARY LARSON

"You know, we're just not reaching that guy."

Assign priorities to each task: A= Important & Urgent actions. B = Important & Not Urgent actions. C = All unimportant actions.

• *Delete C's.* Identify where you are wasting time and cross them off your list.

• *Delegate A's and B's.* Where possible, get another person to complete some of your important tasks. Ask a friend to pick up your dry cleaning. Pay someone to clean your apartment. This choice frees up time do the tasks that only you can do, like your math homework.

• *Complete remaining A's and B's yourself.* Start with your A priorities, such as a looming term paper or a broken refrigerator. Handle them immediately: Visit the library and take out three books to begin researching your term paper topic. Call an appliance repair shop and schedule a service call. Spend time doing only A and B priorities and watch your overwhelm subside.

• *Discover time-savers.* Consciously make better use of your time. For example, keep an errand list so you can do them all in one trip. Or study Q & A cards during the hour between classes.

• *Say "no."* Admit that your plate is full, and politely refuse requests that add to your commitments. If you do agree to take on something new, say "no" to something now on your plate.

• *Keep your finances organized.* A survey of 11,000 adults by *Prevention* magazine revealed that their number one source of stress is worry over personal finances. So curtail unnecessary spending, pay bills when due, balance your checkbook. Use the money-management strategies later in this chapter for stress relief as well as debt relief.

• *Exercise.* Aerobic exercise increases the blood levels of endorphins, and these hormones block pain, create a feeling of euphoria (the exercise high), and reduce stress. One caution: Consult your doctor before dramatically changing your level of exercise.

The sign of intelligent people is their ability to control emotions by the application of reason.

Marya Mannes

Choose new thoughts: Since we create the inner experience of overwhelm in our mind, we can un-create it. Here's how:

• *Elevate.* Rise above the overwhelm and see each problem in the bigger picture of your life, noticing how little importance it really has. From this new perspective, ask, "Will this problem really matter one year from now?" Often the answer is "no."

- *Trust a positive outcome.* How many times have you been upset by something that later turned out to be a blessing in disguise? Since it's possible, expect the blessing.

- *Take a mental vacation.* Picture a place you love (e.g., a white-sand beach, mountain retreat, or forest path) and spend a few minutes visiting it in your mind. Enjoy the peace and rejuvenation of this mini-vacation.

Anger and Resentment   Healthy anger declares a threat or injustice against us or someone or something we care about. Perceiving this violation, our brain signals our body to release catecholamines (hormones) that fuel both our strength and our will to fight. Creators become conscious of oncoming anger through changes like flushed skin, tensed muscles, and increased pulse rates.

With this awareness, Creators can pause and wisely choose what to do next, rather than lashing out impulsively. Emotions don't ask rational questions, so we must. For example, Creators ask, *Will I benefit from releasing my anger, or will it cost me dearly?*

When you perceive a true injustice, use the energy produced by your anger to right the wrong. However, to avoid being hijacked by anger and doing something you will regret later, here are some effective strategies:

Choose new behaviors: Allow the tidal wave of anger-producing hormones about twenty minutes to recede. Here's how:

- *Separate.* Go off and be alone, allowing enough time to regain your ability to make rational, positive choices.

- *Exercise.* Moving vigorously assists in reducing anger-fueling hormones in your body.

- *Relax.* Slowing down also aids in calming your body, returning control of your decisions to you (as long as you don't spend this time obsessively thinking about the event that angered you).

> *No one can create anger or stress within you, only you can do that by virtue of how you process your world, or, in other words, how you think.*
> Wayne Dyer

- *Channel your anger into positive actions.* That's what Marie Tursi did when a drunk driver killed her twenty-year-old son and received only a $151 fine and four years of probation. Tursi turned her anger into action and created Mothers Against Drunk Driving. Now a nationwide organization, MADD strives to end drunk driving and provide support for its victims.

Choose new thoughts: Since thoughts stir emotional responses, revising our anger-producing thoughts can calm us. Here's how:

- *Reframe.* Look at the problem from a different perspective. Search for a benign explanation for the anger-causing event. If you realize you were wronged unknowingly, unintentionally, or even necessarily, you can often see the other person's behavior in a less hostile way.

- *Distract yourself.* Consciously shift your attention to something pleasant, stopping the avalanche of angry thoughts. Involve yourself with uplifting conversations, movies, books, music, video games, puzzles, or similar diversions.

- *Identify the hurt.* Anger is often built upon hurt: Someone doesn't meet me when she said she would. Below my anger I'm hurt that she seems to care about me so little. Shift attention from anger to the deeper hurt. Consider expressing the hurt in writing.

- *Forgive.* Take offending people off the hook for whatever they did, no matter how offensive. Don't concern yourself with whether *they* deserve forgiveness; the question is whether *you* deserve the emotional relief of forgiveness. The reason for forgiveness is primarily to improve *your* life, not theirs. We close the case to free ourselves of the daily self-infliction of poisonous judgments. Of course, forgiveness doesn't mean we forget and allow them to misuse us again.

Fear and Anxiety   Healthy fear delivers a message that we are in danger. Our brain then releases hormones that fuel our energy to flee. Many Victims, though, exaggerate dangers, and their healthy fear is replaced by paralyzing anxiety or even terror about what could go wrong.

Creators become conscious of oncoming anxiety through their body's clear signals, including shallow breathing, increased pulse rate, and "butterflies" in the stomach. With this awareness, Creators can pause and wisely choose what to do next rather than fleeing impulsively from or constantly worrying about a nonthreatening person or situation.

One of the areas where fear hinders academic performance is test anxiety. Unless you minimize this distress, you will be unable to demonstrate effectively what you know. Many colleges offer workshops or courses that offer instruction in anxiety-reducing strategies. Here are some wise choices to avoid being hijacked by fear, especially fear generated by a test.

Choose new behaviors: As with anger, help the anxiety-producing chemicals to recede. Here's how:

- *Relax.* Slowing down helps you reclaim mastery of your thoughts and emotions (but don't spend this time obsessing about the cause of your anxiety).

- *Breathe deeply.* Anxiety and fear constrict. Keep oxygen flowing through your body to reverse their physiological impact.

- *Prepare thoroughly.* If your anxiety relates to an upcoming performance (e.g., test or job interview), prepare thoroughly and then prepare some more. Confidence gained through extensive preparation will diminish anxiety.

- *Bring a piece of home to tests.* For example, bring a picture of your family.

- *Request accommodations.* Visit your college's disability services to see about making special arrangements, such as a longer time to take tests.

Choose new thoughts: Changing our thoughts can soothe irrational anxieties. Here's how:

Living life as an art requires a readiness to forgive.
Maya Angelou

Anxiety . . . sabotages academic performance of all kinds: 126 different studies of more than 36,000 people found that the more prone to worries a person is, the poorer their academic performance, no matter how measured—grades on tests, grade-point average, or achievement tests.
Daniel Goleman

- *Detach.* Once you have prepared fully for an upcoming challenge (like a test), there's no more you can do. Worrying won't help. So do everything you can to ready yourself for the challenge; then trust the outcome to take care of itself.

- *Reframe.* Ask yourself, "If the worst happens, can I live with it?" If you fail a test, for example, you won't like it, but could you live with it? (If not, consider seeking help to regain a healthy perspective.)

- *Visualize success.* Create a mental movie of yourself achieving your ideal outcomes. Play the movie over and over until the picture of success becomes stronger than your fear.

- *Assume the best.* Victims often create fear through negative assumptions. Suppose your professor says, "I want to talk to you in my office." Resist assuming the conversation concerns something bad. In fact, if you're going to assume, why not assume it's something wonderful!

- *Face the fear.* Do what you fear, in spite of the fear. Most often you will learn that your fear was just a <u>F</u>alse <u>E</u>xpectation <u>A</u>ppearing <u>R</u>eal.

- *Say your affirmation.* When fearful thoughts creep into your mind, replace them with the positive words of your affirmation.

If your images are positive, they will support you and cheer you on when you get discouraged. Negative pictures rattle around inside of you, affecting you without your knowing it.

Virginia Satir

Sadness and Depression   Healthy sadness overtakes us upon the loss of someone or something dear. Fully grieving our loss is essential, for only in this way do we both honor and resolve our loss. Unhealthy sadness, however, becomes a lingering depression, a dark, helpless feeling that anesthetizes us, keeping us from moving on to create a positive experience of life despite our loss.

Creators become conscious of oncoming depression through their body's clear signals of low energy, constant fatigue, and lack of a positive will to perform meaningful tasks. With this awareness, Creators wisely take steps to avoid an extended stay in the dark pit of depression. Here are some positive options:

Choose new behaviors: Help your body produce natural, mood-elevating hormones. Here's how:

- *Do something (anything!) toward your goals.* Get moving and produce a result, no matter how small. Accomplishment combats depression.

- *Exercise.* Moving vigorously helps your body produce endorphins, causing a natural high that combats depression.

- *Listen to uplifting music.* Put on a song that picks up your spirits. Avoid sad songs about lost love and misery.

- *Laugh.* Like exercise, laughter is physiologically incompatible with depression. So rent a funny movie, go to a comedy club, read joke books or cartoons, or visit your funniest friend.

- *Breathe deeply.* Like fear, depression constricts. Keep breathing deeply to offset the physiological impact of depression.

- *Help others in need.* Assisting people less fortunate not only distracts you from the source of your sadness, it also reminds you that, despite your loss, you still have much to be grateful for.

Choose new thoughts: As with other distressing emotions, changing our thoughts soothes depression. Here's how:

- *Dispute pessimistic beliefs.* Depression thrives on pessimism. So challenge negative beliefs that make the loss seem permanent, pervasive, or personal. Think, instead, how life will improve over time, how the loss is limited to only one part of your life, and how the cause is not a personal flaw in you, but something you can remedy with an action.
- *Socialize with friends and loved ones.* Isolation usually intensifies depression. Socializing re-engages you with people who matter and helps you gain a healthier perspective on your loss.
- *Distract yourself.* As with anger, consciously replacing depressing thoughts with pleasant ones will help stop the anxiety. So involve yourself with engaging activities that will take your thoughts on a pleasant diversion.
- *Focus on the positive.* Identify your blessings and successes. Appreciate what you *do* have instead of regretting what you don't.
- *Find the opportunity in the problem.* At the very least, learn the lesson life has brought you and move on. At best, turn your loss into a gain.
- *Remind yourself, "This, too, shall pass."* A year from now, you'll be in an entirely different place in your life, and this depression will be only a memory.
- *Identify others who have much more to be sad or depressed about.* Realize by this comparison how fortunate you actually are, changing your focus from your loss to all that you still have.

The greater part of our happiness or misery depends on our dispositions and not our circumstances.
Martha Washington

Choose your attitude

When dealing with stress, the critical issue is, *Do you manage your emotions or do they manage you?* If you have made an honest effort to manage your emotions and they have defied you still, you may want to seek the help of a counselor or therapist. But if it's inspiration you seek, consider Viktor E. Frankl, a psychiatrist imprisoned in the Nazi concentration camps during World War II. In his book, *Man's Search for Meaning,* Frankl relates how he and other prisoners rose above their stressful suffering to create a positive inner experience.

In one example, Frankl tells of a particularly bleak day when he was falling into a deep despair. With terrible sores on his feet, he was forced to march many miles in bitter cold weather to a work site, and there, freezing and weak from starvation, he endured constant brutality from the guards. Frankl describes how he "forced" his thoughts to turn to another subject. In his mind he imagined himself "standing on the platform of a well-lit, warm and pleasant lecture room." Before him sat an audience enthralled to hear him lecture on the psychology of the concentration camp. "By this method," Frankl says, "I succeeded somehow in rising above the situation, above the sufferings of the moment, and I observed them as if they were already of the past."

From his experiences and his observations, Frankl concluded that everything can be taken from us but one thing: "the last of the human freedoms—to choose one's attitude in any given set of circumstances, to choose one's own way."

Creators claim the power to choose their outcomes whenever possible and to choose their inner experiences always. If Victor Frankl could overcome the stress of his lengthy and inhumane imprisonment in a concentration camp, surely we can find the strength to overcome the stresses of our ordinary lives.

The greatest discovery of my generation is that human beings, by changing the inner attitudes of their minds, can change the outer aspects of their lives.

William James

Journal Entry 28

In this activity you will practice identifying positive methods for reducing the stress in your life.

1. **Write about a recent time when you experienced overwhelm, anger or resentment, sadness or depression, fear or anxiety.** Choose an experience different from the one you described in Journal Entry 27. Fully describe the situation that caused your emotional response; then describe the feelings you experienced; finally, explain what you did (if anything) to manage your emotions in a positive way.

2. **Identify three or more strategies that you could use in the future when you experience this emotion.** Explain each strategy in a separate paragraph, and remember the power of the 4 E's—Examples, Experiences, Explanation, and Evidence—to improve the quality of your writing. When you're done, notice if simply writing about your stressors and ways to manage them may have reduced your level of stress. It did for students in a study at Southern Methodist University.

Emotion comes directly from what we think: Think "I am in danger" and you feel anxiety. Think "I am being trespassed against" and you feel anger. Think "Loss" and you feel sadness.

Martin Seligman

I don't consider myself someone who lives in fear, and very few things in life intimidate me. However, the one fear that I could never overcome was my dread of public speaking. When I had to give a speech or read an essay aloud in junior high or high school, I would develop a shaky voice, get sweaty palms, and turn completely red. When I got to college, I took a fundamentals of speech class in which much of our grade depended on two speeches that we had to give using a PowerPoint presentation. My first speech didn't go very well. I hadn't really learned to use PowerPoint, and the slides didn't seem to fit what I was talking about. I began to feel insecure, and I started going all over the place. My teacher said the speech was okay, but I wasn't happy with it, especially because my goal is to work in public relations where I'll need to be able to speak to groups with confidence.

I was taking SLS 1125, Student Support Seminar, at the same time and I discovered many helpful hints in *On Course* to overcome my fears. The first thing I did for my next speech was to make sure I was thoroughly prepared. This time I wrote out my whole speech first and then put my key points on index cards. I learned how to work PowerPoint and made sure all of the

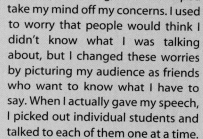

ONE STUDENT'S STORY

Jaime Sanmiguel
Miami Dade College,
Florida

slides went with what I was talking about. I practiced giving my speech a number of times, with my dog as my audience. Another student in my class gave a great speech on the history of watches, and I visualized myself doing some of the things she had done, like using my hands effectively, looking relaxed, smiling, and being more natural and friendly. I also did some relaxing and deep breathing, and that helped take my mind off my concerns. I used to worry that people would think I didn't know what I was talking about, but I changed these worries by picturing my audience as friends who want to know what I have to say. When I actually gave my speech, I picked out individual students and talked to each of them one at a time. These techniques helped me believe in myself more and not be so self-conscious in front of an audience, and in the end I passed the course with a B.

But just as important, in *On Course* I learned, "If you keep doing what you've been doing, you'll keep getting what you've been getting." I took ownership of that fact that if I want to be successful in a public relations career, I have to face and overcome my fears of giving presentations. I think I'm well on my way to achieving this goal.

Creating Flow

FOCUS QUESTIONS   What are you doing when you feel most happy to be alive—when you become so absorbed that time seems to disappear? How can you create more of these peak experiences in college and beyond?

Happiness has been called the goal of all goals, the true destination of all journeys. After all, why do we pursue any goal or dream? Isn't it for the positive inner experience our success will create?

For centuries, explorers of human nature have pondered how we can consciously and naturally create happiness. Psychologist Mihaly Csikszentmihalyi has called highly enjoyable periods of time **flow states.** Flow is characterized by a total absorption in what one is doing, by a loss of thoughts or concerns about oneself, and by a distorted sense of time (often passing very quickly). His studies offer insights into how we can purposely create such positive inner experiences in college and beyond.

Csikszentmihalyi believes that the key to creating flow lies in the interaction of two factors: the **challenge** a person perceives himself to be facing and the related **skills** he perceives himself to possess. Let's consider examples of three possible relationships of skill level and challenge. First, when a person's perceived skill level is higher than a perceived challenge, the result is *boredom:* Think how bored you'd feel if you took an introductory course in a subject in which you were already an expert.

Second, when a person's perceived skill level is lower than that needed to meet a perceived challenge, the result is *anxiety:* Think how anxious you'd feel if you took an advanced mathematics course before you could even add and subtract.

Third, when the individual's perceived skill level is equal to or slightly below the challenge level, the result is often *flow:* Recall one of those extraordinary moments when you lost yourself in the flow—maybe while conversing with a challenging thinker or playing a sport you love with a well-matched opponent. In flow, participation in the activity is its own reward; the outcome doesn't matter. Flow generates the ultimate in intrinsic motivation: We do the activity merely for the positive experience it provides.

> *Being able to enter flow is emotional intelligence at its best; flow represents perhaps the ultimate in harnessing the emotions in the service of performance and learning.*
>
> Daniel Goleman

CREATING FLOW

Skill level HIGH and challenge level LOW = Boredom

Skill level LOW and challenge level HIGH = Anxiety

Skill level EQUAL TO or SLIGHTLY BELOW challenge level = Flow

---

Nadja Salerno-Sonnenberg, one of the world's great concert violinists, describes her own experience of flow this way: "Playing in the zone is a phrase that I use to describe a certain feeling on stage, a heightened feeling where everything is right. By that I mean everything comes together. Everything is one . . . you, yourself, are not battling yourself. All the technical work and what you want to say with the piece comes together. It's very, very rare but it's what I have worked for all my life. It's just right. It just makes everything right. Nothing can go wrong with this wonderful feeling."

College and flow

What if you could have this kind of experience in your college courses? Creators do all they can to maximize that possibility, and how you choose your courses and your instructors is a good first step. Victims typically create their course schedule based on convenience: *Give me a class at 10:00 because I don't like to get up early.*

Creators have a very different approach. They realize that it's worth a sacrifice to get a course with an outstanding instructor, one who creates flow in the classroom. As you plan your schedule for next semester, ask other students to recommend instructors who . . .

1. demonstrate a deep knowledge of their subject,
2. show great enthusiasm for the value of their subject,
3. set challenging but reasonable learning objectives for their students,
4. offer engaging learning experiences that appeal to diverse learning preferences, and
5. provide a combination of academic and emotional support that gives their students high expectations of success.

These are the instructors who are going to create flow in their classrooms, support you to achieve academic success, and inspire you to be a lifelong learner.

Work and flow

Importantly, also consider flow when choosing your academic major and your career. You may be surprised by what Csikszentmihalyi found: Typical working adults report experiencing flow on their jobs three times more often than during free time. When it comes to creating flow, work trumps evenings, weekends, and even vacations. The lesson is clear: If you want to create a positive experience of life, engage in work that appeals to your natural inclinations. When will you have time for boredom if you wake up every morning excited about your day's work?

Carolyn, a twenty-year-old student of mine, was studying to be a nurse, which was the career her mother wanted for her. Carolyn's dream was to dance, but she made keeping the peace at home more important. "If I even mention dancing, my mother goes ballistic," Carolyn confided. "It's not worth the hassle to fight her."

I saw Carolyn some years after our first conversation and asked what she was doing.

"I'm a nurse now," she said.

"Any dancing in your life?"

"I've sort of stopped thinking about that."

As best I could tell, Carolyn had abandoned her dreams.

Have you? Are you headed for a career that represents your passion? Is it the work you would choose if you had absolutely no restrictions, either from outside you or inside you?

We tend to experience flow when we become absorbed in something challenging.

Jere Brophy

The best career advice to give the young is "Find out what you like doing best and get someone to pay you for doing it."

Katherine Whitehorn

For the next couple of decades at least, you'll probably spend many of your waking hours at work. You don't have to settle for just a paycheck. Some people do what they love. Why shouldn't you?

I spent more than a year of my life doing work that wasn't me, and I know how quickly my joy shriveled. I woke up many mornings with a stomachache. I lived for weekends, but by Sunday afternoon I began to dread Monday morning. Finally, I heeded the feedback from my emotional distress and sought work where I was happy. I urge you to follow your bliss. This choice may require self-discipline to get you through the education or training necessary to qualify for your desired career, but it's worth all the discomfort in the present for all the rewards in the future.

One more point remains to be made about the benefits of creating flow in college, at work, and everywhere else in your life. Not only does flow improve your inner experience, but it also promotes your professional and personal growth. Each time you create flow by testing your present skills against a new challenge, your skills improve. To create flow the next time, you have to increase the difficulty of the challenge, which, in turn, offers an opportunity to improve your skills once again. Over time, by creating flow again and again, your skills improve greatly, and this growth adds even more to the success and happiness in your life.

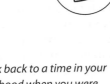

Journal Entry 29

In this activity, you will explore ways to create flow in your life. The more flow you create day to day, the more positive will be your inner experience of life.

1. **Write about a specific past event when you experienced flow in any part of your life.** Remember, flow is characterized by total absorption in what you're doing, an altered awareness of time, and a sense of performing at your very best.

2. **Write about your perfect work of the future, the kind that you believe will create the most flow in your life.** Think about any past or present work experiences. Identify the feelings these jobs generated in you (particularly boredom, anxiety, or flow). Then let your imagination run free. Design your perfect job, its challenges, rewards, fellow workers, hours, location, environment. Consider everything that will make this work something you would love to do *even if you didn't get paid*. Indulge in some no-limit thinking!

Consider illustrating this journal entry with drawings, stickers, pictures cut from magazines, or clip art.

Emotional Intelligence at Work

During nearly twenty years working as a consulting psychologist to dozens of companies and public agencies, I have seen how the lack of emotional intelligence undermines both an individual's and a company's growth and success, and conversely how the use of emotional intelligence leads to productive outcomes at both the individual and the organizational levels.

Hendrie Weisnger,
*Emotional Intelligence
at Work*

Imagine this: The local store manager of a large retail chain sends a one-line email to her department heads: "Quarterly sales figures on my desk by 9:00 A.M. tomorrow!" The head of the men's wear department reads the email, feels insulted by the demanding tone, and fires back an angry email response: "I've been working here a hell of a lot longer than you have, and I don't need your nasty reminders about when sales reports are due. You might try treating people more like colleagues and less like servants awaiting your every command." On an impulse, he copies his response to the company president and the five vice presidents at the store's national headquarters.

How much lost time and productivity do you think will result from this exchange of two emails? How much damage will be done to their professional relationship and their ability to work well together in the future? How might their reputations and careers suffer when others hear rumors of this incident?

Now consider how different this event might have been if the head of the men's wear department had made a different, more emotionally intelligent choice. Suppose he'd read the store manager's email, taken a deep breath, and read it again? Feeling angry at what appeared to be the manager's dictatorial tone, what if he had waited about thirty minutes before responding? During that time, maybe he would have done some deep breathing. Maybe he would have recalled that the store manager has been very respectful of him since she took over the store six months before. Having calmed his initial emotional upset, suppose he now went to the store manager's office and asked for a brief meeting? "You know," he says to her in this revised scene, "I just read your email about turning in the third-quarter sales figures, and I got that you're angry or upset. Is there something we need to talk about?" "What? Oh no," she responds, "there's no problem. I meant to send you a reminder last week, but I'm so far behind in my paper work that I forgot. When I remembered this morning, I wrote the email while I was doing five other things. Sorry if it sounded like I was upset with you. On the contrary, I think you're doing a terrific job!"

Another name for emotional intelligence in the workplace is "professionalism." Professionals are aware of their own feelings. They've developed methods for managing distressing feelings, not allowing themselves to respond impulsively while in their grip. Professionals know how to motivate themselves to do their work with excellence and they consistently meet project deadlines, even when this means delaying gratification in other areas. They're good at perceiving emotions in others, and they know how to communicate effectively, building alliances rather than destroying them. Notice that in the revised scene above, the department head doesn't reply to his manager with another email. He communicates with her in person. Little decisions like this one make all the difference when it comes to building a reputation as a business professional. And that reputation can be destroyed with one careless tantrum.

Your emotional intelligence begins to impact your work life as soon as you consider a career path. If you choose work for which you have no passion or emotional commitment, you're starting your career with a huge handicap. Unmotivated by the outcomes or experiences of your work, you'll likely cut corners, doing less than is necessary to propel your career to success. By contrast, when you match your interests and talents to your career choice, you'll find work stimulating and success more likely. As Shoshana Zuboff, a psychiatrist and professor at Harvard Business School put it, "We only will know what to do by realizing what feels right to us."

Emotional intelligence continues to support your success during your job search. Chances are, every applicant invited for an interview has the training to do the job. So, what will distinguish you from the crowd? One answer lies in what employers are looking for beyond job skills. A 1997 survey of major corporations, done by the American Society for Training and Development, discovered that four out of five companies seek emotional intelligence as one of the qualities they look for in new employees. Realizing this, you'll know to communicate not only your academic and job-related skills, but your emotional intelligence competencies as well.

Employers have good reason to seek employees with emotional intelligence: It's critical to success. In his book *Working with Emotional Intelligence*, Daniel Goleman writes, "We now have twenty-five years' worth of empirical studies that tell us with a previously unknown precision just how much emotional intelligence matters for success." Goleman presents his analysis of what 121 companies reported as the necessary competencies for success in 181 different career positions. He found that two out of three of the abilities considered essential for effective job performance are emotional competencies. Put another way, according to employers themselves, emotional competence matters *twice* as much as IQ and technical expertise in job effectiveness.

You might think that the soft skills associated with emotional intelligence would be less important for those employed in highly technical and intellectual fields like engineering, computer science, law, or medicine. Paradoxically, the exact opposite is true. Since academic success and high intelligence are required of all who enter these careers, virtually everyone in these careers is "book smart." However, not everyone is emotionally intelligent. In these professions, there is more variation in the "soft" domain than there is variation in education and IQ. Therefore, if you're at the top end of the emotional intelligence scale, you have a great advantage over your emotionally illiterate colleagues. As Goleman puts it, "'Soft' skills matter even more for success in 'hard' fields."

While emotional intelligence is important in entry-level positions, as one moves up the ladder into leadership positions, it becomes essential. According to Goleman, employers report emotional intelligence as making up 80 to 100 percent of the skills necessary to be an outstanding leader. As just one example of its importance, leaders are charged with motivating others to move persistently toward company goals and missions. They need to be able to spot and resolve conflicts that happen in their work force, because such upsets, if not dealt with effectively, can get an individual, group, division, or even the whole company off course.

Doug Lennick, executive vice president at American Express Financial Advisors, sums up the case for emotional intelligence in the workplace: "The aptitudes you need to succeed start with intellectual horsepower—but people need emotional competence, too, to get the full potential of their talents. The reason we don't get people's full potential is emotional incompetence."

Believing in Yourself: Develop Self-Love

 FOCUS QUESTIONS   How much do you love yourself? What can you do to love yourself even more?

Ultimately, for most of us, the journey comes down to the same issue: learning to love freely. First ourselves, then other people.

Melody Beattie

S elf-love is the core belief that **I AM LOVABLE.** It's the unwavering trust that, no matter what, I will always love myself and other people will love me as well.

Self-love is vital to success. It empowers us to make wise, self-supporting choices instead of impulsive, self-destructive ones. These wise choices create a rich, full life of outer achievement and inner happiness.

Adults who have difficulty loving themselves typically felt neglected or abandoned as children. Many grew up in families in which they felt unappreciated and unloved. What meager love they did experience was often little more than a short-lived reward for adapting to their parents' expectations and demands. For children who felt unloved, each new day meant a desperate search for something they could say or do to earn approval from others.

A student in my English class once wrote an essay about the outrageous stunts she'd done to become head rabbit for her fifth grade's spring festival. As she read her story, everyone laughed loudly. Afterward, someone asked, "Why did you go to all that trouble just to be the head rabbit?"

The student paused. "Simple. The head rabbit got to wear the best costume." Then a serious look came over her face. "The truth is, I thought people would like me more if I was the head rabbit." She paused again. "And, I guess I hoped that *I* would like me more, too."

Self-esteem is the capacity to experience maximal self-love and joy whether or not you are successful at any point in your life.

David Burns, M.D.

Like my student, we may believe that self-love depends upon our outer accomplishments and what others think of them. This kind of self-love is conditional: *I'll love myself **after** I earn my degree, **after** I get a great job, **after** I marry the perfect person, **after** I buy my dream house . . . .*

If the belief that accomplishment creates self-love were accurate, then why do so many people who appear successful on the outside feel so empty on the inside? Worldly success will not fill all the empty places in our souls. But love for ourselves will.

Design a self-care plan

If we felt unloved as children, we may need to learn how to love ourselves as adults and do so without confusing self-love with egotism, arrogance, or self-righteousness.

First, we might ask, *How do we know when other people truly love us?* Isn't it when they treat us well, when they consider our welfare along with their own, concern themselves with our success and happiness, treat us with respect even when our behavior seems least deserving, give us honest feedback, and make sacrifices for the betterment of our lives? Don't we feel loved when others nurture the very best in us with the very best in them?

Our parents' job was to love and nurture us when we were children. Some parents did a great job; some did a terrible job. Most parents probably fell somewhere in between. Now that we are adults, we are responsible for continuing (or beginning) our own nurturing. The more we care for ourselves, the more we feel lovable. And the more we feel lovable, the more overflow of compassion and love we have for others.

Nurturing yourself can begin today with a conscious self-care plan. As you consider the following options for nurturing yourself, look for choices you could adopt to increase your self-love.

The extent to which we love ourselves determines whether we eat right, get enough sleep, smoke, wear seat belts, exercise, and so on. Each of these choices is a statement of how much we care about living.

Bernie Siegel, M.D.

Nurture yourself physically.   People who love themselves make wise choices to nurture their bodies for a long, healthy life. How's your diet? The next time you're about to eat or drink something, ask yourself: *Would I be proud to offer this to someone I truly loved?* This question will raise your awareness, encouraging you to make wiser choices about eating and drinking. Visit your college's health office or library for valuable information on improving your diet.

Do you exercise regularly? Even moderate exercise done routinely helps most people stay stronger and healthier. Regular exercise strengthens the immune system and produces hormones that give us a natural sense of well-being. Your physical education department can help you begin a safe, effective, and lifelong exercise program.

Do you have habits that harm your body? Do you drink too much coffee, smoke cigarettes, drink alcohol to excess, take dangerous drugs? If so, consider giving up the immediate pleasure of such substances for the improved health you'll gain. Substance abuse is misnamed. You're not abusing the substance—you're abusing yourself. Would you abuse someone you truly loved? Your college's health office can also provide you with information on how to stop these self-destructive habits. Additional community resources include Alcoholics Anonymous (A.A), Narcotics Anonymous (N.A.), Overeaters Anonymous (O.A.), and other twelve-step programs.

Here are additional ways to nurture your body: Get enough rest. Swing on a swing. Have regular medical checkups. Hug someone dear to you. Laugh until your sides ache. Take a bubble bath. Go dancing. Get a massage. Do nothing for an hour. Stretch like a cat. Breathe deeply. Relax.

Nurture yourself mentally.   How you talk to yourself, especially when you're off course, will greatly influence your sense of self-love. Whenever your Inner Critic begins to condemn you, stop. Replace these negative judgments with positive, supportive comments.

You may find it difficult at first to choose self-loving thoughts rather than self-criticism. To help, try separating the doer from the deed. If you fail a test, your Inner Critic wants to label you a failure. But your Inner Guide knows you're not a failure; you're a person who, with many other successes in life, got one F on one test. Keep your self-talk focused on facts, not judgments. When you create an undesired outcome, learn from the experience, forgive yourself for judging your shortcomings, and move on.

Here are additional ways to nurture yourself mentally. Say your affirmation(s) often, read uplifting books (many are listed in the bibliography on pages 255–256), ask a motivating question and seek the answer, learn new words, visualize your success, balance your checkbook, sing or listen to a song with positive lyrics, analyze a difficult situation and make a decision, teach someone something you know how to do.

Nurture yourself emotionally.   The very times you need self-love the most are often the times you feel self-love the least. You may be feeling shame instead of self-acceptance, helplessness instead of competence, self-contempt instead of self-respect, self-loathing instead of self-love.

An emotional antidote for toxic self-judgments is *compassion*. Treat yourself with the same kindness you'd offer a loved one who's struggling to make sense of this huge, confusing, and sometimes painful world. Realize that how you treat yourself as you go through difficult times—judgmentally or compassionately—is what will continue to affect your self-love long after the difficult times have passed.

Here are more ways to nurture yourself emotionally: Feel your feelings, share your feelings with a friend, write about your feelings in your journal, see an uplifting and inspiring movie, spend time with loved ones, listen to inspiring music, do something special for yourself, remind yourself that strong feelings, like storms, will pass.

Deep self-love is the ongoing inner approval of who you are regardless of your current outer results. You are not your results. When you learn to love yourself even when you're off course, your belief in yourself will soar.

> *I believe that the black revolution certainly forced me and the majority of black people to begin taking a second look at ourselves. It wasn't that we were all that ashamed of ourselves, we merely started appreciating our natural selves . . . sort of, you know, falling in love with ourselves just as we are.*
> Aretha Franklin

> *The First Best-Kept Secret of Total Success is that we must feel love inside ourselves before we can give it to others.*
> Denis Waitley

Journal Entry 30

In this activity, you will explore ways to develop greater self-love. Typically, people who love themselves achieve many of their goals and dreams and, regardless of the outer circumstances of their lives, often experience positive feelings.

One of the ways I nurture my own soul is by waking every morning around four-thirty and spending two hours by myself—for myself—doing yoga, visualization, meditation, or working on dreams. . . . Another way I nurture my soul is by keeping a daily journal. . . . This is what my two solitary hours in the morning are about—experiencing the core of my soul and discovering the truth that I have to live.

Marion Woodman

1. **On a blank journal page, draw a circle. Within the circle, create a representation of your most LOVABLE INNER SELF.** If people could get a glimpse of you without your protective scripts, patterns, and habits, this is what they'd see. Such a picture is called a "mandala." Like an affirmation, a mandala represents your ideal self, your greatest potential as a human being, the desired self you are in the process of creating. This picture needs to make sense only to you. Use colors, words, or shapes as appropriate. To create your mandala, feel free to draw, add personal photographs, or clip and paste pictures cut from magazines.

2. **Outside of the mandala circle, write different ways that you could take care of yourself PHYSICALLY, MENTALLY, and EMOTIONALLY.** In this way you are creating a self-care plan for the LOVABLE INNER SELF depicted in your mandala. Look back at the text for examples of ways to nurture yourself physically, mentally, and emotionally. If appropriate for you, add ways to nurture yourself spiritually as well.

3. **On the next page in your journal, write an explanation of your mandala and the Self-Care Plan that you have created.** Think of questions an inquisitive reader would ask you, and let your Inner Guide answer them. For example, What is the significance of the drawings, shapes, pictures, words, lines, and colors that you have chosen to represent your full potential as a human being? What personal characteristics have you depicted as representing your best self? Why are these qualities important to you? In what ways have you decided to take care of yourself? And why have you chosen these particular ways to nurture yourself?

Learning to manage personal finances is a life skill just as important as reading and writing. Few people, however, receive any instruction in managing money. Sadly, the inability to manage money keeps many students from finishing the degrees that would help them earn even more money. And, make no mistake, a college degree is, indeed, money in the bank. According to a recent study by the Employment Policy Foundation, an individual's expected lifetime earnings grow with each additional educational degree. Someone with no high school degree can anticipate an average lifetime earning of $872,396. But a person with a high school degree can expect lifetime earnings of $1,204,343, a person with some college $1,363,031, with a bachelor's degree $2,043,889, with a master's degree $2,402,929, and with a professional degree $2,910,720. Of course, career choice plays an important part in determining income; thus, it's possible for someone with an associate's degree (A.A.) to out-earn even someone with a masters or professional degree. But the bottom line: Earning your degree will literally pay off in the future; and to finance that degree, you'll need to manage money well now.

Getting the Big Picture

1. Create a positive affirmation about money. Many people hold negative beliefs about money and their ability to accumulate it. These doubts keep them from making wise choices that would cause more money to flow in their direction, or reduce the amount of money flowing away from them. Create an affirming statement about money, such as, *I am creating unlimited abundance in my life*. Along with your personal affirmation, repeat this financial affirmation to revise your choices about money.

2. Create a Financial Plan. Like a Life Plan, a Financial Plan gives you the big picture. It helps you make important decisions about the dollars flowing in and out of your personal treasury. Beginning your financial plan is as simple as filling out the form on the next page of this section. As a guideline, some financial experts suggest that expenditures in a healthy financial plan should be close to the following percentages of your net income (i.e., the money remaining after all required federal, state, and local tax deductions):

31% Housing	7% Entertainment
20% Transportation	7% Savings
16% Food	6% Clothing
8% Miscellaneous	5% Health

Obviously, after subtracting all of your expenses from your income, your goal is to have a positive and growing balance. If you have a negative balance, with each passing month, you'll slide deeper into debt. To avoid debt, you need to increase your income, decrease your expenses, or both.

3. Avoid credit blunders. Before we look at ways to develop a positive cash flow, let's look at the negative consequences of being financially irresponsible. Every time you create a debt, national credit agencies are keeping detailed records. When you later apply for credit, potential lenders will have access to how much you owe, who you owe, and how well you pay your debts. In fact, they'll learn your credit history for at least the past seven years, including late payments, underpayments, and lack of payments. This financial record tells lenders whether you are a good or bad risk, and, if you're seen as a bad risk, your application for a house or car loan may be turned down or only offered to you with extremely high interest rates. Your credit report might even wind up in the hands of a potential landlord or employer, affecting your ability to rent an apartment or even get your dream job. So, unwise financial choices in the present will follow you for years into the future, affecting the quality of your life and the life of your family. To see your present credit report and verify its accuracy, order a copy from Equifax at 800-685-1111 (*www.equifax.com*), Experian at 888-397-3742 (*www.experian.com*), or Trans Union at 800-888-4213 (*www.tuc.com*). Depending on where you live, the report will range in cost from free to about $8. If you make a credit blunder, immediately contact the company you owe and work out a payment schedule. The sooner you clean up your credit

My Financial Plan		
Step A: Monthly Income	Amount	Balance
Support from parents or others		
Scholarships		
Loans		
Investments		
Earned income		
Total Monthly Income (A)		
Step B: Necessary Fixed Monthly Expenses		
Housing (mortgage or rent)		
Transportation (car payments, insurance, bus pass, car pool)		
Taxes (federal and state income, Social Security, Medicare)		
Insurance (house, health and life)		
Childcare		
Tuition		
Bank fees		
Debt payment		
Savings and Investments		
Total Necessary Fixed Monthly Expenses (B)		
Step C: Necessary Variable Monthly Expenses		
Food and personal care items		
Clothing		
Telephone		
Gas and Electric		
Water		
Transportation (car repairs, maintenance, gasoline)		
Laundry and dry cleaning		
Doctor and pharmacy		
Childcare		
Books and software		
Computer		
Total Necessary Variable Monthly Expenses (C)		
Step D: Optional Fixed and Variable Monthly Expenses		
Eating out (including coffee, snacks, lunches)		
Entertainment (movies, theater, night life)		
Travel		
Hobbies		
Gifts		
Charitable contributions		
Miscellaneous (CDs, magazines, newspapers, etc.)		
Total Optional Variable Monthly Expenses (D)		
Money Remaining or Owed at End of Month (A-B-C-D = ?)		

report, the sooner your past mistakes will stop sabotaging your future success. If you need help with debt, contact the National Foundation for Credit Counseling (NFCC) for low- or no-cost credit assistance at 800-388-2227 (*www.nfcc.org*).

4. Find a bank or credit union. A bank or credit union helps you manage your money with services such as checking accounts, savings accounts, and easy access to cash through automated teller machines (ATMs). Your ideal financial institution offers a free checking account that requires no minimum balance and pays interest. Further, it offers a savings account with competitive interest rates. And, finally, your ideal financial institution offers free use of its ATMs and the ATMs belonging to other banks or credit unions as well. If you need to pay for any of these services, seek to minimize the yearly cost. Credit unions typically offer lower rates on these services than banks do. If you don't know of a credit union for which you qualify, contact the Credit Union National Association (800-358-5710) to get the phone number of your state's credit union league where you'll get help in finding one you may be able to join. Whether your checking account is with a bank or a credit union, be sure to balance your account regularly. This will save you the embarrassment and expense of bounced (rejected) checks because of insufficient funds.

Increasing the Flow of Money In

5. Apply for grants and scholarships. A great place to get an overview of financial aid sources is provided on the Internet by the U.S. government at *www.ed.gov/offices/OSFAP/Students/student.html*. The process of applying for financial aid dollars begins with the FAFSA: Free Application for Federal Student Aid. Using information you put on this form, the government decides what you or your family can afford to pay toward your education and what you may need in the way of financial assistance. Get copies of the form from your college's financial aid office or online at *www.fafsa.ed.gov*. The deadline for completing the FAFSA form is early

July; however, some colleges use the information from the FAFSA form to determine their own financial aid, so be sure to check your school's deadline or you could be out of luck (and money) for that year! A helpful source for conducting an online search for additional scholarship aid is *www. collegeanswer.com*. The value of qualifying for grants and scholarships is that, unlike loans, they don't need to be paid back. Federal Pell Grants provide financial support to the neediest students with amounts up to about $4,000. You can get comprehensive information from the Federal Student Aid Information Center in Washington at 800-433-3243 (*www.studentaid.ed.gov*). Here you can order a free copy of *The Student Guide*, and learn about programs that make up nearly three-fourths of all financial aid awarded to students. You can also search without cost for scholarships at Internet sites such as *http://collegeboard.com* and *www.fastweb.com* (so, don't waste money paying a private service to find you scholarships). Perhaps most important, spend time with a counselor in your college's financial aid office and let him or her help you get your share of the financial support available for a college education. Ron Smith, head of financial aid at Baltimore City Community College, offers this advice: "Students should apply early, provide accurate information, and follow-up until an award has been received."

6. Apply for low-cost loans. Stafford loans are guaranteed by the federal government so they generally offer the lowest interest rates. Subsidized Stafford loans of up to $2,625 per year for freshman, $3,500 for sophomores, and $5,500 for juniors and seniors are awarded through colleges on the basis of financial need, and the United States government pays interest until repayment begins, usually after graduation. Unsubsidized Stafford loans do not depend on financial need, but the interest accumulates while you are in college. You can apply for them through the Federal Direct Loan Program at 800-848-0979 (*www.ed.gov/offices/OPE/DirectLoan*) or through a private lender like a bank. Other federally guaranteed student loans include PLUS loans (made to students' parents) and Perkins loans (for lower-income students). You may be approved for more loan money than you actually need and be tempted to borrow it all; just remember that what you take now, you'll need to repay later. You don't want to finish your education with the burden of an unnecessarily large debt. The standard repayment plan for student loans is equal monthly payment for ten years. That's a long time to pay for an earlier bad choice.

7. Work. Even with grants, scholarships, and low-cost loans, many college students need employment to make ends meet. If this is your situation, figure out how much money you need each month beyond your financial aid, and set a goal to earn that amount while also adding work experience in your future field of employment. In other words, your purpose for working is both to make money AND to accumulate valuable employment experience and recommendations. In this way, you make it easier to find employment after college and perhaps even negotiate a higher starting salary. One place that may help you achieve this double goal is your campus job center. Additionally, on some campuses, instructors are able to hire student assistants to help them with their research. If you try but can't find employment that provides valuable work experience (or you're not sure what your future employment plans are), then seek work that allows you to earn your needed income in the fewest hours (saving you time to excel in your studies). Since many jobs you'll encounter in the newspaper pay little more than minimum wage, you may do better to create a high-paying job for yourself by using skills you already possess (or could easily learn). For example, one student noticed that each autumn the rain gutters of houses near his college became clogged with falling leaves. With a gasoline-powered leaf blower and a ladder in hand, he knocked on doors and offered to clean gutters for only $20. Few homeowners could resist such a bargain, and averaging two houses per hour, he earned nearly $700 each fall weekend.

8. Save and invest. If you haven't done so already, open a savings account and begin making regular deposits, even if it's only $20 per month (about what you'd pay for a pizza and a movie). Set a goal to accumulate a financial reserve for emergencies equal to three months' living expenses. After that, begin regular deposits in higher-income investments such as stocks, bonds and mutual funds, topics beyond the scope of this book, but well worth your effort to research. (For a brief overview, click on *www.fool.com/60second/indexfund. htm?ref=prmpgid*.) To gain practical experience and guidance, consider joining (or starting) an investment club on your campus. You don't have to be an economics major to realize that, by investing money regularly and benefiting from compound interest (earning interest on interest), even people with modest incomes can accumulate significant wealth. A way to make your savings grow even faster is to invest in a tax-deferred retirement account in which the money you deposit is not taxed until you withdraw it many years later, increasing the amount you can potentially save by many thousands of dollars. You can open such an account through your employer (who may even make additional contributions) or by opening an IRA (Individual Retirement Account) on your own. Some experts even suggest that you invest in such a tax-deferred retirement account before making deposits in a savings account. Your safety net in this approach is your credit cards, which you use only in an emergency (as you would use your savings account, if you had one). Of course, this latter approach depends on your responsible use of credit cards and isn't for everyone, but it is another choice to consider.

Decreasing the Flow of Money Out

9. Lower transportation expenses: Cars are expensive. Beyond car payments, there's also the cost for insurance, registration, regular maintenance, gasoline, repairs, tolls, and parking. And if you're under twenty-five, you'll pay more for insurance than someone over twenty-five (especially young men whose rates are double or triple those of older men). So, if money is tight, consider whether you can get along without a car for now. If you live on campus, this option should be fairly easy; if you commute, you could use public transportation or offer gas money to a classmate for rides to school. If you decide that you do need to buy a car, one expert suggests the following strategy for getting a good purchase price: After determining the model and options you want, call a number of dealers (preferably on the last day of the month when they are more likely to be anxious to make sales quotas), saying, "I'm going to buy this car today from the dealer who gives me the best price, so what's your lowest offer?" After calling at least six to eight dealers, call back the one with the second-to-lowest bid, reveal your lowest bid, and ask if they'll beat it. If so, buy their car. If not, purchase the one with the lowest bid. You can confirm that you're getting a fair price on a new or used car by visiting Kelley Blue Book (*www.kbb.com*) or Edmund's (*www. edmunds.com*).

10. Shop for car loans and insurance. *Before* you shop for your car, check interest rates for car loans with at least two banks and a credit union, and check insurance rates with at least three insurance companies. Knowing available interest rates will protect you from being pressured into signing a high-interest loan contract with the car dealer. On a car purchase, a lower interest rate can mean hundreds (even thousands) of dollars in savings over the life of the loan. You can also check for low interest rates on the Internet at *www.Bankrate.com* or *www.Lendingtree.com*. Likewise, automobile insurance rates for the same coverage can vary significantly from company to company. If you have good grades, tell the agent. A high GPA can reduce your premium by up to 25 percent with some companies! Oh, and think twice about allowing a friend to drive your car; if there's an accident, it's *your* insurance record and premiums that suffer, not your friend's.

11. Use credit cards wisely. You'll very likely be swamped with invitations to open credit card accounts. You're not alone. From 1990 to 2000, the average credit card debt of college students jumped 305 percent, from $900 to $2,748, and nearly 10 percent of college students owe greater than $7,000 on their credit cards, according to a 2000 survey by Sallie Mae, a major national handler of student loans. So, first, consider whether you should even *have* a credit card. Visa, Master Card, and other credit cards provide you with short-term loans to purchase anything you want up to your credit limit. These companies are counting on you to postpone paying off the loan beyond the grace period (the time during which the loan is free) and, thus, to accumulate interest at their high rates. The consequences to your finances can be staggering. Suppose you're twenty years old and owe $3,500 on a credit card that charges 17 percent interest and you regularly pay the minimum charge. You won't pay off that debt until you're fifty-three years old, and the amount you will ultimately pay is nearly $11,000! And if you ever miss a payment, you'll incur a triple penalty. First, you'll be charged a late fee that can be as much as $29 for being even one day overdue. Next, some banks punish late payers by raising their interest rates to "penalty rates" of 20 percent or more. Finally, late payments can show up on your credit report, making it difficult for you to get loans later for a house or car. How serious is the problem of credit card misuse by college students? An administrator at the University of Indiana noted, "We lose more students to credit card debt than to academic failure." So, use a credit card only if you can discipline yourself to pay off most, if not all, of your balance every month. If you can't, a wiser choice would be to cut up your credit cards (or not even apply for one in the first place). To understand the true cost of buying with credit cards, try the exercise "The Cost of Credit" on the *On Course* web site at: *college.hmco.com/pic/downing5e*

12. Choose credit cards wisely. If you decide that you do have the discipline to use a credit card wisely, realize that all credit cards are not created equal. Compare your options and choose the one with the lowest interest rates, the longest grace period (time you get to use the money before paying interest), and the lowest annual fee (preferably free). Some cards offer a reward for using them, such as rebates for purchases or frequent flyer miles that can be exchanged for airlines tickets. To find the best deals on credit cards, visit Internet sites such as *www.bankrate.com* or *www.cardweb.com*.

13. Use debit cards wisely. A debit card is similar to a credit card, except that the funds come not as a loan from a company but as a withdrawal from your own checking account. The danger is that you may not record and track every purchase made on your debit card, as you more likely would if you wrote a check. Consequently, you can easily overdraw your checking account and incur financial penalties for bounced checks (not to mention annoying your creditors). Use a debit card only if you have the discipline to track its every use and keep your checking account balance current.

14. Use ATM cards wisely. An ATM card, like a debit card, draws from your personal account, but here the withdrawal is in cash. ATM cards are so easy to use that some financial experts refer to them as "death cards." Say you withdraw $100 in cash on Monday, and by Thursday the money has dribbled away, so you take out another $100 that disappears by the weekend. After a couple of weeks like this, your money runs out before the month does, and you're slipping ever deeper into debt. Use an ATM card only if you have the discipline to record every withdrawal and track what you do with your cash.

15. Pay off high-rate debt. When you pay off a loan (such as a credit card balance) that charges 17 percent, that's the same as investing your money at a guaranteed 17 percent rate of return. Better yet, the 17 percent return is tax free, so you're actually earning a return of more than 20 percent. Compare that to the puny interest rate you'd be earning in a savings account. If you don't have extra money in savings to pay off money you owe, a variation is to transfer debt from high-interest-rate loans to lower-interest-rate loans (but watch carefully for hidden transfer costs on some accounts).

16. Dispute inaccurate charges. Don't assume all of your bills are correct. Watch your credit card bill, your bank statement, and all of your bills carefully for suspicious charges like a purchase you didn't

make or an inaccurate late fee. Call the number on your statement and explain pleasantly but forcefully why you believe the charge is in error. Typically, the person you talk to is empowered to correct such errors. In fact, if you have a good credit history, it may even pay to question some legitimate charges. I once forgot to pay my credit card bill on time and got charged more than $100 in late fees and interest; I called the credit card company, asked the representative to look at my excellent record of paying on time, and requested that the penalties be waived this once. She agreed, making my five-minute phone call well worth the effort!

17. Use tax credits. Tax credits are expenses you can subtract directly from your federal income tax. If you're paying for college yourself, you may be eligible for a Hope Scholarship Credit of up to $1,500 in each of your first two years. In years you don't claim the Hope credit, you may qualify for up to $1,000 a year in Lifetime Learning Credits, which can be taken in any year of college or graduate school. The credit covers up to 20 percent of your first $10,000 of qualified tuition and related expenses. For details, get a copy of IRS (Internal Revenue Service) Publication 970, *Tax Benefits for Higher Education.*

18. Avoid the "Let's Go Out" trap. You or a friend says, "Let's go out." You go for food or drinks and spend $20 . . . or more. Do this a couple times a week and you'll wind up dropping hundreds of dollars a month into a deep, dark hole. One student reported that even after she ran out of money for the month, friends would say, "Oh, c'mon out with us. I'll loan you the money." That meant she was already spending next month's income. Sure, put entertainment money into your monthly financial plan, but, when it's gone, have the self-discipline to stop going out. Instead, invite friends over and make it BYO—Bring Your Own. Or, you could make a great financial choice by staying home and studying. Studying costs you nothing now and makes a great investment in your future income.

19. Track your expenditures. To plug a leak, you have to know where it is. So, carry a note pad with you and record every penny you spend for at least a week, preferably longer. (Of course your Inner Defender will probably say, "This is stupid and boring." Okay, it is boring, but the benefit is worth it!) Examine your recorded expenses and look for financial leaks that don't show up in your financial plan. One student was shocked to discover that he was averaging $22 per week ($1,144 per year!) on fast-food lunches; he started packing his lunch and saved a bundle.

20. Examine each expense line in your financial plan for possible reductions. Here are some of the money-saving options my students have come up with: Find a roommate to reduce housing costs. Exchange babysitting with fellow students to minimize childcare expenses. Car pool to share commuting costs. Cut up credit cards. Change banks to lower or eliminate monthly checking fees. Exchange music CDs with friends instead of buying new ones. Shop at discount clubs and buy nonperishables (like toilet paper and laundry detergent) in bulk.

Read magazines and newspapers at the library, instead of buying them. Pay creditors on time to avoid penalty charges. Delay purchases until the item goes on sale (such as right after Christmas). Find other money saving ideas on the Internet at *www.lowermybills.com*.

Money-Management Exercise

To help *increase* your flow of money in, make a list of skills you have that you could possibly turn into a high-hourly-wage self-employment opportunity. To help *decrease* your flow of money out, make a list of choices you could make that would each save you $25 or more per year. Compare your two lists with those of classmates to see if you can find additional choices you didn't think of. Add up all of the items on your list (income and outflow) and see how much you could improve your financial picture in one year by making these choices.

Embracing Change

Do one thing different this week

Strong emotions are part of the human experience, but what we do with them is up to us. Victims often let strong emotions become their excuse for making choices that lead to immediate pleasure or escape from discomfort while sabotaging future goals and dream. Creators, however, have learned to weather the storms of strong emotions and refuse to be blown off course by runaway feelings. From the actions below, pick ONE new belief or behavior and experiment with it for one week, seeing if this new choice helps you create more positive outcomes and experiences. After seven days, assess your results. If your outcomes and experiences improve, you now have a tool that will help you stay on course for the rest of your life.

Beliefs and Behaviors	Day 1	Day 2	Day 3	Day 4	Day 5	Day 6	Day 7
Think: "I create my own happiness and peace of mind."							
Write a list of eight emotions and add eight more emotions to the list each day. Afterwards, circle which of the fifty-six emotions you experienced during that week.							
Identify a "strong emotion" as you are experiencing it. Note at the end of the week if you see a pattern in the kind of strong emotions that you experience.							
Identify a "strong emotion" as someone else is experiencing it.							
Talk to someone about emotions, yours or theirs.							
Take the following new action to reduce stress in my life:							
Think the following new thought to reduce stress in my life:							
Notice when I experience "flow," and observe what I am doing at the time.							
Show fellow students the list of five instructor qualities on page 227 that create "flow," and ask them to name the instructor they have had who most demonstrates these qualities. Consider enrolling in a class taught by one of these instructors.							
Do the following to nurture myself physically, mentally, or emotionally (from pages 232–233):							
Use the following money-management strategy (write your choice from pages 235–241):							

(continued on page 243)

During my seven-day experiment, what happened?

As a result of what happened, what did I learn or relearn?

Staying On Course to Your Success

SUCCESSFUL STUDENTS . . .	STRUGGLING STUDENTS . . .
■ **gain self-awareness,** consciously employing behaviors, beliefs, and attitudes that keep them on course.	■ make important choices unconsciously, being directed by self-sabotaging habits and outdated life Scripts.
■ **adopt lifelong learning,** finding valuable lessons and wisdom in nearly every experience they have.	■ resist learning new ideas and skills, viewing learning as fearful or boring rather than as mental play.
■ **develop emotional intelligence,** effectively managing their emotions in support of their goals and dreams.	■ live at the mercy of strong emotions such as anger, depression, anxiety, or a need for instant gratification.
■ **believe in themselves,** seeing themselves as capable, lovable, and unconditionally worthy human beings.	■ doubt their competence and personal value, feeling inadequate to create their desired outcomes and experiences.

Planning Your Next Steps

FOCUS QUESTIONS   How have you changed while keeping your journal? What changes do you still want to make?

Congratulations on completing this part of your life's journey. Your efforts and successes are signs of great things to come! Let's revisit the highlights:

You are the only one who can ever determine whether you are successful or not. . . .
When it comes right down to it, the grades you give yourself are the grades that count.

Shad Helmstetter

First, we saw that our choices create the outcomes and experiences of our lives, and that the foundation of our success is **PERSONAL RESPONSIBILITY**— the ability to make wise choices that keep us on course without interfering with the right of others to do the same. Although in reality we are *not* responsible for everything that occurs in our lives, holding this belief motivates us to find and act upon options we might otherwise overlook. Accepting personal responsibility, therefore, maximizes the control we have over creating the outcomes and experiences of our lives.

Next, we explored how **SELF-MOTIVATION** energizes us from within. We learned that intrinsic motivation results from the interplay of the *value* that we place on any endeavor (both the outcomes and experiences) and our *expectation* of success. We saw that choosing personally meaningful goals and dreams generates a powerful inner drive, and the more specifically we visualize our future life, the more likely we are to make it a reality. Although we can't expect to create every outcome and experience we want, by committing to clear goals and dreams, we generate the positive energy necessary for creating a life worth living.

Then, we considered the power of effective **SELF-MANAGEMENT**. We saw that goals and dreams become reality when we effectively manage our efforts to stay on course, consistently doing first what is important. We explored the illusion of time management, realizing that all we can actually manage is our own choices. To that end, we examined written self-management tools that help us take effective actions toward our goals and dreams. Finally we examined how focus and persistence together create self-discipline, a key to making our dreams come true.

Destiny is not a matter of chance; it is a matter of choice. It is not a thing to be waited for; it is a thing to be achieved.

William Jennings Bryant

Following this, we examined the value of **INTERDEPENDENCE**. In this chapter, we saw how people mature from dependence to independence and finally to interdependence. Interdependent people build networks of mutually supportive people who help one another create lives worth living. By developing effective listening and communication skills, interdependent people strengthen relationships, helping them achieve more in their lives while enjoying the journey.

At this point, we asked how it is that we can do so many things right yet still get off course?. While exploring **SELF-AWARENESS**, we sought to uncover self-defeating patterns of behavior, thought, and emotion, as well as our limiting core beliefs. Now more conscious of some of our Scripts, we began rewriting some of the outdated inner programs that get us off course.

In Chapter 7, we looked at **LIFELONG LEARNING**. We began by exploring how the human brain learns, realizing that for deep and lasting learning to take place, we must be active (rather than passive) learners. Further, we discovered our preferred learning styles so that we can maximize our efforts to learn in college and beyond. Then we looked at how to use feedback to constantly monitor how we are doing, to make course corrections whenever necessary, and to learn the important lessons provided by the University of Life.

Coming near the end of our journey, we reflected on the important part that emotions play in our lives and acknowledged that no worldly success is meaningful without a positive inner experience of life. Therefore, we considered ways for developing **EMOTIONAL INTELLIGENCE**, realizing that we are as responsible for the experiences we create in our inner world as we are for the outcomes we create in our outer world. We learned the components of emotional intelligence and used this knowledge to explore how to reduce distress and create more flow and happiness in our lives.

For each of these important inner qualities, we identified how they are not only the keys to our success in college but also to staying **ON COURSE AT WORK**. The same "soft" skills that allow us to excel in college will propel us to great success in our careers as well.

Throughout our journey, we looked at **WISE CHOICES IN COLLEGE**, learning and practicing study strategies for maximizing what we learn in college, college customs for negotiating the new terrain of higher education, and proven money management skills for making college financially possible.

In a profound sense, each human life has the potentiality of becoming an art work. To that degree, each of us can become an artist-in-life with our finest creation being our own Self.

Ira Progoff

In each chapter we explored the center of our experience—our "selves." There, we discussed the essential nature of **BELIEVING IN OURSELVES**. Unless we believe in ourselves, our outdated Scripts will likely sabotage all of our efforts to succeed. So we looked at various strategies for developing core beliefs such as self-acceptance, self-confidence, self-respect, and self-love. On this transformational journey, we have been slowly but surely rewriting our limiting Scripts so that we can tap our greatest potential and create rich, personally fulfilling lives.

Commencement

Although our travels together are coming to an end, your journey has really just begun. Look out there to your future. What do you want? What are you willing to do to get it? Make a plan and go for it!

Sure, you'll probably get off course at times. But now you have the strategies—both outer and inner—to get back on course. Before heading out again toward your goals and dreams, take a moment to review your tools. Look over the table of contents of this book, which provides an overview of what you've learned. Read the chapter openers, which compare the choices of successful and struggling people. Revisit the Embracing Change activities at the end of each chapter, which list the empowering beliefs and behaviors you have learned. At any time you can return to this book and to your journal to remind yourself of anything you forget.

Assess yourself, again

It isn't where you came from; it's where you're going that counts.

Ella Fitzgerald

On the next page is a duplicate of the self-assessment you took in Chapter 1. Take it again. (Don't look back at your previous answers yet.) In Journal Entry 31, you will compare your first scores with your scores today, and you'll consider the changes you have made. Acknowledge yourself for your courage to grow. Look, also, at the changes that you still need to make if you are to continue evolving into your best self.

You now have much of what you need to stay on course to the life of your dreams. The rest you can learn on your journey. Be bold! Begin today!

Self-Assessment

You can take this self-assessment on the Internet by visiting the *On Course* web site at *college.hmco.com/pic/downing5e*. Select Downing's *On Course* from the list of textbook sites. You'll receive your score immediately . . . and see how others scored as well.

Read the statements below and score each one according to how true or false you believe it is about you. To get an accurate picture of yourself, consider what **IS** true about you (not what you want to be true). Obviously there are no right or wrong answers. Assign each statement a number from zero to ten, as follows:

Totally false   0 1 2 3 4 5 6 7 8 9 10   Totally true

1. ____ I control how successful I will be.
2. ____ I'm not sure why I'm in college.
3. ____ I spend most of my time doing important things.
4. ____ When I encounter a challenging problem, I try to solve it by myself.
5. ____ When I get off course from my goals and dreams, I realize it right away.
6. ____ I'm not sure how I learn best.
7. ____ Whether I'm happy or not depends mostly on me.
8. ____ I'll truly accept myself only after I eliminate my faults and weaknesses.
9. ____ Forces out of my control (like poor teaching) are the cause of low grades I receive in school.
10. ____ If I lose my motivation in college, I know how to get it back.
11. ____ I don't need to write things down because I can remember what I need to do.
12. ____ I have a network of people in my life that I can count on for help.
13. ____ If I have habits that hinder my success, I'm not sure what they are.
14. ____ When I don't like the way an instructor teaches, I know how to learn the subject anyway.
15. ____ When I get very angry, sad, or afraid, I do or say things that create a problem for me.
16. ____ When I think about performing an upcoming challenge (like taking a test), I usually see myself doing well.
17. ____ When I have a problem, I take positive actions to find a solution.
18. ____ I don't know how to set effective short-term and long-term goals.
19. ____ I remember to do important things.
20. ____ When I have a difficult course in school, I study alone.
21. ____ I'm aware of beliefs I have that hinder my success.
22. ____ I don't know how to study effectively.
23. ____ When choosing between doing an important school assignment or something really fun, I usually do the school assignment.
24. ____ I break promises that I make to myself or to others.
25. ____ I make poor choices that keep me from getting what I really want in life.
26. ____ I have a written plan that includes both my short-term and long-term goals.
27. ____ I lack self-discipline.
28. ____ I listen carefully when other people are talking.
29. ____ I'm stuck with any habits of mine that hinder my success.
30. ____ When I face a disappointment (like failing a test), I ask myself, "What lesson can I learn here?"
31. ____ I often feel bored, anxious, or depressed.
32. ____ I feel just as worthwhile as any other person.

Totally false   0 1 2 3 4 5 6 7 8 9 10   Totally true

33. ____ Forces outside of me (like luck or other people) control how successful I will be.
34. ____ College is an important step on the way to accomplishing my goals and dreams.
35. ____ I spend most of my time doing unimportant things.
36. ____ When I encounter a challenging problem, I ask for help.
37. ____ I can be off course from my goals and dreams for quite a while without realizing it.
38. ____ I know how I learn best.
39. ____ My happiness depends mostly on what's happened to me lately.
40. ____ I accept myself just as I am, even with my faults and weaknesses.
41. ____ I am the cause of low grades I receive in school.
42. ____ If I lose my motivation in college, I don't know how I'll get it back.
43. ____ I use self-management tools (like calendars and to-do lists) that help me remember to do important things.
44. ____ I know very few people whom I can count on for help.
45. ____ I'm aware of the habits I have that hinder my success.
46. ____ If I don't like the way an instructor teaches, I'll probably do poorly in the course.
47. ____ When I'm very angry, sad, or afraid, I know how to manage my emotions so I don't do anything I'll regret later.
48. ____ When I think about performing an upcoming challenge (like taking a test), I usually see myself doing poorly.
49. ____ When I have a problem, I complain, blame others, or make excuses.
50. ____ I know how to set effective short-term and long-term goals.
51. ____ I forget to do important things.
52. ____ When I have a difficult course in school, I find a study partner or join a study group.
53. ____ I'm unaware of beliefs I have that hinder my success.
54. ____ I've learned to use specific study skills that work effectively for me.
55. ____ I often feel happy and fully alive.
56. ____ I keep promises that I make to myself or to others.
57. ____ I make wise choices that help me get what I really want in life.
58. ____ I live day to day, without much of a plan for the future.
59. ____ I am a self-disciplined person.
60. ____ I get distracted easily when other people are talking.
61. ____ I know how to change habits of mine that hinder my success.
62. ____ When I face a disappointment (like failing a test), I feel pretty helpless.
63. ____ When choosing between doing an important school assignment or something really fun, I usually do something fun.
64. ____ I feel less worthy than other people.

Transfer your scores to the scoring sheets on the next page. For each of the eight areas, total your scores in columns A and B. Then total your final scores as shown in the sample.

Self-Assessment Scoring Sheet

SAMPLE		SCORE #1: Accepting Personal Responsibility		SCORE #2: Discovering Self-Motivation	
A	B	A	B	A	B
6. __8__	29. __3__	1. _____	9. _____	10. _____	2. _____
14. __5__	35. __3__	17. _____	25. _____	26. _____	18. _____
21. __6__	50. __6__	41. _____	33. _____	34. _____	42. _____
73. __9__	56. __2__	57. _____	49. _____	50. _____	58. _____
__28__ + 40 − __14__ = 54		_____ + 40 − _____ = _____		_____ + 40 − _____ = _____	
SCORE #3: Mastering Self-Management		SCORE #4: Employing Interdependence		SCORE #5: Gaining Self-Awareness	
A	B	A	B	A	B
3. _____	11. _____	12. _____	4. _____	5. _____	13. _____
19. _____	27. _____	28. _____	20. _____	21. _____	29. _____
43. _____	35. _____	36. _____	44. _____	45. _____	37. _____
59. _____	51. _____	52. _____	60. _____	61. _____	53. _____
_____ + 40 − _____ = _____		_____ + 40 − _____ = _____		_____ + 40 − _____ = _____	
SCORE #6: Adopting Lifelong Learning		SCORE #7: Developing Emotional Intelligence		SCORE #8: Believing in Myself	
A	B	A	B	A	B
14. _____	6. _____	7. _____	15. _____	16. _____	8. _____
30. _____	22. _____	23. _____	31. _____	32. _____	24. _____
38. _____	46. _____	47. _____	39. _____	40. _____	48. _____
54. _____	62. _____	55. _____	63. _____	56. _____	64. _____
_____ + 40 − _____ = _____		_____ + 40 − _____ = _____		_____ + 40 − _____ = _____	

Carry these scores to the corresponding boxes in the chart on the next page, writing them in the "Your Score" column.

Choices of Successful Students

Your score	Successful students...	Struggling students...
Score _____	**accept self-responsibility,** seeing themselves as the primary cause of their outcomes and experiences.	see themselves as Victims, believing that what happens to them is determined primarily by external forces such as fate, luck, and powerful others.
Score _____	**discover self-motivation,** finding purpose in their lives by discovering personally meaningful goals and dreams.	have difficulty sustaining motivation, often feeling depressed, frustrated, and/or resentful about a lack of direction in their lives.
Score _____	**master self-management,** consistently planning and taking purposeful actions in pursuit of their goals and dreams.	seldom identify specific actions needed to accomplish a desired outcome. And when they do, they tend to procrastinate.
Score _____	**employ interdependence,** building mutually supportive relationships that help them achieve their goals and dreams (while helping others do the same).	are solitary, seldom requesting, even rejecting, offers of assistance from those who could help.
Score _____	**gain self-awareness,** consciously employing behaviors, beliefs, and attitudes that keep them on course.	make important choices unconsciously, being directed by self-sabotaging habits and out dated life Scripts.
Score _____	**adopt lifelong learning,** finding valuable lessons and wisdom in nearly every experience they have.	resist learning new ideas and skills, viewing learning as fearful or boring rather than as mental play.
Score _____	**develop emotional intelligence,** effectively managing their emotions in support of their goals and dreams.	live at the mercy of strong emotions, such as anger, depression, anxiety, or a need for instant gratification.
Score _____	**believe in themselves,** seeing themselves as capable, lovable, and unconditionally worthy human beings.	doubt their competence and personal value, feeling inadequate to create their desired outcomes and experiences.

Interpreting your scores: A score of . . .

0–39   Indicates an area where your choices will **seldom** keep you on course.
40–63   Indicates an area where your choices will **sometimes** keep you on course.
64–80   Indicates an area where your choices will **usually** keep you on course.

Journal Entry 31

*And the end of all our
exploring
Will be to arrive where we
started
And know the place for the
first time.*

T. S. Eliot

In this activity, you will examine the changes you have made since the beginning of this course, and you'll plan your next steps toward success in college and in life.

1. In your journal, write the eight areas of the self-assessment and transfer your two scores from the chart on page 9 (first score) and the chart on page 251 (second score), as follows:

First Score	Second Score	
_____	_____	1. Accepting personal responsibility
_____	_____	2. Discovering self-motivation
_____	_____	3. Mastering self-management
_____	_____	4. Employing interdependence
_____	_____	5. Gaining self-awareness
_____	_____	6. Adopting lifelong learning
_____	_____	7. Developing emotional intelligence
_____	_____	8. Believing in myself

2. Comparing the results from the two self-assessment questionnaires, write about the area(s) in which you have raised your score. Remember to answer questions that a thoughtful reader would have about what you are writing, diving deep by using the four E's!

3. Further comparing the results from the two self-assessment questionnaires, write in depth about the area(s) in which you most want to continue improving. Remember the saying "If you keep doing what you've been doing, you'll keep getting what you've been getting." With this understanding in mind, identify the specific changes you'd like to make in your behaviors, thoughts, emotions, and beliefs in the months and years to come.

By the way, if one of your scores went down over the semester, consider that this result may indicate not that you became less effective but that you are now more aware of what's necessary to excel in this area.

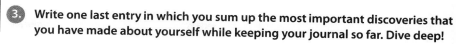

3. Write one last entry in which you sum up the most important discoveries that you have made about yourself while keeping your journal so far. Dive deep!

Onward!

APPENDICES

Autobiography in Five Short Chapters

Bibliography

Acknowledgements

Quick Coach Guide to Avoiding Plagiarism

Index

AUTOBIOGRAPHY IN FIVE SHORT CHAPTERS

CHAPTER ONE

I walk down the street.
> There is a deep hole in the sidewalk.
> I fall in.
> I am lost...I am helpless.
> It isn't my fault.
>> It takes forever to find a way out.

CHAPTER TWO

I walk down the same street.
> There is a deep hole in the sidewalk.
> I pretend I don't see it.
> I fall in again.
I can't believe I am in the same place.
> But it is my fault.
It still takes a long time to get out.

CHAPTER THREE

I walk down the same street.
> There is a deep hole in the sidewalk.
> I *see* it is there.
> I still fall in...it's a habit...but, my eyes are open
>> I know where I am,
It is *my* fault.
I get out immediately.

CHAPTER FOUR

I walk down the same street.
> There is a deep hole in the sidewalk.
> I walk around it.

CHAPTER FIVE

I walk down another street.
>> —Portia Nelson

Bibliography

Adams, Kathleen. *Journal to the Self: Twenty-Two Paths to Personal Growth.* Warner Books, 1990.

Allen, David. *Getting Things Done.* Viking, 2001.

Bradshaw, John. *Homecoming.* Bantam Books, 1990.

Brandon, Nathaniel. *How to Raise Your Self-Esteem.* Bantam, 1988.

Burns, David, M.D. *Feeling Good.* William Morrow & Company, 1980.

Buzan, Tony. *Make the Most of Your Mind.* Simon and Schuster, 1977.

Cappacchione, Lucia. *The Creative Journal.* Newcastle, 1989.

Carnegie, Dale. *How to Win Friends and Influence People.* Pocket Books, 1936.

Chapman, Joyce. *Live Your Dream.* Newcastle, 1990.

Ciarrochi, Joseph. *Emotional Intelligence in Everyday Life.* Psychology Press, 2001.

Covey, Stephen R. *7 Habits of Highly Effective People.* Simon and Schuster, 1989.

Csikszentmihalyi, Mihaly. *Flow: The Psychology of Optimal Experience.* Harper & Row, 1990.

Davis, Martha, Elizabeth Robbins Eshelman, and Matthew McKay. *The Relaxation and Stress Reduction Workbook.* New Harbinger, 2000.

deBono, Edward. *deBono's Thinking Course.* Facts on File, 1982.

Dyer, Wayne. *You'll See It When You Believe It.* Morrow, 1989.

Firestone, Robert W., Lisa Firestone, Joyce Catlett, and Pat Love. *Conquer Your Critical Inner Voice.* New Harbinger, 2002.

Frankl, Viktor E., M.D. *Man's Search for Meaning.* Washington Square Press, 1959.

Garfield, Charles. *Peak Performers.* Avon Books, 1986.

Gawain, Shakti. *Creative Visualization.* Bantam Books, 1979.

Glasser, William. *Reality Therapy.* Harper and Row, 1978.

Goleman, Daniel. *Emotional Intelligence.* Bantam Books, 1995.

———. *Working with Emotional Intelligence.* Bantam Books, 2000.

Griessman, B. Eugene. *The Achievement Factors.* Dodd, Mead, 1987.

Harmon, Willis, and Howard Rheingold. *Higher Creativity.* J.P. Tarcher, 1984.

Harris, Thomas. *I'm OK, You're OK.* Harper and Row, 1967.

Helmstetter, Shad. *Choices.* Simon and Schuster, 1989.

Herrmann, Ned. *The Creative Brain.* Brain Books, 1989.

James, Muriel, and Dorothy Jongeward. *Born to Win.* Addison-Wesley, 1978.

Jensen, Eric. *Brain-Based Learning.* The Brain Store, 2000.

Keirsey, D., and M. Bates. *Please Understand Me.* Prometheus Nemesis Books, 1978.

Keyes, Ken, Jr. *Handbook to Higher Consciousness.* Living Love Publishing, 1975.

Leyden-Rubenstein, Lori. *The Stress Management Handbook*. Keats Publishing, 1998.

Mandino, Og. *A Better Way to Live*. Bantam Books, 1990.

Mazlow, Abraham H. *Toward a Psychology of Being*. Van Nostrand Reinhold, 1968.

McKay, Matthew, Patrick Fanning, Carole Honeychurch, and Catherine Sutker. *The Self-Esteem Companion*. MJF Books, 2001.

Merlevede, Patrick E., Denis Bridoux, and Rudy Vandamme. *7 Steps to Emotional Intelligence*. Crown House, 2001.

Merrill, A. Roger. *Connections: Quadrant II Time Management*. Publishers Press, 1987.

Moore, Thomas. *Care of the Soul*. HarperCollins, 1992.

Myers, David G. *The Pursuit of Happiness*. Avon Books, 1992.

Myers, Isabelle. *The Myers-Briggs Type Indicator*. Consulting Psychological Press, 1962.

Ostrander, Sheila, and Lynn Schroeder. *Super-learning*. Dell, 1979.

Peck, M. Scott, M.D. *The Road Less Traveled*. Simon and Schuster, 1978.

Progroff, Ira. *At a Journal Workshop*. Dialogue House Library, 1975.

Remen, Rachel Naomi, M.D. *Kitchen Table Wisdom*. Riverhead Books, 1996.

Restak, Richard, M.D. *The Mind*. Bantam Books, 1988.

Richardson, Cheryl. *Turning Inward: A Private Journal for Self-Reflection*. Hay House, 2003.

Robbins, Anthony. *Awaken the Giant Within*. Simon and Schuster, 1991.

Rogers, Carl. *Freedom to Learn*. Charles E. Merrill, 1969.

Satir, Virginia. *The New People-making*. Science and Behavior Books, 1988.

Schiraldi, Glen R., Patrick Fanning, and Matthew McKay. *The Self-Esteem Workbook*. New Harbinger, 2001.

Segal, Jeanne. *Raising Your Emotional Intelligence*. Henry Holt, 1997.

Seligman, Martin. *Learned Optimism*. Alfred A. Knopf, 1991.

Smith, Hyrum W. *The 10 Natural Laws of Successful Time and Life Management*. Warner Books, 1994.

Sousa, David A. *How the Brain Learns*. Corwin Press, 2006.

Steiner, Claude M. *Scripts People Live*. Bantam Books, 1974.

Stone, Hal, and Sidra Stone. *Embracing Your Inner Critic*. HarperCollins, 1993.

Tobias, Sheila. *Overcoming Math Anxiety*. W.W. Norton & Co., 1993.

vonOech, Roger. *A Whack on the Side of the Head*. Warner Books, 1983.

Waitley, Denis. *Seeds of Greatness*. Pocket Books, 1983.

Ward, Francine. *Esteemable Acts: 10 Actions for Building Real Self-Esteem*. Broadway Books, 2003.

Zilbergeld, Bernie, and Arnold A. Lazarus. *Mind Power*. Ballantine Books, 1987.

Acknowledgements

Page 82: Outline sample from Carol Kanar, The Confident Student, Third Edition, p. 353. Copyright (c) 1998 by Houghton Mifflin Company. Used by permission.

Page 83: From Walter Pauk, How to Study in College, Sixth Edition, p. 205. Copyright (c) 1997 by Houghton Mifflin Company. Used by permission.

Page 177: Inspired by "Take This Fish and Look at It" by Samuel J. Scudder, 1874.

Page 144: Notecard sample from Carol Kanar, The Confident Student, Third Edition, p. 353. Copyright (c) 1998 by Houghton Mifflin Company. Used by permission.

Page 144: From James F. Shepard, College Study Skills, Sixth Edition, p. 191. Copyright (c) 1997 by Houghton Mifflin Company. Used by permission.

Page 213: Adapted text (Components of Emotional Intelligence) from Daniel Goleman, Emotional Intelligence (New York: Ballantine Books, 1994), p. 43.

Contents
The Quick Coach Guide to Avoiding Plagiarism

Preface   v

1   Introduction   1
In this Guide   1
Why this Guide is Important   1
Defining Plagiarism   2
Understanding When to Give Credit   3
Knowing the Rules   4
Knowledge Check   5

2   Avoiding Plagiarism   6
Doing Your Own Work, Using Your Own Words   6
Allowing Enough Time   7
Keeping Track of Sources   8
Taking Notes   8
Clarifying Who is Speaking   9
Crediting the Source   9
Citing Sources Correctly   10
Quoting   12
Paraphrasing   12
Avoiding Patchwriting   12
Summarizing   13
Avoiding Using Other Students' Papers and Paper Mills   13
Knowledge Check   14

3   Quotations and Parenthetical Citations   15
Understanding Citations   15
Using Parenthetical Citations   17
Using Direct Quotations   19
Using Indirect Quotations   20
Using Ellipses and Brackets   21

Using Block Quotations   21
Knowledge Check   22

4   Paraphrasing   23
Defining a Paraphrase   23
Giving Credit to the Source   24
Sample Paraphrases   25
Citing Paraphrases   29
Knowledge Check   30

5   Summarizing   31
Defining a Summary   31
Sample Summary   32
Knowledge Check   34

6   References and Works Cited Lists   35
Citation Content   35
Basic Format   36
MLA Citations   36
APA Citations   39
MLA and APA Citations for Web Publications   41
Types of Reference Lists   43
Knowledge Check   44

7   Practice Quiz   45

8   Additional Sources of Information   49
Citation Style Overviews   49
Documentation Styles by Discipline   49
Free Citation Generators   50
Reference Tracking   50
Plagiarism   50
Style Guides   51

Works Cited   53

Answers to Exercises   54

Preface

"It is better to fail in originality than to succeed in imitation."

Herman Melville (1819–1891)

This guide is the culmination of years of working with students and their writing assignments in classrooms, learning labs, and online classes. When students were caught using the writing and research of others—plagiarizing—we found most cases to involve students with weak writing, poor English skills, or students who did not understand how to use citations. Rather than see students make uninformed mistakes that were setbacks to their education and future, we looked for ways to help them successfully author their own work and avoid plagiarizing.

As educators, we emphasized the educational aspects instead of academic integrity. We did not want to be punitive to our students. Our goal was to prevent them from making citation errors in the first place and getting punished for what was really not intentional. By making sure students had the knowledge to create honest work, we could improve their skills and motivation, reducing the incidents of plagiarism in our classes. This also made it much easier to separate the honest students from those who were not. Once we employed this model, the students we caught plagiarizing knew what they were doing. It became obvious that an educational approach weeded out the accidental cheaters from the intentional cheaters, making honor code enforcement easier.

Student response to the educational model of academic integrity has been excellent and this guide is the result. We hope it helps students learn the importance of doing honest work and gives them the necessary tools to write essays, reports, term papers, and the like with pride and confidence.

ABOUT THE AUTHORS

Rosemarie Menager, Ed.D. is a psychology professor at Foothill College. A graduate of USC's Rossiter School of Education Human Performance Technology cohort, she did her dissertation on student success in online learning. After discovering that many of her students were inadvertently plagiarizing because they lacked a clear understanding of how to correctly cite their work, Dr. Menager created "Educate First and Enforce Next," an educational approach to preventing plagiarism that informs the content of this *Quick Coach Guide.* Dr. Menager has also served as a consultant for the "Stressed-Out Student (SOS)" conference at Stanford University and is currently working on a plagiarism intervention for students in grades K-12. In her spare time, Dr. Menager is a mom, impressionist oil painter, and member of a sheriff's mounted search and rescue group.

Lyn Paulos is an assistive technology lab technician at Santa Barbara City College. She is currently completing her B.S. in psychology and will be pursuing an M.S. through the University of Phoenix. Ms. Paulos currently manages a state-of-the art adaptive technology learning lab at Santa Barbara City College. A frequent presenter at technology conferences and passionate advocate for student academic integrity, she has also authored an online tutorial on plagiarism prevention and education entitled "Authoring Your Own Work." In her extracurricular life, Ms. Paulos is a celebrated lampwork glass artist whose creations are collected internationally.

1
Introduction

IN THIS GUIDE

This guide is designed to help students avoid the pitfalls of plagiarism. The chapters cover the correct way to credit sources, quote, cite, paraphrase, summarize, create a list of references, and more. Knowledge checks are provided at the end of each section for your review.

WHY THIS GUIDE IS IMPORTANT

What do you want from college? There are many answers to this question, and certainly one of them is to succeed in your coursework. Probably the last thing you would want is to fail a class for cheating or plagiarizing by mistake. If you are unfamiliar with the practices and rules of incorporating work from other sources, then you will find this short guide useful. We've tried to make the information and skills you need clear and simple.

You can use the Knowledge Checks at the end of the main chapters and the final quiz to practice all the skills necessary to correctly use and cite your research material. Citing your sources—what to cite, when, how—can be confusing. Most colleges have very specific requirements about giving references, depending on the subject or instructor. Correct citation is more involved than just inserting footnotes or listing references at the end of a paper. Including punctuation with quotes, using extracts, and a number of other considerations are necessary to distinguish your sources from your writing. This guide provides information and samples of the kinds of citations that are necessary to correctly reference different types of academic work.

DEFINING PLAGIARISM

Plagiarism is using someone else's work and passing it off as one's own. The term comes from the Latin word ***plagiarius***, which means *kidnapper*. It also has another root word in Greek, ***plagios***, which means *crooked* or *treacherous*. (Reader's Digest Great Encyclopedic Dictionary 1031).

This means that if a student uses another writer's work without giving credit, it may be considered deceptive, even if it is an honest mistake. Knowing the definition of plagiarism and when to cite sources is the best way to avoid problems.

Preventing plagiarism is also a critical part of the academic integrity that is expected, or even required, by educational institutions. Many schools and colleges have well-defined codes of honor or conduct that prohibit dishonesty, including cheating and plagiarizing. You should be aware of the rules and consequences for dishonesty in your academic setting.

The right to protect and profit from one's originality was recognized and codified by the founders of this country. Regulations about ownership and the right to profit from an individual's creations, including written work, is in Article 1, Section 8 of the U.S. Constitution, Title 17 of the U.S. Code, and parts of other copyright laws. Violators of copyright laws have faced severe consequences, including legal prosecution, loss of jobs, and damage to their reputations. Newspaper editors, college presidents, professors, and many other successful professionals have been discredited and subject to severe penalties for plagiarism. Countries that want to profit from originality must also respect it and enforce owners' rights. Some countries consider it a moral imperative as well as a commercial right (Chavez 127). There are many practical reasons for academic integrity, as well. Your safety, and confidence in doctors, mechanics, and other service providers might be in serious question if you did not assume they had integrity and honesty.

UNDERSTANDING WHEN TO GIVE CREDIT

Because information, pictures, and music are now easy to copy from the Internet, it's more tempting than ever to find and freely use those materials. How can you tell when it is appropriate to use something without a citation and when it isn't?

Generally, any time you use someone else's work as a source of ideas or inspiration, credit is required. There are a few exceptions, such as when the information is common knowledge. An example of common knowledge is the fact that Christopher Columbus crossed the Atlantic Ocean in 1492. To be safe, if you consult a source and that source's ideas become part of your work, then you need to cite that source. If you use a direct quotation, then you need to reproduce it accurately and cite it correctly. These practices prevent inadvertent plagiarizing, and this guide provides the basics to get you started.

Tip
When you consult a source, cite it correctly.

There are also limitations on how much of someone else's work can be used as part of an assignment. Exclusively, excessively, or inappropriately using another author's work by copying, paraphrasing, summarizing, or directly quoting is plagiarizing. It is important to use your own words and ideas in a paper. One suggested rule of thumb for the acceptable amount of outside source content to use in an assignment is no more than 10 percent provided it is properly cited (Zaharoff). Make sure to check your instructor's preferences.

Many students worry that their own words do not sound as professional as those used by the original author. The point of using a source in the first place is to give you an opportunity to bring in outside authorities to support your *own* ideas, as expressed in your *own* words. Instructors do not give assignments so that students can give them back in someone else's words. Instructors want to read *your words.* If instructors wanted to read only the professional author's words and ideas, they could go directly to the original source and skip yours. It's important for you to work with ideas and to express them in writing so that you can develop your own writing style, perspective, voice, and analytical skills. This is a big investment of time and effort. Often when students risk plagiarizing, they haven't allowed themselves sufficient time to complete an assignment. This miscalculation can lead to trouble.

Tip

Know the rules about plagiarism; ignorance is no excuse.

KNOWING THE RULES

Because academic integrity and the validity of a college degree are vitally important to institutions of higher learning, schools create codes and policies governing instances of dishonesty. These policies come under various headings: Academic Integrity, Academic Honesty, Honor Code, Cheating, Student Conduct Code, or Plagiarism. They list rules, definitions, and specific behaviors that are considered cheating. These codes also describe consequences and the various procedures that occur when a student is caught cheating. **It is your responsibility to know the rules of your institution and to follow them.** Rules are usually published in school catalogs and are considered a part of the enrollment agreement for the college. If you have any questions about academic policies, check with your instructor or the dean's office to get the facts.

When instructors suspect plagiarism, they are obligated to follow steps prescribed by the institution to address the problem. These steps include contacting the student and forwarding a report to the dean or a disciplinary committee, and a possible hearing before either or both.

Consequences to the student can include failing the assignment or even the entire course. Some institutions assign community service or some other restitution to the campus community as part of the punishment. Some students have been unhappily surprised to learn that the consequences for a first-time offense of plagiarism can be as severe as expulsion. Being caught as a plagiarizer is humiliating and can also be costly. It can directly affect a student's progress toward a degree. And it is entirely avoidable.

Don't gamble with your academic future. Taking this risk with the expectation that you won't get caught can result in consequences much worse than a warning or a simple fail on an assignment. This kind of high stakes gambling can make you a loser. Keep the odds in your favor. If you aren't prepared, it's better to get a poor grade on one assignment than to fail in a class (or worse) because you panicked and plagiarized.

Knowledge Check

True or False?

1. Most students who plagiarize do so inadvertently. T/F

2. Students cannot be accused of plagiarizing if they don't know the citation style expected by the instructor. T/F

3. Using sources for educational purposes means that those sources are exempt from citation rules. T/F

Check your answers on page 54.

2
Avoiding Plagiarism

This chapter lists and describes twelve guidelines to help you avoid plagiarizing, good practices when writing a paper:

1. Do your own work and use your own words.

2. Allow yourself enough time to research the assignment.

3. Keep careful track of your sources.

4. Take careful notes.

5. Make it clear who is speaking.

6. Credit the source.

7. Cite sources correctly.

8. Quote accurately and sparingly.

9. Paraphrase and cite.

10. Do not patchwrite.

11. Summarize.

12. Avoid using other students' papers and paper mills.

DOING YOUR OWN WORK, USING YOUR OWN WORDS

College gives you the opportunity to be exposed to new ideas, to formulate ideas of your own, and to develop the skills necessary to communicate your ideas. Strengthening your writing skills requires hard work and practice, but you learn thinking and communicating skills that will benefit both your studies in college and your career.

Expressing a thought in your own words may seem overwhelming. The difficulty may stem from not understanding the language, not understanding the research material, or lacking confidence in expressing ideas and concepts. Don't be discouraged by the thought that your paper may not sound as professional as you would like. By creating and practicing your own personal style, you improve your ability to state ideas clearly and support your arguments, as well as increase your vocabulary.

These skills are not built by using another researcher's or student's words or by paying a service to write a paper for your class. Attempting to cheat on your paper cheats you the most because you are depriving yourself of the thinking, learning, and writing practice that benefits every aspect of your education and beyond.

Cheating also creates the risk of humiliation and punishment. Most professors are so familiar with the work in their field that they can spot a fake quickly. New plagiarism detection methods are also making it easier for professors to catch cheaters electronically. Finally, as discussed in Chapter 1, all institutions punish students who plagiarize. Doing honest work is the way to avoid the negative consequences of cheating.

ALLOWING ENOUGH TIME

Often, students caught plagiarizing claim that they didn't have time to do the work. This excuse rarely works. Allow sufficient time to do all the steps necessary in an assignment. The best way is to plan for each part: selecting the topic, doing the research, then writing and refining your ideas. Minimizing the time it will take to do the work, or procrastinating because you feel that you do better work when you are anxious, more often than not leads to trouble.

The most productive strategy is to begin the assignment as soon as it is given and try to complete it early. This allows you to adjust the schedule if you encounter any research difficulties, provides time for questions or clarification, and offsets other events that can interfere or cut into study time. If you are unsure about how to plot out your time for each step, then ask your instructor to help you plan your schedule.

KEEPING TRACK OF SOURCES

As you look through books, articles, online sources, and other materials, you will be able to identify which content is relevant to your paper. The sources from which you decide to take notes are the ones for which you will need to keep careful records.

Create a master list of all your sources that contains detailed bibliographic information for each item. (You need to record the author, the title of the source, its publisher, the date, and page number. Chapter 6 has more detailed information on what to cite and how to format it.) As you conduct your research, you will likely add or delete sources from this list, but keeping it current and complete will make your work much easier when it comes time to format your list of Works Cited or References. This list of references enables your readers to locate the exact content you discuss in your paper—as well as assists you in finding it again.

TAKING NOTES

Some students find they take better and more easily referenced notes if they make photocopies of relevant pages from their sources. If you decide to use this method for print sources such as articles and books, photocopy the copyright page and make a copy of the relevant table of contents pages for each source. Make sure the page numbers or other identifiers are visible on each page. For electronic sources, such as websites, databases, CDs, or even blogs, print out both the home or copyright page and the relevant content pages, making sure that identifiers such as page numbers—and (for online sources) the URL and access date—are visible.

If you take notes instead on note cards or in computer files, then make sure to keep a detailed record of where each note came from and take down the information carefully and accurately.

Next, scrutinize your resources, thinking about the ideas expressed, noting and recording the relevant points, and adding to the notes your reactions, questions, and thoughts. If you find a particular phrase that you want to quote, then highlight it to separate it from the regular notes.

CLARIFYING WHO IS SPEAKING

As you write the first draft of your paper, make sure you express your thoughts and ideas in your own voice. Use the thoughts or words of others only to support your thoughts, not to make your point for you. Your writing should make clear at all times who is speaking.

Decide from your notes whether you need to quote, summarize, or paraphrase the source. (Chapters 3, 4, and 5 discuss each method.) Then make sure to introduce the guest voice (the source) and explain why the source's information is relevant to your topic.

CREDITING THE SOURCE

When you draft your paper, if you are stating another person's thought, make the source or origin of that thought clear. Identify the source of any and all borrowed content in your paper. Your readers need to know where to find the original source if they want to explore the idea further.

The academic departments of virtually every college and university recommend that their students use a particular style guide. The guides issued by the Modern Language

Association (MLA) and the American Psychological Association (APA), as well as the University of Chicago's *Manual of Style* (CMS), are the most common. Each features a method to identify your source by inserting a brief parenthetical citation where the source's content appears and then creating a list with the complete source information placed at the end of the paper. Follow whichever style your instructor specifies.

CITING SOURCES CORRECTLY

A **citation**—a statement of the source of an idea, a conclusion, or a specific collection of information—of another person's work is the highest form of respect that a serious writer can make. It is also the single best way to avoid accusations of plagiarism and cheating. Properly citing sources involves acknowledging them both in the body of your work (when and where your writing borrows from a given source) and in a list of all the sources at the end of your paper.

Check with your instructor or writing center for the proper format style of your writing project. Citation styles differ by subject or discipline—and many overlap in the areas of study and writing for which they were originally intended. For English and the other humanities, the MLA style is typically used. Psychology, Sociology, Business, Economics, and similar disciplines typically follow APA. More specialized style guides exist for other disciplines, including the Council of Science Editors (CSE) style, which is used in scientific writing.

Chapters 3 through 5 discuss how to use parenthetical citations and quotations, paraphrases, and summaries (respectively). Chapter 6 surveys the various methods of compiling references as well as presenting basic examples. For more detailed information, you can purchase the style guides for MLA, APA, and CMS styles, available at most bookstores. Online citation generators can also help you with listing references in the correct format.

MLA
APA
TURABIAN
CHICAGO

About • Register • School • Blog

CITATION MACHINE
Serving Students & Teachers
K-12, College, & University

Citation Machine is an interactive web tool designed to assist high school, college, and university students, their teachers, and independent researchers in their effort to respect other people's intellectual properties. To use Citation Machine, simply...

1. Click the citation format you need and then the type of resource you wish to cite,
2. Complete the Web form that appears with information from your source, and
3. Click Make Citations to generate standard bibliographic and in-text citations.

The primary goal of this tool is to make is so easy for high school, college, and university students and other researchers to credit information sources, there is virtually no reason not to -- because SOMEDAY THE INFORMATION THAT SOMEONE WANTS TO USE, WILL BE YOURS.

LINKBOT

Save the following link in your bookmarks or links bar to create a clickout version of Citation Machine, available to you any time.

[CMachine]

There will be copies in your school or public libraries.

This is the main page for a citation generator that helps create citations in different styles.

QUOTING

Quotations should be used only to emphasize your point, which you have already stated in your own words. A good quotation from an original source can underscore a theme and introduce thoughts or direction, but quotations should be relevant, necessary, accurate, and limited.

Using too many direct quotations (more than ten percent) is a sign both that you have not developed your own idea enough and that you are relying on others to make your point for you. Over-quoting is also an opportunity for plagiarism to creep in. If you are using several sources, then limit how much those sources contribute, and give a correct citation and credit every time you use them.

PARAPHRASING

The practice of taking another writer's sentence and then looking up words and replacing them with synonyms is a common way for students to think they are paraphrasing from a source (see Chapter 4). Merely changing some of another writer's words, or reversing the order of the clauses in the sentences, is still copying. This is another way you can inadvertently plagiarize. Use paraphrase to state in your own words what another writer believes or argues.

AVOIDING PATCHWRITING

Patchwriting consists of mixing several references together and arranging paraphrases and quotations to constitute much of a paper. In essence, the student has assembled others' works—with a bit of embroidery here and there—but with very little original thought or expression. Work that has been simply patched together is very likely to contain plagiarism.

To avoid patchwriting, develop a position and bring in sources only as needed to support your viewpoint or argument. Read the material several times to make sure you understand what the source is saying. Then put it aside and think about it. Analyze the readings and what they mean, and then try to organize the main points. Create an outline of what you want to say and go back and pull in the supporting information from the sources. Good writers think of the reader as listening to what is being said; this process will help you create and organize your own original work and find your own voice in your writing.

SUMMARIZING

Most word processors have an automatic summarize function that can take 50 pages and turn them into ten. The problem with this feature is that it condenses material by selecting key sentences. Therefore, a summarized version is still in the exact words of the original source, only shorter, and does not necessarily make the same point as the original. The auto-summary feature is intended for writers to summarize their own work, not the work of others. If a paper uses any portion of an auto-summary generated from another writer's work, then it is plagiarism.

If you wish to summarize another writer's work, then describe briefly in your own words the writer's idea, identifying who that writer is and providing a citation of the work, and state how it relates to your own ideas (see Chapter 5).

AVOIDING USING OTHER STUDENTS' PAPERS AND PAPER MILLS

Don't cross the line from looking at someone else's paper to presenting it as original work. A paper written by another student can be an example of how to do the assignment. Reworking or rewriting that person's paper for submission is plagiarism.

Similarly, buying papers from paper mills, or paying for someone else to write a paper, is obviously dishonest and is a clear example of plagiarizing. Databases of written papers are often kept by colleges and by plagiarism detection services, so instructors who question the authenticity of a student's paper can easily verify its source.

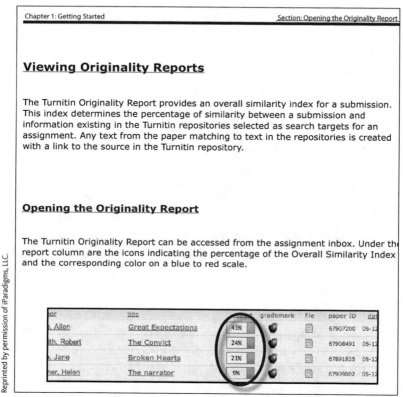

TurnitIn's® "Originality Reports" help faculty detect plagiarism in student papers.

Knowledge Check

True or False?

1. One way to avoid plagiarizing is to give yourself enough time to do a good job on the assignment. T/F

2. As long as you put everything in quotation marks, you are not plagiarizing. T/F

3. Getting a paper from a friend or the Internet is a good way to get a head start on your assignment. T/F

Check your answers on page 54.

3
Quotations and Parenthetical Citations

UNDERSTANDING CITATIONS

This chapter shows you how to use the work of others and correctly credit it in the body of your own. Citation is an accolade to the original writer and a way to acknowledge his or her influence on your research or thinking. It is also the single best way to avoid accusations of plagiarism and cheating. "Plagiarizing doesn't just mean borrowing someone else's words. It also means borrowing someone else's ideas" (Lipson 46). The general policy in acknowledging sources is to cite a source if it had an influence on your work. This allows people who read your work to follow a path back to original ideas and sources. Citation of sources can be a very confusing process.

There are different styles of citations for different areas of academics. You have already learned that **MLA** style is commonly used for English, literature, and other humanities classes. **APA** style is used for psychological research, sociology, and even environmental science. There are other styles specialized for math, physics, chemistry, and other disciplines. The styles have many things in common. In this guide, we present the basics of the MLA and APA styles, which both employ the **author-date** convention. While this guide will not cover all the nuances of each style—you should consult their respective guides in print and online—it will give you an introduction.

There are several basic rules to citations. These rules include such things as alphabetizing author lists including their names and publications, and also specify what should be cited and how.

Knowing these rules and the basics of different citation forms will help you to properly cite your sources and give credit to the authors that have helped you and influenced your work.

While these styles have things in common, fundamental differences exist in presentation and format. For example, one style will use italics for the title of a book or journal in your paper, while another has you underline these same elements. If you have the option of either, you must choose one and be consistent. As we examine the different styles, take note that while the basic information presented in different styles can be the same, the order of presentation can be quite different.

Tip

Always check with your instructor for the style format they prefer.

Citation styles contain basically the same information, just in different formats. The basic information that is included in all citations styles follows:

- Author's name
- Article title
- Book title
- Publisher information
- Year of publication
- Place of publication
- Page numbers when applicable

Listings of References or Works Cited for all styles are placed at the end of the paper. They are often separated from the body of the paper on a separate page or pages—and each listing is typically set with a hanging indent so that the author names can easily be seen. (Examples of how to create reference lists are given in Chapter 6.)

USING PARENTHETICAL CITATIONS

We have already mentioned that citations are presented at the end of your work, but you need to indicate within the written text or body of the work what references are being used at any given instance. A bibliography, in which you only list the works you researched to compose your paper, is typically not enough for higher-level coursework. Correctly noting or referencing begins in the body of the text and points to the full citation at the end of the work. If you use an idea, paraphrase, or direct or indirect quote, you need to insert a **parenthetical citation**. Parenthetical citations can be considered the roadmap to your Works Cited or References list. There are several ways in which to acknowledge your sources correctly. Only work that is cited in the body of the paper is included in the list at the end. Some examples of how to use parenthetical citations with quotations follow. (There are additional examples of parenthetical citations for paraphrasing and summarizing in Chapters 4 and 5, respectively.)

Quotations with parenthetical citations

Using quotations is an effective way to support your arguments and add credibility to your research paper. Quotations are most useful when they highlight or help to refine a point you are making. However, you should quote selectively and sparingly. Inserting too many quotations in your paper distracts your readers from the argument you are trying to construct and makes your paper sound as if others are speaking for you.

You can use a **direct quotation** (a word-for-word repetition from another source) or an **indirect quotation** (a restating in your own words of the ideas of another person, which is also called paraphrasing). Each time you insert a direct or indirect quotation into your paper, you must add a citation to the source following the quotation. The necessary citation is called a parenthetical citation because of the use of parenthesis and a brief reference to the source within the referenced, quoted, or paraphrased text. A parenthetical citation, used after a quotation, may look like the following.

The following is a parenthetical citation that uses APA style:

(Houston, 2008, p. 323)

This is an MLA version of a parenthetical citation:

(Houston 323)

Both in-text citations are for direct quotation and follow an abbreviated, parenthetical format that points the reader to the full citation in a Works Cited or References list at the end of the paper (see Chapter 6).

Quotations can be used in various ways within a research paper. This chapter will cover some of those uses and the proper citation styles needed for each. Some examples of how to use parenthetical citations with quotations are included.

Basic In-Text Citation Rules

In MLA style, referring to the works of others in your text is done by using what's known as parenthetical citation. Immediately following a quotation from a source or a paraphrase of a source's ideas, you place the author's name followed by a space and the relevant page number(s).

⊞ Teaching Writing

⊞ Tutoring Writing

⊞ About the OWL at Purdue

⊞ Suggested Resources for You

```
Human beings have been described as "symbol-using
animals" (Burke 3).
```

When a source has no known author, use a shortened title of the work instead of an author name. Place the title in quotation marks if it's a short work, or italicize or underline it if it's a longer work.

Your in-text citation will correspond with an entry in your Works Cited page, which, for the Burke citation above, will look something like this:

```
Burke, Kenneth. Language as Symbolic Action: Essays on
        Life, Literature, and Method. Berkeley: U of
        California P, 1966.
```

We'll learn how to make a Works Cited page in a bit, but right now it's important to know that parenthetical citations and Works Cited pages allow readers to know which sources you consulted in writing your essay, so that they can either verify your interpretation of the sources or use them in their own scholarly work.

Multiple Citations

To cite multiple sources in the same parenthetical reference, separate the citations by a semi-colon:

```
...as has been discussed elsewhere (Burke 3; Dewey 21).
```

Many college websites, such as the OWL at Purdue University, provide information on preparing citations.

Follow these basic rules for using quotations:

- Use quotations sparingly.

- Make sure the quotation exactly fits the idea of your paragraph.

- Make sure direct quotations stay identical to the original passage. Do not change the wording, the spelling, or the punctuation of the original passage.

- Cite the source! Include a parenthetical citation for all quotations.

- If a direct quotation is longer than four lines, use a block quotation.

USING DIRECT QUOTATIONS

A direct quotation is an exact copy of the original author's work. Make your point first, and then enclose the quote in quotation marks (or if it is long, set it apart as a block quotation) and provide a parenthetical citation directly after.

The MLA style of citing a quotation includes the author's last name followed by the page number directly after the quotation. Note that no comma separates the name from the page number.

> Personal growth is a painful process, and part of that process is taking personal responsibility for your actions. This includes remembering that "you can't talk your way out of problems you behaved yourself into" (Covey 186).

The APA style of citing the same quotation includes the publication year as well as the author's last name and page number. Note that no comma separates the name from the date, but that a comma does follow the date and that the abbreviation "p." precedes the page number.

> Personal growth is a painful process, and part of that process is taking personal responsibility for your actions. This

includes remembering that "you can't talk your way out of problems you behaved yourself into" (Covey 1989, p. 186).

Notice that in both cases the citation is included in the sentence, with the period after the citation.

Alternatively, you can introduce the name of the author in the text and then cite the page number for reference.

> Noted author Stephen Covey suggests that to be effective, one must "begin with the end in mind" (97).

Note that the APA style includes the year of publication directly after the author's name and the page number at the end for easy reference.

> Weeks (1994) believes that "we need to celebrate diversity, not fear it or perceive it as a threat" (33).

USING INDIRECT QUOTATIONS

When using research sources, it is common to find that the original author has quoted a **secondary source**, another author, in his or her work. The following example shows such a quotation and the proper citation for it.

In MLA style, the addition of "qtd. in" (abbreviated for "quoted in") shows that a quote (in this case, by Jung) was found in a secondary resource (here, Byrne).

> Psychology has had its masters of theory and quite a bit of humor as well. C. G. Jung, a noted psychologist, once claimed, "Show me a sane man and I will cure him for you" (Jung, qtd. in Byrne 453).

In APA style, notice the change in wording as well as the addition of the date the source was published.

> Psychology has had its masters of theory and quite a bit of humor as well. C. G. Jung, a noted psychologist, once claimed, "Show me a sane man and I will cure him for you" (as cited in Byrne, 1996).

USING ELLIPSES AND BRACKETS

An **ellipsis** (shown by three evenly spaced periods: [. . .]) is a break or omission of words within a direct quote. Using only part of a quotation is common practice, especially if the entire quotation is too long or cumbersome. But make sure to use ellipses cautiously so you don't present the author's words out of intended context.

> We can now plainly and painfully see that "components of human interaction . . . often lead to conflict" (Weeks 33).

Sometimes a quote is worded in a way that could read awkwardly or make an incomplete sentence when inserted in a paper. If you need to add a word or phrase within a quotation to make your sentence grammatically correct or clearer, then put brackets around your insertion.

> There are many examples of how "components of human interaction . . . [can] often lead to conflict" (Weeks 33).

In this instance the word "can" was added to clarify the thought for the reader.

USING BLOCK QUOTATIONS

A quotation from poetry, plays, or any text longer than four lines should be set apart in block quotation format. A block quotation is indented about one inch (ten spaces) from the left margin and double-spaced. A block quotation needs no quotation marks and is introduced by a complete sentence. Often a colon, rather than a period, follows the introductory words.

Tip

Block quotations do not require quotation marks.

The block quotation is introduced by a sentence that contains the author's name and ends with a colon, and uses an ellipsis to show that it is not complete. Note that the page is included in parentheses after the period for easy reference.

> As Shein and Bernstein explain, discovering you could be a twin is a shocking yet fascinating experience:
>
> > Imagine that a slightly different version of you walks into a room, looks you in the eye, and says hello in your voice. You discover that she has the same birthday, the same allergies, the same tics, and the same way of laughing. . . . This identical individual has the exact same DNA as you and is essentially your clone. (vii)

Knowledge Check

True or False?

1. Quotations must be used in original form. T/F

2. Quotation marks are required for all direct quotations. T/F

3. Brackets indicate that a word has been added that is not in the original text. T/F

Check your answers on page 54.

4
Paraphrasing

DEFINING A PARAPHRASE

A **paraphrase** is a restatement of an author's writing that uses your own words and accurately conveys the original information. You paraphrase another author's words when you want to explain the content of the quote or to maintain your own voice and rhythm in your paper. You might also paraphrase after you have introduced a source earlier in your paper and wish to continue to discuss that source's ideas without needing to quote the source verbatim.

The length of a paraphrase should be about equal to the length of the original work. (This is not to be confused with a summary—explained in Chapter 5—which describes in a few words the ideas or points made in another author's long passage or large work.) Also, a paraphrase, because it's an indirect quotation, requires a parenthetical citation, as seen in the examples that follow.

Tips

Do

1. Use your own words.

2. Present the author's ideas without changing, adding to, or deleting from the original meaning.

3. Make the paraphrase about equal in length to the original.

4. Give credit to the source.

(continued)

> *Don't*
>
> 1. Keep the author's sentences and just replace the words with synonyms.
> 2. Flip-flop clauses and leave the words the same.
> 3. Lose track of original sources.

GIVING CREDIT TO THE SOURCE

Restating an author's ideas accurately in your own words and writing style can be difficult. And it can be confusing to know when—and how—to add a citation. The thing to remember is this: If a sentence or idea came from an outside source, then it should be acknowledged with a parenthetical citation.

You might be tempted to shift some words around from the original, but doing so would be plagiarizing because those words and the idea still belong to the author. Remember that improving your writing skills is part of the goal of using others' works. Instructors want you to learn to write and think, not just hand back what someone else created.

One way to develop paraphrasing skills is to read the material several times to make sure that you understand completely what the writer is saying. Next, put aside the author's work and try to explain the passage in your own words. This will help you develop a personal voice and style. Compare the explanation with the original and decide whether it is accurate and conveys the original ideas. Is something missing from your paraphrase that a person who hadn't read the source passage would need to know to understand it? If so, revise your paraphrase. It is vital that the paraphrase not alter the original meaning of the source. Adding words that distort the intention of the author or leave out significant parts can misstate or misrepresent what that author intended.

Also make sure to explain how the paraphrased content relates to your idea. Once you have worked the paraphrase into your draft, be sure to cite the original.

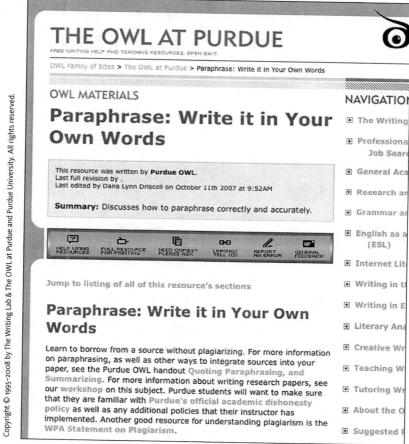

THE OWL AT PURDUE

FREE WRITING HELP AND TEACHING RESOURCES. OPEN 24/7.

OWL Family of Sites > The OWL at Purdue > Paraphrase: Write it in Your Own Words

OWL MATERIALS

Paraphrase: Write it in Your Own Words

This resource was written by **Purdue OWL**.
Last full revision by .
Last edited by Dana Lynn Driscoll on October 11th 2007 at 9:52AM

Summary: Discusses how to paraphrase correctly and accurately.

| HELP USING RESOURCES | FULL RESOURCE FOR PRINTING | NEED COPIES? PLEASE ASK | LINKING? TELL US! | REPORT AN ERROR | GENERAL FEEDBACK |

Jump to listing of all of this resource's sections

Paraphrase: Write it in Your Own Words

Learn to borrow from a source without plagiarizing. For more information on paraphrasing, as well as other ways to integrate sources into your paper, see the Purdue OWL handout Quoting Paraphrasing, and Summarizing. For more information about writing research papers, see our workshop on this subject. Purdue students will want to make sure that they are familiar with Purdue's official academic dishonesty policy as well as any additional policies that their instructor has implemented. Another good resource for understanding plagiarism is the WPA Statement on Plagiarism.

NAVIGATION

- The Writing
- Professiona
  Job Sear
- General Aca
- Research an
- Grammar an
- English as a
  (ESL)
- Internet Lit
- Writing in t
- Writing in E
- Literary Ana
- Creative Wr
- Teaching W
- Tutoring Wr
- About the O
- Suggested

The OWL at Purdue University website has information to help you correctly paraphrase.

SAMPLE PARAPHRASES

Paraphrase with citation, MLA

Original work

Poll after poll indicates that one of the primary concerns of contemporary U.S. citizens is violence. Terrorism is obviously one part of this concern, but there is also considerable concern about non-terrorist forms of violence. Violence among the nation's youth is especially troubling and difficult to explain. This difficulty is frequently the reason that social psychologists are often asked to make sense of seemingly senseless acts of violence. Why are there so many shootings in the U.S. high schools? Why are there so many gangs, and why are they growing at such alarming rates? (Potter 306)

Incorrect paraphrase

<u>Survey</u> **after** <u>survey show</u> **that one of the** <u>big things</u> that <u>people</u> in the **U.S.** <u>worry</u> about <u>today</u> is **violence.** **Terrorism is** <u>clearly</u> a <u>reason</u> **but there is also** <u>a lot of</u> worry **about** other **forms of violence. Violence** from the <u>young people in this country</u> **is** <u>very confusing</u> **and** <u>hard</u> **to** <u>understand</u>. **This** <u>problem</u> **is** <u>often</u> **the** <u>issue</u> **that** <u>researchers</u> are <u>frequently required</u> to <u>explain incomprehensible violent crimes. What is the reason for the number of gun related crimes in schools in America? Is it because the number of</u> **gangs** <u>are going up</u>?

This paraphrase copies the content and writing style of the source passage. It is plagiarized, not paraphrased. Sentence by sentence, the information is exactly restated using different words. The substituted words in exact sequence are <u>underlined</u>. The sequence of each idea and structure of each sentence is the same, and words have been replaced with synonyms. In some cases, original phrases have been kept in order (shown in **bold**). This "patchwork paraphrasing" merely uses synonyms for words in the original text, but everything is essentially identical. Finally, there is no citation as the end of the paraphrase. Now consider the following:

Correct paraphrase

Many recent **polls** have suggested that people in the United States are very concerned about **terrorism** and other acts of violence. Increasing **violence**, including **shootings**, among **high-school**-aged children is one of these concerns. People in the community want to understand why this is happening. **Social psychologists** have been asked to explain this troubling trend. It is difficult to understand why young people may be joining **gangs** and committing acts of violence in greater numbers. (Potter 306)

This example—which uses MLA citation—maintains the ideas of the original piece, but the style of writing is different. Instead of following an identical sequence to the original work, the correctly paraphrased paragraph conveys the information but does not pull out words and substitute them with synonyms. It uses *some* of the words from the original to accurately present the author's ideas and is complete in presenting the original author's ideas, but it uses the student's original sentences. It also cites the author of the original work. The following is another example:

Paraphrase with citation, MLA

Original work

At first glance, there appears to be little justification for telling the story of California's early Indian wars. Aside from the brief Modoc conflict of 1873, and possibly the Mariposa war of 1851, few people are aware that California had any Indian troubles during the Gold Rush days of the 1850s. Certainly the Far West never had a Custer's Last Stand or a grand retreat such as that made by Chief Joseph of the Nez Perce. There were no Sitting Bull or Geronimo, no spectacular uprisings, like Adobe Walls or Beecher's Islands. On the contrary, many California tribes were generally peaceful by nature, few having even a war club or a tomahawk as part of their culture. Yet in California, the bloodiest drama in the settlement of the West took place, a brutal disruption and destruction so devastating that by the 1870s many native groups were extinct. (Secrest xi)

Incorrect paraphrase

Unless you know about the events, you would think there isn't much reason to write about what happened in the **Indian wars** in **early California**. There were two conflicts, one in **1873** with the **Modoc** and another in **Mariposa in 1851**. But most people don't know anything about California having trouble with Indians during the **1850s Gold Rush**. The **Far West** didn't have any famous Indian conflicts like **Custer's Last Stand** or any other Indians that were well known like **Chief Joseph of the Nez Perce, Sitting Bull, or Geronimo**. It didn't have Indian revolts like **Adobe Walls or Beecher's Islands**. In California the Indians were peaceful and didn't carry weapons. But California had the **bloodiest** wars in the **West**. It was harsh and destructive and annihilated the Indians to the point where by the 1870s many of the groups were dead and gone.

This paragraph is plagiarized. Notice that the writing style of the original piece was copied. Sentence by sentence the information is restated using different words, and the sequence of each idea is the same. In most cases, words have been substituted for synonyms (see underlined), while in others, words have been kept (see **bold**). This is another example of patchwork paraphrasing. In addition, no indication of the source of this paraphrase is provided in the text.

Correct paraphrase

If history books are to be believed, there is little to say about the California Indian conflicts. Indeed it would seem that all of the great battles such as Custer's Last Stand and the great chiefs were only far away. While history shows us the Gold Rush and its subsequent effect on California, it also leaves us with the false impression that California Indians were peaceful, with no weapons or conflicts with the intruding whites. This type of historical omission negates the devastation and annihilation that the California Indians suffered; annihilation so complete "that by the 1870s many native groups were extinct" (Secrest xi).

In this example, the ideas of the original piece are maintained, but the style of writing is different and belongs to the writer of the paper. Instead of following an identical sequence to the original work, the correctly paraphrased paragraph conveys the information. Once more, it does not use synonyms in place of the original author's words. It still uses some of the phrasing from the original, but this instance is identified by quotation marks and is used to accurately convey and emphasize the ideas of the original author. It also cites the author of the original work using MLA style.

To avoid the errors of adding information that wasn't in the original work or omitting something important to the original meaning, carefully track your sources and acknowledge them in your writing. You need to correctly present the meaning, and you need to cite the source accurately. Sometimes it is difficult to work with many different ideas, but remember that your professor is very familiar with many of the ideas and sources you'll use and can help you work out how best to present them.

CITING PARAPHRASES

Like direct quotations, the only difference between APA and MLA styles is the citation at the end.

MLA style includes the name of the author and the page number.

> . . . Yet in California, the bloodiest drama in the settlement of the West took place, a brutal disruption and destruction so devastating that by the 1870s many native groups were extinct (Secrest xi).

APA style includes the name of the author, the date of publication, and the page number.

> . . . Yet in California, the bloodiest drama in the settlement of the West took place, a brutal disruption and destruction so devastating that by the 1870s many native groups were extinct (Secrest, 2003, p. xi).

For electronic sources, consult the applicable style guide. What is important to know, however, is that you don't need to include page numbers because there aren't any. Your citation only needs the author's name (and the date if applicable) and points to the Works Cited or References list, where readers can find additional information—such as a URL—to check a source.

Tip

When citing online sources, you do not include the page numbers of your printout.

Knowledge Check

True or False?

1. Keeping the writing style of the original passage when you paraphrase is appropriate as long as you change most of the words. T/F

2. Correct paraphrasing includes a citation for the original source after the paraphrased passage. T/F

3. A paraphrase should be roughly the same length as the original. T/F

Check your answers on page 54.

5
Summarizing

DEFINING A SUMMARY

A **summary** condenses the size of an original piece of writing while retaining its author's essential message. A summary enables you to comment briefly on another writer's ideas and express how they relate to your own. Summarizing shortens the length of the original passage, whereas paraphrasing nearly matches the original in length.

To summarize another writer's passage, read it several times—taking notes if necessary—to make sure you understand what the writer is saying. It might help to read it aloud so you can hear the words. Then say to yourself, "In other words . . ." and complete the thought. If you use almost as many words to explain or express the thought, then you need to revise it and make it simpler and briefer. Reduce the original passage to its basic idea. And make sure to explain for your reader how the writer's idea relates to the point you are making in your paper.

Tips

Do

1. Be accurate to the original meaning.
2. Cite the original source.
3. Make your summary significantly shorter than the original.
4. Use your own words and explain how the writer's idea relates to yours.

(continued)

> *Don't*
> 1.   Copy the original writing style; use your own.
> 2.   Replace the original words with synonyms.
> 3.   Change the meaning of a passage.

SAMPLE SUMMARY

Original work

Polls show that large majorities of Americans believe that anyone who works hard can succeed, and even higher percentages of Americans say they admire people who get rich by their own efforts. Those who fall behind, meanwhile, are often blamed for their misery. In a typical recent survey finding, three quarters of Americans agreed with the statement that if a person is poor, their own "lack of effort" is to blame. In other words, Americans tend to make moral judgments about people based upon their level of economic success. Everybody loves a winner, the saying goes, and nowhere is that more true than in America. Winners are seen as virtuous, as people to admire and emulate. Losers get the opposite treatment— for their own good, mind you. As Marvin Olasky, . . . has said: "An emphasis on freedom should also include a willingness to step away for a time and let those who have dug their own hole suffer the consequences of their misconduct." The prevalence of a sink-or-swim mentality in the United States is unique among Western democracies, as is the belief that individuals have so much control over their destiny. Elsewhere people are more apt to believe that success or failure is determined by circumstances beyond individual control. Scholars attribute the difference in outlook to the "exceptionalism" of America and, especially to the American Dream ethos that dominates U.S. culture—an ethos at once intensely optimistic and brutally unforgiving. (Callahan 124–25)

Incorrect summary

Polls show that large majorities of Americans believe that anyone who works hard can succeed, and even higher percentages of Americans say they admire people who get rich by their own efforts. Winners are seen as virtuous, as people to admire and emulate. Elsewhere people are more apt to believe that success or failure is determined by circumstances beyond individual control.

The above summary was created using the AutoSummarize feature of Word set for 25%. It selects key sentences from the original document and puts those sentences together to form an abbreviated copy. (Note that the AutoSummarize feature is intended for writers to provide summaries of their own work, not the work of others.) This is not an acceptable summary because it is entirely copied, word for word. It is plagiarism. It does not change the writing style of the original author, nor does it give credit with a correct citation to indicate the source. Additional problems with this method of summary may be the altering of the original meaning of the piece. Note that the original piece was about the difference between how Americans view winners and losers, but the summary does not mention how losers are viewed. That thesis has not been mentioned in the summary. It is important to connect a summary to the point you are making in your paper and the reason why you referred to the source you are summarizing.

Correct summary

According to Callahan, Americans, unlike people in other Western democracies, take the moral perspective that success is the result of individual effort. Most believe that a person's success is a product of his or her labor and thus deserved. Conversely, a person's poverty or failure is viewed as the outcome of his or her lack of sufficient effort and is therefore also deserved (124–25).

In the correct summary, which uses MLA citation, the ideas of the original passage are maintained, but the style of writing is different from the original passage, and the summary is shorter than the original. In a paper, the summary should also clearly address your thesis or argument. It should convey the main points of the original, but it does not copy full sentences or substitute words with synonyms. It can have some material in common with the original as long as it accurately presents the author's ideas—and it should be cited correctly.

Knowledge Check

True or False?

1. You can keep the writing style of the original passage when you summarize as long as you significantly shorten the length and leave out some of the original. T/F

2. Correct summarizing includes a citation for the original source next to the summarized passage. T/F

3. A summary should convey the same meaning as the original. T/F

Check your answers on page 55.

6

References and
Works Cited Lists

As you draft your paper, you will assemble a complete list of source materials that correlate with the quotations and paraphrases that you use. This list, as discussed in previous chapters, appears at the end of your paper. You will also need to format this list in the style required by your instructor.

This chapter presents the basics of formatting an **author-date** reference list in MLA and APA style. (Referencing sources with footnotes is not covered here. But if you want to learn more, consult the *Chicago Manual of Style*.) The guidelines here will help get you started and make you aware of this important part of writing a paper. For additional information, you should consult the appropriate style guide. You can also get more help from your instructor, your school's library or writing center, and the online resources listed in Chapter 8.

CITATION CONTENT

While the information presented in all styles is the same, the order of the information and how it is shown can be quite different. The basic information contained by all citation styles includes the following:

- Author name

- Title of article, essay, book, or website

- Publisher information

- Year of publication

- Place or form of publication

BASIC FORMAT

All documentation styles place the list of references at the end of the paper. Follow these basic formatting rules for all citation styles:

- Arrange all citations in alphabetical order by the author's last name.

- Arrange authors' names in a multiple-author work exactly as they appear in the source.

- Reverse the author's name so that the last name appears first.

- Double-space your list of references, as you would your paper.

- Use a hanging indent so that the second and subsequent lines of a citation allow the author's name to appear by itself in the left margin. The typical indention is one-half inch (five spaces).

- Include in your list of references only the works to which your paper refers.

Tip

Always check with your instructor for the required documentation style.

MLA CITATIONS

Books

The basic elements of an MLA citation of a book include the following:

- Author name (last name, first name) followed by a period.

- Book Title—underlined, followed by a period.

- City of publication, followed by a colon.

- Publisher's name, followed by a comma. Use only the first name of the publisher, and abbreviate University Press to UP.

- Year of publication, followed by a period.

An example of a single-author book is presented below:

Ross, JoAnn. <u>Legends Lake</u>. New York: Pocket Books, 2001.

Multiple authors

When you are citing a book that has two or three authors, list them in the order in which they appear on the title page. Invert the first author's name (last name first), but not the names of the second or third author. Separate all the authors by commas. For a book by four or more authors, MLA allows the listing to include either all the authors listed in order or just the first author followed by the Latin words **et al.,** which is short for *et alia*, meaning "and others." Check with your instructor about the form that he or she prefers.

The following example is for a book by two authors:

Schein, Elyse, and Paula Bernstein. <u>Identical Strangers</u>. New York: Random House, 2007.

These examples are for a book with four or more authors:

Kauffman, James, Mark Mostert, Stanley Trent, and Daniel Hallahan. <u>Managing Classroom Behavior</u>. Boston: Allyn & Bacon, 2002.

or

Kauffman, James, et al. <u>Managing Classroom Behavior</u>. Boston: Allyn & Bacon, 2002.

Articles or essays

You might use an article from a periodical or an essay from an anthology. While the basic structure of citations for articles is the same as for books, there are some significant differences. You need to list both the title of the article or essay, the journal or book in which it was published, and the page range.

The information in a citation of a source from an anthology follows this order:

- Author of the article or essay (last name first) followed by a period.

- "Title of the article or essay" in quotation marks, followed by a period.

- Title of the Book—underlined, followed by a period.

- Comp. (for "compiled by") or Ed. (for "edited by").

- Author of the book (first name first), followed by a period.

- City, followed by a colon.

- Publisher, followed by a comma.

- Year, followed by a period.

- Page range (separated by a hyphen or en dash) followed by a period.

- The word "Print," followed by a period (if your instructor is using the *MLA Style Manual and Guide to Scholarly Publishing*, 3rd edition).

Anson, Chris. "Taking Off." Finding Our Way: A Writing Teacher's Sourcebook. Ed. Wendy Bishop and Deborah Coxwell Teague. Boston: Houghton Mifflin, 2005. 44–51. Print.

Tip

Citations from an anthology or magazine should include the page numbers.

Popular magazine and newspaper articles include the month, either spelled out or abbreviated, of publication in the citation.

Smith, Julian. "Endangered Destinations." U.S. News and World Report May 2008: 36–43.

Landmark's Citation Machine makes preparing references in different styles easy.

For scholarly journals, the volume number is included after the journal title. The year is placed in parentheses. A colon follows the year and the page range.

Houston, Linda "Teaching English in the Two Year College." Urbana 35 (2008): 323–26. Print.

APA CITATIONS

The APA style contains the same information as MLA, but it formats the content differently, putting more emphasis on the date of publication.

Books

The basic APA style of citation for a book is as follows:

- Author (last name first) then first initial, followed by a period. For a work by more than one author, invert all names, use initials instead of first names, and insert an ampersand (&) before the last author.

- Year of publication in parentheses, followed by a period.

- Book title and volume number *italicized* (capitalize the first word of the title, the first word of the subtitle, and any proper nouns), followed by a period.

- City and full publisher's name, separated by a colon and followed by a period.

The following example is for a single-author book:

Maguire, G. (1995). *Wicked: The Life and Times of the Wicked Witch of the West*. New York: HarperCollins.

Articles

The basic APA style of citation for a scholarly journal article by a single author is as follows:

- Author last name and first initial followed by a period. For a work by more than one author, invert all names, use initials instead of first names, and insert an ampersand (&) before the last author.

- Year (in parentheses) with a period.

- Title of article (capitalize only first word, the first word after a colon, and any proper nouns; and no quotation marks), followed by a period.

- Title of journal in *italics,* followed by a comma.

- Volume number in *italics,* followed by a comma.

- Full page range of article, followed by a period.

Here is an example of a journal article by a single author:

Houston, L. (2008). Teaching English in the two year College. *Urbana, 35,* 323–26.

For a journal article by two to five authors, use the following example as a guideline:

Brown, C., A., Dickson, R., Humphreys, A., McQuillan, V. & Smears, E. (2008). Promoting academic writing/referencing skills: Outcome of an undergraduate e-learning pilot project. *British Journal of Educational Technology, 39,* 140.

MLA AND APA CITATIONS FOR WEB PUBLICATIONS

(From sec. 6.7.1: "Citing Web Publications: Introduction")

In the past, the *MLA Style Manual and Guide to Scholarly Publishing* recommended including URLs of Web sources in Works Cited entries. Inclusion of URLs has proven to have limited value, however, for they often change, can be specific to a subscriber or a session of use, and can be so long and complex that typing them into a browser is cumbersome and prone to transcription errors. Readers are now more likely to find resources on the Web by searching for titles and authors' names than by typing URLs. You should include a URL as supplementary information only when the reader probably cannot locate the source without it or when your publisher requires it. If you present a URL, give it immediately following the date of access, a period, and a space. Enclose the URL in angle brackets, and conclude with a period.... (212–13)

Provide the following information for Web publications and similar electronic sources. This example uses those elements listed by the MLA. APA style includes most of these with some exceptions.

- Author, director, editor, performer, etc. of work (if available)

- Title of full work (if available), set in quotations marks if the work is part of a larger work, and italicized if the work is independent

- Title of overall website set in italics

- Date of work (if available)

- Name of institution/organization that sponsors the site

- Date of publication (day, month, and year)

- Web (medium of publication)

- Date that you accessed it

- Optional: URL (set in angle brackets (< >))

MLA online citation

The MLA citation shows the author's full name and the date after the title. Note that the year of publication is followed by a period, that the date of access is day, month (abbreviated, except May) and that no punctuation follows it. The word "Web" precedes the access date and is separated by a period. The final element is the URL, which is set in angle brackets. For longer Web addresses, the line break of the URL falls after a slash, and a period closes the entry.

The following example is for an MLA Web publication citation with an author:

Warlick, David. "Landmarks Son of A Citation Machine." The Landmark Project. 2000. Web. 19 Mar. 2005 <http:// www.citationmachine.net>.

For an online citation without an author, the title replaces the author as the element that is alphabetized in the Works Cited list, as shown in the following example, which has other differences. Here the sponsor of the website is listed. Note again the placement of the medium (Web), access date, and URL.

DSPS Policies and Procedures, 2003. Santa Barbara City College. Web. 3 Jan. 2004 <http://www.sbcc.edu/dsps/>.

APA online citation

APA electronic citations follow the rules of normal APA style of formatting such as capitalization, first initial, year placement, and italics. Note that the retrieval date is spelled out, that a comma follows it, and that no punctuation follows the URL. The full URL is normally given. This example shows an article that has an author:

Lee. I. (1998). *A Research Guide for Students: Research, Writing, and Style Guides*. Retrieved March 19, 2005, from http://www.aresearchguide .com/styleguides.html

This next example shows an online citation without an author:

DSPS policies and procedures. (2003). Santa Barbara City College. Retrieved January 3, 2004, from http://www.sbcc.edu/dsps/

Tip

Both APA and MLA Web publication citations require the date of access because websites often change, are archived, or even disappear from the Web.

TYPES OF REFERENCE LISTS

This section features examples of an MLA Works Cited list, including the Works Cited list for publications used as examples in this book. Consult your instructor as to whether to use underline or italics.

MLA Works Cited list

Works Cited

Anson, Chris. "Taking Off." *Finding Our Way: A Writing Teacher's Sourcebook*. Ed. Wendy Bishop and Deborah Coxwell Teague. Boston: Houghton Mifflin, 2005. 44–51.

DSPS Policies and Procedures, 2003. Santa Barbara City College. 3 Jan. 2004 <http://www.sbcc.edu/dsps/>.

Kauffman, James, Mark Mostert, Stanley Trent, and Daniel Hallahan. *Managing Classroom Behavior*. Boston: Allyn & Bacon, 2002.

Maguire, Gregory. *Wicked: The Life and Times of the Wicked Witch of the West*. New York: Harper Collins, 1995.

Norman, Michael, and Beth Scott. *Historic Haunted America*. New York: Tor, 1995.

Warlick, David. "Landmarks Citation Machine." *The Landmark Project*. 2000. Web. 19 Mar. 2005 < http://citationmachine.net/>.

Schein, Elyse, and Paula Bernstein. *Identical Strangers*. New York: Random House, 2007.

APA References list

References

Brown, C., A., Dickson, R., Humphreys, A., McQuillan, V. & Smears, E. (2008). Promoting Academic Writing/Referencing Skills: Outcome of an Undergraduate E-Learning Pilot Project. *British Journal of Educational Technology*. 39, 140.

DSPS Policies and Procedures. (2003). Santa Barbara City College. Retrieved January 3, 2004, from http://www.sbcc.edu/dsps/

Houston, L. (2008). Teaching English in the Two Year College. *Urbana*, 35, 323–26.

Lee, I. (1998). *A Research Guide for Students: Research, Writing, and Style Guides*. Retrieved March 19, 2005, from http://www.aresearchguide .com/styleguides.html

Maguire, G. (1995). *Wicked: The Life and Times of the Wicked Witch of the West*. New York: HarperCollins.

Knowledge Check

True or False?

1. Works Cited or References lists should be single-spaced. T/F

2. Only works actually cited in the body of the paper should be listed in the Works Cited page. T/F

3. Works Cited or Reference lists should be listed in alphabetical order by author's last name. T/F

Check your answers on page 55.

7
Practice Quiz

1. **Cheating may include**

   a.   plagiarizing or copying without attribution.

   b.   using an essay or paper from someone who has previously taken the course.

   c.   using answers to an exam from someone who has previously taken the course.

   d.   all of the above.

2. **Plagiarism is**

   a.   quoting someone else's work and giving credit to them.

   b.   using someone else's ideas, work, sentences, research, or information and presenting it as your own.

   c.   using original ideas in your written work.

   d.   using Web sources.

3. **Citation of sources is required**

   a.   whenever paraphrasing or summarizing an idea.

   b.   only in the Works Cited section of your paper.

   c.   when using your own ideas in an original paragraph.

   d.   a and b

4. **The word *paraphrase* means**

   a.   to replace original words with synonyms.

   b.   to maintain the writing style of the original author.

    c.   to give an exact idea of the original author's meaning in your own writing style.

    d.   to give a general, but not exact, idea of the original author's meaning.

5. **A paragraph is not properly paraphrased when**

    a.   only a few words are different.

    b.   you express in your own words the general idea of what the author is saying.

    c.   the sentences have been rearranged but not changed much.

    d.   a and b

    e.   a and c

6. **Correct summarizing includes**

    a.   a copy of the original writing style.

    b.   replacing the original work with synonyms.

    c.   the accurate meaning of the original work but significantly shorter than the original.

    d.   using the autosummarize feature of your word processing program.

7. **Citation of sources is required**

    a.   when quoting a source in your paper that you use word for word.

    b.   when browsing the Internet.

    c.   when describing another writer's idea in your paper.

    d.   a and c

8. **Over-quoting in your work**

    a.   shows you have not synthesized or analyzed the material from your resources.

    b.   is acceptable because it shows the amount of work and research you have done.

c.   means using too many direct quotes from your sources.

d.   a and c

e.   a and b

9.   **John's paper is based on several different sources, including a research paper from a friend who took the same class last summer. Seeing that his friend's research closely matches his own, does John need to cite his friend in his final draft?**

a.   No, he just needs to cite the other sources.

b.   Yes, anything John consulted needs to be cited.

10.   **Look at the original and choose which paraphrase is correct.**

Original

Because there are many ways to cheat, and there is temptation to do so, students may assume that this is something that everyone is doing. Surveys of college students show that cheating is a common occurrence, and some students consider it an accomplishment to get away with this type of behavior. These kinds of attitudes and behaviors are unethical and have consequences. (Menager, 2003, 12)

a.   Students can be tempted to cheat by the many resources available to them that make it easy. They may believe that a majority of students cheat in some form or another. Surveys done in colleges suggest that cheating is more rampant than once thought and that students see it as a triumph to cheat and not get caught. This shows a serious lack of ethics in behavior and can lead to repercussions from the academic institution (Menager, 2003, 12).

b.　Because there are so many different ways to cheat, and temptations for students are great, a lot of students think everyone is doing it. Students surveyed say that cheating is a common occurrence and it is an accomplishment to get away with it. This kind of attitude is unethical and can have some consequences.

8
Additional Sources of Information

Reference the following Web and print resources to learn more about plagiarism and proper citation using the various styles in use at institutions of higher learning in the United States, Canada, and elsewhere.

CITATION STYLE OVERVIEWS

University of California–Berkeley: Citing Your Sources

http://www.lib.berkeley.edu/instruct/guides/citations.html

DOCUMENTATION STYLES BY DISCIPLINE

Anthropology

http://www.aaanet.org/publications/guidelines.cfm

Chemistry

http://pubs.acs.org/books/references.shtml

Law

http://www.law.cornell.edu/citation/?

Math

http://www.longwood.edu/mathematics/stylesheet.html

Physics

http://www.aip.org/pubservs/style.html

Sociology

http://www.calstatela.edu/library/bi/rsalina/asa.styleguide.html

FREE CITATION GENERATORS

Son of Citation Machine

http://www.citationmachine.net

Style Wizard

http://www.stylewizard.com

REFERENCE TRACKING

EasyBib

http://easybib.com

RefWorks

http://www.refworks.com

PLAGIARISM

University of Indiana: Plagiarism

http://www.indiana.edu/~istd/definition.html

Center for Academic Integrity

http://www.academicintegrity.org

TurnitIn®.com

http://www.turnitin.com

Samford University Library

http://library.samford.edu/topics/plagiarism.html

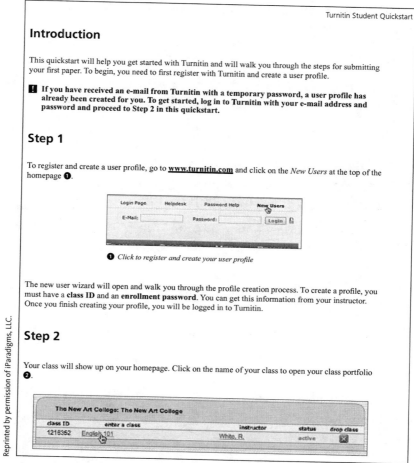

This is the student page for establishing a TurnitIn account and posting papers to check for authenticity.

STYLE GUIDES

American Psychological Association. *Concise Rules of APA Style.* Washington: APA, 2005.

http://books.apa.org/subpages/apastyle.cfm

The Chicago Manual of Style. 15th ed. Chicago: U of Chicago P, 2003.

http://www.chicagomanualofstyle.org/about.html

Gibaldi, Joseph. The MLA Style Guide for Writers of Research Papers. 6th ed. New York: MLA, 2003.

http://www.mla.org/store/CID24/PID159

Huth, Edward J. Scientific Style and Format: The CBE Manual for Authors, Editors and Publishers. 6th ed. New York: Cambridge UP, 1994.

http://www.councilscienceeditors.org

Works Cited

Byrne, Robert. *The 2,548 Best Things Anybody Ever Said*. New York: Galahad, 1996. sec. 453.

Chavez, J. Carolina. "Copyright's 'Elephant in the Room': A Realistic Look at the Role of Moral Rights in Modern American Copyright." Washington, D.C.: *American Intellectual Property Law Association Quarterly Journal*, 36 (2008): 125–45.

Covey, Stephen. *The Seven Habits of Highly Effective People*. New York: Simon, 1989. 97, 186.

Houston, Linda "Teaching English in the Two Year College." *Urbana* 35 (2008): 323–26.

Kauffman, James, Mark Mostert, Stanley Trent, and Daniel Hallahan. *Managing Classroom Behavior*. Boston: Allyn, 2002.

Lathrop, Ann, and Kathleen Foss. *Student Cheating and Plagiarism in the Internet Era: A Wake-up Call*. Englewood, Colorado: Libraries Unlimited, 2000.

Melville, Herman. Quotation 4797 in *Cole's Quotables*. 30 Mar. 2005 <http://www.quotationspage.com/ quote/4797.html>.

Potter, W. James. "Is Media Violence Harmful to Children?" *On Media Violence*. Thousand Oaks: Sage, 1999. [Rept in Brent Slife, *Taking Sides: Clashing on Controversial Psychological Issues*, 13th ed. New York: McGraw, 2004. 306.]

Reader's Digest Great Encyclopedic Dictionary: Standard College Dictionary 2nd Ed. New York: Funk & Wagnalls, 1967. 1031.

Secrest, William B. *When the Great Spirit Died: Destruction of the California Indians, 1850–1860*. Sanger, California: Word Dancer, 2003.

Schein, Elyse, and Paula Bernstein. *Identical Strangers*. New York: Random House, 2007.

Weeks, Dudley. *The Eight Essential Steps to Conflict Resolution*. New York: Penguin, 1994. 33.

Zaharoff, Howard. "A Writer's Guide to Fair Use in Copyright Law." *Writers Digest* Jan. 2001. 3 Mar. 2005 <http://www.writersdigest.com/articles/zaharoff_fair_copyright_law.asp>.

Answers to Exercises

Chapter 1

1. (True) Don't be one of them. This can be a costly mistake!

2. (False) It is your job to find out.

3. (False) All sources should be cited.

Chapter 2

1. (True) Most people who plagiarize use poor time management and even worse judgment.

2. (False) If you quote more than 10 percent of your paper, you may be graded down for overquoting.

3. (False) Using a friend's paper or an Internet paper is plagiarizing and considered to be academic cheating.

Chapter 3

1. (True) Quotations should be identical to the original passage.

2. (False) Block quotations do not require quotation marks.

3. (True) Brackets show that text was added to the original passage.

Chapter 4

1. (False) This is a common mistake students make because they don't know the rules and they lack confidence in their own writing ability. You should restate the writer's idea in your own words.

2. (True) Always acknowledge when you've used ideas from someone else, no matter whether it's a clause, sentence, or paragraph.

3. (True) A paraphrase restates another person's idea in your own words.

Chapter 5

1. (False) A summary should be in your own words and writing style but convey the message of the original. Do not use autosummarize for someone else's work because it is just an abridged copy.

2. (True) Always acknowledge when you've used ideas from someone else, no matter what.

3. (True) Do not alter the meaning; just express it concisely and in your own words.

Chapter 6

1. (False) All references should be double-spaced.

2. (True)

3. (True)

Chapter 7

1. d   2. b   3. a   4. c   5. e   6. c   7. d   8. d   9. b
10. a

Index

Abbreviations, 84
Acronyms, 205–206
Active learning. *See also* Learning;
    Learning style
    choices for, 183
    journal entry on, 183–184
    keys to, 180–182
    strategies for, 176
Active listening
    in college classes, 133
    example of, 134–135
    importance of, 132
    journal entry on, 134–135
    steps to, 132–133
Advisors, college, 18, 127
Affirmation
    about memorizing, 205
    about money, 235
    about note taking, 81
    about reading, 48
    about strengthening desired
        qualities, 77–78
    about stress reduction, 222
    about studying, 142
    about test taking, 170
    about writing, 113
    development of, 75–77
    function of, 77
    journal entry on, 78–79
    living your, 78
Alcoholics Anonymous (A.A.), 232
Ali, Muhammad, 76
Allen, David, 94, 96
Amygdala, 150
Angelou, Maya, 30, 123, 190, 202, 221
Anger, 220
Anxiety, 221, 226
Arnold, Karen, 212
Artistic personalities, 165
Assertiveness
    effective requests as, 139–140
    ineffective communication affecting,
        137–138
    journal entry on, 140–141
    leveling as form of, 138–139
Assignments, late, 23
ATM cards, 240

Attendance
    on first day of class, 18
    importance of, 167
Attitude, 223–224
Attributions, 154
Audio recordings, 206
Automatic teller machines (ATMs), 237
Automobile insurance, 239
Automobile loans, 239

Banks, 237
Bannister, Roger, 4
Beal, Louise, 128
Beattie, Melody, 231
Beck, Lindsey, 216
Behavior
    choice of, 3–4
    in classes, 20–21
    to reduce stress, 218–223
    self-defeating, 157
    of successful students, 167–168
Behavior patterns, 153
Beliefs
    choice of, 3–4
    core, 15–16, 155
    disputing irrational, 43–44
    impact of outdated, 159–160
    of successful students, 9
Bell, Terrell, 55
Benjamin, Neal, 131
Berne, Eric, 152, 154
Bissonette, Robert, 25
Blaming, 138, 139
Bolles, Richard, 73
Bradshaw, John, 76
Brain, 179
Brainstorming
    during tests, 172
    before writing, 114
Brandon, Nathaniel, 15, 25, 35,
    124, 135
Brophy, Jere, 58, 227
Brown, Les, 62
Bryant, William Jennings, 36, 245
Budda, 159
Burns, David, 231
Burns, Thomas, 41

Caldwell, Taylor, 183
Calendars, monthly, 94, 98
Campbell, Joseph, 65
Campus life, 19
Career center, 128, 164
Careers
    education requirements for, 57
    flow and, 226–227
    learning preferences and
        compatible, 199
    resources for learning about, 136,
        198–199
Career success
    effects of, 13
    personal responsibility in, 38–40
    requirements for, 14
    self-management for, 107–109
    self-motivation for, 73–75
    skills for, 14–15, 64–166
    supportive relationships for,
        136–137
Carney, Clarke G., 164
Carroll, Lewis, 63
Change
    checklist for embracing, 51–52,
        85–86, 118–119, 145–146, 174–175,
        208–209, 242–243
    lifelong learning and, 195–196
    self-awareness and courage for,
        194–195
    stress as result of, 215–216
Chapman, Joyce, 24, 36, 77
CHOICES, 198
Choices
    case study on strange, 148–149
    making successful, 34–37
    moment of, 26
    personal responsibility and, 26–28
    power of, 3–4
    of successful students, 9–10,
        251–252
CIS, 198
Clark, Karen Kaiser, 195
Classes
    active listening in, 133
    asking questions in, 19
    attendance in, 18

Classes (*contd.*)
   behavior in, 20–21
   seating in, 18
   withdrawals from, 19–20
Classmates
   discuss reading material with, 50
   to help with information on missed
     classes, 19
   study groups with, 128–130
Cochise, 139
Codependence, 123, 124
Cole, Johnetta B., 91
College
   effective reading in, 48–50
   effective studying in, 45–47, 142–144
   effective writing in, 113–117
   experiences gained in, 58–60
   financial assistance for, 127,
     237–238
   flow and, 226–227
   learning customs of, 18–21
   predictors of success in, 96
   support services in, 127–128
   transportation expenses for,
     238–239
   value of graduating from, 57–58
College advisors, 18, 127
College catalogues, 18
College courses, 18
Commitments
   to goals, 68–69
   importance of honoring, 202–204
Communication
   effective requests during, 139–140
   leveling in, 138–139
   patterns of ineffective, 137–138
Compassion, 233
Concept maps
   explanation of, 81
   as memory technique, 206
   for writing, 114, 115
Conventional personalities, 165
Core beliefs
   explanation of, 15–16
   in scripts, 155
Corey, Irwin, 196
Cornell note-taking method, 81, 83
Counseling office, 127
Courage, for change, 194–195
Covey, Stephen, 89, 133, 161
Cramming, 182
Creativity, in journal writing, 5
Creators
   adopting role of, 22, 24–25
   choice as, 27
   communication style of, 138–140

as embracers of change, 51
explanation of, 25–26, 89
language of, 22, 29–33
saying "no" as tool of, 140
self-talk of, 31–33
time management by, 90, 91
in workplace, 38–40
Credit, 235, 240
Credit cards, 239
Credit reports, 235–236
Credit unions, 237
Critical thinking case studies
   on choices, 148–149
   on emotional intelligence, 211–212
   on interdependence, 121–122
   on late papers, 23
   on learning, 177–178
   on motivation, 54–55
   on procrastination, 88
Cross, K. Patricia, 56
Csikszentmihaly, Mihaly, 59, 167,
   225–226
Cues, 82

D'Angelo, Anthony J., 200
DAPPS rule
   application of, 66, 73, 95, 139
   explanation of, 63–64
Darben, Althea Gibson, 125
Data Dump, 142
Debit cards, 240
Debt, 240
Deci, Edward, 140
Decisions, making wise, 22, 34–37
Deep processing, 181
Deep-processing strategies, 181–182
Delany, Bessie, 112
Denny, Terry, 212
Dependence, 123, 124
Descartes, René, 188
Dewey, John, 181
Dictionaries, use of, 49
Dictionary of Occupational Titles
   (DOT), 198
Directions, for journal writing, 5
DISCOVER, 198
Distributed practice, 181
Doing learners, 189–190, 199
Dominitz, Ben, 69
Donne, John, 122
Do-Not-Disturb signs, 142
Douglas, Clair, 42
Dreams, 53, 65
Dryden, John, 155
D'Souza, Alfred, 10
Dunham, Katherine, 33

Edelman, Marian Wright, 105
Edison, Thomas, 89
Editing, your writing, 116
Edwards, Tryon, 188
Einstein, Albert, 189
El Guerrouj, Hicham, 4
Eliot, Charles W., 134
Ellis, Albert, 40–41, 43, 155
Emotional intelligence
   case study in, 211–212
   components of, 213–214
   development of, 9, 244, 246
   elements of, 210, 212–213
   foundations of, 214
   journal entry on, 215
   in workplace, 229–231
Emotional patterns, 153
Emotions, knowing your own, 214
Empathy, 213–214
Employee training, 198
Enterprising personalities, 165
Errors, 116–117
Essay questions, 172
Expectations, 56, 57
Expenditures, 240–241

Fanning, Patrick, 16, 30, 42
Fear, 221
Federal Direct Loan Program, 237
Federal Pell Grants, 237
Feeling learners
   career preferences for, 199
   explanation of, 190–191
Fill-in-the blank questions, 171
Financial aid, 127, 237
Financial aid office, 127
Financial Plans, 235, 236, 241
First-day handout, 19
Floriolli, James, 158
Flow
   college and, 226–227
   creation of, 225–226
   journal entry on, 228
   work and, 227–228
Flow states, 225
Focus, importance of maintaining,
   102–103
Ford, Henry, 134
Frankl, Viktor E., 223–224
Franklin, Aretha, 233
Free writing, 5
Fritz, Robert, 27, 89

Gabler, June E., 130
Gandhi, Mohandas, 59, 201
Garfield, Charles, 71, 78, 110–111, 194

Garvey, Marcus, 112
Gawain, Shakti, 79
General education requirements, 18
Givens, Charles J., 38, 69, 90, 102
Glasow, Arnold H., 60
Glasser, William, 35
Goals
    commitment to, 53, 68–69
    guidelines for setting, 63–65
    journal entry on visualizing, 71–72
    resistance to setting, 62–63
    visualizing your, 69–70
Goleman, Daniel, 214, 221, 226, 230
Google.com, 113
Grade point averages (GPA), 19, 20
Grants, 127, 237
Graphic organizers, 50, 143
Grasseth, Dominic, 45
Guided journal writing, 5
*The Guide for Occupational Exploration
    (GOE)*, 198

Habits
    changing your, 168
    self-defeating, 155–156
Hard skills, 164
Harman, Willis, 151
Haskins, Joseph, 12
Hatch, Betty, 203
Hayes, Dennis, 94
Health services, 128
Hearn, Lefcadio, 95
Helmstetter, Shad, 35, 160, 245
Hemingway, Ernest, 131
Hendricks, Gay, 34, 138, 212
Hendricks, Kathlyn, 34, 138, 212
Henley, William E., 24
Herrmann, Ned, 186
Hill, Napoleon, 64
Hoffer, Eric, 180
Holland, John, 165
Holland Code, 165
Holmes, Oliver Wendell, 152
Holt, John, 191
Honesty, 5, 138
Hooks, in writing, 114
Hope Scholarship Credit, 240
Hubbard, Elbert, 67
Huigens, Brandeé, 169
Hulnick, Mary, 195
Human brain, 178–179
Huxley, Thomas Henry, 103, 182

Iacocca, Lee, 95
Identity, creation of, 109–110
I-messages, 138–139

Independence, 123–124
Injunctions, 154–155
Inner Critic
    explanation of, 30
    placating and, 137
    self-judgments of, 41–42
    separating from, 43
Inner Defender
    blaming and, 138
    function of, 30–31, 76
    self-esteem of, 42
    separating from, 43
    stress and, 218
Inner Guide
    function of, 31, 76
    to help with persistence, 103
Inner voice
    changing your, 40–44
    of creators, 31–33
    of victims, 29–31, 33
Innovating learners
    career preference for, 199
    explanation of, 191–192
Instructors
    identifying cues from, 82
    making appointment with, 19
    relating anticipated absence to, 19
    seeking help from, 116, 127
Integrity, 201–202
Interdependence. *See also* Supportive
    relationships
    benefits of, 123, 245
    case study on, 121–122
    creating network for, 126–130
    development of, 1, 9, 120
    in workplace, 135–137
Internet, using search engines on, 113
Investigative personalities, 165
Irrational beliefs, 43–44

Jacobs, Robert, 179
James, Henry, 134
James, Muriel, 66, 132, 153
James, William, 224
Jeffers, Susan, 33, 79, 212
Jensen, Eric, 179
Job interviews, 200
Jobs. *See* Careers
Job search, 136
Johnson, Earvin (Magic), 129
Johnson, Lynn, 171
Jongeward, Dorothy, 66, 132, 153
Jordan, Michael, 103
Journal entries
    on active learning, 183–184
    on active listening, 134–135

on assertiveness, 140–141
on course corrections, 196
on creating support network, 130
on creator role, 28
on desired outcomes and
    experiences of college, 60–61
on flow, 228
on giving and receiving, 125
on Inner Critic and Inner
    Defender, 44
on language of personal
    responsibility, 33–34
on learning style, 192–193
on life plans, 67–68
on personal affirmation, 78–79
on rewriting scripts, 160–163
on self-assessment, 12, 252–253
on self-awareness, 151–152
on self-confidence, 112
on self-defeating patterns, 157
on self-discipline, 105
on self-love, 233–234
on self-management, 92–93, 97–100
on self-respect, 204
on strengths and weaknesses, 17
on stress reduction, 224
on visualizing goals and dreams,
    71–72
on Wise Choice Process, 37–38
on writing your own rules, 168–169
Journal writing, 4–5
Jung, Carl, 17

Katz, Lillian Vernon, 110
Keller, Helen, 127
Keyes, Ken, 31, 138
Kiam, Victor, 14
King, Martin Luther, Jr., 65, 89
Kübler-Ross, Elisabeth, 26
Kumin, Maxine, 160

Langer, Ellen J., 153
Language
    of creators, 22, 29–33
    of responsibility, 32–34
Lansing, Sherry, 104
Lazarus, Arnold A., 43
Learners
    doing, 189–190
    feeling, 190–191
    innovating, 191–192
    thinking, 187–188
Learning. *See also* Lifelong learning
    active, 178–179
    adopting to, 9
    choices for, 183

Learning. *See also* Lifelong learning
   (*contd.*)
   critical thinking skills for, 177–178
   journal entry on, 183–184
   keys to deep and lasting, 180–182
   prior, 180
   skills for, 176
   study skills for, 45–47
Learning style
   assessment of your, 184–187
   discovery of, 176
   journal entry on, 192–193
   problem solving and, 194
LeDoux, Joseph, 150
Lee, Spike, 194
Lennick, Doug, 231
LePage, Allysa, 101
Lerner, Harriet Goldhor, 65
Leveling, strategies to promote,
   138–139
Libraries, use of, 113
Lifelong learning. *See also* Learning
   adopting to, 9, 244
   change and, 195–196
   importance of, 246
   in workplace, 198–200
Life plans
   design of, 65–67
   dreams for, 65
   elements of compelling, 53, 62
   journal entry on, 67–68
   roles and goals for, 62–63
   setting goals for, 63–65
Lifetime Learning Credits, 240
Lightner, Candy, 65
Lincoln, Abraham, 68
Listening. *See* Active listening
Lists
   of assignments, 142
   next action, 94–95, 98
Loans
   automobile, 239
   educational, 237–238
Loci technique, 205
Loden, Jason Matthew, 126
Logan, Richard, 24
Ludwick, Donna, 80

Maggard, Jessie, 197
Main ideas, 49, 114
Major, choice of, 18
Malcolm X, 184
Maltz, Maxwell, 111
Mamchur, Carolyn, 187
Mankiller, Wilma, 123
Mannes, Marya, 219

Martinelli, Bobby, 67
Matching questions, 171–172
Maxwell, Elaine, 35
McCall, Nathan, 110
McCullers, Carson, 154
McKay, Matthew, 16, 30, 42
McLuhan, Marshall, 200
Memorization strategies, 181,
   205–207
Memory cards, 205
Mentors, 137
Millay, Edna St. Vincent, 156
Miller, Richard, 217
Money management, 235–241
Montagu, Ashley, 3
Monthly calendars, 94, 98
Moore, Brian, 29
Morely, Christopher, 3
Mother's Against Drunk Driving
   (MADD), 65
Motivation. *See also* Self-motivation
   creating inner, 53, 55–60
   critical thinking case study on, 54–55
   formula for, 56–57
   lack of, 55–56
Multiple-choice questions, 171
Munson, Patricia J., 203
Murray, William Hutchison, 71
Myer-Briggs Type Indicator ″®
   (MBTI), 164
Myers, Rochelle, 132, 149

Narcotics Anonymous (N.A.), 232
Networking, 136, 137
Neurons, 178–179, 181–182
Next action lists, 94–95, 99
Niebuhr, Reinhold, 16
Nietzsche, Friedrich, 59
Nin, Anais, 159
No, method for saying, 140
Nolen, William A., 2
Note cards, 114, 143, 144
Note taking
   guidelines for effective, 81–84
   while reading, 48, 49

Obstacles, types of, 10
Occupational Outlook Handbook
   (*OOH*), 198
Oech, Roger von, 59
Office Depot, 74
Onaga, Jalayna, 13
Opportunities, making choices
   about, 10
Organization, of documents, 20
Outlines, 81, 114

Overeaters Anonymous (O.A.), 232
Owens, Jessie, 11

Patterns
   of ineffective communication,
    137–138
   in scripts, 153
   self-defeating, 157
Peck, M. Scott, 102, 152
Pell Grants, 237
Penfield, Wilder, 150
Persistence, importance of, 103–104
Personal expenditures, 240–241
Personality types, 165
Personal responsibility. *See also*
   Responsibility
   acceptance of, 1, 9, 24
   benefits of taking, 25–26, 245
   choice and, 26–28
   journal entry on, 33–34
   language of, 32–33
   at work, 38–40
Placating, 137, 139
Postage stamp method, 143
Powell, Colin, 104
Prerequisites, 18
Prior learning, 180
Procrastination, 88
Professionalism, 229
Progoff, Ira, 150, 246
Proofreading, 172

Quadrant II Time Management System,
   89–91
Question & Answer cards, 143, 144
Questions
   answering readers, 116
   asking people, 113
   in class, 19
   end-of-chapter, 50
   essay, 172
   fill-in-the blank, 171
   on homework assignments, 81
   matching, 171–172
   multiple-choice, 171
   short-answer, 171
   true-false, 171
   while reading, 48

Ray, Michael, 132, 149
Reading
   guidelines for effective, 48–50
   importance of, 48
Realistic personalities, 165
Reciting
   as memory technique, 206
   while reading, 49

Reframing, 220, 222
Reich, Robert B., 198
Relationship management, 214
Repetition
    as memory technique, 206
    as study technique, 143
Requests, style of, 139–140
Resentment, 220
Responsibility. *See also* Personal
    responsibility
    in communication, 138–139
    language of, 32–34
Restak, Richard, 150
Résumés, 107–108
Riley, Pat, 25, 127, 129
Robbins, Anthony, 213
Rockefeller, David, 107
Rogers, Carl, 51
Roles, live, 63
Roosevelt, Eleanor, 65
Rules
    function of, 166
    journal entry for writing your own,
        168–169
    for success, 167–169

Salary, 57, 235
Salerno-Sonnenberg, Nadja, 226
Sandburg, Carl, 93
Sanmiguel, Jaime, 225
Satir, Virginia, 15, 93, 137, 166, 222
Savings accounts, 238
Schmeling, Amanda, 72
Scholarships, 127, 237
Scholastic Aptitude Test (SAT) scores, 96
Schultz, Will, 37
Scripts
    anatomy of, 153–154
    choices in writing, 154–155
    explanation of, 152
    getting rid of outdated, 155–156, 166
    journal entry on rewriting, 160–163
    revision of, 159–160, 165
Scrudder, Samuel J., 178
Search engines, 113
Seating, in class, 18
Secretary's Commission on Achieving
    Necessary Skills (SCANS), 14
Self-acceptance, development
    of, 15–17
Self-assessment
    of career skills, 164–165
    importance of, 5–6
    journal entry on, 12, 252–253
    of learning style, 184–187
    of your feelings, 10–12

Self-assessment list, 6–8, 248–249
Self-awareness
    benefits of, 4–5, 9, 244
    change as result of, 194–195
    elements of, 147, 245–246
    emotional intelligence and, 213
    identifying scripts as element of,
        152–156
    to identify when you are off course,
        149–151
    journal entry on, 151–152
    rewriting scripts as element of,
        159–160
    when you are off course, 149–151
    in workplace, 164–166
    writing your own rules as element of,
        166–169
Self-care plan, 232–233
Self-confidence
    development of, 109–111
    journal entry on, 112
Self-defeating behavior, journal entry
    on, 157
Self-Directed Search (SDS), 164
Self-discipline
    to be persistent, 103–104
    development of, 87, 101–102
    journal entry on, 105
    to stay focused, 102–103
    in workplace, 107
Self-esteem
    explanation of, 16
    of Inner Defender, 42
    personal power and, 166
Self-judgments
    effects of, 30
    of Inner Critic, 41–42
Self-love
    development of, 231
    journal entry on, 233–234
    plan for, 232–233
Self-management
    benefits of, 245
    as element of emotional
        intelligence, 213
    journal entry on, 97–100
    mastery of, 1, 87
    monthly calendars for, 94
    next actions list for, 94–95
    Quadrant II Time Management
        System for, 89–91
    rewards of, 96–97
    tools for, 93
    tracking forms for, 95–96
    in workplace, 107–109
Self-management tools, use of, 87

Self-motivation. *See also*
    Motivation
    discovery of, 1, 9
    in workplace, 73–75
Self-respect
    explanation of, 201
    honoring commitments as element
        of, 202–204
    integrity as element of, 201–202
    journal entry on, 204
Self-sabotage, 149–150
Self-talk
    of creators, 31–33
    importance of, 29
    of victims, 29–31
Seligman, Martin, 224
Selye, Hans, 167, 217
Senses, use of, 206
Sentence acronyms, 206
Seuss, Dr., 193
Shakespeare, William, 78, 201
Sher, Barbara, 139
Shield, Benjamin, 123
Short-answer questions, 171
Short-term memory, 182
Siebert, Al, 96
Siegel, Bernie, 70, 141, 228, 232
SIGI PLUS, 198
Simmons, John, 97
Sinetar, Marsha, 5, 110, 228
Skills
    hard, 164
    soft, 14–15, 164
Sleeping, 207
Smith, Francie Larrieu, 62
Smith, Hyrum W., 204
Smith, Ron, 237
Social personalities, 165
Soft skills
    of emotional intelligence, 230
    self-assessment of, 164
    for workplace, 14–15
Sources, citing your, 116
Sousa, David, 179, 182
Spencer, Edmund, 40
Spontaneity, in journal writing, 5
SQ3R Method, 48
Stafford loans, 237
Stine, Jean Marie, 133
Stinkin' thinkin', 40–41
Stone, Hal, 29, 41
Stone, Sidra, 29, 41
Strengths, acceptance of, 16–17
Stress
    explanation of, 216–217
    persistence of, 217

Stress reduction
  healthy, 218–223
  unhealthy, 218
Strong Interest Inventories (SII), 164
Student activities office, 128
Student loans, 127
Study groups
  benefits of, 142, 143
  suggestions for starting, 128–130
Study schedules, 170
Study sheets, 143
Study skills
  reasons to learn, 45–47
  strategies to develop, 142–144
Study space, 142
Success
  celebration of, 110
  inner, 2
  meaning of, 2–3
  outer, 2
  role of choice in, 3–4
Successful students
  choices of, 9–10, 251–252
  motivation as element of, 55–56
  rules for, 167–168
  study skills for, 45–47
Supporting ideas, reading for, 49
Supportive relationships. *See also*
    Interdependence
  active listening to strengthen,
    131–133
  assertiveness in, 137–140
  creating network for, 126–130
  development of, 122–125
  with instructors, 116, 127
  in workplace, 135–137
Support networks
  creation of, 126–130
  during job search, 136
  journal entry on, 130
Syllabus, 19

Talents, 110
Tardiness, 1
Tax credits, 240

Teams, creating project, 128
Tecumseh, 28
Tests, skills for taking, 170–173
Textbooks, purchase of, 19
Thesis, 114
Thinking learners
  career preferences for, 199
  explanation of, 187–188
32-Day Commitment, 105, 106, 218
Thomas, Debi, 105
Thompson, Melissa, 193
Thoreau, Henry David, 90
Thought patterns, 153
3 x 5 cards, 114, 143, 144
Time management
  monthly calendars for, 94
  next actions list for, 94–95
  rewards of, 96–97
  tools for, 93
  tracking forms for, 95–96
Time management system (Covey),
    90–93
Tomlin, Lily, 64
Tracking forms, 95–96, 100
Tracy, Brian, 62
Transitions, in writing, 114
Transportation expenses, 238–239
True-false questions, 171
Turner, Cathy, 69–70
Tutoring labs, 127

Unconscious forces, 150–151
Underwood, Blair, 167

Vallerand, Robert, 25
Value
  of college experiences, 58–60
  of college outcomes, 57–58
  of education, 56, 57
VanDerveer, Tara, 109
Vang, Chee Meng, 61
Victims
  choice as, 27
  communication style of, 137–140
  explanation of, 25

self-talk of, 29–31
  in workplace, 38
Visualization
  of career choice, 75
  of ideal future, 69–70
  keys to effective, 70–71
  as memory technique, 206
  of purposeful actions, 110–111
  to reduce stress, 222
Vonnegut, Kurt, Jr., 75

Waitley, Denis, 4, 233
Walter, Tim, 96
Ware, Eugene F., 12
Washington, Harold, 70
Washington, Martha, 223
Weakness, 16–17
Weisnger, Hendrie, 229
Wells, Cinda Field, 164
Welty, Eudora, 157
Whistling Elk, Agnes, 32
Whitehorn, Katherine, 227
Wilson, Woodrow, 126
Winfrey, Oprah, 27, 124, 151
Wise Choice Process, 35–38
Woodman, Marion, 234
Word acronyms, 205–206
Workplace
  emotional intelligence in, 229–231
  interdependence in, 135–137
  lifelong learning in, 198–200
  personal responsibility in, 38–40
  self-awareness in, 164–166
  self-management in, 107–109
  self-motivation in, 73–75
  soft skills for, 14–15
Work-study programs, 127
Writing
  guidelines for effective, 113–117
  importance of, 113

Yahoo. com, 113

Ziglar, Zig, 128
Zilbergeld, Bernie, 43
Zuboff, Shoshana, 230